THE PRESIDENTS' WAR

ALSO BY CHRIS DEROSE

Congressman Lincoln: The Making of America's Greatest President

Founding Rivals: Madison vs. Monroe, The Bill of Rights, and The Election that Saved a Nation

THE PRESIDENTS' WAR

*Six American Presidents and the
Civil War That Divided Them*

CHRIS DEROSE

LYONS PRESS
Guilford, Connecticut
An imprint of Globe Pequot Press

For Nolan Davis, mentor and friend, with profound appreciation for the life you made possible, this book is gratefully inscribed by the author.

Lyons Press is an imprint of Globe Pequot Press.

Project editor: Meredith Dias
Layout: Adam Caporiccio

Library of Congress Cataloging-in-Publication Data

DeRose, Chris (Christopher)
The presidents' war : six American presidents and the Civil War that divided them / Chris DeRose.
   pages cm
Includes bibliographical references and index.
ISBN 978-0-7627-9664-9
1. Lincoln, Abraham, 1809-1865—Adversaries. 2. United
States—Politics and government—1861-1865. 3. Ex-presidents—Political
activity—United States—History—19th century. 4. United
States—Politics and government—1815-1861. I. Title.
E458.D45 2014
973.7092—dc23
                         2014011002

Printed in the United States of America

10 9 8 7 6 5 4 3 2 1

CONTENTS

Would it promote the peace of the community, or the stability of the government to have half a dozen men who had had credit enough to be raised to the seat of the supreme magistracy, wandering among the people like discontented ghosts, and sighing for a place which they were destined never more to possess?
—ALEXANDER HAMILTON, FEDERALIST 72

Whatsoever God willeth must be, though a nation mourn.
—EPITAPH OF THE ONLY CIVILIAN KILLED AT GETTYSBURG

PROLOGUE

In Jackson's Time

April 13, 1830

Brown's Indian Queen Hotel

Washington City, District of Columbia

A Toast.

The banquet in honor of Thomas Jefferson's birthday was a splendid one, even by the standards of the national capital, "unsurpassed for richness and variety, elegance and abundance." More than one hundred congressmen, leaders of the American military, and members of the president's cabinet sat at two tables the length of the hall terminating in a perpendicular head table occupied by the president of the United States.

By tradition, the hosts of the gala would share their sentiments, called the "regular toasts." Subsequently, "volunteer toasts" were given in order of standing.

As members of an ascendant political party presiding over a prosperous, growing country, the banqueters should have been enjoying a night of pure celebration. But an uneasy tension hung over the room, perhaps more palpable than the scent of the evergreen branches that adorned the walls. Dividing this once happy family was the doctrine of nullification, the principle that a state could refuse to be bound by national laws with which it disagreed. The tariffs of 1828 and 1832, which boosted northern manufacturers but burdened southern agriculture, gave rise to a movement in South Carolina to "veto" what was believed to be an unconstitutional policy. The planners of this event had chosen to use it to make a statement. The regular toasts, twenty-four in all, embraced this controversial new doctrine, even seeking to give it Jefferson's imprimatur.

When the regular toasts had concluded, the president of the United States was called on to give the first volunteer toast. Andrew Jackson had listened long enough. Though known as an ardent supporter of states' rights, Jackson's remarks would sorely disappoint the nullifers.

"Our Union—" Jackson said "—it must be preserved."

The president's toast "electrified the country," recollected one senator, who had chosen to stay at the dinner while others walked out. The tough old general had issued a challenge, setting forth the terms of debate in what would become the gravest crisis yet presented to the young Union. Jackson had chosen his words carefully. The day before, he had read a newspaper article alerting him that the nullifiers had hijacked the gala. He drafted three possible toasts and, after consulting with trusted friends, decided on the one that "fell among the nullifiers like an exploded bomb!" as one biographer put it.

Vice President John Caldwell Calhoun of South Carolina, the leading exponent of nullification, was next in order. He did not shrink from the challenge offered by the chief executive. "The Union—next to our liberty the most dear; may we all remember that it can only be preserved by respecting the rights of the states and distributing equally the benefit and burden of the Union."

Next was the secretary of state, Martin Van Buren of New York. "Mutual forbearance and reciprocal concessions; through their agency the Union was established—the patriotic spirit from which they emanated will forever sustain it."

Three toasts at the end of a long evening. From the president came the view that the Union was sacred and permanent, paramount to other considerations. From the vice president, the Union was important but subject to the South's unique standard of liberty, dissolvable in the event that the Union was no longer advantageous. From the secretary of state, a reminder that the Union in its origins and preservation had always been the product of compromise. These divergent perspectives would clash, compete, and come to define the presidency of Jackson and those of his successors, not to be resolved until the close of a great war, some seeds of which were planted that evening at the Indian Queen.

Several days later a South Carolina congressman came to visit the president on his way out of town. Jackson "received him with great kindness, offering his hand, and begging him to be seated."

After a brief conversation, the congressman rose to leave. Was there anything the president wished to convey to his friends in South Carolina?

"No, I believe not," said Jackson. After a moment, however, the president reconsidered. "Please give my compliments to my friends in your state," he said. "And say to them, that if a single drop of blood shall be shed there in opposition to the laws of the United States, I will hang the first man I can lay my hand on engaged in such treasonable conduct, upon the first tree I can reach."

—◦—

But neither Calhoun's threat nor Jackson's promise would be tested until another generation. Rather, Van Buren's philosophy of compromise would rule the day, in the presidency of Jackson and in that of his successors. Beginning with Van Buren himself, the heirs to Jackson saw the role of president as conciliator-in-chief, containing the elements that threatened the Union, often by concessions made to southern interests. But a surprise victor in a bitterly divided presidential election, at the head of a new political party, would upset the old order of things, and redefine the nature of the presidency.

George Nicolay and John Hay, the young private secretaries of the president-elect, Abraham Lincoln, observed that beneath their boss's quiet demeanor, he was "undergoing most anxious and harassing labors. Day by day the horizon of politics gathered gloom, and the theory of secession became the theme of every newspaper and the staple question of his daily visitors."

Lincoln shared with them his thoughts on the gathering crisis as southern states considered leaving the Union, and what he believed he would have to do. "The very existence of a general and national government," Lincoln said, "implies the legal power, right, and duty of maintaining its own integrity. This, if not expressed, is at least implied in the Constitution. The right of a state to secede is not an open or debatable question. It was fully discussed in Jackson's time, and denied not only by him, but by the vote of Congress. It is the duty of a president to execute the laws and maintain the existing government."

The *Springfield Journal*, Lincoln's party newspaper, summarized his thinking on the day South Carolina seceded. Its headline: The Union— It Must Be Preserved. Soon Lincoln would take the oath of office as the sixteenth president of the United States. He would face the greatest military, moral, and political crisis of anyone to hold that office. Living witnesses to the Civil War included five of his presidential predecessors. Each, in their way, had attempted to arrest the gathering storm. And each, in their way, had brought it about. All had opposed Lincoln's candidacy, for in him they saw a threat to the institution itself. These five former presidents, who had occupied the highest of roles in a former epoch, now searched for their place in a new one.

CHAPTER 1

I Met Nullification at Its Threshold

The season for animated debate is rapidly passing by, our politicians possessing a more fervid and glowing heat in the winter than in the summer. This would lead one to conclude that the fire which blazed within them was not from heaven.

—John Tyler

Van Buren ~ Buchanan ~ Tyler

As far as exiles go, the Court of St. James's would not be without its charms.

A year and four months after his toast to compromise, Martin Van Buren was on a ship bound for England, the familiar scenes of home yielding to the dark and choppy waters of the North Atlantic. Van Buren believed his life's ambition to the presidency faded along with his view of the coast.

Nearly two decades earlier Van Buren had been aboard a ship when he learned of his first great political victory. He and his legal colleagues were sailing down the Hudson to attend court in New York City. At one of the stops came the news that he had become the youngest member of the New York Senate—by 200 votes out of 30,000 cast.

Van Buren was born in upstate New York in 1782, after the decisive siege of Yorktown but before the Treaty of Paris recognized American independence, growing up with three children by his mother's previous marriage and six siblings from his parents' union, along with six slaves his mother had inherited. His father was a farmer who operated a tavern on his property. For Van Buren, working in a barroom was an appropriate apprenticeship for politics. No doubt he could remember debates over the proposed Constitution of 1787, which bitterly divided the state of New York as well as his own Columbia County. As he grew older, he remembered he "had been a zealous partisan, supporting with all my power the administrations of Jefferson and Madison."

Van Buren began his legal training at age fourteen, doing menial work in his employer's office to earn his place. The archaic method of recording property titles was a persistent source of litigation, and after a time learning his trade in New York City, Van Buren returned home to Kinderhook and made a name for himself defending small landholders.

The New York Senate was scene to Van Buren's first attempts at a "science of politics" to manage competing ideological and ethnic factions. Working with allies, he helped create a statewide network of political leaders and newspapers, slating candidates for office and managing the affairs of their party, a group that would become known as "The Albany Regency," the first true statewide political machine. His tremendous political skill gave rise to nicknames such as "The Little Magician," a reference to his diminutive height, or the "Red Fox of Kinderhook," a nod to his hair color in younger days. A strong supporter of the War of 1812, Van Buren was appointed attorney general three years later (a position he held concurrently with his state senate seat). At age thirty-eight, with the Regency ensconced in power, the New York legislature appointed Van Buren a member of the US Senate.

It was the "Era of Good Feelings," with President James Monroe in his second term. Successor to Jefferson and Madison, completing the most durable dynasty in presidential history, Monroe's presidency was believed by some to make party politics a relic of the past. Van Buren knew better. Though now on a bigger stage with more complex factions, Van Buren tried to re-create the coalition building that had led him to the top of New York politics.

As the 1824 presidential election approached, Van Buren reached out to the leaders of emerging political organizations throughout the country, from New Hampshire to Georgia, attempting to unite the friends of limited government against supporters of a more active federal role, led by Secretary of State John Quincy Adams. General Andrew Jackson ultimately won a majority of the popular vote and the lion's share of the Electoral College, but fell short of a majority there, casting the race to the House of Representatives where he was defeated. Adams's victory did not deter Van Buren's efforts. Jackson had not been his first choice for president, and perhaps was not now, but promising the greatest chance of electoral success, Van Buren offered him an early endorsement in 1826.

As 1827 began, Van Buren sat down to write a letter to Thomas Ritchie, a powerful newspaper editor and political boss in Richmond, Virginia. In it he proposed an alliance between the "planters of the south and the plain republicans of the north." Together with "General Jackson's personal popularity," he believed they could unseat Adams. Van Buren, who had married a childhood acquaintance, may have believed that a romantic marriage was strengthened by similitude. But he knew that a durable political marriage relied on disparate groups uniting. Later that year the New Yorker traveled south, whipping up support for Jackson and assisting in the building of new party operations.

Sparing no effort to win the presidential election, Van Buren agreed to run as the Jacksonian candidate for governor of New York, where his friends believed that his personal popularity would boost the entire ticket. This time Jackson would win the state, by a margin of 8,000 votes out of 270,000 cast, on his way to winning a landslide across the country. From these efforts and the presidential victory they produced would emerge the Democratic Party, with Jackson generally considered its first chief executive.

Van Buren had not sought out the governorship, but a reprieve would not be long in coming. Jackson rewarded him with the first place in his administration as secretary of state. The previous four presidents had all held the preeminent position in the cabinet. Why would Van Buren, with his great political skill, fail to reach the summit as they had? And so it must have been with great surprise that he found himself out of the cabinet and on a ship bound for England a little more than two years later.

Jackson's presidency, commenced with such promise, had a congenital defect. Van Buren would remember the scandal "kept alive by feelings of the bitterest character" for two years, "a plague to social intercourse, destructive in many instances of private friendship, deranging public business . . . disparaging the character of the government."

Secretary of War John Henry Eaton, a dear friend of Jackson from Tennessee, had married Margaret O'Neill Timberlake shortly after the death of her husband, and in the process scandalized certain quarters of Washington. Floride Calhoun, wife of Vice President John C. Calhoun, led the other cabinet wives in ostracizing the Eatons. The Eaton Affair paralyzed the cabinet, divided the city, and caused the president "daily anguish."

Van Buren, son of a country tavern keeper, had no use for the protocols so harshly applied to the young couple. As a widower he had no worry of a wife to drag him into the wrong side of the quarrel. His support for the Eatons solidified his relationship with the president, who in turn became increasingly estranged from Calhoun. Within the cabinet, aside from Eaton himself, only the postmaster general joined Van Buren in supporting Margaret.

This seemingly silly concern implicated questions of great magnitude, perhaps none more so than the question of who would be Jackson's successor. Congressman James Buchanan of Pennsylvania noted, "Disguise it as we may, the friends of Van Buren and those of Calhoun are becoming very jealous of each other." John Quincy Adams, the former president now serving in the House of Representatives, wrote, "It is the prevailing opinion . . . that Mr. Van Buren is about to scale the Presidency of the United States by mounting upon the shoulders of Mrs. Eaton."

The 1829 social season that preceded the meeting of Congress brought these hostilities to the fore. Van Buren, determined to integrate the Eatons into Washington social life, held an event of his own, but none of the other cabinet wives attended. Van Buren and Jackson turned to the diplomatic corps for support, ensuring the Eatons were invited to balls given by the British and Russian ministers. When the wife of the minister from the Netherlands tried to exclude the Eatons from a ball, Van Buren attempted to persuade her in Dutch, his first language, while Jackson threatened to expel her husband from the country, differing approaches emblematic of their varying temperaments.

By the end of his first year in office, Jackson was permanently estranged from Calhoun and had settled on Van Buren as his successor. Encouraged to write a letter that could be used in case of his death, Jackson penned a political last will and testament and praised Van Buren in the strongest terms. The bequest referred to him as "well qualified to fill the highest office in the gift of the people, who in him will find a true friend and safe depository of their rights and liberty. I wish I could say as much for Mr. Calhoun."

In the summer of 1831, on one of their regular horseback rides, Van Buren mustered the courage to tell Jackson of the decision he had already made privately.

"General, there is but one thing that can give you peace."

- "What is that, Sir?"

"My resignation." It would not be enough to dismiss the Calhoun faction; doing so would make Jackson as well as Van Buren an object of wrath for the disappointed party. They would all have to go. And he would be the first to fall on his sword.

"Never, Sir! Even you know little of Andrew Jackson if you suppose him capable of consenting to such humiliation of his friend by his enemies."

Van Buren spent four hours trying to convince him, interrupted only occasionally by questions from the president. It was in his best interests to have a harmonious cabinet, Van Buren argued, something he would not achieve with the current composition. What had he planned for the future? Jackson asked. When Van Buren suggested returning to practice law, Jackson refused to countenance it. Perhaps, Jackson offered, the prestigious post of minister to England would allow him a face-saving departure.

Taking his hand, Jackson said that he had much to think about and asked him to come to the White House in the morning. There he found a careworn president who had not slept since their conversation. Van Buren noticed Jackson yielding "to the obvious force of the truth as I spread it before him."

Van Buren and Eaton resigned from the cabinet. Jackson soon dismissed the Calhounites, who had failed to follow in kind. The minister to

Great Britain was recalled to create an opening for Van Buren, who was appointed to the post in August. He would keep it subject to the consent of the Senate, which heretofore had been customarily given.

—~—

Arriving in September, Van Buren went quickly to work, the country lawyer gliding easily through the gilded halls of British government. On the day of the king's first formal reception of the season, Van Buren felt too ill to attend. He asked for his mail to be brought to his bedside, where at once he noted its unusual volume. He first opened the letter of a friend, a congressman from New York, which contained the shocking news. "I most sincerely congratulate you on your rejection by the Senate." Van Buren's enemies had finally gone too far, frontally challenging the popular President Jackson. The friend predicted that Van Buren would now be selected vice president "in spite of yourself." Encouraging him to hasten home, he wrote, "we have no triumphal arches as in ancient Rome, but we'll give you as warm a reception as ever a conqueror had."

Though stung and embarrassed by this rebuke, Van Buren reconsidered and attended the king's levee rather than staying in bed. At the palace, Lord Palmerston, foreign affairs secretary, conveyed the king's condolences, remarking that "no class of her [England's] public men were exempted from experiencing the excesses of party spirit."

Van Buren's rejection had come after two days of fiery debate. Senators Daniel Webster of Massachusetts and Henry Clay of Kentucky arranged for the balloting to end in a tie, thus handing the knife to Vice President Calhoun. "It will kill him sir," Calhoun jeered triumphantly, "kill him dead. He will never kick, sir, never kick." Senator Thomas Hart Benton of Missouri overheard him and disagreed. "You have broken a minister," he predicted, "and elected a Vice President."

Senator John Tyler of Virginia agreed with Benton. "Jackson is invincible; Van Buren is elevated by the silly thing of rejecting him; Calhoun is greatly injured." So it was.

The first Democratic National Convention would meet in May 1832 to re-nominate Jackson and select his running mate. With Van Buren at a safe, transatlantic distance, the question of the vice presidency would in reality be about whether to sustain Jackson. In March Van Buren wrote Senator William Marcy, his old ally in the Albany Regency, that if "my elevation to the Vice Presidency [is] the most effectual mode of testifying to the world their sentiments with respect to the act of the President and the vote of the Senate, I can see no justifiable ground for declining to yield to their wishes."

Jackson was convincingly re-elected over Henry Clay with his chosen successor as his running mate. But he would not be sworn in for a second term before seeing off the greatest crisis to face the Union. On November 24, 1832, an ordinance was unanimously carried by a convention of the most prominent citizens of South Carolina. The tariff of 1828 and the 1832 amendments were declared "null, void, and no law, nor binding upon this state, its officers or citizens," and after February 1, 1833, the state would no longer pay federal duties. Nullification, begun in whispers, persisting in rhetoric, was now a reality. But more dangerous still was the fifth section of the ordinance, which held that if the federal government attempted to enforce the tariff, South Carolina would withdraw from the Union, severing all political connections and establishing an independent nation. South Carolina lawmakers immediately passed legislation adopting the ordinance. The governor was empowered to accept volunteer soldiers. Calhoun resigned the vice presidency and returned to Washington as a senator to press the case for nullification.

The nullifiers would meet formidable opposition. In the words of one biographer, "If ever a man was resolved to accomplish a purpose, General Jackson was resolved on this occasion to preserve intact the authority with which he had been entrusted." Jackson ordered the collector of the Port of Charleston to "resort to all means provided by the laws." If necessary, he was to seize and even sell cargo to satisfy the duty.

As the standoff began, General Sam Dale of Mississippi, who had served under Jackson at the Battle of New Orleans, arrived in Washington on other business. Sent for by his old friend, Dale arrived to find Jackson on the lawn of the White House, from where the president conducted him to a reception room with Senator Benton and several others. They discussed the only subject on anybody's mind. "General Dale," Jackson said, "if this thing goes on, our country will be like a bag of meal with both ends open. Pick it up in the middle or endwise, and it will run out. I must tie the bag and save the country." When everyone left, Jackson asked his old comrade to remain. He instructed his servants to bring up whisky and turn away visitors. They talked briefly of their time together in the War of 1812. "Sam, you have been true to your country," Jackson said, "but you have made one mistake in life. You are now old and solitary, and without a bosom friend or family to comfort you. God called mine away. But all I have achieved—fame, power, every thing—would I exchange if she could be restored to me for a moment." Jackson "trembled with emotion, and for some time covered his face with his hands, and in tears dropped on his knee." He said, "they are trying me here; you will witness it; but, by the God of heaven, I will uphold the laws."

Dale expressed his hope that all would go right.

"They shall go right, sir," Jackson said passionately, smashing his pipe to splinters on the table.

Jackson hurriedly prepared an address to the upcoming session of Congress, writing so quickly that he was forced to spread out the pages in order for them to dry. Jackson replaced the Charleston garrison with more reliable troops, put the War and Navy Departments on notice, and dispatched a spy to learn if federal officers in the Palmetto State had gone over to the nullifiers.

On December 12, Jackson issued the proclamation that had so rapidly poured from his head to the page. "I consider the power to annul a law of the United States assumed by one state incompatible with the existence of the Union, inconsistent with every principle on which the Constitution was founded, and destructive of the great object for which it was formed. No state or states has a right to secede," he said. "The Union must be preserved without blood if possible, but it must be preserved at all hazards and at any price." The government of South Carolina responded with hostile remonstrances of their own, showing no signs of backing down. On January 16, the president asked Congress for authorization to use force against South Carolina.

Senator John Tyler now faced a question that not only carried the possible fate of the country, but one with the potential to destroy his political future. Tyler, though only forty-three, was well into a very full career. A graduate of William and Mary and a lawyer by training, he had served ten years in the General Assembly of Virginia; five years in the US House, where he had voted against the Missouri Compromise; governor; and for the past nine years a member of the Senate. Tyler was of the first families of Virginia, his father a classmate of Thomas Jefferson who had served with Madison and Monroe in the state's legislature before pre-dating his son as governor.

In keeping with his upbringing, Tyler had a dignified bearing. "Half the success in life depends on manners," he once told his son, "and the first and highest conquest is for him to obtain a mastery over his passions." Tyler looked the part: thin and over six feet tall, blue eyes, "silky brown" hair, and an angular nose befitting his aristocratic roots. While riding in a carriage on the road to Washington, a passenger complained that he could smell the city before it came into view. "Why, sir," Tyler responded, "if you can smell Washington with your nose, my nose must be there already."

Tyler had a history of independence from the popular Jackson that had cast doubt on his re-election even before the current crisis. The Virginia legislature had originally scheduled the Senate election for January 30, 1832. Now it was postponed for two weeks to force Tyler to show his hand on the president's request to use the military in South Carolina.

Tyler believed the nullifiers had made a mistake. But he did not condone coercing them by force and determined to lose his seat in opposition if necessary. On February 6, Tyler spoke out against "An act further to provide for the collection of duties on imports," known popularly and to its opponents as the "Force Bill." His discourse on the Senate floor was a revealing look at his views on the United States and the proper relationship between federal and state governments. "If I could hesitate as to my course, now that the storm is raging, the battlements rocking, and our institutions trembling to their foundations, I should be derelict to my highest duty, and recreant to the great trust confided in me.

"Let us learn to admire the beautiful system under which we live, and not seek to convert it into what it is not. Everything, Mr. President, is running into nationality. You cannot walk along the streets without seeing the word on almost every sign—national hotel, national boot-black, national blacksmith, national oyster-house." Here he was interrupted by a senator who added "The newspapers" to the list. "I let them alone," Tyler explained. "No man gets anything by intermeddling with them." Continuing, he said, "The government was created by the states, is amenable to the states, is preserved by the states, and may be destroyed by the states. I owe no responsibility, politically speaking, elsewhere than to my state.

"To arm him [Jackson] with military power is to give him authority to crush South Carolina, should she adopt secession. When the question comes up (I trust it never will), should the decision be formally pronounced against the right of secession, it would come to be a subject worthy of all reflection, whether the military arm should be exerted, or other measures of a milder nature, but equally efficacious, be resorted to.

"I would that I but moral influence enough to save my country in this hour of peril . . . I stand here manacled in a minority, whose efforts can avail but little. You, who are the majority, have the destinies of the country in your hands. If war shall grow out of this measure, you are alone responsible."

Jackson's policy of coercion cost him support in Virginia. Tyler's opposition dramatically increased his standing among the people. The Virginia Senate election, delayed to undermine Tyler, resulted in his reappointment by a wide margin. When the Force Bill came to a vote, Calhoun led a walkout of southern senators. Tyler held his ground and registered the lone dissent.

By this time Tyler and Henry Clay had already been conferring on a compromise. Budget surpluses as well as southern agitation compelled a reduction in the tariff. But northern manufacturers needed time to prepare for the increased competition of less expensive foreign goods. "Time," Tyler told Clay, "is of little importance to us." Tyler believed the real issue for southerners was crafting a tariff solely to raise revenue and not for protection. Tyler agreed to sound out the South about whether this tack would resolve the crisis. Clay's proposal kept the current rates in place until July 1, 1842, followed by a substantial reduction to 20 percent, and articulated the principle that the tariff existed simply to fund the government. When it finally passed the Senate, Tyler and Clay shook hands on the floor, congratulating one another.

Into this maelstrom of tariffs, secession, and nullification, Martin Van Buren made his triumphal return to office. He later wrote, "It is difficult to imagine a more critical condition than that in which I found the country involved at the moment of my arrival in Washington on the 26th of February, 1833." President Jackson picked him up in his own carriage and brought him to the gates of the Capitol. He then entered the Senate where he would preside as vice president, over friends and enemies alike.

On March 2, as his first term drew to a close, Jackson signed both the Force Bill and the Compromise Tariff. South Carolina responded by repealing the offensive ordinance. On the day he learned of his victory, the old general wrote his minister to Russia, James Buchanan. "I met nullification at its threshold. My proclamation was well timed, as it at once opened the eyes of the people to the wicked designs of the nullifiers, whose real motives had too long remained concealed.

"Although the tariff was made the ostensible object, a separation of the confederacy was the real purpose of its originators and supporters." The reaction, Jackson believed, all throughout the country, was "that it is not probable that we shall be troubled with them again shortly."

Buchanan had passed a cold winter in St. Petersburg, anxious for updates that were in short supply. He replied to the president, "I sincerely rejoice that our domestic differences seem almost to have ended. Independently of their fatal influence at home, they had greatly injured the character of the country abroad . . . God grant that the restless spirits which have kindled the flame in South Carolina may neither be willing nor able to promote disunion by rendering the Southern States generally disaffected towards the best of governments."

CHAPTER 2

The Freshmen

I never knew what it was to be so constantly pressed with engagements.
—FRANKLIN PIERCE

Pierce ~ Fillmore ~ Tyler ~ Van Buren

In the autumn of 1833, two future presidents arrived in the city of
Washington. Franklin Pierce of New Hampshire and Fillmore of New
York were newly elected members of the 23rd Congress, the first to
meet in Jackson's second term. Fillmore was thirty-three years old and
Pierce had just turned twenty-nine, but aside from youth the two had
little in common.

The polished appearance and impeccable manners of Millard Fillmore masked an upbringing of extreme poverty. The son of an itinerant
farmer, Fillmore was raised to backbreaking labor in western New York.
He watched his father struggle to scrape out a living, only to be thrown
off his land following a title dispute. The desperate feelings of poverty and
helplessness before the law would serve as powerful motivators.

At fourteen Fillmore took an apprenticeship in a textile mill, but
aspired to something better. "While attending the carding machines," he
would later recall, "I used to place the dictionary on the desk—by which
I passed every two minutes in feeding the machine and removing the
rolls—and in this way I would have a moment in which to look at a word
and read its definition and could then fix it in my memory." As an adult,
the boy who practiced with his dictionary would own a personal library of
more than four thousand volumes. Fillmore left his apprenticeship early,
remembering his journey home "on foot and alone with a knapsack on my
back." From there he attended school in the winter and worked on a farm

in the spring. By 1818, he taught school for three months in Cortland County, a testament to his rapid development as well as the desperate need for teachers on the frontier. When the academic year was over, he supported himself by working in a sawmill in New Hope. He remembered that the establishment of a small library at Kelloggsville, perhaps a mile from where he worked, "gave me my first knowledge of books, and though I had little leisure, I enjoyed the reading very much."

A greater opportunity appeared when his father became a tenant farmer of Cayuga County's Judge Walter Wood, whom he persuaded to take on Fillmore as a law clerk. The young man who had read the dictionary for elucidation was now reading *Blackstone's Commentaries*. When it was time to return to the mill, the judge offered him a seven-year clerkship. Fillmore used his teacher's salary to pay his way out of his previous apprenticeship, and in 1820 was finally able to accept Judge Wood's offer. While studying in his office, he worked as a land surveyor to cover his expenses. In the wintertime, he resumed teaching at a school eight miles distant. At a local Fourth of July gathering Fillmore was asked to give a speech, greatly impressing the audience. It led to his being hired to handle a suit before the Justice of the Peace, a lower court where advocates did not need to be lawyers. Judge Wood disapproved and ordered him not to repeat his offense. It then dawned on Fillmore with horror. "He did not intend that I should be a lawyer; but a dependent on him and a drudge in his business. But what could I do? I was friendless and penniless but my pride was instantly aroused, and I told him I would leave and at once settled up and I gave him my note for the balance I owed him." Once again, he found himself with a broken apprenticeship, trudging on foot back to his father's home. Fillmore resumed teaching in Aurora, handling the occasional dispute before Justices of the Peace. In 1823, he taught in Cold Springs, and "assisted some in the Post Office" at Buffalo. In the Law Offices of Rice and Clary, he finally completed the training to become a lawyer. In 1826, he married Abigail Powers, a minister's daughter. He bought a lot for them near East Aurora and built a sturdy home, one that stands to this day.

In 1828, Fillmore was elected to the state legislature as an Anti-Mason, a populist party focused on eliminating the secret societies that had begun in his home region of western New York. There, while tending closely to the issues affecting his district, he helped create a bankruptcy law that abolished imprisonment for debt.

Many presidents of the United States are intimately associated with places. None more so than Fillmore with Buffalo, where he finally moved in 1830, after opening a new law practice and renting a wooden tenement on Main Street above Mohawk. The first directory of the city misspelled both his first and last name, but in time he would become the best known of its citizens. He had first seen the city in 1818, five years after the British torch had been laid to it. One writer noted, "It was just rising from the ashes and there were many cellars and chimneys without houses, showing that its destruction by the British had been complete." Now it was a thriving, prosperous city on the western terminus of the Erie Canal. The former farm and factory worker embraced the active civic and social community he found there. For four months a year, when ice prevented shipping on the canal, the people of Buffalo opened their homes to one another. Millard and Abigail were frequent guests and hosts. Rapid growth meant great opportunity, and in 1832 Fillmore withstood the Jackson and Van Buren landslide in the state to win a seat in Congress.

Franklin Pierce's path to prominence was short and straight, especially by contrast with Fillmore. As a twelve-year-old attending New Hampshire's prestigious Hancock Academy, a homesick Pierce decided to return to his parents. He was shocked to find that his father, a stern veteran of the Revolution, did not rebuke him for desertion. The two had dinner, where the subject went unmentioned, and afterward Benjamin Pierce silently drove his carriage back toward Hancock. At a juncture in the woods, Franklin was ordered to walk the rest of the way, a significant part of the journey in the rain. And so he began the day where he had started, only wetter, colder, and more fatigued.

Pierce entered college at Bowdoin, in Maine, in 1820. Returning for his sophomore year by stagecoach, he met an incoming freshman, Nathaniel Hawthorne, beginning what would become the most important friendship of his life.

Pierce returned to his hometown of Hillsborough after graduation, an appointment arranged by his father to provide him a salary while studying law. In 1827, Benjamin Pierce was elected New Hampshire's governor after two previous defeats. The following year Franklin followed his father into politics, and was convincingly elected presiding officer of the Hillsborough Town Meeting. Pierce and his allies—ardent Jacksonians—defeated the old guard loyal to John Quincy Adams. Pierce campaigned hard for Jackson, and in the process helped create the New Hampshire Democratic Party.

Pierce was elected at twenty-five to the Great and General Court of New Hampshire, the state's legislature, where he chaired a committee to overhaul control of the local schools. In his second term, the affable, popular Pierce was chosen from New Hampshire's legislative body of 230 to serve as speaker. With seemingly little effort, Pierce leapt from one honor to the next, all the while struggling within himself to be content, writing, "Is it not the present that we cling to but something that sparkles in the distance and beckons us on—to find what? Disappointment."

The following year the Democratic state convention nominated him for the Congress. New Hampshire elected its five members at-large, giving an advantage to Pierce's party. Pierce was "gratified," but not "elated," when he won, and wondered whether he should not have shifted focus to the law. While at Bowdoin he and a friend had pledged not to marry young, worried "that our union with a lovely woman would interfere with and check the course of our ambition." His youth waning, at least for matrimonial purposes, Congressman-elect Pierce proposed marriage to Jane Appleton, the sister-in-law of one of his Bowdoin instructors. "Shy, retiring, frail and tubercular," in the words of one historian, Jane seemed less than an ideal fit for the hard-drinking, gregarious politician. They would be married in a quiet affair at the home of her family in Amherst, New Hampshire, during a congressional recess. A half hour after the nuptials, the newlyweds were on the road for Washington and the next session of Congress.

Partisan rancor would typify their later careers, but Fillmore and Pierce arrived in Congress in an era without crisp partisan divisions, when members were largely classified by their support or opposition to Jackson. In the House there were 143 "Jacksons," 63 "Anti-Jacksons," with 25 Anti-Masons and 9 Nullifiers. Fillmore and Pierce joined two other presidents in the House, one future, James K. Polk of Tennessee, and one past, John Quincy Adams. Fillmore and Pierce had incredible demands on their time, socially and professionally. Pierce wrote, "I never knew before what it was to be so constantly pressed with engagements." Their first days of federal service would later be known as "The Panic Session" of Congress. President Jackson was opposed to the Bank of the United States—a federally chartered institution that received government deposits and set monetary policy—believing it an anti-democratic concentration of power and a corrupting influence on politicians. First Jackson had vetoed the reauthorization of the bank, which gave it an expiration date but one that was too distant for his liking. He then turned to depleting its funds; federal expenditures were made with the bank's deposits, while new revenues were placed in various state banks.

Fillmore remembered, "the chief topic was the removal of deposits from the Bank." Pierce wrote, "the debate upon the deposit question seems to be interminable."

The future presidents found themselves on opposite sides of numerous votes on the bank. Fillmore in the House and Tyler in the Senate presented petitions from their constituents protesting the president's actions. Tyler, who personally opposed the bank, objected to the withdrawals, reasoning that Jackson could legally put the money in his own pocket as easily as in the state banks. For him, the question was not whether to have a national bank; it was whether the separation of powers would be preserved.

Vice President Van Buren, presiding over the Senate, feigned disinterest in the bromides against Jackson. Hoping to get a rise out of him, Clay, in one of his many speeches on the removals, asked Van Buren to go to the White House to "extend his well known influence" over the president. Van Buren, who had been reading a book, set it aside and walked down onto the Senate floor. Anxious senators and spectators alike watched as the vice president headed for Clay. Arriving at his desk, Van Buren said, "Mr. Senator, allow me to be indebted to you for another pinch of your aromatic Maccoboy [tobacco]."

The fight culminated in March, when Tyler joined a 26–20 Senate majority in favor of censuring Jackson. By that summer the fragmented

opposition groups became known as the Whigs, after the English political faction that opposed monarchial rule, and a new era of political parties
was born.

On January 30, 1835, the luminaries of Washington were at the Capitol for the funeral of a congressman. As the mourners walked down the
Capitol steps headed to the burial site, Tyler felt unwell and stood off
to the side. Then, an explosion. Startled, he turned to see a man, "about
four steps off, with a pocket pistol pointed at the President." The man
produced a second gun and again pulled the trigger at point-blank range.
Both misfired. Jackson raised his cane to strike him as he was tackled to
the ground.* "The old General sprung at him like a tiger," Tyler recalled,
"and manifested as much fearlessness as one could possibly have done."
Tyler visited the White House the following day. "Why, Mr. President,"
Tyler said, "when I looked at you yesterday while springing on that man
with your cane, I could have taken you for a young man of twenty-five."
So heated were the politics of the hour that Jackson blamed his Whig
opponents for complicity in the crime. Fillmore wrote to his law partner,
"The city is all in commotion at the outrageous attempt to assassinate the
president." It was on account of that same partner that Fillmore would
retire from Congress after only one term. In his absence, their firm had
been engaged in a number of lawsuits, representing the Holland Land
Company against ordinary settlers. While remunerative, the backlash
among the voters was such that Fillmore chose not to run again.

During the next congressional session slavery would come to the
fore. Congress set aside one or two days a week for the reading of petitions from constituents, and many of these entreaties related to abolition
or the limitation of slavery. Unhappy southern members and their allies
in Congress proposed a "gag rule," which would prevent these petitions
from being printed, read, or referred to a committee. Pierce was on the

---

* This was the first presidential assassination attempt. Jackson would also receive what was probably
the first presidential death threat the following year, over his refusal to pardon two men: "You damned
old scoundrel . . . I will cut your throat while you are sleeping," and a later sentence that ended with
the phrase "burnt at the stake in Washington." Its author was an actor, destined for less notoriety than
his son, Junius Brutus Booth.

committee that drafted this proposal and denounced abolitionists on the House floor. He wrote to Polk, now Speaker of the House, "I do not believe there is one person out of a hundred who does not wholly reprobate the course of the few reckless fanatics who are only able to disturb occasionally the quiet of a village." Rather than quiet the village, authors of the gag rule had guaranteed their opponents a rallying cry, with nine years of spirited debate to follow.

Meanwhile, a possible fight with France and the liberal use of patronage had realigned Jackson with his base of support in Virginia. Tyler's opposition to the president went from being an asset to a liability, coinciding with a movement in the Senate to lift the censure against Jackson. The Virginia legislature was preparing instructions to Tyler to support the measure. Tyler, who believed that senators were ambassadors of their states, would not defy his instructions. Nor would he vote against his conscience. If directed to lift the censure, he would resign. "I look daily for my walking papers from the legislature," Tyler wrote. His friends argued that the censure was of no moment, that he should vote to remove it or simply vote against it, but encouraged him in any event not to let the legislature drive him from the Senate. But Tyler was sanguine. As he once told his son, who was struggling with school, "adopt my motto, *Perserverando,* and all difficulties will vanish."

Tyler believed that public opinion, with its fluctuations, was not a useful compass. "The Duke of Marlborough, after being idolized by England, was turned adrift, hated and despised," he wrote. "This teaches us not to place our hopes of happiness on others, and least of all, to rest it upon popular favor. The purest and the best of men have been neglected and abused. Aristides was banished, and Socrates was poisoned." The Virginia legislature was not looking to make Tyler a martyr; offered a judgeship to go away quietly, he declined. Finally receiving his instructions to repeal the censure, Tyler resigned from the Senate in February 1836. "I shall set an example to my children which shall teach them to regard as nothing place and office, when either is to be attained or held at the sacrifice of honor."

CHAPTER 3

The Setting Sun

. . . perhaps the greatest, of the prominent sources of discord and disaster supposed to lurk in our political condition was the institution of domestic slavery.

—MARTIN VAN BUREN, INAUGURAL ADDRESS

Van Buren - Fillmore - Pierce - Buchanan - Tyler

After the vicious infighting that had opened Andrew Jackson's presidency, perhaps no one would have guessed that Van Buren would unanimously be nominated by the Democratic Party as his successor. The New Yorker ran strong in the South, promising non-interference with slavery where it existed, including attempts to abolish it in the District of Columbia. The Whigs nominated four regional candidates, hoping to send the election to the House of Representatives, but Van Buren prevailed, winning the presidency in the election of 1836. But in his victory were signs of trouble ahead; Van Buren's electoral vote collapsed from Jackson's 219 to 170, and this against badly divided opposition. His strategy of symbiosis with Jackson had brought him to this point, but he would have to work to carve out his own identity. Referring to Jackson's presence at the inauguration, one senator wrote, "For once, the rising was eclipsed by the setting sun."

The American economy had overheated. Slavery, which had so concerned Van Buren while he wrote his inaugural address, receded as an issue in the face of the first national economic collapse. The state banks, flush with federal deposits, were instructed to lend it freely, leading to runaway land speculation. Less than two weeks after the inauguration, the New York financial services firm of I. and L. Joseph collapsed. European lenders curtailed their lending and liquidated American assets.

Banks began to fail, triggering a run on accounts. In just one day in New York, $2 million in coins were withdrawn.

Confronted with this unprecedented crisis, Van Buren called a special session of Congress, the first in twenty-four years. Van Buren proposed issuing treasury bonds to cover the deficit, and the placement of revenue in an independent treasury, essentially making the government its own banker. James Buchanan, now a senator from Pennsylvania, approved of Van Buren's plan, writing Jackson, "It was every thing it ought to have been; and whilst it delighted his friends it extorted the respect of his enemies." Also considering these proposals were Millard Fillmore who had won election to his old congressional seat, riding a wave of increasing economic frustration, and Franklin Pierce, who at thirty-three became the nation's youngest senator.

The Whigs demonstrated strength at Van Buren's expense during the midterm elections. In his home state Democratic legislators became an endangered species while William Seward was elected the first Whig governor. Fillmore traveled through the western part of the state with Seward, and "no stump in five counties was too small for him to mount" on his behalf. The young political party could now taste the ultimate prize. The Whigs met early to select their nominee—December of 1839—and held their first national convention in Harrisburg, Pennsylvania. Henry Clay, twice defeated in his great pursuit for the presidency, was the choice of states' rights Whigs, who supported him due to his work on the Compromise Tariff. John Tyler, who had returned to the Virginia House and served as speaker, was a Clay delegate, "first, last and all the time . . . whether he could be elected or not." Clay's chief rival was William Henry Harrison, a former senator, congressman, minister to Colombia, and governor of the Indiana Territory, who gained fame as the Indian-fighting general at the Battle of Tippecanoe. Harrison had the backing of national republican Whigs (successors to John Quincy Adams, who favored a more energetic federal government) as well as the Anti-Masons and those who wanted a war hero of their own to best the party of Jackson. When Harrison prevailed, Tyler was rumored to have shed tears, something he laughed off as nonsense. But the reports had their effect on Clay supporters looking to be mollified. Tyler had been the vice presidential nominee of the southern Whigs in 1836, carrying four states. Now, to balance the ticket with a states' rights supporter and Clay man, he was the vice presidential nominee of the national party. The Whigs, who came together from divergent backgrounds and for different reasons, facing a badly wounded foe, did not attempt to put together a platform.

In May, Martin Van Buren was re-nominated by the Democrats for a second term. Taken for granted in modern times, his ability to win re-nomination would baffle his successors for twenty-four years.

The Jacksonian era had seen a dramatic expansion of the electorate, as various barriers to voting were reduced or removed, triggering a need for vastly different campaigns. The 56 percent average turnout in 1836 and 1832 was dwarfed by 80 percent in 1840, with an increase from 1.5 million to 2.5 million voters. The Whigs portrayed Harrison as a log-cabin-dwelling, coonskin-cap-wearing, hard-cider-drinking frontier farmer. The opposite was true. Harrison was from one of the oldest and most prosperous families in Virginia, and his log cabin was in reality a mansion in Indiana. His father, Benjamin Harrison V, had been a member of the Continental Congress, signer of the Declaration of Independence, and governor. The Whig campaign conveyed its message as never before through parades, barbecues, pole raisings, rallies, and printed pamphlets. The Whigs of Buffalo erected a Harrison log cabin, where on October 23, Millard Fillmore made a speech on behalf of the ticket, condemning the high-handedness of the president, criticizing his approach to the financial crisis, and advocating federal public works. Van Buren was crushed 234–60 in the Electoral College, winning only 47 percent nationally while losing his home state to Harrison.

Van Buren would leave office shortly after his fifty-eighth birthday. He easily could have retired, spending the rest of his life enjoying family, rest, and relaxation. He could do so secure in his record of service in New York, in the US Senate, in the legacy of the Democratic Party he had played a principal role in founding, and in holding the three highest offices in the national government. But what promise did retirement have for a man whose entire adult life was at center of action?

The Whigs were euphoric. The reign of the Jacksonians was over and they had elected a president of their own, and with him massive majorities in both chambers of Congress. But their joy would be short-lived. For all the rallies, the marches, the speeches, the brilliant sloganeering, the long-sought hard-fought victory of the opponents of Andrew Jackson would be for nothing.

CHAPTER 4

... And Tyler, Too

I am under Providence made the instrument of a new test which is for the first time to be applied to our institutions.

—JOHN TYLER

Tyler ~ Fillmore ~ Pierce ~ Van Buren ~ Lincoln

Vice President John Tyler was at home in Virginia, on his knees playing marbles with his young sons, when two messengers arrived at his door. President William Henry Harrison had died, thirty-one days after assuming office. Tyler hastily prepared himself and his family and by 5:30 that evening was on his way to Washington, departing on a train from Richmond reserved specially for that purpose. In the predawn hours of April 6, 1841, he took the oath of office at Brown's Indian Queen.

Harrison was the first president to die at his post; seven others would join him over time. The swift and unquestioned transfer of power and continuity of government are now taken for granted. It is much to the credit of John Tyler, the first to confront this problem. The Constitution, as originally written, provides that "In case of removal of the President from office, or of his death, resignation, or inability to discharge the powers and duties of said office, the same shall devolve on the Vice President." At a minimum, there is ambiguity as to the title, if not the responsibilities of the office. Was Tyler "President," "Acting President," still "Vice President?" Some would even argue that a special election was required to complete Harrison's term.

In the hours after his swearing in, Tyler called a meeting of the cabinet. Daniel Webster, the prominent former senator and now secretary of state, argued that Harrison had intended to govern through his department heads, submitting questions for consensus approval, with the president serving as but one vote among the group. "I beg your pardon, gentlemen," Tyler responded. "I am very glad to have in my cabinet such able statesmen as you have proved yourselves to be. And I shall be pleased to avail myself of your counsel and advice. But I can never consent to being dictated to as to what I shall or shall not do. I, as President, shall be responsible for my administration. I hope to have your hearty co-operations in carrying out its measures. So long as you see fit to do this, I shall be glad to have you with me. When you think otherwise, your resignations will be accepted."

Having moved to consolidate his position in Washington, Tyler published an address to the nation on April 9. Congressional recognition of him as president was soon to follow, despite a spirited fight from former president John Quincy Adams.

President John Tyler's next challenge came from an unexpected quarter: Henry Clay, with whom he had worked so closely on the Compromise Tariff, whom he had stood behind through the Bank Wars, and whose presidential hopes at the 1839 Whig Convention he had so strongly supported. Tyler's very presence on the Harrison ticket, after all, was in part a consolation to the defeated Clay faction. For Clay, who had already accomplished more than most American presidents, all feelings were subservient to his desire for the nation's highest office. Tyler was now the tenth president, and at age fifty-one, the youngest, replacing Harrison, sixty-eight, the oldest.* Only three of Tyler's predecessors had not won re-election. None had been denied re-nomination by their own party. Harrison had pledged in his inaugural to serve but one term, and now Tyler was very much in Clay's way. No previous feelings of comity could compensate for that.

Despite their familiarity, Clay badly misjudged his opponent, whose tenure he thought "will be in the nature of a regency." Congress, which usually convened in the December following the presidential inauguration, would gather on May 31, in response to a call by President Harrison. Taking office suddenly and under unprecedented

---

* Harrison would hold this record until Ronald Reagan's inauguration in 1981.

conditions, Tyler would now have to deal with Congress far earlier than most of his predecessors.

With Van Buren gone and financial affairs in disarray, many Whigs wanted to move forward in creating a new national bank. Their new president, however, had come to the Whigs over states' rights and in response to Jackson's executive overreaches. He did not then and had never in the past favored a national bank. But Tyler was not eager for a frontal assault on his party's cherished objective. And while he believed many aspects of a national bank unconstitutional, he could support the idea of a bank in the District of Columbia, chartered pursuant to Congress's general legislative power over the capital, empowered to set up branches in states that agreed. The Whigs in Congress were similarly disinclined to take on their new president. But Clay, its most powerful member, was determined to force the issue.

A week before the opening of the special session, Clay went to see the president. Tyler asked that the issue be continued until December, with the regular meeting of Congress. Tempers and voices were raised and Clay would not yield. "Then, sir," the president said, "I wish you to understand this—that you and I were born in the same district [Virginia]; that we have fed upon the same food, and have breathed the same natal air. Go you now, then, Mr. Clay, to your end of the avenue, where stands the Capitol, and there perform your duty to the country as you shall think proper. So help me God, I shall do mine at this end of it as I shall think proper."

Clay proceeded to push a bill that he knew the president would not accept. According to one biographer, Clay "almost single-handedly shattered his own party by his obsessive desire to fashion a third national bank." And before long Tyler would find a bill to re-charter the national bank on his desk.

Daniel Webster recalled that every member of the cabinet "earnestly recommended" Tyler sign it into law. But on August 16, the president issued his veto. The Whigs were deflated. "Egad," said one Democrat, "he has found one of old Jackson's pens."

Tyler was serenaded by a mob outside the White House, banging drums and blowing trumpets while firing blunderbusses, shouting "Huzza for Clay!" "A Bank! A Bank! Down with the Veto!" Through windows the president watched himself burned in effigy.

But the break was not permanent. A delegation of Whigs visited the White House in search of a compromise. Tyler was glad to receive them and explained the kind of bank he could approve, dropping all of his objections, except for the power of banks to discount notes* without state concurrence. But Tyler, motivated by presidential concerns of his own, began to reconsider the plan that he had agreed to. Perhaps his fortunes lay not with the Whigs, but with the Democrats.

Less than a month later, Tyler would veto a second bill to incorporate a national bank. Two days later, the White House was a funereal scene. Letter after letter arrived from the cabinet, the first at 12:30 p.m., the last at 5:30, announcing their resignations. All but Webster had signaled their intentions. Later in the day he came in person to the White House.

"Where am I to go, Mr. President?" Webster asked.

"You must decide that for yourself, Mr. Webster."

"If you leave it to me, Mr. President, I will stay where I am." Webster had vied with Clay for leadership of the Whigs and shared his overwhelming desire to be president. Rather than return to the Congress where Clay was ascendant, the less distasteful option was to stay where he was.

Rising and extending his arm, the president said, "Give me your hand on that, and now I will say to you that Henry Clay is a doomed man." Tyler moved quickly to fill his cabinet, choosing Whigs who had fallen out with Jackson for the same reasons as himself.

On September 13, 1841, fifty Whig members of Congress stood on Capitol Square and formally kicked Tyler out of the Whig Party. Their published address "created a great sensation throughout the country," Fillmore wrote. "I have heard of but two Tyler men in this city . . . I need not add that both of these are applicants for office."

Six months into his presidency, Tyler may be fairly said to have had as little party support as anyone in his position. Tyler's son, who served

---

* "Discounting notes" is the process by which central banks loan money to local banks at favorable, or discounted, rates. In effect, it gives the central bank the power to control the money supply and thus to dictate monetary policy.

as his father's personal secretary, attempted to arrange train travel for the president.* The railroad superintendent, a strong Whig, refused, saying that he was not presently running any special cars for presidents. "Did you not furnish a special train for the funeral of General Harrison?" Tyler asked. "Yes," said the superintendent, "and if you will only bring your father here in that shape you shall have the best train on the road."

In February, Franklin Pierce resigned from the Senate, pledged to give up alcohol, and returned to New Hampshire and his family. Jane—who hated politics, despised Washington, and regretted prolonged absences from her husband—would finally get her wish. As a thirty-seven-year-old senator embarked on an unlikely retirement, a sixty-year-old former president was energetically resisting the same.

On June 16, 1842, Martin Van Buren was on a western campaign tour, building support for another presidential bid, when muddy roads stranded him for the night in Rochester, Illinois. Despite the setback, Democrats were determined to show their guest a good time. This meant inviting a humorous and interesting dinner guest of the opposite party, a state legislator and lawyer named Abraham Lincoln. Lincoln did not disappoint, with "a constant supply" of entertaining stories, "each more irresistible than its predecessor." Van Buren had many stories of his own, of old New York politics in the days of Alexander Hamilton and Aaron Burr, and from his tumultuous life in government. The group stayed together until after midnight. Van Buren admitted that his sides were sore from laughter for days afterward. Upon parting, Van Buren promised that he would never forget that night. (Nearly twenty years later, at a critical moment for Lincoln and the country, he would prove that he never did.) Lincoln—who from his impoverished childhood "was just awful hungry to be somebody," and was dubbed by his law partner "the most ambitious man in the world"—was no doubt affected by his first meeting with a president. Lincoln had more than kept up with his distinguished visitor, and could not have helped but come away from that experience believing his grand ambitions were not so unrealistic after all.

---

* This story comes to us from President Abraham Lincoln, who repeated it to memorable effect while planning his first train trip in office.

Meanwhile in Washington, a familiar fight over the tariff was about to heat up. Fillmore ran for Speaker of the House, losing in the Whig Caucus to John White of Tennessee. As the runner-up, by tradition, Fillmore was appointed chairman of the powerful Ways and Means Committee. In this capacity Fillmore had several successes, requiring departments to reconcile their estimated spending with congressional authorizations to stay within their budgets, a practice continued to the present day. As he had in the New York legislature, he backed a successful bankruptcy bill. Fillmore was also critical in securing a $30,000 appropriation for Samuel Morse to lay the first telegraph line from Washington to Baltimore, a feat that proved the feasibility of this revolutionary new technology. But his greatest task would be reducing the runaway budget deficit. Fillmore had authored two tariff bills that were vetoed by Tyler over the issue of sharing the proceeds of public land sales with the states. Under Fillmore's third proposal, the revenue sharing was dropped, the average tariff would be 30 percent, higher for products that competed directly with American-made goods, and preferential tax treatment would be given to the cargo of American versus foreign ships. Arguing for his plan, Fillmore was a "plain, matter of fact debater," aiming at logic but not emotion, in the words of one reporter. On August 30, 1842, President Tyler signed Fillmore's tariff. By January 1, Fillmore was able to report the deficit had become a surplus of five million dollars. Satisfied with this and other important victories, Fillmore resolved to leave the field to others, writing his "utmost ambition has been satisfied . . . I aspire to nothing more, and shall retire from the exciting scenes of politics strife to the quiet enjoyments of my own family and fireside."

As Fillmore headed for home, President Tyler confronted a crisis that set an important precedent for his successors. The state of Rhode Island was still using the constitution designed by King Charles II in 1663, one that severely restricted voting rights. A convention of the disaffected met and declared themselves the lawful representatives of the state. Fearful of the upstarts, the ironically named Governor Samuel King wrote President Tyler for help. Tyler responded "however painful the duty, I have to assure your excellency that, if resistance is made to the execution of the laws of Rhode Island by such force as the civil posse shall be unable to overcome, it will be the duty of this government to enforce the constitutional guaranty." At the same time, Tyler advised the governor to call a convention to address these matters and to pardon the leaders of the convention. Tyler sent the secretary of war to Rhode Island when he became aware that the convention was armed and planning an overthrow. In that event, he was to call out the Massachusetts and Connecticut militia to defend the state government. The breakaway faction backed down, and a convention was called by the state that met and amended the constitution to increase voting rights.

John Tyler, as other presidents dealing with a difficult Congress, would turn his attention to foreign policy, where he could act decisively. His efforts led to the first trade treaty with China and the settlement of a number of disputes with Great Britain. But his foreign policy focus would not be overseas. The Republic of Texas, largely populated by American emigrants, had effectively won its independence from Mexico in 1836. Talk of annexation was immediate on both sides of the Sabine River. On the last day of his presidency, Jackson sent a diplomat to the Republic, giving them official recognition. Van Buren had struggled with the complexities of the issue; northern states were concerned about new slave territory, while Mexico, who refused to acknowledge that Texas was independent, threatened war. For Tyler, not only was union with Texas the right thing to do, but it captured the American imagination, and just might propel him to another term as president. In December 1843, Tyler's message to Congress reviewed annexation's advantages. Privately he enlisted Andrew Jackson to lobby Texas president Sam Houston, a protégé of the former president, who had been burned by Van Buren's snubbing of Texas's overtures. Webster, who opposed the addition of Texas, left the cabinet—a decision that preserved whatever chance he retained to be president and may have saved his life.

As Tyler moved to acquire Texas, the man dubbed "the Accidental President" was about to see his personal and political fortunes upended by another twist of fate. On February 28, 1844, the leading men and women of Washington boarded the USS *Princeton* to watch the firing of what was billed the most powerful cannon in the world. As Tyler headed to watch the display from the deck, he was detained below by a woman who wished to give him a toast, causing him to miss the demonstration. It did not go as planned. The gun exploded, killing the secretary of state, secretary of the navy, and six others, injuring many more. Congressman John Hardin, who had defeated his fellow Whig Abraham Lincoln the year before, remembered "the ghostly countenances of the dead, the shattered limbs, the gashes in the wounded and the mournful moaning" that "can neither be described or imagined." Julia Gardiner, a young heiress from New York, had been traveling with her family, first throughout Europe, then to Washington, for a fateful appointment aboard the *Princeton*. Hearing of her father's death, she collapsed in the arms of John Tyler.

Tyler replaced the cabinet vacancies with Democrats, a clear signal that he hoped to be their nominee in 1844. His new secretary of state, John C. Calhoun, was determined to acquire Texas for the United States, and would ultimately devise a successful strategy when all appeared lost. Tyler had brought the question to the fore. The opinions of all presidential aspirants were sought. Clay believed that annexation meant war with Mexico, maybe even war backed by a European power. Van Buren penned a thoughtful, nuanced letter, explaining his opposition to immediate annexation. In so doing he took a major detour from the royal road he had been traversing back to the presidency. Clay and Van Buren had put themselves on the wrong side of popular opinion in an ambitious young country.

April was a month of courtship, personal and political, for John Tyler. Calhoun quickly concluded negotiations with Texas, and on April 22 a treaty of annexation was sent to the Senate. There it was defeated, by the lopsided margin of 16–35. With more success, Tyler, who had been widowed eighteen months earlier, asked Julia Gardiner's mother for her daughter's hand in marriage. That June, Tyler would become the first president to wed while in office. Tyler, fifty-four, and Julia, twenty-four, went on a month-long honeymoon in July.

Tyler knew that his best chance to retain the presidency lay as the nominee of a major political party. The Whig bridge had been burned. The Democratic Party seemed a real possibility. But he would have to find his way around Martin Van Buren. As the election year dawned, twelve state party conventions had endorsed Van Buren, while four of the remaining six did not commit to any candidate. Through a mutual friend, Tyler offered his opponent a seat on the Supreme Court, an appointment rejected by Van Buren. But being the front-runner for the Democratic nomination was a mixed blessing, both for Van Buren and those who followed. The difficulty stemmed from the "2/3 Rule" of the Democratic Party, requiring a supermajority for nomination, perhaps the most consequential rule in American history to be so little remembered. On the first ballot at the May convention, Van Buren won roughly 55 percent of the vote, 146 out of 266 delegates. Though the clear preference of a strong majority of Democrats, he was forced to withdraw after nine ballots. It appears he would have easily achieved the nomination but for his position on Texas. The 2/3 Rule produced the first "dark horse" nominee for president, James K. Polk of Tennessee, the former Speaker of the House, protégé of Jackson, and a strong supporter of Texas annexation.

Unable to force Van Buren from the field, Tyler chose not to participate in the convention, realizing that losing there meant he would be bound to support the nominee. In May, an independent "Tyler Convention" met in Baltimore and nominated him for another term. In accepting their endorsement, he wrote "I do not feel myself at liberty to decline the nomination tendered me under such circumstances. There is much in the present condition of the country which would forbid my doing so." Throughout the summer pressure built for Tyler to retire from the general election. There were growing fears that he would split the pro-Texas vote and allow Henry Clay to win the presidency. Jackson wrote, "Mr. Tyler's withdrawal at once would unite all the Democrats into one family without distinction. This would render our victory easy and certain." Eventually, reluctantly, Tyler came to realize this as well, and withdrew. Clay and others had achieved their wish of making him a one-term president, but at their own expense. Tyler—with just a few months left in office—would return to the Texas question with all of his might, armed with a creative solution from Calhoun. In his final address to Congress, he proposed a bill to bring Texas into the Union as a state, requiring a simple majority, rather than relying on a formal treaty such as the one the Senate had rejected. As his presidency drew to a close, Tyler proudly put his signature to the bill admitting Texas to the Union. All that remained to achieve was for Texas to give her consent.

᠆ ᠊

Julia Tyler's time as first lady was both short and energetic.* Jackson and Van Buren had been widowers, while Tyler's first wife Letitia had been sick for much of his presidency. In these cases the duties of first lady had devolved to others. Now for the first time in many years the president's wife fulfilled the role. Opening the White House for one final gala, the Tylers found many callers, prompting the first lady to tell her husband that he could no longer be called "a President without a party." Addressing his guests, Tyler said, "when called from the plow by an act of Divine Providence, to assume the high and responsible duties which devolved upon him, he knew he was leaving a bed of down to repose upon a bed of thorns—and was happy that he was about to return from this bed of thorns to one of down." People's eyes were filled with tears. Julia remembered, "His voice was more musical than ever; it rose, and fell, and trembled, and rose again."

Tyler's "bed of down" could be found on the James River in Charles City County, thirty-five miles from Richmond, an estate he had bought during his presidency. Tyler named it Sherwood Forest, after the wooded residence of Robin Hood, a facetious nod to his outlaw status after his expulsion from the Whigs. Julia Tyler witnessed her new Virginia home "with a feeling of pleasurable excitement and agreeable surprise. The house had been opened by their slaves, and everything appeared neat and beautiful." The twelve-hundred-acre plantation was maintained by sixty to ninety slaves living in twenty cabins on the property. Furniture was coming from the White House by ship, to be joined by furnishings from her home state of New York, including "rugs, a chandelier, French mirrors," and an assortment of other necessities.

Tyler's public life seemingly behind him. "Everything he desired in the future was to have his motives and actions properly vindicated," his son remembered. But his legacy would haunt him even in his secluded

---

* At Julia Tyler's request, "Hail to the Chief" was first played for a president on official occasions.

retirement, as "Nearly every neighbor, and most of his countrymen were Whigs and followers of Clay, and who had learned to hate Tyler as a traitor, a renegade, and everything that was esteemed bad in their party creed." Neighbors refused to visit him, a courtesy due even a stranger. One day the clerk of the court interrupted the isolation at Sherwood Forest to announce that Tyler's neighbors had voted him overseer of roads. Even the newspapers noted that it had been done to insult Tyler, who would have to pay a fine if he declined, which they fully expected him to do. Instead, the former president expressed his honor at this favor, and promised to fulfill his duty as faithfully as he had all of his other offices.

His son noted, "Mr. Tyler commenced his duties with the same faithful purpose as had ever characterized him. The road being very undulating, he resolved to cut down the hills, fill up the ravines, and make it an example to the state. He summoned to all the hands in the township. Day by day he applied himself to his work, the law of Virginia specifying no limited time for working on the roads." His one power to meet his responsibilities was the ability to requisition his neighbors' slaves at his discretion. "The effect of his diligence was seen, not only on the road, but in the mournful silence that prevailed on the various plantations, which were chiefly owned by the Whigs." When the harvest was ready to be picked, "The hands were all upon the road. The smiles that lately illuminated the countenances of the Whigs turned to dismay." Finally, Tyler's neighbors graced him with their presence at Sherwood Forest, commending his work and asking him to let someone else have a chance. Tyler declined, citing a solemn obligation to continue his duty.

And so it was John Tyler—as he had time and again before—who had the last laugh at the expense of his antagonists.

CHAPTER 5

War in Mexico!

Neither of us probably supposed that he would ever be President. He has since greatly improved.

              —JAMES BUCHANAN ON JAMES K. POLK

Buchanan ~ Tyler ~ Pierce ~ Fillmore

President-elect Polk asked James Buchanan to serve as his secretary of state. The letter bearing the offer appeared to carry with it the condition that Buchanan not run for president. Buchanan responded carefully. "I do not know that I shall ever desire to be a candidate of the Presidency," but "I could not, and would not, accept the high and honorable office which you have called me, at the expense of self-ostracism. My friends would unanimously condemn me were I to pursue this course." If put forward as a candidate, "I cannot declare in advance that I would not accede to their wishes." The two eventually found language that made both of them comfortable, and Buchanan prepared to enter the cabinet.

At the age of fifty-three, Senator James Buchanan of Pennsylvania climbed yet another step on the steadiest ascension to the apex of American politics. Buchanan's resume, which included a decade in the House of Representatives, another decade in the Senate, and service as Jackson's minister to Russia, concealed a less auspicious beginning.

Buchanan was the son of an Irish immigrant farmer and a mother who was the daughter of a country farmer. His well-read mother liked to argue with her children, sharpening their debating skills. Buchanan entered Dickinson College in 1807. "There was no efficient discipline," he remembered, "and the young men did pretty much as they pleased. To be a sober, plodding, industrious youth was to incur the ridicule of the mass of the students." To fit in, Buchanan "engaged in every sort of extravagance and mischief in which the greatest proficients of the college indulged." On a Sunday during an autumn break from school, Buchanan remembered, a letter was delivered to his father. Upon reading it, "his countenance fell." Passing it to his son, he left the room. Its contents—details of Buchanan's misbehavior—were devastating. If not for his father's reputation, he would have been expelled. Buchanan was requested not to return, which would spare the family the mortification of his being sent away while school was in session. Buchanan reached out to the pastor of his church, a trustee of Dickinson, and pledged to refrain from shenanigans if he could only be readmitted. In this he succeeded, but his conduct was not forgotten, and at graduation, when the faculty had to choose between two students on whom to bestow the highest honors, Buchanan was unfairly passed over. His father's advice would be valuable for his future career in politics. "Often when people have the greatest prospects of temporal honor and aggrandizement, they are all blasted in a moment by a fatality connected with men and things; and no doubt the designs of Providence may be seen very conspicuously in our disappointments, in order to teach us our dependence on Him who knows all events, and they ought to humble our pride and self-sufficiency."

Buchanan qualified as a lawyer and served in the War of 1812 as a private in a company that went to Baltimore, in preparation for a British invasion of the city that never materialized. Upon his return he was elected to the Pennsylvania legislature. There he gained fame in the impeachment trial of Judge Franklin, who had vacated the state conviction of a man who refused to be drafted into federal service. Buchanan successfully argued for his acquittal before the Senate.

With success at the Bar, service in time of war, and a record in politics, Buchanan next turned his attention toward finding a wife. Of all those to serve as president, he was the only one never to succeed in doing so. Ann Coleman, his fiancée, was remembered as a "very beautiful girl, of singularly attractive and gentle disposition," from a prominent family in Lancaster, Pennsylvania. It appears, however, that from the machinations of others a wedge was driven between the young lovers. In the summer of 1819, she wrote Buchanan a letter asking to be released from their engagement. If it was her wish, he replied, he would acquiesce. Months later, at the age of twenty-three, she died while visiting Philadelphia, before an expected reconciliation could come to pass, with suicide often suspected as the cause. An obituary, which one witness claimed was written by Buchanan, closed with the poem "The spider's most attenuated thread/Is cord, is cable to man's tender tie/On earthly bliss—it breaks at every breeze."

Buchanan wrote to her father. "You have lost a child, a dear, dear child. I have lost the only earthly object of my affections, without whom life now presents to me a dreary blank. My prospects are all cut off, and I feel that my happiness is buried with her in the grave." Buchanan said that someday he would learn that they both had been the victims of interference by others in their relationship. "God forgive the authors of it." He pleaded with the grieving father to "Afford me the melancholy pleasure of seeing her body before its interment." He asked also that he be allowed to attend the funeral. "I would like to convince the world, and I hope yet to convince you, that she was infinitely dearer to me than life." The letter was returned to him, unopened. Buchanan would never marry or again come close to marriage. Several years before becoming secretary of state, his sister and her husband died, leaving him the guardian of Harriet Lane, his young niece. She would later serve as first lady, as well as the closest thing Buchanan would experience to having a child of his own. In his grief, he accepted the urging of his friends to run for a seat in Congress, which he won. He was sworn in in December of 1821, during the presidency of James Monroe.

An active supporter of Jackson in 1824 and again in 1828, Buchanan's earnest efforts helped Old Hickory win Pennsylvania. Though still very young, his abilities led to his being talked about for the vice presidency. In December of 1831, President Jackson proposed Buchanan as the minister to Russia, and he was confirmed by the Senate a month later. He would not depart until the icy water unfroze, giving him time to learn French, the universal diplomatic language. Buchanan remembered his time at the Tsar's Court as a series of encounters with princes, counts, dukes, and other assorted noblemen. He remembered the double-paned windows and fireplaces that made the winter bearable, as well as the northern summer nights that never seemed to end. Buchanan successfully concluded a treaty of commerce and navigation with Russia, departing in August of 1832 in an unsuccessful attempt to see his ailing mother one final time.

Entering the Senate in December 1834, he declined to serve as Van Buren's attorney general five years later. Buchanan was considered for president in 1840, but most delegates were committed to Van Buren, the incumbent. "If I should ever run for the Presidency," he told his supporters, "I would like to have an open field and a fair start." But if Van Buren somehow stumbled, Buchanan had empowered his friends to put him forward. Four years later came another disappointment for Buchanan, as the dark horse from Tennessee garnered the Democratic nomination and the presidency.

Buchanan remembered serving with Polk in the House, remarking to a former colleague "neither of us probably supposed that he would ever be President. He has since greatly improved." The president and his secretary of state had recently shared a meal and afternoon together, and Buchanan came away satisfied that the best choice had been made under the circumstances. Besides, Buchanan was certain that Van Buren would have lost to Clay.

Polk and Buchanan had three pressing challenges in the realm of foreign affairs. The first was to make sure that Texas ratified the resolution, adopted at the close of Tyler's term, to join the Union. The second was to manage the fallout with Mexico that would result. Third was a potential war with Britain over the Oregon Territory. This massive region included all of modern-day Washington, Oregon, Idaho, and parts of Montana and Wyoming. Remote and sparsely populated, the area was jointly administered by Britain and the United States, a stopgap since neither could agree on a northwestern boundary. Either country could withdraw from the treaty after a one-year notice. In addition to the prospects of losing the territory to Britain or forcing a war on the subject, Polk faced the predominantly American settlers clamoring for protection and threatening to create their own government in the event the United States did not find a way to bring them in.

The president and his secretary of state had radically different personalities; where Polk was bellicose, Buchanan was cautious. Ultimately,

Buchanan would prevail upon the president to accept a more moderate settlement with Britain, allowing the administration to focus on the deteriorating situation with Mexico.

Late one September evening Buchanan visited Polk to discuss the rumors then circulating about his being considered for appointment to the Supreme Court. Buchanan swore that he was not the source, but that he "had long desired to have a seat on the Bench of the Supreme." He noted that he had passed up chances in the past, none having come at the right time. He added that it would save them from an awkward situation if Polk moved to reduce the tariff, which Pennsylvania manufacturing relied upon.

Polk expressed his satisfaction with Buchanan at State and questioned whether he could find a suitable cabinet replacement. Buchanan promised that if the situation with Mexico worsened he would stay. The two agreed that nothing had to be decided now, and to revisit the question when Congress convened in December.

But as Congress met, tensions with Mexico were high. Buchanan wrote to Louis McLane, American minister to England, "I should this day have been on the bench of the Supreme Court, had it not been for the critical state of our foreign relations. I very much desire the position, because it would have enabled me to spend the remainder of my days in peace. I have now been on the stormy deep nearly a quarter of a century." And so James Buchanan narrowly missed a life of peaceful judicial decision-making and continued on the track that would lead him to the calamitous final hours of his life in politics. Polk's Supreme Court nominee failed in the Senate, amid rumors that Buchanan had helped orchestrate his defeat, underscored by the votes of Buchanan's closest allies. Buchanan later tried to enlist the attorney general to back his Supreme Court claim, unsuccessfully. Polk recorded in his diary, "Mr. Buchanan will find that I cannot be forced to act against my convictions, and that if he chooses to retire I will find no difficulty in administering the government without his aid."

In addition to the dispute over Texas, America was aggrieved by millions of dollars in outstanding claims against the Mexican government. For years, corrupt officials had seized American vessels and goods, and Americans traveling or doing business in the country were arrested or placed in slavery. Louisiana congressman John Slidell (the only one who spoke Spanish) had been sent to Mexico to adjust the difficulties between the two countries. He was rejected by the Mexican government, who relied on a technicality to send him back to Washington. Polk had begun the year by ordering General Zachary Taylor and his men to the Rio Grande, to protect Texas from Mexican aggression. Polk informed his cabinet that attempts at diplomacy had failed, and that Mexico had refused to make good on the wrongs done to the United States. He then asked the opinion of his cabinet, starting with Buchanan. The secretary of state agreed and urged Polk to seek a declaration of war. The consensus was that a message should be drafted by Buchanan and sent to Congress.

The cabinet met again on May 9. Everyone agreed that if any hostile action were taken against Taylor's forces, a declaration of war should be sought immediately. Buchanan believed America had more than enough cause for war, but would "feel better satisfied in his course" in the event of aggression against Taylor. At 7:30 that night, the cabinet returned to the White House in summons to an emergency meeting. Since their earlier gathering, Polk had received a dispatch explaining that Mexican forces had crossed the Rio del Norte, killing or capturing sixty-three of Taylor's men. Buchanan was tasked with hastily preparing a history of the wrongs committed by Mexico and assisting the president in his message to Congress.

On May 13, the United States Congress declared war on Mexico. Soon thereafter, the US Army advanced from three directions; Taylor drove south into Mexico's interior, while two separate forces proceeded west, capturing California and New Mexico with little difficulty (these two Mexican territories included all or part of the present-day states of California, Nevada, Utah, Wyoming, Colorado, New Mexico, and Arizona). On August 8, 1846, President Polk asked Congress for authority to purchase land from Mexico as part of a settlement. Before now, the inextricable issues of slavery and territorial acquisition had been settled by the Missouri Compromise of 1820. Missouri was admitted as a slave state, Maine as a free state; in territories created from the Louisiana Purchase, slavery was otherwise prohibited north of the 36' 30" parallel (roughly the southern border of Missouri), and permitted to the south of that line. What would be the fate of the vast new territory expected to be acquired from Mexico?

The president's request created bedlam in the House of Representatives. In the heat of the debate, the Speaker recognized David Wilmot of Pennsylvania, a little-known, pro-administration Democrat, who would now offer one of the most divisive proposals in American history. Wilmot supported slavery where it existed, he said, but where it did not, "God forbid that we should be the means of planting this institution upon it." The Wilmot Proviso, as it would be known, would forbid slavery in the territory gained from Mexico. "As if by magic," one newspaper noted, "it brought to a head the great question which is about to divide the American people." It would pass the House but die in the Senate, taking Polk's request down with it.

John Tyler, who had opposed the Missouri Compromise as a congressman, wrote a newspaper editorial on the Wilmot Proviso. Former presidents were expected to remain out of politics, which may account for its anonymous publication. "What is it that excited in the northern states such distrust of the south as shall produce on their part a desire to exclude the southern states from an equal participation in the full benefits of Union?" Tyler believed that ten northerners would move to the new territory for every southerner. He believed no man would bring his slaves there and risk losing them upon statehood. Tyler argued that the Wilmot Proviso was an abstract question to the North, but a serious insult to the South.

At the opening of the war, Polk had marginalized General Winfield Scott, a Whig thought to harbor presidential ambitions, in favor of Taylor. After Taylor's signal successes, the Whigs began to mention his name as a candidate for president in 1848. Whether politics or military strategy was his guide, Polk decided to open a second phase of the war. A significant part of Taylor's army would be given to Scott, who, with ten new regiments, would land at Veracruz and drive west to Mexico City to capture the capital. Polk attempted to place Democratic senator Thomas Hart Benton of Missouri in a new role of lieutenant general, over Scott and Taylor, to deny them their military laurels and to strengthen his party in the next presidential election. But even the Democrats in Congress resisted this move, unable to justify replacing the leadership that had not lost a single battle. Buchanan, it appears, administered the coup de grace to this plan through his congressional supporters, unwilling to see Benton elevated as his rival for the nomination. After Scott's expedition left, Taylor was left hundreds of miles inside of Mexico with 4,073 men, only a tenth of whom were professional soldiers. General Santa Anna, eager to undermine American support for the war, approached him with a force of twenty thousand, intending to crush Taylor's army. Taylor refused to surrender, inflicting on his opponent a catastrophic defeat in the Battle of Buena Vista. Rather than undermine Taylor, Polk had inadvertently made him the most popular man in America. Less than a month later, Scott executed the largest amphibious landing in history, and aided by officers such as Ulysses Grant, Robert E. Lee, George Meade, James Longstreet, and Thomas Jackson, shelled the city of Veracruz into submission in a matter of days. Scott marched westward, where he would await the rest of his regiments before proceeding to Mexico City.

On July 14, Brigadier General Franklin Pierce and his twenty-five hundred men left Veracruz with eighty-five wagons to join Scott's army. To his wife's horror, Pierce had lobbied fiercely for the appointment and worked hard to raise men for the war effort. He had grown up listening to his father's Revolutionary War stories and those of his brothers' service in the War of 1812 and was eager for martial glory of his own. Five years earlier, he had reluctantly agreed to leave politics, to focus on his wife, the practice of law, and raising children. He had even turned down Polk's offer to serve as attorney general. But he resolved that Jane would not deny him this.

At the National Bridge, spanning the Antigua River, Pierce learned by careful reconnaissance that Mexican soldiers were lying in wait, fortified on a bluff on the other side. After an artillery barrage, Pierce sent an infantry division to capture their position. But the sight of US forces sent the defenders to flight. Before fleeing, they had managed to shoot Pierce's hat from his head while killing the horse next to him. At another river crossing, the bridge was destroyed to block American reinforcements.

Pierce ordered a new bridge constructed, and five hundred men working together accomplished exactly that within three hours.

Three weeks after leaving Veracruz, with skirmishing, sniper fire, and sickness all confronted successfully, General Pierce joined General Scott in Puebla, and together marched toward their final destination. At Contreras, they encountered the main Mexican army under Santa Anna. Pierce's brigade was directed to attack head on, while Scott and the rest of his men took a circuitous route to attack on their flank. Pierce's brigade was greeted with artillery fire, startling his horse, which had been a gift from the people of New Hampshire. Pierce suffered a groin injury from being thrown against his saddle, when his mount stumbled before finally falling on its rider. Slowly regaining consciousness, Pierce declined to leave the field while attempting to find his men. The next day, his soldiers were ordered to resume the attack on foot. Pierce, with a badly injured knee, turned over command. The operation was successful, forcing a Mexican retreat. The Mexicans regrouped at Churubusco, where Scott intended to give a decisive blow. Before the attack, Scott ordered the injured Pierce to the rear. "For God's sake General," Pierce implored of the man he would later defeat for president, "this is the last great battle, and I must lead my brigade." Scott relented, ordering him to lead his men behind the Mexican army to block their escape. Along the way, Pierce was required to dismount and lead his horse, but the pain of walking three hundred yards on his injured knee was so severe that he lost consciousness. When he came to, Pierce ordered his men to leave him there, and when the Mexicans arrived to check their movement, some of the bloodiest fighting of the war ensued. Santa Anna and his men successfully retreated into Mexico City. On September 8, Pierce had sufficiently recovered to lead his men in reinforcing a successful attack against the defenders of Chapultepec Castle, a strategic outpost for the defense of the capital. Pierce and his men guarded the supplies while the rest of the army triumphantly entered Mexico City.

As the American army captured the Mexican capital, the Whigs were winning major offices throughout the country. Fillmore, who had been unwillingly nominated for New York governor in 1844 and defeated, was now put forward for comptroller. This office, elected by the people for the first time in 1847, had more power than the governor. "Much against my wishes, I was nominated for Comptroller and elected," he wrote. Fillmore won by 38,000 votes, the largest margin of any Whig in state history, capping a year of Whig successes throughout the country, as the party took control of the House of Representatives.

CHAPTER 6

The 30th Congress

We are at a crisis of some importance.

—DANIEL WEBSTER

Lincoln - Van Buren - Fillmore - Tyler - Buchanan

The 30th Congress gathered on December 6, 1847. Robert Winthrop of Massachusetts, the Whig nominee for Speaker, was challenged by a southern Democrat who opposed the Wilmot Proviso, a northern Democrat who opposed the Wilmot Proviso, and a northern Democrat who favored the measure. With the Whigs in the majority and the Democrats so divided, it should have been an easy accomplishment for Winthrop. But five Whigs did not vote for their party's candidate: two abolitionists who believed Winthrop too eager to accommodate slavery, and three southerners who disagreed with his support of the Proviso. The balloting ended only when a southern Whig left the chamber, reducing the number Winthrop needed for a majority.

The following day, Polk sent his annual message to Congress, calling for vast new territory from Mexico as part of any settlement, and increased military funding, despite the collapse of the Mexican military. The president could not have been more at odds with the Whigs in the House, who were eager to bring the war to a conclusion. First-term congressman Abraham Lincoln thought Polk's address "the half insane mumbling of a fever dream . . . He is a bewildered, confounded, and miserably perplexed man. God grant he may be able to show, there is not something about his conscience, more painful than all his mental perplexity!"

The Whigs wasted little time in attempting to rein in the war. Some proposals called for immediate peace, some for peace without any territorial gains, while some focused on condemning the war itself and the president who conducted it. On December 22, Lincoln introduced eight resolutions regarding the origins of the war. Did it begin on American soil, as Polk had alleged? Mexican soil? Disputed territory? In a January 17 speech on his resolutions, Lincoln said that the president would not answer because "he feels the blood of this war, like the blood of Abel, is crying to Heaven against him; that he ordered General Taylor into the midst of a peaceful Mexican settlement purposely to bring on a war, that, originally having some strong motive . . . to involve the two countries in war, and trusting to escape scrutiny by fixing the public gaze upon the exceeding brightness of military glory—that attractive rainbow, that rises in the showers of blood—that serpent's eye, that charms to destroy—he plunged into it, and has swept on and on till disappointed in this calculation of the ease with which Mexico might be subdued, he now finds himself he knows not where." The speech produced an uproar in Illinois, where the war was extremely popular.

By the time Lincoln spoke, the House had adopted a resolution that the war was "unnecessarily and unconstitutionally begun by the President of the United States." It passed 82–81, with Lincoln voting in favor; a subsequent attempt to reverse it failed 105–95. Polk's request for a loan to underwrite the war was delayed and finally reduced, a signal that the president was now on an increasingly short tether. In their quest to end the war, the Whigs in the House would soon be aided by a renegade diplomat, in one of the more remarkable events in American foreign policy.

Nicholas Trist was sent with Winfield Scott to negotiate a peace treaty with Mexico. Frustrated at the pace of negotiations and wishing to impose harsher terms than he had initially proposed, including perhaps the conquest of all Mexico, Polk recalled his emissary. Initially Trist complied, waiting for a replacement or an escort to bring him safely to Veracruz. But none arrived, and Scott could not spare any men for the dangerous journey. Eventually, through the encouragement of moderates in the Mexican government, the British diplomatic corps, and a visiting newspaper reporter, Trist decided he would continue negotiations for peace, despite Polk's order. On February 2, Trist signed the Treaty of Guadalupe Hidalgo, and sent it to a furious president.

Meanwhile Congress had turned into "a great President making machine," in the words of one member. Lincoln joined six others in forming "The Young Indians," committed to promoting General Zachary Taylor's candidacy. Taylor, who had never held elected office or even voted, was the perfect cipher for a party and a country divided over slavery. Lincoln supported Taylor over Henry Clay, his "beau ideal of a statesman" whom he "almost worshipped." But as Lincoln wrote, "I go for him, not because I think he would make a better President than Clay, but because I think he would make a better one than Polk, or [Senator Lewis] Cass, or Buchanan, or any such creature, one of whom is sure to be elected, if he is not."

While the Young Indians took advantage of Taylor's ambiguity on the Wilmot Proviso, a former president wanted to make clear where he stood. On April 11, a member of the New York legislature took the floor to read an address from Martin Van Buren into the record. Van Buren had watched with concern as the Democratic Party, which he had helped create, became increasingly identified with the spread of slavery. The first draft of his response ran fifteen thousand words. It was a comprehensive treatment of the issue, starting with the Articles of Confederation through the present day, a complete constitutional and political history of the subject, thoroughly refuting the Democratic arguments. The division between Democrats over the Proviso played out in the states as well, and none more so than New York. The Barnburner faction, which favored it, included Van Buren. The Hunkers opposed it, preferring to focus on other issues. A contentious Democratic state convention the previous year had resulted in the Barnburners walking out. In 1848 both Barnburners and Hunkers held their own state conventions, each claiming to be the official Democratic meeting. Both sent their own slate of delegates to the national convention in Baltimore. Van Buren wrote instructions to the Barnburner delegates, encouraging them to be constructive members, and to avoid raising the Proviso issue. He urged them to vote against several candidates, including Buchanan, and Polk in the unlikely event that he was placed for re-nomination.

On June 7, Lincoln joined thousands of his fellow Whigs in Philadelphia for their national convention. On the fourth ballot, the popular general and political novice defeated Clay, a founder and senior statesman of the Whig Party. Now it was time to find him a running mate. Taylor, a slaveholding southerner, would need a credible partner from the North to have any hope of keeping the party unified.

John Collier of New York obtained the floor, explaining that he had been a Clay delegate, but that Taylor could be assured of the support of New York should Millard Fillmore be nominated for vice president. Collier's motives have been variously ascribed; it has been argued that he aspired to the Senate and believed Fillmore his main obstacle. It has also been said that with Fillmore as vice president, the influence of New York Whig leaders William Seward and Thurlow Weed would be diminished, since patronage would presumably go through Fillmore rather than them. The last time the Whigs had won the White House, their chosen president had barely lasted a month, replaced by John Tyler, who obstructed his party's priorities before being formally expelled. Despite this, there was precious little debate over the vice presidential spot. After a close first ballot, Millard Fillmore was nominated with 173 votes to 87 for Abbott Lawrence of Massachusetts. Fillmore's New York was the biggest electoral prize with 36 electoral votes, 10 more than its nearest rival, and 24 percent of the total needed for victory. Fillmore, with a solid eight-year congressional voting record, was well known to the delegates, who now had to decide whether to support Taylor, who had avowed himself "not an ultra Whig." From his retirement at Sherwood Forest, John Tyler observed that Democratic nominee Lewis "Cass is greatly open to attack. Taylor admits of being highly lauded, and yet the issue is doubtful . . . Fillmore is a dead weight, but nous verrons . . . Clay is dead, and none of the conspirators will succeed."

On June 22, the Barnburners met in Utica, New York, and despite his wishes, nominated Martin Van Buren for president as an independent on a platform supporting the Wilmot Proviso. There was dissatisfaction with both the Whigs' Taylor and the Democrats' Lewis Cass from Proviso supporters in both parties. These disaffected groups, along with members of the abolitionist Liberty Party, met in Buffalo on August 8, as representatives of the new Free Soil Party. Van Buren wrote a letter to the delegates, praising it as the first meeting of its kind, "composed of individuals who have all their lives been on different sides of public questions and politics, state and nation, and who still differ regarding most of these questions but who feel called upon to unite on one issue, slavery extending into the territories." So they did unite, on that issue and on their nominee—Martin Van Buren. Charles Francis Adams, the son and grandson of presidents, was selected as his running mate. Van Buren accepted the nomination, hoping to advance the cause of Free Soil, to vindicate the Barnburners, and to defeat the Democratic nominee, running on an anti-Proviso platform. He had won a presidential election as a defender of slavery in the District of Columbia, a position he now reversed, and on a policy of non-interference in the places where it existed, which he maintained. The Little Magician of Kinderhook, nearly fifty years after his first campaign for office, would take the field one final time, with no hope of victory, to vindicate a cause he believed in. Van Buren, who had once believed the president should serve as the national pacifier, capitulating to the South when necessary, was condemned by President Polk as "the most fallen man I have ever known."

Lincoln devoted the summer and fall to electing Taylor and Fillmore. From the House floor he made the case for Taylor and Fillmore, systematically addressing Democratic criticisms while taking apart the rationale for Cass's candidacy. Lincoln, who had consistently voted for the Wilmot Proviso, expressed his hope that Taylor would sign it. But he also knew that Cass would veto it. "One of the two is to be President; which is preferable?" As to the charge that the Whigs had mistreated Clay, "like an old horse to root," Lincoln asked whether the Democrats had done the same, perhaps to "a certain Martin Van Buren . . . and is he not rooting a little to your discomfort about now?" The folksy, humorous, yet devastating speech caused a Democratic member to interrupt, shouting, "We give it up!"

During the recess, Lincoln worked at the Central Rough and Ready Club, the Washington headquarters of Taylor's presidential campaign, corresponding with supporters throughout the country and coordinating the national effort. As Election Day approached, Lincoln traveled throughout Massachusetts making numerous speeches for Taylor and Fillmore. "I had been chosen to Congress then from the Wild West and with hayseed in my hair I went to Massachusetts, the most cultured state in the Union, to take a few lessons in deportment," he would remember. For the first time, Lincoln would find himself winning over the audiences he would need to achieve his life's ambition. Lincoln's great concern was that Van Buren would win enough in Massachusetts to throw the state to Cass. "All agreed that slavery is evil," he told the Whig Club of Boston, "but that we were not responsible for it and cannot affect it in states of this union where we do not live. But the question of the extension of slavery to new territories of this country is a part of our responsibility and care, and is under our control." The Free Soilers, he argued, were working against the only issue that united them. They had "hitched their skirts to the artful dodger of Kinderhook and could only spoil the election."

Lincoln's Massachusetts campaign was a critical success, generating many positive stories. From there he headed to Buffalo, where he would depart to Illinois over the Great Lakes. On his way, Lincoln and Thurlow Weed paid their respects to Millard Fillmore at Delevan House in Albany. Lincoln and Fillmore would not meet again for more than twelve years, under very different circumstances for both men and for the country.

"And so Taylor is the president-elect," Tyler wrote his son on November 14. The Whigs would have their first president since he had been drummed out of the party. Though he voted for Cass, Tyler said, "I shall not shed many tears at the result. Poor Van! He is literally a used-up man; and Clay, let him shed tears over the fact that anybody can be elected but himself." His wife Julia, he noted, was a Taylor supporter.

Van Buren won 10 percent of the national vote, despite receiving no support in the southern or border states. Van Buren had won 26 percent in his own state, relegating Cass to third place in New York, as he did in several other states in the North, helping tip the election to Taylor.

The 30th Congress, which had been so divided by war, slavery, and presidential politics, would meet for one more session. Vast new territory had been added to the United States, which was now a Pacific power. But questions of how the new territory would be organized—free, slave, or some division between the two—would haunt Congress to the final moments of the session. On March 1, with only three days left, the normally non-controversial Civil and Diplomatic Appropriations Bill, vital to the funding of the federal government, became an explosive political device when the Senate amended it to allow the president to organize the new territory as he saw fit. Polk was on the record as favoring an extension of the Missouri Compromise line west to the ocean. Therefore, a vote to fund the government became a bill to open millions of new acres to slavery. When it came to the House the following day, representatives adopted an amendment to keep slavery out of the new territory. Lincoln, who earlier that session had unsuccessfully proposed a bill to eliminate slavery in the District of Columbia, voted "yes." The House then voted down the Senate amendment. The disagreement was far from resolved on March 3, the final day of the 30th Congress.

At sunset, James Knox Polk observed his empty desk. After four tumultuous years he was returning to private life.* One last obligation remained. He and his cabinet headed for the Capitol for the last-minute consideration of legislation. Armed with a veto message, Polk was determined to reject any law that excluded slavery from the territories. "I did not hesitate for a moment in my course," he wrote. A conference committee between the Senate and House was unable to come to an agreement. Late in the evening, a government shutdown appeared likely. In the Senate, Daniel Webster decried that "important bills connected with the continuance of the government, which for sixty years have never failed to be passed in time to carry on the government, are now to some degree in jeopardy . . . we are at a crisis of some importance." There was a vote in the House to withdraw its disagreement from the Senate bill, allowing the measure to be sent directly to the president. This failed by the narrow margin of 110–107, with Lincoln voting "no." An amendment was then offered to maintain the laws of Mexico in the territories until changed by Congress, which passed 111–105, with Lincoln voting "yes." Since Mexico forbade slavery, this arrangement would have the same effect as passing the Wilmot Proviso. Southern members flocked to see Polk "in great excitement." Polk cleared the room in order to consult with his cabinet.

---

* Polk's long-awaited retirement would last little more than three months, the shortest post-presidency in history.

First of all, since it was after midnight, was he even still president? He argued that he had won a four-year term, and therefore had until noon the following day. Then came the question of whether to sign the appropriations bill if it came to him in its current form. Secretary of State Buchanan urged the president to sign, arguing that keeping the present laws was distinct from agreeing to the Wilmot Proviso. Buchanan was joined by three others, against only one member who wanted it vetoed. The fighting continued through the night and into the morning. At 4:00 a.m., Polk retired to the Willard Hotel. Finally the Senate blinked, receding from their own amendment, sending a clean appropriations bill to the president, who signed it, thus leaving the issue of slavery in the new territories to his successor. "Thus concluded my duties as President of the U. States," Polk wrote.

CHAPTER 7

A Final Settlement

My only object is to save the country [and] to save the Whig party, if possible.

—MILLARD FILLMORE

Fillmore ~ Tyler ~ Pierce ~ Buchanan ~ Van Buren

From his perch as presiding officer of the Senate, Vice President Fillmore had a unique vantage point of the mess he was about to inherit. In the wake of the 30th Congress, the country continued to divide along sectional lines. With the encouragement of President Taylor, California was preparing to apply for admission as a free state, without any offsets for the South. Texas claimed a significant part of New Mexico as its own, threatening military force against its territorial neighbor. The South was clamoring for an expansion of slave territory and furious over the increasing refusal of northern states to surrender fugitive slaves.

Buchanan noted with trepidation the increasingly toxic feeling throughout the South. "They are preparing for the impending struggle with far more unanimity, determination, and intensity of purpose than they have ever yet displayed."

Despite another presidential defeat, Henry Clay had returned to the Senate with one final service left to render. As he had with the Missouri Compromise and the Compromise of 1833, he put together a proposal to prevent catastrophe. His plan called for the admission of California as a free state; organization of the remainder of the Mexican cession without any reference to slavery; to fix Texas's western border without any new territory, and in exchange Texas's debts would be assumed by the national government; to end the slave trade in the District of Columbia but to maintain the legality of slavery there for as long as Maryland did so; a pronouncement by Congress that it had no power to interfere with the interstate slave trade; and a stronger fugitive slave law.

On March 4, a gravely ill John C. Calhoun reappeared in the Senate after some time away. His mind still sharp but his body otherwise, the task of delivering his address fell to Senator John Mason of Virginia. The South was faced with a choice between abolition and secession, he argued. There was no compromise to make. The South had nothing left to give. Calhoun had once toasted, "The Union—next to our liberty most dear." Nothing could save that Union now, he argued, but for slavery in the territories, a stronger fugitive slave law, and for the North to cease agitating the slavery issue. With weeks to live, these words served as a coda to a career that had begun under President James Madison.

"Calhoun's speech does him no credit," Tyler thought. "It is too ultra, and his ultimata impracticable." Even Tyler, opponent of the Missouri Compromise, would publicly lend his support to Clay's proposals, giving critical cover to southern members who wished to vote in favor.

But what would the North say? On March 7, the leading voice of that region weighed in for Clay's compromise. Senator Daniel Webster of Massachusetts argued that since the climate of the New Mexico Territory would never permit slavery, why "reenact the will of God?" To adopt the Wilmot Proviso over land where slavery was impossible was a gratuitous insult to the South. His speech was a candid acknowledgment of the bad feelings that pervaded the country. It was an honest prediction of the horrors that would result in the event of secession. And it was a masterful case for the advantages that all regions enjoyed from being in one Union. Webster's speech was widely discussed throughout the country. His credibility was the product of decades of opposition to slavery. The three most influential senators of the past twenty years, Clay, Calhoun, and Webster, had now all spoken. Calhoun's "all or nothing" tack sounded even more discordant after Webster's generous address.

The leading northern voice against compromise would be William Seward, now a senator from New York. He called for the immediate admission of California, the abolition of slavery in the District of

Columbia, and the Wilmot Proviso for the territories. He spoke of a "higher law" than the Constitution, a terrifying prospect to southerners who believed that document provided the surest protection for slavery.

President Taylor was stridently opposed to any compromise. His firmness threatened to break the presidential mold, which called for mollifying the South. A delegation from Dixie lobbied Taylor at the White House, to no avail. Southern political leaders called for a June convention in Nashville to consider secession. Taylor promised to raise an army and personally ride at its head to put down any rebellion in the South. Matters seemed destined for a collision.

Fillmore told Taylor that if required to break a tie in the Senate, he would support the compromise. "I wished him to understand," Fillmore wrote, "that it was not out of any hostility to him or his administration but the vote would be given, because I deemed it for the interests of the country."

On July 9, Fillmore was presiding over the Senate when a messenger came from the White House—the president was deathly sick. The day Zachary Taylor died, Millard Fillmore passed the only sleepless night of his life, consumed by the enormous responsibility that would now devolve on him. Eighteen months earlier, he had been the comptroller of New York. That night he was president of the United States, facing the most formidable threat that had ever been presented to the Union.

The cabinet offered their resignations; Fillmore accepted them all. Taylor's cabinet had been far from effective; several were about to be fired over a conflict of interest scandal. President Fillmore moved quickly to surround himself with high-caliber men representing different regions of the country. For the first position he chose Daniel Webster, who had fulfilled the role of secretary of state for Harrison and Tyler.

The death of Taylor may well have created the most abrupt about face of presidential policy in history. Would his opposition to the compromise have brought Civil War a decade earlier? Would the South have been unified in secession? Would the popular, southern slaveholding general have seen off the crisis, preventing the Civil War entirely? Such things can never be known. But with Taylor's passing the presidential tradition of conciliation remained intact. Fillmore favored the compromise; now it was a matter of getting it to his desk. Due to Taylor's veto threat, Clay had been forced to combine his proposals in a single bill, in the hopes that he could be induced to sign it. Extreme factions north and south working together succeeded in killing the legislation. Clay, exhausted after seventy speeches over six months, took a leave of absence. Into the void stepped Stephen Douglas of Illinois. With a supportive president, the legislation could move in pieces, with the sectional blocs voting for or against bills as they pleased, but with a core group of centrists providing the majority for every measure. This strategy would require a careful sequencing of bills, but it was the only way.

While the tactics of compromise were being worked out, Texas moved aggressively to establish civil authority over New Mexico. In a message to Congress, Fillmore promised to respond to this for what it was—a criminal invasion. He underscored his words by dispatching 750 additional troops to the region.

Bill by bill, the compromise measures passed, in substantially the same form that Clay proposed, and Fillmore rapidly signed them into law—all but one, where he hesitated. The requirement that runaway slaves be returned to their masters can be found in the Constitution and was critical in securing southern ratification. The particulars were left to Congress, which passed the first Fugitive Slave Act in 1793. Ultimately, the northern states resisted, withholding the use of their police and jails, and adopting "personal liberty laws," guaranteeing jury trials for accused slaves, who were likely to be acquitted. A tougher fugitive slave law was an indispensible component of the compromise. Years later, Fillmore replied to an autograph seeker who asked for a sentiment on the measure, revealing his thoughts as the bill sat on his desk. "Permit me to speak frankly," he answered. "I am and ever have been opposed to slavery and nothing but a conviction of Constitutional obligation could have induced me to give my sanction to a law for the reduction of fugitive slaves. I knew that when I signed it I signed my political death warrant, and by its execution arranged against myself the most fanatical hostility . . . but that man is not worthy of public confidence, who hesitates to perform his official duty, regardless of all consequences to himself." The new act required federal law enforcement to assist in the capture of runaway slaves; it prohibited jury trials for accused slaves, and made it a federal crime to interfere with a slave capture. Fillmore hated the bill, but he hated the prospect of civil war more. A month earlier, Fillmore had solicited funds for his coachman to purchase the freedom of his wife and children, even contributing his own money to the project. But his private sentiments would yield to what he saw as the national interest.

Resistance to the new fugitive slave law was widespread throughout the North. Committees of Vigilance were established to protect runaway slaves. One of these groups freed an alleged fugitive from a Boston courtroom and from the custody of federal marshals. In September a slaveowner from Maryland arrived near Buchanan's home in Pennsylvania, looking for two of his slaves. The master was killed, and his son gravely injured. In western New York, an armed mob broke into the building where an accused slave was awaiting trial, freeing him and sending him on his way to Canada.

Certain elements of the South believed that they had been on the losing end of the compromise. Fillmore learned that extremists in South Carolina planned on seizing federal installations at Charleston. As he had with Texas, Fillmore acted decisively, inviting General Winfield Scott to cabinet meetings. He poured federal troops into South Carolina and positioned others in North Carolina that could strike if necessary. The South Carolina legislature, through their governor, demanded an explanation. Fillmore, through his State Department, made clear that he was the commander-in-chief of the army and navy, that the decision to direct troops was entirely within his discretion, and that he was not answerable to the governor, the legislature, or anyone else. In his first year in office, Fillmore had successfully pushed for the Compromise of 1850, which had settled the threat of civil war, and responded with authority to military action threatened by two different states. Fillmore had not entered national politics as a supporter of Andrew Jackson, like Franklin Pierce, or advanced his career as an ally of Jackson, like Buchanan, Polk, or Van Buren. Fillmore, as an Anti-Mason and Whig, had always been a political opponent of Jackson. Tyler, in his war on the bank and pursuit of Texas, may be said to have served out Jackson's third term. Nor was Fillmore a general, like Harrison or Taylor. But by finding the right balance of firmness and flexibility, Fillmore had prevented civil war and ironically was the most Jacksonian of any president of the era.

———

Historian Allen Nevins once remarked, "Ideas rule the world, and ideas conjoined with art make the swiftest conquest of men." Harriet Beecher Stowe, encouraged by her husband, had for ten years struggled in literary pursuits, to no great effect. Her fortunes changed in March 1852 with the publication of her first book, *Uncle Tom's Cabin*. By 1853, "300,000 copies had been sold and eight power presses were running night and day to keep pace with the demand." Stowe's depiction of slavery horrified readers throughout the North and around the world, and was ultimately published in half of all known languages. The Duchess of Sutherland, joined by other British women with similar titles, wrote "The Stafford House Address," a plea to the ladies of the South to help bring about slavery's demise. Julia Tyler responded, in what the *New York Times* referred to as the extension of the Monroe Doctrine from our shores to our institutions. "If you wish a suggestion as to the suitable occupation of your idle hours," Julia wrote, "I will point you to the true field of your philanthropy—the unsupplied wants of your own people of England. In view of your palaces, there is misery and suffering enough to excite your most active sympathies.... The negro of the South," Tyler argued, "lives sumptuously in comparison with the 100,000 of the white population of London." She reminded slavery's English critics of the plight of Ireland. "Spare from the well fed negroes of these states one drop of your superabounding sympathy, to pour into that bitter cup which is overrunning with sorrow and with tears."

Despite Julia's charges of hypocrisy against slavery's critics, *Uncle Tom's Cabin* would have an immeasurable effect on the country, increasing support for abolition in the North and defensiveness of the institution in the South.

———

For ten years, Franklin Pierce had acceded to his wife's wishes, focusing on his family and the practice of law in Concord (his military exploits in Mexico excepted). As the Democratic Party searched for a candidate to take back the White House in 1852, his friends were interested in putting him forward. Formidable candidates such as Douglas and Buchanan were the names most mentioned, but with the front-runners engaged in a pitched battle and the 2/3 rule for nomination in place, all signs pointed to another compromise candidate. Pierce had been reticent, but finally gave his supporters what they needed, writing in April that if "the success of the cause" could be promoted by his nomination, "then you must judge for me in view of all the circumstances." Pierce signed off on the strategy of presenting his name after the leading candidates had bloodied each other for several rounds.

On an otherwise ordinary day, Pierce and his wife were out in their carriage when a fast-riding messenger overtook them. "Mr. Pierce, you've been nominated for United States President." Jane, who had married an ambitious young congressman only to push him out of politics, was now looking at his potential return, at the highest level of government. She fainted at the news. The plan of Pierce and his supporters had worked out; Pierce, whose name did not appear until the thirty-fifth ballot, was the nominee on the forty-ninth.

John Tyler felt it was "obvious . . . from an early hour . . . that none of those who had been most prominently spoken of could be selected.

"While I hold all the gentlemen whose names were before the convention in the highest respect, yet I must say, without disparagement to any, that the nomination which has been made is destined to carry with it quite as much, if not more, influence in the election than any other that could have been made," he said, predicting Pierce's election "as next to certain." This letter was published nationally in support of Pierce's candidacy.

From his fellow Whigs, Fillmore received support north and south for another bid. Conventions throughout the South nominated him for re-election. He had even won a deathbed endorsement from Henry Clay. But Fillmore had resolved not to seek another term. His desire for a peaceful retirement had twice been disturbed, first by Whigs in his home state and then by the 1848 convention. After his turbulent time in office, no one could begrudge his return to private life. He also doubted whether he could win, since the Compromise of 1850 had been tough medicine for both North and South. Fillmore had planned to announce his retirement in his annual message, but was dissuaded by supporters in Virginia, where he was popular, in order to help the Whigs win the upcoming state elections. On two other occasions, Fillmore was deterred from bowing out. Supporters of the compromise believed he was the only Whig who could win. While refusing to rule himself out, Fillmore did nothing to promote his candidacy, despite control of patronage, or to check the efforts of Daniel Webster, his secretary of state, who was running again despite having only months to live. Webster, who believed himself a failure for not having won the presidency, was running for this reason, rather than because of any serious support. The same could not be said for Winfield Scott, commanding general of the army. Scott won support from those who opposed the compromise as well as those who believed that, yet again, a general presented the best chance for victory. Seward hoped to nominate Scott, driving southerners from the Whigs, and creating a new northern party that would then elect him to the presidency in 1856. Fillmore, who had determined to save his country by any means necessary and his party if possible, could have had the nomination if he had only grasped for it. But he did not. On the first ballot, he won 133 delegates to 131 for Winfield Scott and 29 for Daniel Webster. Scott prevailed on the fifty-third ballot. The Whigs were finished; Fillmore would be successful only in saving his country.

Pierce's defeated rival, James Buchanan, had become good friends with Robert Tyler, the former president's son, who had moved north and become a prominent Philadelphian. Buchanan, who had been talked about for national office for two decades, was sanguine about the Pierce nomination, writing "For the first time I have had a fair trial and have been fairly defeated."

Buchanan wrote, "General Pierce is a sound radical Democrat of the old Jeffersonian school, and possesses highly respectable abilities. I think he is firm and energetic, without which no man is fit to be President." Buchanan went out on the stump for Pierce, who came under fire for his actions in Mexico. "Frank Pierce a coward! That man a coward, who, when his country was involved in a foreign war, abandoned a lucrative and honorable profession and all the sweets and comforts of domestic life in his own happy family, to become a private volunteer soldier in the ranks!

A FINAL SETTLEMENT

How preposterous!" Pierce's friend from college days, Nathaniel Haw-thorne, now the bestselling author of *The Scarlet Letter*, wrote a campaign biography on his behalf.* Martin Van Buren, returned from his Free Soil dalliance, endorsed Pierce in a letter.

Pierce prevailed in a landslide, winning 254–42 in the Electoral College, and carrying twenty-seven states to Scott's four. Buchanan watched yet another of his colleagues overtake him, this one thirteen years younger. With the presidency seeming forever out of reach, Buchanan focused on his niece, who was making the rounds in Philadelphia society. She wrote him after "an elegant dinner," where she met a former president. "Mr. Van Buren treated me with *marked attention*—drank wine with me first at table—talked a great deal of you, & thinks you treated him shabbily last summer, by passing so near without stopping to see him. I tell you these things, as I think they show a desire on his part to meet you."The next day Harriet was headed to dinner at Robert Tyler's.

Buchanan wrote her back, saying "your sentences ran into each other without proper periods," admonishing her on her writing and reminding her to mind her social etiquette.

Franklin Pierce, president-elect of the United States, sat toward the front of the train car, his wife Jane to his side, his boy Benny in front of him. Surrounded by his family, he steamed out of Andover. He was on his way to New Hampshire to put some affairs in order. From there, he would proceed to Washington to be sworn in. Without warning the train was off the tracks hurtling toward a cliff. Pierce grabbed Jane with one arm and reached forward for Benny in the seat ahead. As his arm swept forward for his son, the car slammed on its side and slipped over the edge. The fifteen-foot fall must have seemed an eternity, ended by the crashing of the train on the rocks below. The sixty passengers quickly moved to assess the damage, perhaps shocked to be alive and mostly unhurt. But

---

* Nathaniel Hawthorne was appointed consul at Liverpool by President Pierce. The position paid a good salary and accrued to its holder a fee from every ship heading to or from the United States, while giving him time to write. The product of this trip, *Our Old Home,* would later be the subject of much controversy regarding Pierce.

the window next to Benny had fallen upon a giant rock, the impact of which removed the top part of his head. Before their very eyes, the Pierces lost their only child.

A journey that had begun with such bright prospects had ended in tragedy.

CHAPTER 8

A Hell of a Storm

Gentlemen, you are entering a serious undertaking, and the ground should be well surveyed before the first step is taken.
—FRANKLIN PIERCE

Pierce - Fillmore - Buchanan - Van Buren - Tyler - Lincoln

Jane Pierce was in a state of mourning that would last throughout her time as first lady, while her husband was forced to soldier on with preparations to assume the presidency. His predecessor welcomed him upon his arrival in Washington, and the two took a cruise together on the Potomac. The Compromise of 1850 was considered by its supporters "a final settlement" of the problems that had so formidably threatened the Union just two years earlier. No president of the era had passed to his successor such a favorable state of affairs. Secure in this, Fillmore was trying to figure out his future. "It is a national disgrace," he would later tell a reporter, "after having occupied the highest position in the country, that our Presidents should be cast adrift, and perhaps be compelled to keep a corner grocery for subsistence. We elect a man to the presidency, expect him to be honest, to give up a lucrative profession, perhaps, and after we have done with him we let him go into seclusion and perhaps poverty."

Franklin Pierce, at forty-eight the youngest president yet, delivered his inaugural address without notes, a first. The high hopes for the administration were at odds with the darkness in the White House. The staterooms were draped in black, and Jane Pierce wore a black veil on her infrequent excursions.

On March 30, the cabinet meeting was suspended by news of the death of Abigail Fillmore. Pierce, who had known his share of suffering since that fateful train ride, wrote Fillmore with his condolences. The temporary suspension of business also gave Pierce the chance to write James Buchanan a letter "already so long deferred," offering him the position of minister to England.

Pierce invited him to the White House, where Buchanan showed up "determined to decline." After dinner they retired to the library, where Pierce said, "You know very well that we have several important questions to settle with England and it is my intention that you shall settle them all in London. The country expects and requires your services as a minister to London. You have had no competitor for this place, and when I presented your name to the cabinet they were unanimous. I think that under these circumstances I have a right to ask you to accept the mission."

Buchanan then pointed out that "In all your appointments for Pennsylvania, you have not yet selected a single individual for any office for which I recommended him . . . if I were now to accept the mission to London, they might with justice say that I had appropriated the lion's share to myself, and selfishly received it as an equivalent for their disappointment. I could not and would not place myself in this position."

"I can assure you," Pierce replied, "if you accept the mission, Pennsylvania shall not receive one appointment more or less on that account. I shall consider yours as an appointment for the whole country."

Could he share that assurance with the public, Buchanan asked?

Pierce said that he would rather it stay private, but that he could reassure his friends of the promise.

Buchanan added that he could not stay for more than two years. Pierce agreed to honor that request, and that if the issues with England could be settled in less time, then Buchanan could apply to return as early as eighteen months.

The new secretary of state, William Marcy, was not someone Buchanan wanted to work for. "He would have succeeded in any other Department of the Government," Buchanan thought. Buchanan wanted to manage British relations without interference from State. At the time, there were two major questions: one regarding Canadian fisheries, and another over British involvement in Central America. Would Marcy really permit him to handle these on his own?

Pierce said, "with some apparent feeling," that he would handle Marcy, pledging to write the secretary of state and meet with him before re-conferring with Buchanan.

It was not long before Buchanan asked to be relieved of the mission. He learned that Marcy intended to handle the fishery matter in Washington; Buchanan believed he needed to leverage that issue to win concessions on Central America. Pierce responded that Buchanan's declining the post at this stage would be embarrassing to him. Buchanan countered that the fishery treaty could be perfected at Washington, but not executed until he could get to London, where he could then hold it until the Central American question could be resolved. Pierce argued that a delay might mean war between Britain and the United States. Buchanan then flatly declined the appointment.

Pierce attempted another tactic. A State Department aide arrived at Wheatland, Buchanan's Pennsylvania estate, on June 6, with a package containing his commission and instructions as minister as though nothing had ever happened. More written exchanges followed. When Pierce misplaced some of his letters, Buchanan believed that he had succeeded in fending him off. Finally, Buchanan offered to meet him in Philadelphia, where Pierce was scheduled to appear.

Buchanan's allies urged him to accept. One pointed out that if he declined, people would see it as ducking an important responsibility to the country.

On Sunday, April 10, the Senate adjourned without his name going forward. Buchanan assumed that Marcy had refused the terms he needed and the matter was settled. That evening, Buchanan called on Jefferson Davis of Mississippi, Pierce's secretary of war. Buchanan pointed out that since Van Buren's rejection by the Senate in 1832, American envoys were seen as "half a minister" if they, too, lacked Senate approval. Later that same night a messenger found all the straggling senators who were still in Washington, asking them to stay. On Monday, Buchanan received a message at 10:00 a.m. asking him to see the president at once. Back at the White House, Pierce offered to send the nomination to the Senate. If a quorum could not be mustered, he was prepared to let the matter drop. With thirty-three members present, Buchanan was confirmed.

Buchanan soon learned that various Pennsylvanians were being denied consulates by the administration on account of his appointment. On May 19, he again met with Pierce, who promised to enforce his assurances. Buchanan realized quickly that Pierce and his cabinet were actively pursuing re-election. One of the reasons Pierce had been so adamant about Buchanan shipping out was to remove him from the presidential field.

On May 21, Buchanan was at Brown's Hotel, with Marcy, Davis, and other members of the cabinet. Davis began to joke with Marcy and Buchanan about the next presidential election. Buchanan said to Marcy, "You and I ought to consider ourselves out of the list of candidates. We are both growing old, and it is a melancholy spectacle to see old men struggling in the political arena for the honors and offices of this world, as though it were to be their everlasting abode. Should you perform your duties as Secretary of State to the satisfaction of the country during the present Presidential term, and should I perform my duties in the same manner as Minister to England, we ought both to be content to retire and leave the field to younger men. President Pierce is a young man, and should his administration prove to be advantageous to the country and honorable to himself, as I trust it will, there is no good reason why he should not be re-nominated and re-elected for a second term." That summer, Pierce met with the last president who had tried to keep the office. Traveling to White Sulphur Springs, Virginia, he conferred with John Tyler, who had been president when Pierce retired from the Senate. Julia remembered "Pierce's generous extolling language in regard to the President [Tyler], and his conduct of public affairs was received with absolute emotion by some, and with gratification by all." Pierce would soon find himself in Tyler's position, confronted with a challenge from Congress that would define his presidency.

Stephen Douglas, as chairman of the Senate Committee on Territories, reported a bill to organize the territories of Kansas and Nebraska with or without slavery as decided by the people. The area was home to only three white settlers, aside from those who worked for the federal government, but treaties with various Indian tribes had removed the last barrier to significant settlement. Douglas was an exponent of "popular sovereignty," the idea that territories could decide for themselves whether to be free or slave. But located exclusively above the Missouri Compromise line, Kansas and Nebraska would be free unless a different decision was made at state-hood. Or unless Congress repealed the Missouri Compromise.

Slave state senators, who now numbered thirty out of a sixty-two-person body, were opposed, and had succeeded in killing a similar bill the previous session. On January 18, 1853, Kentucky senator Archibald Dixon and Douglas went for a carriage ride. Dixon explained that without a specific law permitting slavery in these non-slave territories, the popular vote would be a foregone conclusion. For popular sovereignty to work, one side—in this case slaveowners—could not be excluded before the vote. "By God, sir, you are right," Douglas said, "and I will incorporate it in my bill, though I know it will raise a hell of a storm."

On Sunday, January 22, Douglas and a contingent of southern senators approached Jefferson Davis to obtain an urgent meeting with the president, who observed the sabbath out of respect for his religious first lady. They explained their plan; the two territories would be open to all and would later vote whether to be free or slave, setting aside the Missouri Compromise.

"Gentlemen, you are entering a serious undertaking," Pierce said, "and the ground should be well surveyed before the first step is taken." The following day Pierce met with his cabinet. If he resisted the plan, he feared retribution against the rest of his agenda. Meanwhile, settlers were eager to move into the new territories, and the Senate would not permit an organization of these lands that outlawed slavery. By the next day, the administration's newspaper was reporting that Pierce would be "directly involved" in securing passage of the bill.

The "final settlement" of 1850, which was to end the slavery agitation for all time, had lasted for four years. The Missouri Compromise, adopted thirty-four years earlier, was now targeted for repeal. A week later, Tyler wrote, "I perceive a new storm is about to break out in Congress and the country," over the territorial question, predicting it would end "in the despoilment of the South ... These agitations cannot end in good." He blamed the North for the controversy, arguing that the bill was simply "a recognition of their equality with the other states," based "on the principle ... the right of the people of colonies or territories to regulate their own domestic concerns," something found in the bedrock of the revolution.

"Never have I witnessed a more bitter feeling in Congress," wrote one reporter. On March 3, after an all-night debate, the Senate voted at 5:00 a.m., 37–14, to pass the Kansas-Nebraska Act. How would the voters react? Pierce's New Hampshire would hold the first state elections after the Senate vote. The Democratic governor held on with 1,500 votes, down from 5,500 in the previous election, and a majority of the eighty-nine Democrats in the state House were eliminated. Democrats in the US House, especially those from northern states, could see that to vote for Kansas-Nebraska was to risk ending their career.

To push the bill through the House, the Pierce administration announced that federal patronage would be leveraged to the hilt. Pierce's efforts were enough to win half of the northern Democrats, barely enough to pass the bill, 113–100. Forty-one northern Democrats voted in favor; 42 were opposed. Southern Democrats went for the bill 57–2; southern Whigs, already an endangered species, 12–7. Every single northern Whig opposed the bill, 45 in all.

Into the fire stepped Anthony Burns, a slave from Alexandria, Virginia, who had stowed away aboard a ship bound for Boston. Safe in Massachusetts, Burns sent a letter to his brother. His master traced his location and had him arrested. While his trial was ongoing, a substantial crowd attempted to free him from the jail, killing a deputy marshal in the process. Other marshals successfully dispersed the crowd. President Pierce sent two militia companies of artillery, one company each from the army and marines, to supplement the 120 marshals deputized to secure Burns's presence. There was no question as to his status, and the judge ordered him returned to Virginia.

On May 30, 1854, Franklin Pierce signed the Kansas-Nebraska Act, proposed by Stephen Douglas nearly five months earlier. According to one historian, "Douglas had converted more men to intransigent freesoil doctrine in two years than" the leaders of the movement "had converted to abolitionism in twenty years."

—

For the past five years, since leaving Congress and failing to secure an appointment in the Taylor administration, Abraham Lincoln had returned to Springfield and resumed the practice of law. He would later write that the Kansas-Nebraska Act had "aroused him as he had never been before." While traveling the judicial circuit with his fellow lawyers and judges, Lincoln discussed slavery, which Judge Dickey argued was protected by the Constitution and therefore could not be interfered with. Lincoln took the position that slavery would have to be made extinct. After dinner, Lincoln and the judge retired for the night, taking their places respectively in the two beds in the room. Wearing his nightshirt, Lincoln continued to press the point. When Dickey awoke, Lincoln was sitting up in bed. "Dickey, I tell you this nation cannot exist half slave and half free," Lincoln said.

"Oh Lincoln," said Dickey, "go to sleep!"

Initially taking the stump that year to promote the Whig congressional candidate from his district, Lincoln increasingly found opportunities throughout the state to voice his opposition to Kansas-Nebraska. Douglas, facing withering criticism for his bill, mounted a three-hour defense at Peoria. When he was finished, Lincoln took the stage to make his own argument. Lincoln defended the Missouri Compromise, giving a lengthy history of the acceptance and effectiveness of that measure. He acknowledged the difficulty of the slavery issue, but argued that "no man is good enough to govern another man, without that other's consent. I say this is the leading principle—the sheet anchor of American republicanism." He was not advocating for political equality, he stressed, but he was "arguing against the extension of a bad thing."

As the summer rolled on, politics throughout the United States realigned along the fault line created by Kansas-Nebraska. Fusion movement conventions were held across the North uniting Whigs, Free Soilers, and Democrats. Many abandoned their existing affiliations for an embryonic new party, the Republicans. But of the upcoming elections, perhaps none would matter more than those in the new territory of Kansas. On the day Pierce signed the Kansas-Nebraska Act, there were fewer than eight hundred white settlers. Within nine months, there would be more than eight thousand. Kansas was, and should have remained, a testament to American industry; at Fort Leavenworth roughly thirty settlers had picked a site, spent $2,400 to clear 320 acres, and within days had a "sawmill, printing office, stores, hotel, and boarding houses." Before long, the Kansas experiment would serve as evidence of something far darker about the nation it inhabited. Pierce appointed an inexperienced lawyer named Andrew Reeder as the territorial governor. He arrived at Fort Leavenworth on October 7. By then the state had between fifteen hundred and two thousand adult males.

The New England Emigrant Aid Company, which favored a free Kansas, sent armed settlers to the territory, and they concentrated in and around the town of Lawrence. Capitalized at $200,000 by private subscriptions, it received an additional $1 million from the Massachusetts legislature. Various transportation interests provided discounted fares over rail and steam. Slaveholders, meanwhile, mostly from neighboring Missouri, settled near the towns of Leavenworth and Lecompton.

On November 29, Kansas went to the polls to elect their territorial representative to Congress. Of the 2,871 votes cast, 1,114 were legal. "The whole country was overrun on the day of the election by hordes of ruffians from Missouri," one witness remembered, "who took entire possession of the polls in almost every district, brow-beat and intimidated the judges, forced their own votes into the ballot-box for [the pro-slavery candidate], and crowded out and drove off all who were suspected of being in favor of any other candidate." It was an organized effort, with so-called Blue Lodges offering "a free ferry, a dollar a day, and liquor" to vote in Kansas. Over the protests of free state supporters, Governor Reeder allowed the results to stand.

The fall elections elsewhere signaled the birth of a new era in party politics. The Democrats fell from 157 seats in the House to 83. The Republicans, along with other opponents of the Kansas-Nebraska Act, made up 108. Forty-three were members of a secretive party referred to as the "Know Nothings," who opposed Catholicism and immigration.

Meanwhile, popular sovereignty continued to fail in Kansas. On March 30, 1855, Kansans went to the polls to select their legislature. One report listed eight hundred men a day being ferried across the river from Missouri for three days leading up to the election. The voting was distributed strategically throughout the territory to ensure control of the legislature, and the reach of these illegal votes extended 120 miles into the territory. The results were 5,427 for pro-slavery candidates, 791 for free soil candidates, and 92 votes for others. Despite being badly outnumbered by free state settlers in the territory, the pro-slavery faction had won all but three seats. A census taken a month earlier had recorded just 2,905 legal voters.

Missouri newspaper editors who criticized the obvious fraud found themselves under fire. One had his printing press thrown in the river and was ordered out of the state. Another was put on public trial by a mob who contemplated hanging him, instead setting him adrift on the river. A Leavenworth attorney who complained found himself captured and taken to Missouri, where he was tarred and feathered, and sold at a fake slave auction for a dollar.

Governor Reeder did not turn a blind eye as he had before. He set aside the results in six districts, but this constituted a meaningless percentage of the legislature and of the actual fraud. Incredibly, the pro-slavery element in Kansas condemned Governor Reeder for his actions. Returning to Washington, Reeder asked President Pierce to send a military presence to the territory where he intended to have new elections.

The first territorial legislature of Kansas met in June, moving the capital nearer to Missouri, adopting Missouri's laws as their own, and restricting officeholding to those in favor of slavery. A criminal statute was enacted; anyone who disagreed with the legal existence of slavery would be sentenced to hard labor for two years. Anyone who assisted a slave or circulated any material that could incite rebellion, a broad definition to be sure, would face the death penalty. Reeder issued vetoes but found them overridden. When the six districts where Reeder had found fraud held their special elections, free state candidates were successful. But the pro-slavery legislature refused to seat them, instead awarding the seats to the candidates who had originally won.

On August 15, Reeder received word that he was being dismissed for ethical violations. He had, in fact, invested money in Kansas land, and had even forced the legislature to convene on property that he owned. But it was his antagonism toward the pro-slavery forces in Kansas that sealed his fate. William Shannon was sent to replace him. A politician from Ohio, Shannon had declined to run for re-election there after his support for Kansas-Nebraska.

In September, shut out from Kansas government after two stolen elections, anti-slavery citizens held a "Free State Convention" in Big Springs. There they decided to hold their own election for territorial representative and to boycott the election scheduled by the legislature. Later that fall the free staters held a constitutional convention in Topeka to establish their own government.

The politics of Kansas then turned to violence. Pro-slavery resident Franklin Coleman had squatted on land abutting his own property, a plot that had been abandoned by others. The original owners sold it to Jacob Branson, a free stater, who attempted to claim his purchase. Arriving, he found an armed Coleman none too ready to let him have it. Branson was awarded the claim by arbitration, but now he had Coleman as a neighbor. Charles Dow later became a tenant of Branson. While running errands in town, he verbally quarreled with one of Coleman's friends. Passing Coleman on his walk back to the Branson property, Dow ended up with a chest full of buckshot. Coleman claimed self-defense and hastened to Missouri.

On November 26, a militia organized by free state Kansans burned several houses of pro-slavery men and Coleman's abandoned homestead. The sheriff of Douglas County, Samuel Jones, arrested Branson in bed for "disturbing the peace." A group of the militia encountered Jones's posse on the road, removing Branson from his custody and taking him to Lawrence. Jones reported the event to Governor Shannon, who called up the territorial militia. More than two thousand Missourians poured into Kansas in response to the governor's call, while Lawrence swelled with a similar number of defenders. When one of these defenders, Thomas Barber, left to return to his home, he encountered pro-slavery men and was murdered.

The following day, Governor Shannon traveled to Lawrence, meeting with leaders at the Free State Hotel, where Barber was lying in state. From there he traveled to Franklin to talk to the other side. While negotiations continued, Shannon authorized the free staters of Lawrence to raise a militia, as the Missourians camped outside the town seemed unlikely to disband.

The Illinois legislature had been transformed by the elections of 1854. Only four members would return. Candidates opposed to Kansas-Nebraska had won a majority. Lincoln wrote a friend in the legislature, "I have really got it into my head to be a United States Senator, and if I could have your support my chances would be reasonably good." Lincoln made a list of every legislator, writing down as much as he knew about their leanings. The status of the parties were greatly confused, but two things were clear; he had a real chance, and it would be a close fought thing.

—◦—

Shut out of the political process, despite their superior numbers, Kansas's free state supporters ratified their own constitution, drafted in Topeka, by a margin of 1,731 to 46, with the pro-slavery element boycotting the election. A month later elections were held for state officers. The pro-slavery authorities had outlawed voting for what they considered a renegade government, and polling places were secretly established in homes. At 2:00 a.m., Stephen Sparks, his son, and his nephew were leaving the polls when a group of pro-slavery men insulted and then fired upon them. His son ran to the polling place to get help. Fifteen or so free staters engaged in a ten-minute firefight with pro-slavery men, with one wounded on each side. The following day, free state supporter Reese Brown was captured and tortured by pro-slavery men, before being dropped on his own doorstep, where he was found by his two-year-old daughter and his wife. "They murdered me like cowards," he told them as he lay dying.

On January 24, President Pierce issued a special message to Congress about Kansas. He dismissed the stolen elections as garden-variety problems, "prone to exist in all imperfectly organized and newly associated communities." He condemned the free state movement and promised "to exert the whole power of the Federal Executive to support public order in the territory." Some two weeks later, he issued a proclamation ordering the free state movement to disperse, warning that their "attempted insurrection . . . will be resisted not only by the employment of the local militia, but also by that of any available forces of the United States." Pierce had recently told his cabinet that he intended to seek re-election, a decision with which they heartily concurred. With the 2/3 rule in place, his path to re-nomination ran through the South.

While Kansas bled, Pierce plotted re-election, and Lincoln ran for the Senate, Fillmore, Van Buren, and Buchanan were in Europe. The two ex-presidents were treated with great distinction throughout the continent. In London they dined together with Queen Victoria and sat in on the House of Commons. John Bright, Member of Parliament, remarked on this unusual event, saying "I think the House will be of opinion that it is one worth notice—of two of the distinguished men being present listening to the debates in this House who have occupied the position of President of the United States, a position I venture to say, not lower in honor and in dignity than that of any crowned monarch on the surface of the globe."

Tyler, meanwhile, was content at Sherwood Forest. "If you are half as merry as we are here," he wrote a family member, "then you are all as merry as I could wish you to be. It is on the morning of Christmas that one realizes the happiness of having a house well filled with children. The children last night hurried to bed at an early hour in order to sleep away the tedious hours which were to elapse before the dawning of day." Tyler went to their rooms around eleven to find two of them awake, watching for Santa Claus, "complaining of his tardiness." Tyler told the kids that Santa did not like to be seen, which helped them fall back to sleep.

On February 2, 1856, two months and 133 ballots after they began, the House of Representatives concluded the longest election for Speaker in history. The new House was divided north and south, among party lines old and new, Republican, Democrat, Free Soil, and Know Nothing—all divisions being for and against Kansas-Nebraska, the bill that had obliterated the old system but that had not yet crystallized the new one. The Whig Party, torn apart by the Compromise of 1850 and the electoral disaster of 1852, had all but ceased to exist. Joshua Giddings, the stalwart abolitionist and Free Soil founder, administered the oath to Nathaniel Banks, a Know Nothing opponent of Kansas-Nebraska. "I have attained the highest point of my ambition," Giddings said. "I am satisfied."

The clash of the old dynamics against the new would play out in similar fashion in the Illinois Senate election. Lincoln began with 44 votes to 41 for James Shields, a supporter of Kansas-Nebraska. Five members voted for Lyman Trumbull, an anti-Kansas Democrat. These handful of legislators indicated that they "could never vote for a Whig." As the ballots went on and a pro-Kansas candidate gained steam, Lincoln threw his support to Trumbull, who prevailed. "I regret my defeat moderately," he wrote, tempered by seeing a senator who reflected his beliefs. But to have been so close and to have had so much support, only to yield to a candidate with little strength because of his obstinate supporters, must have stung. Lincoln, who from his earliest youth believed he was destined for great things, had been frustrated yet again.

As the elections of 1856 continued, the Know Nothing Party was ascendant, believing along with many voters that only they could keep the country together. Avoiding the slavery issue, they demonstrated an increasingly rare strength in all regions of the country, from the North, where they swept House races in Massachusetts, New Hampshire, Connecticut, and Rhode Island, to the border states, to the Deep South. This movement, in response to increasing concerns over immigration and Catholicism, had grown out of Nativist clubs. Styling themselves "The Order of the Star Spangled Banner," they took an oath to support native-born American citizens for office, excluding foreigners and Roman Catholics. Members, who knew the secret passwords and handshakes of the organization, pledged to support the candidates endorsed by the Order. Branches grew throughout New York City and eventually up and down the eastern seaboard.

"Nothing has puzzled me more than the Know-nothing party," Tyler wrote, speaking for many. "The secrecy of its organization is only exceeded by the certainty with which it marches to victory." Tyler predicted a short life span for the party, and expressed regret to see their hostility toward immigrants gaining popularity. Meeting in February to nominate their presidential candidate, the Know Nothings made a surprise choice: former president Millard Fillmore. Hearing of his nomination in Europe, he returned to the United States to campaign. Fillmore did not share their antipathy for immigrants or Catholics. In fact, he had just met with Pope Pius IX in Rome. But Fillmore saw the Know Nothings as a safe repository for Union sentiment throughout the country.

Back in Kansas, smarting from his failure to arrest Jacob Branson, Sheriff Jones arrived in Lawrence with one deputy to arrest one of Branson's rescuers. But the lawmen were disarmed and sent on their way. Returning the next day with more men, the sheriff suffered the same result. Several days later, Jones returned with a contingent of US Army personnel and arrested six men, still missing the person he was searching for.

Then, while camping outside of Lawrence, Jones was shot in the back. Though the action was denounced by free state leaders, it was trumpeted by the pro-slavery forces. The Kansas-Nebraska Act, on which Pierce and the Democrats had staked everything, was proving to be a terrible and bloody mistake.

James Buchanan had mightily resisted Pierce's efforts to send him to London. Ironically, this very thing would bring Buchanan the honor he had coveted for so long. Buchanan, a serious contender in the last three Democratic National Conventions, was untainted by the blood of Kansas. Returning in April, he received a warm welcome in the city of New York. He had left the United States as an old public servant in the last station of life and returned to a welcome consistent with his status as a front-runner for president.

On May 5, the chief justice of Kansas instructed a grand jury to indict the entire free state government. Between five and seven hundred Missourians surrounded Lawrence, and the Topeka governor was arrested on his way out of town. Sheriff Jones arrived with his men and Lawrence's Committee of Public Safety turned over their weapons. Their peaceful disarmament would come at a cost. Jones responded by setting up four cannon on Massachusetts Street. The Free State Hotel, which had been built to withstand a siege, resisted the cannon fire, and so it was torched to the ground. Newspaper presses were thrown in the river, and houses were looted and burned, including that of the governor.

On May 19, Senator Charles Sumner of Massachusetts, a leading abolitionist, took the Senate floor. It was ninety degrees inside the chamber, which was filled to capacity. Over two days, he condemned the "Crime against Kansas," castigating in particular Senators Douglas and Andrew

Butler of South Carolina. Shortly after adjournment on May 21, Congressman Preston Brooks of South Carolina, Butler's nephew, crossed the Capitol and found Sumner sitting at his desk, handling correspondence. Fearing a physical confrontation with Sumner, Brooks pounded him on the head with his cane, nearly blinding him, and then continued to strike him repeatedly. Sumner struggled to rise, ripping his desk from the floor, falling forward ten feet and collapsing. One witness attested that Senator John Crittenden of Kentucky was the first to restrain Brooks. It would be fitting, in light of the peacemaking role he would seek in less than four years' time.

The House censured Brooks, who resigned but was again elected, resuming his seat seven weeks after the attack. Every southern member of Congress, "without conspicuous exception," defended Brooks, who had beaten a trapped, unarmed man with a cane until it broke, and nearly killed him. Sumner would be incapacitated for three years, but re-elected by the Massachusetts legislature despite his absence.

On May 24, a thousand miles to the west, the Doyle family had retired for the evening in their small home on Potowatomie Creek, Kansas. As midnight approached, the silence of the remote farmhouse was broken by a knock on the door, which was opened by James Doyle, the family patriarch who thought nothing of it. On the other side were men, armed with pistols and knives who forced their way into the house. They removed James and his two oldest sons in front of their weeping mother, who successfully begged them to spare her next oldest son. It must have seemed like forever, though it could not have been long before she heard pistol shots, followed by "moaning, as if a person was dying." Doyle and his sons were slave catchers, and their killers were led by John Brown, an abolitionist incensed by the news of the sacking of Lawrence and the attack on Sumner. Brown and his party would visit two more homes before sunrise, killing two more pro-slavery Kansans.

CHAPTER 9

The Final Election of the Old America

If this sectional party succeeds it leads inevitably to the destruction of this beautiful fabric reared by our forefathers, cemented by their blood, and bequeathed to us, a priceless inheritance.
—MILLARD FILLMORE

Lincoln ~ Buchanan ~ Fillmore ~ Tyler ~ Pierce

On May 29, 1856, the Republicans of Illinois had their first state convention in Bloomington. After a long list of speakers, the crowd called for remarks from Abraham Lincoln. "A tall figure rose in the back of the audience and slowly strode down the aisle," reported the *Chicago Tribune*. The expression on his face was one "of intense emotion." His hands on his hips, he walked toward the front of the stage, "his eyes blazing, his face white with passion, his voice resonant with the force of his conviction." People wept and cheered.

"The audience rose to its feet en masse, applauded, stamped, waved handkerchiefs, threw hats in the air, and ran riot for several minutes." Lincoln "looked like the personification of political justice."

Joseph Medill, the *Tribune*'s managing editor, was too absorbed to write anything down. Once "calm had succeeded the tempest, I waked out of a sort of hypnotic trance." Worried that he would be "scooped" by his competitors, he was relieved to know "that each had been equally carried away by the excitement caused by the wonderful oration." John Scripps wrote: "Never was an audience more completely electrified by human eloquence. Again and again during its delivery they sprang to their feet and upon the benches and testified, by long continued shouts and the waving of hats, how deeply the speaker had wrought upon their minds and hearts." Another witness said "that is the greatest speech ever made in Illinois, and puts Lincoln on the track for the Presidency."

As the Democrats prepared to nominate a presidential candidate, Buchanan had written to Robert Tyler, one of his campaign managers. "I fully appreciate your friendly services, and they are recorded in my heart . . . I say to you now, what I would not have said to you last night, that should the 'Old Dominion' stand firm, it is my opinion my friends will succeed in Cincinnati," site of the upcoming convention.

Pierce had led his party to a landslide defeat and proved unequal to managing affairs in Kansas. For this he would be denied re-nomination, the first and last elected president to suffer this fate. Buchanan led him on every ballot with increasing decisiveness. The convention adjourned for the night after fourteen ballots. In the morning, the chair of the New Hampshire delegation withdrew Pierce's name, deferring to what the delegates saw as "the more practicable method of advancing cherished principles . . . an offering upon the altar of our common cause." New Hampshire then endorsed Douglas. The latter withdrew after two more ballots where he demonstrated serious strength but badly trailed Buchanan. To have any hope of victory, the beleaguered Democrats needed someone free of Kansas-Nebraska.

On June 10, John Tyler wrote his son, "I suppose this will reach you rejoicing in the glories of your trip to Cincinnati. If rumor speaks truly, Pennsylvania has a prospect of giving a President to the United States. I hope it may be all realized, my opinion being that if the Democratic party shall succeed in giving the factions a good sound drubbing, it will go further towards settling the distractions of the country than all else combined. The Know Nothing party will entirely melt away, and the Black Republicans will either have to rush into the embraces of the Abolitionists . . . or go into so violent and rabid a course as to abandon and disgust all reflecting men."

Robert wrote back, "Mr. Buchanan is nominated, and he is clearly indebted to Virginia for the nomination." He told his father "your name was mentioned always with praise and admiration," while lamenting that his current financial status was preventing his own entry into politics. "If I were a rich man, and the Union does not 'slide,' I might be something yet. But as it is, I float helplessly on the waves of doubt and debt."

Lincoln was at court in Urbana while the first national Republican Convention met in Philadelphia. That morning, like every morning, the innkeeper had roused his guests at dawn by banging a gong, whose reverberations summoned them to breakfast. The judges and lawyers of the Eighth Judicial Circuit concluded that "the offending instrument" had to be removed. His colleagues voted Lincoln as the man for the job. Shortly before noon, Lincoln slipped out of the courthouse and stealthily into the dining room of the hotel. Undetected, he grabbed the gong, hid it under his coat, and began his getaway. In his escape he encountered David Davis and another lawyer, who was holding a copy of the *Chicago Tribune*, whose pages brought the news that Lincoln had won 110 votes and was the runner-up for the vice presidential nomination in Philadelphia.

"Great business this," said Davis about Lincoln's obvious thievery, "for a man who aspires to be Vice President of the United States."

Days later, Fillmore returned to New York, addressing enthusiastic crowds on his way to Buffalo. In Albany, the Know Nothing nominee for president touted his ability to "rise above sectional prejudice, and look to the welfare of the whole nation." Fillmore warned of the Republican nominees, men from free states committed to preventing the expansion of slavery. He wondered whether "they have the madness or the folly to believe that our southern brethren would submit to be governed by such a chief magistrate." Fillmore asked his listeners to consider what would happen if the South had a majority of the electoral votes, and elected a president and vice president exclusively from slave states. "Do you think we would submit to it? No, not for a moment," he declared. "If this sectional party succeeds it leads inevitably to the destruction of this beautiful fabric reared by our forefathers, cemented by their blood, and bequeathed to us, a priceless inheritance."

President Pierce had meanwhile ordered the army to break up the free state legislature in Topeka. The force's commanding officer, mounting the rostrum in the Kansas free-state House of Representatives, announced that while it was "the most painful duty of my whole life," he must "command you to disburse." In response to the recent murders, some three to four hundred pro-slavery forces converged on the town of Osawatomie, killing an unsuspecting Frederick Brown, son of John. John Brown and a much smaller contingent held them off before evacuating the town, which was burned and looted.

Such engagements were increasingly common. Free staters attacked Fort Titus, a pro-slavery stronghold, outside of Lecompton. It has been said that making peaceful protest impossible makes violent protest inevitable. Never was this more true than in the attack on Fort Titus, which free staters bombarded with cannonballs melted down from the newspaper presses in Lawrence, which had been destroyed during the siege. Above the din of cannon fire, the leader of the free state forces shouted, "This is the second edition of The *Herald of Freedom*. How do you like it?"

That fall yet another governor was appointed for Kansas. John Geary had been the first mayor of the rough and tumble boomtown of San Francisco. Surely, he thought, he was prepared for whatever he saw in Kansas. He was eager to make peace, appealing to "Men of the North—men of the South—of the East, and of the West . . . Will you not suspend fratricidal strife?" Outside of Lawrence, Geary disbursed a band of Missourians who were planning on a second sacking of the town, promising them that they would have to fight the army first. The departing mob murdered a man who worked in his fields as they left.

On November 6, at his Wheatland estate, James Buchanan addressed a group that had come to congratulate him on winning the presidency. He thanked them, adding, "It is my sober and solemn conviction that Mr. Fillmore uttered the words of soberness and truth when he declared that if the Northern sectional party should succeed, it would lead inevitably to the destruction of this beautiful fabric reared by our forefathers, cemented by their blood, and bequeathed to us as a priceless inheritance." To a great extent, such was the Democratic message in 1856. The party responsible for undoing the Missouri Compromise and the Compromise of 1850, for the oppression of the people of Kansas at the hands of an illegitimate pro-slavery government, ultimately prevailed because the public understood that things could get a good deal worse. Buchanan had been held to 45 percent of the popular vote in this three-way race, far from an endorsement of Democratic policy. Fillmore had won 28 percent of the vote nationally, but 48 percent in the border states (carrying Maryland) and 43 percent in the South. As one biographer noted, a shift of eight thousand votes would have swung three more states to Fillmore, casting the race into the House of Representatives, where he may have stood the best chance of being chosen president.* Fremont, as the first Republican nominee, had swept New England, captured the biggest prize of New York, and won Iowa, Wisconsin, Michigan, and Ohio. If the next Republican nominee could carry Buchanan's Pennsylvania, plus Indiana or Illinois, he would win the White House without any support from the border states or the South.

In Kansas, the pro-slavery legislature scheduled the election of delegates to the constitutional convention at Lecompton. An early cutoff was established for registering, so that anyone who wished to move to Kansas to influence the election was more likely to come from Missouri. The census to determine voter eligibility did not include half of the counties in Kansas. Free state voters were omitted from the rolls. No polling place was established at Lawrence.

After the presidential election, Abraham Lincoln addressed a Republican banquet in Chicago. The chair of the meeting toasted, "First the Union—the north will maintain it—the south will not depart therefrom." Lincoln said that he "could most heartily endorse the sentiment," defending the party against charges of being enemies to the Union. Interrupted frequently by cheers and applause, he mocked Pierce's revelry in Buchanan's victory, comparing him to "a rejected lover, making merry at the wedding of his rival." Lincoln noted that Buchanan had received less than a majority of the popular vote and predicted the future success of the Republican Party.

"All of us who did not vote for Mr. Buchanan, taken together, are a majority of four hundred thousand. But, in the late contest we were divided between Fremont and Fillmore. Can we not come together, for the future? Let every one who really believes, and is resolved, that free society is not, *and*

---

* When the House chooses a president, every state has equal suffrage. The Know Nothing Party controlled a number of delegations outright, had the majority in others, and carried widespread support throughout the country. On account of this strong starting position, his standing as a former president, and as the second choice for most Republican/Opposition members, it is easier to see a path for Fillmore than either of his competitors in this scenario.

shall not be, a failure, and who can conscientiously declare that in the past contest he has done only what he thought best—let every such one have charity to believe that every other one can say as much. Thus let bygones be bygones. Let past differences, as nothing be; and with steady eye on the real issue, let us reinaugurate the good old 'central ideas' of the Republic. We *can* do it. The human heart *is* with us—God is with us. We shall again be able not to declare, that 'all States as States, are equal,' nor yet that 'all citizens as citizens are equal,' but to renew the broader, better declaration, including both these and much more, that 'all *men* are created equal.'"

Pierce's political obituary appeared in the *New York Herald*, which reported "the worst of the United States presidents will retire into private life. He has satisfied no one and disgusted all." His friend Nathaniel Hawthorne recorded him "without one true friend, or one man who will speak a single honest word about him." It was hard for Pierce's friends to reconcile this public attitude with their personal experiences with the man. Varina Davis, wife of the secretary of war, was surprised one evening to find the president of the United States as a guest. Pierce walked for hours in a blizzard and through six feet of snow, and showed up unannounced after hearing she was unwell. Nobody doubted him when he said, "I am so tired of the shackles of presidential life that I can scarcely endure it." Throughout his life, honors he had sought, honors he had not sought, were his, often at a younger age than anyone before him. Now, when he needed his magic the most, he was despised, abandoned, isolated, and utterly unable to control events around him, the first and only elected president in American history to be denied re-nomination by his own party.

The last redoubt of Pierce supporters may have been within his own cabinet, the only one to remain intact over a four-year term. Jefferson Davis wished that his "days be many, your happiness great and your fame be in the minds of posterity as elevated and pure as the motives which have prompted your official action."

Pierce replied, "I can scarcely bear the parting from you who have been strength and solace to me for four anxious years and never failed me."

President-elect James Buchanan arrived in Washington on the day Preston Brooks's funeral was held in the House. The Boston *Atlas* called

Brooks's death "a signal instance of Divine retribution," to which the Richmond *Whig* responded that they thought death was sacred, and had supposed not even "the most fanatical party . . . could so far forget what is due to our common humanity as to cast reproach and insult upon the pale tenants of the grave."

"After the White House," Franklin Pierce reflected, "What is there to do but drink?" Charles Mackay, the Scottish author, was traveling the United States, carrying a letter of introduction from Nathaniel Hawthorne to the former president. Finding that he was in Boston at the same time, Mackay presented the letter, and Pierce "very cordially" received him. Mackay remembered him as a "man of polished and courtly manners, of a cultivated mind, and of wide and varied information." Pierce invited him to dinner the following evening, but he declined, having already engaged to dine at the private monthly meeting of an exclusive social club. Pierce indicated that he too would like to come, and perhaps Mackay could ask the gentleman who had invited him to include him? Mackay saw the host that day, and he agreed to invite Pierce. At the dinner, Mackay noticed thirty or forty guests, many of whom asked to be introduced to him. "Not one, however, made any attempt to obtain an introduction to Mr. Pierce, whom they suffered to enter the room unwelcomed, and almost unobserved, and some few were rude enough to turn their backs upon him, in so unmistakable and offensive a manner that it could not fail to attract his notice." Pierce "took an early opportunity" to make his exit. Mackay was astounded; in such social environs with such refined guests, he had never seen such a thing. Was this how Americans treated their ex-presidents?

CHAPTER 10

General Jackson Is Dead!

I have learned more of the depravity of my fellow man than I ever
before knew.

—Governor Geary, on his time in Kansas

Buchanan ~ Tyler ~ Pierce ~ Fillmore

A month before his sixty-fifth birthday, James Buchanan had finally ascended to the most distinguished destination on his course of honor—the presidency. Two days after his inauguration came an eagerly awaited Supreme Court decision in the case of *Dred Scott v. Sandford.* The case and its controversy had originated in Jackson's second term, when an army surgeon from Missouri took his slave, Dred Scott, from that state to his post in Illinois, and from there to Fort Snelling, in the Louisiana Territory north of the Missouri Compromise line. While at Snelling, Scott married another slave, Harriet, and together they had two children. In the second year of Van Buren's presidency, the Scott family were removed by their owner to Missouri. Unsuccessfully attempting to purchase his freedom in 1846, Scott resorted to legal action under the theory that his previous presence in free territory had ended his status as a slave. After a series of unsuccessful proceedings in the lower courts, Scott's case was appealed to the Supreme Court in 1854. What followed was a complicated series of decisions featuring different combinations of justices, sometimes a plurality and sometimes a majority, coming together or apart over the various issues involved. Of the many purported holdings of the case, only three received a majority. By a vote of 7–2, the court ruled that Scott was still a slave. Five slaveholding justices ruled that the Missouri Compromise itself was unconstitutional. The same five declared that slaves were like any other property, and therefore could be brought to any territory of the United States, regardless of laws to the contrary. Four justices, a plurality, held that Congress had no power to regulate slavery in the territories. The decision caused an immediate national schism. No issue in American history had been more divisive than the expansion of slavery, which had been at the heart of the Missouri Compromise, the Wilmot Proviso, the Compromise of 1850, and the Kansas-Nebraska Act. Now the Supreme Court claimed to have removed the issue from the political realm, where voters through their elected representatives could determine the outcome.

In his inaugural address, Buchanan reported that this question was now before the Court, and that he would "cheerfully submit" to its result. But Buchanan, who had corresponded with friends on the Supreme Court, not only knew the probable result, but had lobbied them for a more expansive decision, which he believed would settle the slavery issue once and for all.

Kansas's governor, John Geary, perhaps looking for Buchanan's affirmation or recognizing his prerogative to name his own candidate, tendered his resignation, hopeful of reappointment. Instead Buchanan chose Robert Walker, a Pennsylvanian who had made his life in Mississippi and served as secretary of the treasury under Polk. A committed Unionist, he seemed to be exactly the man to succeed where his three predecessors had failed. But he failed in his efforts to convince free staters to vote for delegates to the Constitutional Convention at Lecompton, with only an estimated 10 percent turnout.

With America's future shrouded in uncertainty, John Tyler spoke at the 250th anniversary of the Jamestown settlement, noting, "A small body of men planted on this spot the seed of a mighty empire." After reciting a long history of Virginia and the United States, he took note of the problems of the country, closing by saying, "we renew our pledges to those principles of self-government, which have been consecrated by their examples through two hundred and fifty years; and implore that great Being who so often and signally preserved them through trials and difficulties, to continue to our country His protecting guardianship and care."

Franklin and Jane Pierce headed for the island of Madeira, conveyed by the steamship *Powhatan*, which President Buchanan had put at their disposal.* From there they traveled throughout Europe, as

---

* The *Powhatan* would later figure prominently in Lincoln's plan to resupply Fort Sumter.

Fillmore and Van Buren had done before them, summering at Lake Geneva, Switzerland. Pierce did not give up on politics, observing from afar the travails of his successor with abundant schadenfreude. He had been baffled by the presidency, but his seasoned successor appeared to manage the affairs of state with no greater effect. Pierce wrote, "considering the promise of what large experience and statesmanship, at the helm, were to accomplish—the change for the better—the palpable improvement, which was to be at once apparent," yet nowhere to be found, "is quite notable."

In October, Kansas held elections for the legislature, the first election in three years in which both sides participated. The military was able to keep the peace, which is not to say the election was fair. One example of the tainted vote was the poll book of the 1,601 alleged voters in Oxford, Kansas, who had all signed in using the exact same handwriting and voted in alphabetical order (corresponding exactly to the Cincinnati Directory). But Governor Walker would not accept this fraud, personally visiting Oxford to see six houses, and found no witnesses to the 1,600 voters who had allegedly come and gone. The free staters had triumphed and would dominate the upcoming legislature. But this still left open the problem of the Lecompton Constitution, drafted a month earlier by pro-slavery delegates after a thoroughly fraudulent election. Knowing they would lose a referendum on the constitution, they were reluctantly persuaded to allow the voters to choose between the constitution "with slavery" or "without slavery." Even this distinction was qualified; the vote would not affect slaves currently living in the territory. Walker returned to Washington to convince Buchanan that the choice was unacceptable.

That fall, Edward Ruffin* visited his friend John Tyler at Sherwood Forest. Julia appeared "young and blooming . . . though now the mother of six children."

Tyler was more "thin, or gaunt, than formerly, but still is ruddy, and seems hale and hearty . . . It is to me no subject for surprise, but it would be to every stranger, to see the man who once occupied the station and

---

* Ruffin would fire one of the first shots on Fort Sumter and committed suicide when the Civil War ended.

wielded the power of a Constitutional King—as truly does a President of the United States—to be since, the plain and unassuming country gentleman and farmer, pretending not in the least to anything in position or appearance, because of his former place and power." Which is not to say that Tyler was not watching developments outside Sherwood Forest. "I do not think we differ much as to the expediency of a separation of the Union," Ruffin wrote in his diary.

On December 7, the first freely elected Kansas legislature convened, reflecting the free state beliefs of its people. They quickly scheduled a second ratification vote on the Lecompton Constitution for January 4, an up or down measure on the entire document, not just the slavery components. Incredibly, Buchanan fired the territorial secretary, the man who had been acting as governor while Walker had traveled to Washington, and who had signed off on the measure.

That same week, Senator Stephen Douglas arrived at the White House to see President Buchanan. Pro-slavery forces had made an absolute mockery of his cherished popular sovereignty. He had carried their water at great political expense, and all the tragedy that had followed was attributable to their crimes. Now, he would do whatever it took to oppose the admission of Kansas under Lecompton, the very fruits of their actions. As he would later tell a journalist, "In making the fight against this power, I was enabled to stand off and view the men with whom I had been acting; that I was ashamed I had ever been caught in such company; they were a set of unprincipled demagogues, bent upon perpetuating slavery, and by the exercise of that unequal and unfair power, to control the government or break up the Union; and I intend to prevent their doing either." Despite Douglas's intentions, the president fancied that he could bring him into line.

During a visit at the White House, Buchanan reminded Douglas of the many powers at his command, including the power of patronage, and the influence of administration-controlled newspapers. "No Democrat ever broke with a Democratic administration without being crushed," he warned, reflecting on the methods by which Andrew Jackson had brought dissenters to heel.

"Mr. President," Douglas replied, "I wish to remind you that General Jackson is dead."

—◦—

In his first annual message, Buchanan blamed the free staters for Lecompton, as though he had no idea why they might have boycotted the elections that produced the constitution. He pronounced the upcoming referendum on "slavery" or "no slavery" perfectly sufficient, despite the lack of effect it would have on slaves already present. Governor Walker resigned, accusing the president of malfeasance.

One week later, Tyler wrote words of advice to an ambitious young politician. "So much of the future of the country is overcast, that the future of political pursuit becomes a mere myth. Is it worth the pursuit?" he asked. "A long political life opens me to this truth, that those who pursue political advancement are almost always disappointed. Who ever ran the chase with more eagerness than Clay, Calhoun, and Webster? And the goal, always in view, was never reached . . . I have come to the conclusion, therefore, that the surest means of advancement is to discharge faithfully the duties of the position which you may be, and leave the future to take care of itself." Stephen Douglas could just as easily have written this letter, having pursued the presidency for so long, having previously come so close, and at age forty-four being the front-runner for the 1860 nomination. He would now risk everything to defend the freedom of Kansas.

On December 18, Douglas proposed a bill to scrap both the free state Topeka Constitution and the pro-slavery Lecompton Constitution and to start afresh. Three days later came the scheduled vote in Kansas on the Lecompton Constitution, with pro-slavery forces winning 6,226 to 569 in an election boycotted by free staters. The free state election, held January 4, saw 10,226 voting to reject the Lecompton Constitution entirely while 138 supported it without slavery and 24 with slavery.

Also held that day were elections to offices under the Lecompton Constitution. Once again there were allegations of fraud, with one election judge adding a "5" in front of "35" and 900 voters being accounted for at one location when the real number was closer to 250. Names found in the poll books included those of famous actors, Horace Greeley, and James Buchanan. An investigation was made impossible by the disappearance of polling books shortly after the election. A search discovered three hundred forged ballots buried like treasure. Buchanan's newly appointed governor, James Denver, told the president that absent the fraud, the free state party had won control of government. Denver proposed a new election of delegates to a new constitutional convention. But on February 2 Buchanan transmitted the application of Kansas to Congress with a proposal for admission as a state under Lecompton. Three months of debate would follow. According to Nevins, "About fifty set speeches were delivered, which changed not one vote in Congress and not a thousand outside."

The Senate voted first, on March 23, sustaining the administration 33–25. Douglas had held his ground, delivering powerful speeches and voting "no," but party discipline prevailed, and Douglas was joined by only three northern Democratic senators. All but two southern senators of either party voted "yes."

But Buchanan would not have the same success in the House, despite a Democratic majority. A compromise fashioned by Senator John Crittenden, which would have admitted Kansas but scheduled a new vote on the constitution, carried 120–112. Lecompton was effectively dead. Many were eager for a face-saving resolution. When applying for statehood, a territory must request a grant of public land. Compromisers supported sending the bill back to Kansas for revision and revote on the pretext that they had requested too much land. Allowing everyone to claim victory, the tactic prevented an embarrassing defeat. When finally before the people of Kansas in a fair election, the Lecompton Constitution was crushed, 11,812–1,926.

Though retaliation could achieve nothing, Buchanan was determined to make good on his threat to Douglas. The president attacked the senator in the administration newspapers, and removed his supporters from federal jobs. He also ordered government employees to attend state nominating conventions to send anti-Douglas delegates to the national presidential convention.

The Buchanan-Douglas feud, initiated by the president to impose a fraudulent pro-slavery constitution upon an unwilling people, and continued out of revenge, would ultimately result in the fall of the Democratic Party. The last truly national organization, with supporters in all parts of the country, its collapse would mean uncharted waters for the United States. But what would rise to fill the void?

CHAPTER 11

The First and Only Choice of the Republicans of Illinois

From this time forward, until the Senatorial question shall be decided, [Illinois is] the most interesting political battleground in the Union.
—*NEW YORK TIMES*

Lincoln ~ Buchanan

The Illinois Republican Convention met on June 16, 1858, to nominate Abraham Lincoln as "the first and only choice of the Republicans of Illinois for the United States Senate." The Republicans hoped that by a direct appeal to the voters they could win the legislature and thereby the Senate seat.

The result was no surprise; ninety-five county conventions throughout the state had resolved that Lincoln would be the candidate, instructing their delegates to the state meeting accordingly. At the end of the convention, Lincoln stood to deliver remarks to 578 delegates and fifteen hundred spectators at the State Capitol. "We are now far into the fifth year," he said, "since a policy was initiated, with the avowed object, and confident promise, of putting an end to slavery agitation," he said. "Under the operation of that policy, that agitation has not only not ceased, but has constantly augmented. In my opinion, it will not cease until a crisis shall have been reached, and passed. 'A house divided against itself cannot stand.' I believe this government cannot endure permanently half slave and half free. I do not expect the Union to be dissolved—I do not expect the house to fall—but I do expect it will cease to be divided. It will become all one thing, or all the other. Either the opponents of slavery will arrest the further spread of it and place it where the public mind shall rest in the belief that it is in course of ultimate extinction; or its advocates will push it forward, till it shall become alike lawful in all the states, old as well as new—north as well as south."

Lincoln went on to condemn *Dred Scott,* Kansas-Nebraska, and Lecompton, and to argue that before long the Supreme Court would rule that no state could exclude slavery from its limits. "Welcome or unwelcome, such decision *is* probably coming, and will soon be upon us, unless the power of the present political dynasty shall be met and overthrown . . . To meet and overthrow the power of that dynasty is the work now before all those who would prevent that consummation. . . . Two years ago the Republicans of the nation mustered over thirteen hundred thousand strong. We did this under the single impulse of resistance to a common danger, with every external circumstance against us. Of strange, discordant, and even hostile elements, we gathered from the four winds and formed and fought the battle through, under the constant hot fire of a disciplined, proud, and pampered enemy.

"Did we brave all then, to falter now?—now—when that same enemy is wavering, dissevered and belligerent? The result is not doubtful. We shall not fail—if we stand firm, we shall not fail."

Lincoln and Stephen Douglas, his opponent for the open Senate seat, had met in the Illinois legislature twenty-four years earlier. "We were both young then," Lincoln remembered, "he a trifle younger than I. Even then, we were both ambitious; I, perhaps, quite as much so as he." Douglas never knew his father—a Vermont physician—who died while reportedly holding his infant son in his arms. Financial pressures forced Douglas as a young man to head west. "When shall we expect you to come home to us, my son?" his mother asked. "On my way to Congress, Mother," he wrote at age twenty. Eventually he found himself in Illinois, where the doors of opportunity opened wide for him. Douglas was elected district attorney, state legislator, and was Van Buren's appointee as the head of the Illinois Land Office by age twenty-four. After a narrow loss for Congress to Todd Stuart, Lincoln's first law partner, Douglas was appointed a justice of the Illinois Supreme Court. A congressman by age thirty, Douglas was sworn into the US Senate at thirty-three. In the 1852 Democratic Convention, the thirty-nine-year-old Douglas had demonstrated considerable strength, posting strong second-place showings to James Buchanan across many ballots until both were trampled by the dark horse, Franklin Pierce. A leader of great renown in the Senate, his association with Kansas-Nebraska held him back in 1856, but he was the presumed front-runner for president in 1860. This formidable resume contrasted sharply with that of his opponent in 1858.

On the eve of his Republican Party nomination for Senate, Lincoln had written a biography for a man compiling the personal data of everyone who had ever served in Congress. It read as follows:

Born, February 12, 1809, in Hardin County, Kentucky.
Education, defective.
Profession, a lawyer.
Have been a captain of volunteers in Black Hawk war.
Postmaster at a very small office.
Four times a member of the Illinois legislature, and was a member of the lower house of Congress.

Of Douglas, Lincoln could not help but observe, "With *me*, the race of ambition has been a failure—a flat failure; with *him* it has been one of splendid success. His name fills the nation; and is not unknown, even, in foreign lands." Ward Hill Lamon, Lincoln's friend, recalled, "Mr. Douglas's great success in obtaining place and distinction was a standing offense to Mr. Lincoln's self-love and individual ambition. He was intensely jealous of him."

Lincoln and Douglas would begin making their cases for the Senate seat in the face of challenges from their own parties. In Lincoln's case, many Republican voices (though mostly out of state) called for giving Douglas a pass on Kansas-Nebraska and rewarding his redemptive work against Lecompton. Douglas, for his part, was beset by a vengeful administration, who busily purged the senator's stalwarts from top patronage jobs in Illinois.

Douglas far from underestimated Lincoln. "I shall have my hands full," he wrote. "He is the strong man of his party, full of wit, facts, dates, and the best stump speaker, with his droll ways and dry jokes, in the west. He is as honest as he is shrewd; and if I beat him my victory will be hardly won."

The state Republican Party urged Lincoln to challenge Douglas to debates, rejecting his current strategy of following Douglas throughout the state and speaking after him as a pathetic ploy. On July 24, Lincoln wrote to Douglas, "Will it be agreeable to you and myself to divide time, and address the same audiences during the present canvass?"

Douglas, like incumbents before and after him, recognized that he had little to gain by sharing a stage with his challenger. Still, after initially laughing off the invitation, he ultimately accepted, proposing debates in the seven congressional districts where neither candidate had yet spoken.

Reporters from out of state came to Illinois to cover the Senate race between Lincoln and Douglas, their accounts widely reprinted throughout the country. Ten thousand people attended the first debate in Ottawa.

Each debate featured much of the same points and counterpoints as those before it. Douglas accused Lincoln of being an abolitionist; chastised him for "taking the side of the common enemy against his own country" by opposing the war in Mexico; and sharply disagreed with his claim that Americans could not live divided between slave and free, as they had always done. Lincoln disclaimed any purpose of interfering with slavery where it existed, and any desire to create civil equality between blacks and whites, but he did not deny the humanity of blacks, as Douglas had done. And Lincoln argued that all men were entitled to the promises of the Declaration of Independence, "life, liberty, and the pursuit of happiness." Lincoln also took note that not all whites had equal abilities, but that the inferior among them were not made slaves. Lincoln dismissed popular sovereignty, in the wake of *Dred Scott*, saying that all it did was allow people who wanted slavery to approve it, and prevent people who did not want it from disapproving it.

Lincoln was much more sure-footed in the second debate at Freeport than he had been in Ottawa. He posed a series of questions to Douglas, one of which was designed to separate him from his Democratic base. Could a territory outlaw slavery before statehood? Douglas argued that it could, simply by not enacting a slave code, since slavery needed the positive support of the government to survive. Lincoln knew the answer Douglas would offer, but also knew that it ran counter to *Dred Scott*'s plurality opinion, as well as the position of many Democrats.

These debates, between a national star and his eloquent challenger, captivated the nation, extensively covering as they did the greatest issues of the moment. In his final words at the last debate in Alton, Lincoln placed the debates in their historical context. "It is the eternal struggle between these two principles—right and wrong—throughout the world. They are the two principles that have stood face to face from the beginning of time; and will ever continue to struggle. The one is the common right of humanity and the other the divine right of kings. It is the same principle in whatever shape it develops itself. It is the same spirit that says, 'You work and toil and earn bread, and I'll eat it.' No matter in what shape it comes, whether from the mouth of a king who seeks to bestride the people of his own nation and live by the fruit of their labor, or from one race of men as an apology for enslaving another race, it is the same tyrannical principle."

Turnout in Illinois was high on November 2, 1858. For the legislature, there were more votes for Lincoln Republicans than Douglas Democrats, and Republicans won both statewide offices. But Douglas would keep his Senate seat. From the 1856 election there were thirteen state senators who were not up for re-election until 1860; eight of them were Democrats. The legislators who won in 1858 did so under maps drawn on the 1850 Census, before massive population gains in the northern part of the state. And so the Republicans, with 50 percent of the popular vote, carried 47 percent of the legislative seats, and the Democrats, with 47 percent of the vote, won 53 percent.

Douglas had emerged from the battle unbroken. He had withstood the best efforts of his opponents in Illinois and Washington to unseat him, while the entire North was a killing field for Democrats. Most Democrats who were still standing were pro-Douglas and anti-Lecompton. Buchanan's own Keystone State was no exception. "Well!," he wrote his niece, "We have met the enemy in Pennsylvania and we are theirs." Of twenty-five representatives elected in the state, only two supported Lecompton. Buchanan's own floor leader in the House had lost his seat.

In Ohio, the delegation would be eighteen Republicans to four Democrats, three of whom were Douglasites; in Indiana, seven Republicans to two Douglas Democrats, with two for the administration; New Jersey, three Republicans and two anti-Lecompton Democrats. New York Republicans and anti-Lecompton Democrats took twenty-nine of thirty-three seats. The states of Pennsylvania, Illinois, Indiana, and New Jersey, which had eluded Fremont, were clearly in play for the right Republican presidential nominee.

Lincoln, having exhausted his personal resources in his senatorial campaign, was back on the legal circuit. His ambition had been checked once more, despite his having done everything possible to win, and it hurt him deeply. He wrote a number of letters, to encourage others as well as himself, at turns humorous and serious. To one, "'This too shall pass away.' Never fear." To another, "I am glad I made the late race. It gave me a hearing on the great and durable question of the age, which I could have had in no other way; and though I now sink out of view, and shall be forgotten, I believe I have made some marks which will tell for the cause of liberty long after I am gone." Lincoln also wrote, "The fight must go on. The question is not half settled. New . . . divisions will soon be upon our adversaries; and we shall have fun again," and "The cause of civil liberty must not be surrendered at the end of one, or even one hundred defeats." He predicted the ultimate triumph of their cause. "We are right, and can not finally fail . . . let all Republicans stand fast by their guns." Lincoln expressed "an abiding faith that we shall beat them in the long run. Step by step the objects of the leaders will become too plain for the people to stand them."

But following his defeat, Lincoln found it hard to see his place in that victory. Such despondency was evident when he encountered his friend Jesse Fell, who had been traveling throughout the country during the election. "Very frequently I have been asked," Fell told him, "'Who is this man Lincoln of your state, now canvassing in opposition to Senator Douglas?'" Fell pointed out "Judge Douglas being widely known, you are getting a national reputation through him, and the truth is I have a decided impression that if your popular history and efforts on the slavery question can be sufficiently brought before the people, you can be made a formidable, if not a successful, candidate for the Presidency."

"What's the use of talking of me for the Presidency," Lincoln asked. "Seward, Chase, and others . . . are so much better known to the people" and had done so much more for the party. "Everybody knows them; nobody scarcely outside of Illinois knows me."

Fell pressed the point and asked Lincoln to provide him with a biography he could distribute back east.

Lincoln rose to leave, wrapping his gray shawl around his shoulders. "Fell, I admit that I am ambitious and would like to be President. I am not insensible of the compliment you pay me and your interest in the matter, but there is no such good luck in store for me as the Presidency of these United States. Besides, there is nothing in my early history that would interest you or anybody else." Bidding him goodnight, Lincoln "disappeared into the darkness."

CHAPTER 12

A Startling Tide of Reckless Fanaticism

*I, John Brown, am now quite certain that the crimes of this guilty
land will never be purged away but with blood.*

—JOHN BROWN

Fillmore ~ Buchanan ~ Tyler ~ Van Buren ~ Lincoln ~ Pierce

Defeated in his bid to return as president, Millard Fillmore resumed
his comfortable retirement. He served on the board of the Mutual Life
Insurance Company of New York, and entertained various invitations,
such as those to celebrate the bicentennial of Norwich, Connecticut,
or from the Detroit and Milwaukee Railway Company for a one-week
steamship cruise on the Great Lakes to celebrate the opening of a new
route.

His sister wrote, "Only yesterday we were little children by the fireside of our parents, listening to Father's stories and songs," while "today
we are old folks, with frosted hair, weakened eyesight and impaired vigor,
for us whose craft is not yet moored in the Eternal Haven. Nearly half our
number have already."

The Know Nothing Party that had exploded on the national scene in
1854 was now almost gone, its members subsumed into the other existing
parties. Fillmore's supporters were trying to figure out where they lined
up, often seeking his advice. "The political parties north and south are in
a great measure divided and cannot unite upon any one man," wrote one.
But he told Fillmore that his supporters "will ever look to you as the great
standard bearer of our nationality. In all candor, what shall the remnant of
your party do? Point out the road and we will follow it and strike it boldly."

"I am taking no part in politics," Fillmore wrote his friend Dorothea Dix, "but looking at the world from the outside, delighted that I have no responsibility."

———

On October 16, 1859, John Brown officially brought his war against slavery from Kansas to Harper's Ferry, Virginia. With seventeen men, he approached under the cover of darkness. Telegraph wires were cut; bridges into the city were secured. The federal armory and arsenal, worth millions of dollars in weapons and ammunition, were seized. From there Brown's plan called for freeing slaves to join his army, and the taking of slaveowners as hostages. Two local planters, including the great-grandnephew of George Washington, were captured in their homes and along with their slaves, brought to Harper's Ferry. News of the raid soon reached points outside the town, and local militia as well as the Jefferson Guard from Charleston quickly descended on Harper's Ferry, seizing the entry routes. Brown sent an emissary to negotiate a truce, but the man was captured and ultimately killed. Coming out under a white flag, another of Brown's men was shot dead while yet another was captured. Buchanan sent three companies of artillery and roughly ninety marines to Harper's Ferry to end the standoff, putting Colonel Robert E. Lee in command. Throughout the long night, Brown, his men, and his hostages, surrounded in an engine house, watched his son die from injuries sustained earlier in the day. Brown's grand scheme to move south, liberating slaves, increasing his army, driving into Tennessee and Alabama, would never happen. Lee planned on taking the engine house at daylight, using bayonets to avoid harming the hostages. He sent his subordinate J. E. B. Stuart to the door. Brown opened it a crack to hear Stuart ask for his surrender. Brown refused, unless permitted to leave the city. Stuart gave the signal, and the marines burst forward, using a ladder to break down the door as rifles fired at them through the walls. Two marines were killed, one shot in the face. One of Brown's men was stabbed through with a bayonet against the wall, another as he hid under a fire engine. Brown was beaten unconscious.

The fear of a slave revolt reverberated throughout the South. Charles City County raised a cavalry unit and a company of home guards to protect themselves, with John Tyler chosen as commander. President Buchanan felt the raid "made a deeper impression on the southern mind against the Union than all former events." Not for the act itself, "but the enthusiastic and permanent approbation of the object of his expedition by the abolitionists of the north." Van Buren called Brown "a man of lawless . . . disposition." Fillmore thought it a "foolish and criminal invasion of Virginia."

An unrepentant John Brown stood upon the scaffold, his last view of earth a crowd of angry faces there to watch him die, with a military complement present to see the deed done without incident. In the last moments of his life, he betrayed no signs of nervousness or fear. He was confident in what he had done, and in the end result of the conflict that had brought him to that place. He had no final words, and if he had, his executioners would not have permitted him to speak. His final thoughts he recorded on a note and handed to a guard that morning: "I, John Brown, am now quite certain that the crimes of this guilty land will never be purged away but with blood. I had, as I now think vainly, flattered myself that without very much bloodshed it might be done." A white cap was placed over his head, and the platform beneath him opened, the noose tugging at his neck until his death. He was left hanging for forty minutes, as if to make absolutely sure that John Brown could never again disturb the peace of Virginia.

— ⌢ —

Abraham Lincoln may have been surprised by the invitations he received after his Senate campaign, to places such as Indiana, Iowa, Wisconsin, and Ohio. His forceful condemnation of slavery and its advance had captivated people throughout the country. In December 1859, he traveled throughout Kansas making a number of speeches, praising the free staters, condemning popular sovereignty and *Dred Scott*. There he also denounced John Brown, stating that "no man, north or south, can approve of violence or crime." He emphasized that the ballot box was the mechanism for opposing slavery. He addressed southern threats to leave the Union if an opponent of slavery was elected president. "Old John Brown has just been executed for treason against a state. We cannot object, even though he agreed with us in thinking slavery wrong. That cannot excuse violence, bloodshed, and treason . . . So if constitutionally we elect a President, and therefore you undertake to destroy the Union, it will be our duty to deal with you as old John Brown has been dealt with."

Lincoln's trip to Kansas closed a busy year for him, in which he traveled four thousand miles and delivered twenty-three speeches. Shortly after returning to Illinois, he wrote Jesse Fell the autobiography he had requested, and it was printed throughout the country. He collected the transcripts of his Senate debates and had them published as *Political Debates Between Hon. Abraham Lincoln and Hon. Stephen A. Douglas, in the Celebrated Campaign of 1858, in Illinois*. It was an instant bestseller.

The raid of John Brown had raised tensions north and south. Hundreds of miles away in New Hampshire, Franklin Pierce had no doubt that the North was responsible for the tension. "Scarcely had we completed emancipation in our own state, before a clamor was raised for the repeal of the law, permitting citizens of other states . . . to bring with them the servants of their household." Pierce believed "The serpent of sectional discord had cradled into this Eden, where songs of redeeming grace and dying love were sung by children of a common father together." To Pierce, everyone was responsible but the pro-slavery forces themselves; even the churches were at fault. "Pulpits have been desecrated to the base service of sectionalism, missionaries have been sent forth to war upon slavery."

Pierce believed that anti-slavery sentiment had caused the raid on Harper's Ferry and lamented that it had been invested by so many "with saintly and brave and heroic virtues." To Pierce, Brown's time in Kansas "was marked by every species of wrong and violence . . . his pathway can be traced by bloody foot prints along the whole career from theft to murder," yet upon his death, "bells were tolled, minute guns were fired, and gatherings were invoked, as though the spirit of a patriot or sage was about to pass from Earth to Heaven."

In the wake of Brown's execution, Pierce regretfully declined to attend a bipartisan meeting in Massachusetts, called to condemn the raid at Harper's Ferry. But he offered some hopeful words. "The invasion and evil acts of treason and murder are openly justified and applauded at large meetings of men and women in your midst . . . We may all have regarded with too much indifference the startling tide of reckless fanaticism, but we are not too late to hear it now . . . I have faith, above all, that the continued favor of the God of our fathers who watched over our feeble beginnings, who preserved us through the innumerable perils of the struggle for nationality, will yet make the wrath of man subservient to the peace and durability of this Union."

Pierce would receive similar invitations, and in his replies did not always strike such an optimistic tone. "The present status cannot be maintained," he wrote to a group in Hartford, Connecticut. "The condition of affairs must, of necessity, soon become a great deal better or a great deal worse." But Pierce would "rejoice in these public and timely manifestations, now being made throughout the north, bringing out the true sentiment, and the true loyalty, of so large a portion of our common country."

Millard Fillmore believed that Pierce did not have to look far to find the party responsible for Harper's Ferry. Writing to a group in New York City, he surmised that "in an evil hour this Pandora's box of slavery was again opened but what I conceive to be an unjustifiable attempt to force slavery into Kansas by a repeal of the Missouri Compromise, and the flood of evils now swelling and threatening to overthrow the constitution and sweep away the foundations of the government itself and deluge the land with fraternal blood, may all be traced to this unfortunate act. Whatever might have been the motive, few acts have ever been so barren of good, and so fruitful of evil . . . the lamentable tragedy at Harper's Ferry is clearly traceable to this unfortunate controversy about slavery in Kansas." Fillmore credited "an Overruling Providence" with settling the Kansas question "in favor of freedom."

These unity meetings, which sprang up throughout the North in response to the raid on Harper's Ferry, were eager for the presence of their past presidents. On December 16, Fillmore responded to a group in New York City planning a meeting "The North and the South—Justice and Fraternity." In his letter he would break his silence on politics, if only for a moment. The "objects of the meeting have my most hearty approval," Fillmore wrote, "but I have long since withdrawn from any participation in politics beyond that of giving my vote for those whom I deem the best and safest men to govern the country; and I have uniformly since I was at the head of the government declined an invitation to attend political meetings; yet in view of the present stormy aspect and threatening tendency of public events, did I feel that my presence at your meeting could, in the least, tend to allay the growing jealousy between the north and the south, I should at some personal inconvenience, accept your invitation, and cordially join you in admonishing the country, north and south, to mutual forbearance towards each other; and to cease crimination and recrimination on both sides, and endeavor to restore again the fortunate feeling and confidence which have made us a good and happy people." Fillmore said that his silence, in part, had been due to a fear of being misquoted and misunderstood. "My sentiments on the unfortunate question of slavery and the constitutional rights of the south in regard to it have not changed since they were made manifest to the whole country by the performance of a painful official duty in offering and enforcing the fugitive slave law." But Fillmore pledged to "stand by the Constitution of my country at every hazard . . . prepared to maintain it at every sacrifice." And then, as though changing his mind in the middle of his reply, Fillmore noted that since he left office there had been developments on which his positions were not known. The former president was about to make national news with a letter that had begun as a standard refusal.

Despite southern fears, Fillmore argued, "there are few, very few of the north who would justify in any manner an attack upon the institutions of the south which are guaranteed by the Constitution . . . We are all antislavery in sentiment, but we know that we have nothing to do with slavery in the several states, and we do not intend to interfere with it." To the North, Fillmore said, "respect the rights of the south—assure them by your acts that you regard them as friends and brethren. Let harmony be restored between the north and the south . . . rally around the national flag and swear upon the altar of his country to sustain and defend it."

Once the letter was published, the praise poured in for Fillmore. Various writers called the message "sound and just," "admirable and timely," "sentiments [that] cannot fail to meet the approbation of all right thinking men." Another said "there was never anything better said or in better time." Fillmore's mailbox would continue to fill up with invitations. But in the year for choosing Buchanan's successor Fillmore recorded his presence "very quietly and very happily at home without a single wish to be anywhere else . . . how quietly and contentedly we live." But he acknowledged this tranquility was not evenly distributed across the land. The "ill will and jealously that has been engendered between the North and the South, growing out of this slavery agitation, is greatly to be deplored, and I greatly fear that it will eventually destroy this government."

On February 29, Abraham Lincoln took the stage in New York City, at the Cooper Institute. The event's promoters were auditioning him as a potential presidential alternative to William Seward. The audience was skeptical of their western guest. Despite buying an expensive new suit, Lincoln's appearance was noticeably less polished than that of his distinguished auditors. Appearance, however, quickly yielded to substance as Lincoln utterly won them over with his defense of Republican policy, tying their thoughts about containing slavery to the Founding Fathers. He addressed southern threats to secede in the event of a Republican victory, comparing secessionists to robbers. He closed with an eloquent appeal: "Neither let us be slandered from our duty by false accusations against us, nor frightened from it by menaces of destruction to the government nor of dungeons to ourselves. Let us have faith that right makes might, and in that faith, let us, to the end, dare to do our duty as we understand it." It is hard to overstate the effect Lincoln had on his audience. Horace Greeley's influential *New York Tribune* recorded it "as one of the happiest and most convincing political arguments ever made in this city . . . addressed to a crowded and most appreciating audience . . . No man ever before made such an impression on his first appeal to a New York audience." One reporter called Lincoln "the greatest man since St. Paul." The Illinois politician, whose support was soft in the Northeast, was now invited to speak throughout the region. From there Lincoln went to Rhode Island, New Hampshire, and Connecticut, eleven different cities in twelve days. After another event in Brooklyn before returning west, the *New York Tribune* put it simply: "Mr. Lincoln has done a good work and made many warm friends."

CHAPTER 13

Five against Lincoln

The defeat of Lincoln was the great matter at issue, and that all others were subordinate.

—John Tyler

Pierce ~ Fillmore ~ Lincoln ~ Tyler ~ Buchanan ~ Van Buren

It was a season for choosing a new chief executive. The former presidents knew how much depended on the result.

From the Clarendon Hotel in New York City, Pierce wrote Jefferson Davis a confidential letter that would later become known to millions. The New Hampshire Democrat encouraged his former secretary of war to run for president, citing support that came not only from their friends but from a movement "rapidly gaining ground in New England." He added, "Without discussing the question of right—of abstract power to secede, I have never believed that actual disruption of the Union can occur without blood, and if through the madness of northern abolitionism that dire calamity must come, the fighting will not be along Mason and Dixon's line merely. It will be within our own borders, in our own streets, between the two classes of citizens to whom I have referred." The Union meetings to which Pierce had addressed so many letters "are all in the right direction and well enough for the present," but "they will not be worth the paper upon which their resolutions are written, unless we can overthrow political abolitionism at the polls and repeal the unconstitutional and obnoxious laws which in the cause of 'personal liberty' have been placed upon our statute-books." Davis, for his part, supported Pierce for the presidency and responded that it was a sentiment shared by many in Mississippi.

Fillmore, who had captured 22 percent of the vote four years earlier, was also receiving calls to seek his old job, though he too was not interested. As the last president who was neither a Democrat nor a Republican (a distinction he carries to the present day), Fillmore's choice was less predictable than that of the others. In the House of Representatives, a member stated "on the best authority" that Fillmore would not support the Republican nominee. Yet it was also reported that Fillmore would support "Bates, Lincoln, Chase, or Seward," or whoever else the Republicans put forward. One incredulous correspondent called such a claim "a libel on your good name," written "to injure your friends and to lure them into the Republican camp." While he did not act publicly to challenge the story, Fillmore did tell one correspondent, "There is no probability that any nomination will be made at Chicago which I can support." Fillmore would see a number of these reports, including one published in his hometown newspaper, and receive a number of requests for clarification, which he generally disregarded. Which is not to say that he was detached from the outcome. Later that summer he clipped out a newspaper item headlined DISUNION TICKET, quoting supporters of Vice President John C. Breckinridge, "If I had the power, I would dissolve this government in two minutes," and "Let the Union rip! My voice is for war!"

John Tyler was happy to stay the course. Buchanan "has acquitted himself well in his high office, and if re-nominated I should go to the polls and vote for him with alacrity." Tyler, for his part, actively sought a return to the presidency. His wife recorded, "The politicians talk of him very freely as being the second choice of at least three candidates." Tyler had sent a delegation of friends to Charleston to offer his name should there be a Democratic deadlock. After a speech earlier that year at the restoration of the College of William and Mary, he said "Never have I witnessed more enthusiasm on my being toasted. The cheering was immense. I never spoke better. Every sentence was followed by loud applause." If his name were offered at Charleston, he believed, "the whole south would rally with a shout."

At the end of April 1860, Democrats met in Charleston's Institute Hall. In less than eight months, in that very room, South Carolina delegates would formally secede from the Union. The two events were directly related. At the nominating convention, delegates decided to first fight over a platform. There was a majority report, holding that slavery would be allowed in the territories, and at statehood a state could decide to be slave or free. The minority argued simply that the Democratic Party would abide by decisions of the Supreme Court. Balloting for president finally began on May 1. Stephen Douglas dominated the first ballot with 145½ votes, his next closest opponent at 42. Twelve more ballots would follow that night and then forty-five the following day. Douglas never received more than 152½, needing 202. Once again the 2/3 rule had returned to wreak havoc with the Democrats. What could the party do? Douglas's support was solid. It would also never be enough. The Democrats decided to adjourn, to meet again in Baltimore in six weeks' time.

John Tyler wrote, "The times are so much out of joint as to have excited even with me, secluded as I am from the political world, an extraordinary degree of interest." The failing of the convention, he said, "filled me with apprehension and regret."

Meanwhile, the Republicans gathered in Chicago to choose their nominee. All of the strongest candidates had significant weaknesses. Seward, dating from his "higher law" speech against the Compromise of 1850, was seen as too radical, and therefore not competitive in the northern states won by Buchanan. Chase, a former Democrat and ardent abolitionist, was problematic on similar grounds, and did not have the united support of the Ohio delegation. Edward Bates, a Missouri Whig, who had not formally joined the Republicans, had the opposite problem, seen as insufficiently concerned about the expansion of slavery. Lincoln's dedicated team of managers worked diligently to make him everyone's second choice. The home state advantage was leveraged to the fullest; the Chicago press strongly advocated for his candidacy in newspapers available to arriving delegates. Lincoln supporters were given counterfeit tickets to the convention, adding to the enthusiasm in the room. The New York and Pennsylvania delegates were seated across the hall from one another, with Lincoln supporters in between, to prevent them from reaching any sort of agreement.

Lincoln was waiting at the Springfield telegraph office when balloting began. The first ballot had gone Seward 173½, Lincoln 102, Simon Cameron 50½ (a temporary placeholder for Pennsylvania's votes), and

Bates 48. Seward narrowly led on the second ballot, 184½ to 181, with a drop for all other candidates. On the third ballot, Lincoln won 231½, 33 short of victory. Lincoln crossed the square to run an errand for his wife Mary. Standing in the door of the shop engaged in conversation, he heard a cry rise up from the crowd outside the telegraph office. A little boy ran across the square yelling, "Mr. Lincoln, Mr. Lincoln, you are nominated!" He was soon corroborated by the rush of the crowd toward Lincoln, cheering, "half laughing, half crying, shaking his hand when they could get it, and one another's when they could not."

"My friend," Lincoln said to one, "I am glad to receive your congratulations, and as there is a little woman down on Eighth Street who will be glad to hear the news, you must excuse me until I inform her."

The Democrats were quick to grasp the brilliance of the Republican pick. Thomas Seymour, the former governor of Connecticut, wrote to Pierce, "In putting up Lincoln they get rid of the odium which attaches to Seward without giving up Seward's views! We ought to beat them—but madness rules the hour, and no one can tell what is to be our future."

Jefferson Davis continued to believe that Pierce should be nominated. "We all deplore the want of unanimity as to the candidates among our Southern friends and I do not see any satisfactory solution of the difficulty ... Our people will support any sound man, but will not vote for a 'squatter sovereignty' candidate any more than for a 'free-soiler.' If northern men insist upon nominating Douglas, we must be beaten and with such alienation as leaves nothing to hope for in the future of nationality in our organization. I have urged my friends to make an honest effort to save our party from disintegration as the last hope of averting ruin from the country. They would gladly unite upon you ... I have never seen the country in so great danger, and those who might protect it seem to be unconscious of the necessity."

Pierce firmly resisted attempts to push him forward for the presidency. "A proposition to use my name at Baltimore, come from what quarter it may, is one which neither you nor any other personal friend understanding my wishes and the reasons for them, can for a moment entertain ... I cannot doubt that the convention from the names already prominently before it can make an acceptable selection under the established rule, and that such a nomination could be the sure harbinger of victory."

On June 18, the Democratic National Convention reconvened in Baltimore, at the same church where Martin Van Buren had first been nominated for president. Only South Carolina boycotted. Douglas's forces resisted seating the delegates who had withdrawn at Charleston, holding their resignation to be irrevocable. In the meantime, pro-Douglas forces in the states that had withdrawn substituted slates of pro-Douglas delegates. The Committee on Credentials was firmly in Douglas's hands, replacing his previous detractors with their pro-Douglas substitutes. With that, five southern states withdrew, along with Maryland, California, and Oregon. Douglas, in a moment but not a manner in which he could have envisioned, was finally nominated for the presidency. Meanwhile, 231 delegates from nineteen states met in a separate convention across town. Consisting mainly of delegates who had been shut out of the convention, they nominated Vice President John C. Breckinridge of Kentucky for president. The Democratic Party was officially broken.

One newspaper printed the obituary for the once mighty organization. "The Democratic party is now in a deplorable condition. It is in fact no longer a party. It has no coherence, no strength, no organization." Another newspaper weighed in on the debate over the party's cause of death. "Who killed the Democratic Party? You, says Douglas to Breckinridge. You, says Breck to Douglas. You, says Old Buck [Buchanan] to both of them. You, say both to Old Buck. You, say the south to the Democratic allies north. And you, shout back the allies north to the south. You! Thunder out the slave codites to the Douglas repealers of the Missouri compromise. No, you! Echo back the Douglas Repealers and Squatter sovereigntyites."

Franklin Pierce wrote one of the rejected delegates to Baltimore, a letter published in the *Boston Post* and widely reprinted, assuring him that his exclusion "looks, in my judgment, a clear violation of right . . . It was vain to hope for harmony after the election of the majority upon the report of the Committee on Credentials." He said, "It would gratify me exceedingly if our friends in all sections of the land could unite earnestly and cordially in support of Mr. Breckinridge and Gen. Lane, and thus insure for our cause signal victory; but this cannot even be hoped for."

The Republican ascendency in the summer of 1860 depressed the hopes of all five ex-presidents in equal measure. With the Democrats unable to agree on a nominee, Abraham Lincoln increasingly looked like a winner. By August, Douglas told a Republican senator that he was sure Lincoln would win. His campaign would be therefore dedicated to convincing the South to accept the result. Though nearly destitute, Douglas administered strong medicine to hostile audiences throughout the South, an endeavor one historian would refer to as his finest hour. In Norfolk, Virginia, he addressed a group of seven thousand, telling them plainly that a Lincoln presidency was insufficient to justify secession. He added that the next president "should treat all attempts to break up the Union . . . as Old Hickory treated the Nullifiers in 1832." In Raleigh he promised to "hang every man higher than Haman who would attempt to resist by force the execution of any provision of the Constitution which our fathers made and bequeathed to us."

Meanwhile, the 1860 election featured the first and only presidential efforts of the new Constitutional Union Party. Earlier that summer they had nominated former House Speaker John Bell of Tennessee on a ticket dedicated to preserving the Union. At a June 9 Bell rally in New York, a speaker read a letter from Fillmore pledging his support "if his were the only vote in the state." And it appeared that it might be. Lincoln's supporters were confident of carrying New York. One especially enthusiastic letter writer to the *New York Herald* claimed that Fillmore and one other person were the only holdouts in Erie County. "Put that in your pipe, Mr. Bennett [the anti-Lincoln editor of the *Herald*], and take a good smoke on it under a shady tree, in the cool evening twilight, at Washington Heights." The day that letter appeared, the *Tribune* recorded a large gathering of Fillmore supporters who seemed to be coalescing around Lincoln. It would take a significant alliance between the anti-Lincoln factions to win New York, and the *Tribune* reported that this "formidable combination" headed by "skillful managers" were already "at work to form such a coalition."

President James Buchanan, titular head of what remained of the Democratic Party, addressed a crowd outside the White House on July 9. "Every Democrat is at perfect liberty to vote as he thinks proper, without running counter to any regular nomination of the party," he argued to cheers. He strongly preferred Breckinridge to arch-nemesis Douglas. But "The main object . . . is to defeat the election of the Republican candidates; and I shall never oppose an honest and honorable course calculated to accomplish this object." The Democratic Party was not dead, and would not die, he continued, but "like one of the ancient cedars of Lebanon, it will flourish to afford shelter and protection to that sacred instrument, and to shield it against every storm of faction." The crowd interrupted with applause. "Now friends and fellow-citizens, it is probable that this is the last political speech that I shall ever make." The crowd responded with cries such as "We hope not!" But Buchanan, who had entered politics at age twenty-three as a Federalist, knew that he indeed was giving his valedictory. "It is now nearly forty years since I first came to Washington as a member of Congress, and I wish to say this night, that during that whole period I have received nothing but kindness and attention from your fathers and from yourselves. Washington was then comparatively a small town; now it has grown to be a great and beautiful city; and the first wish of my heart is that its citizens may enjoy uninterrupted health and prosperity. I thank you for the kind of attention you have paid to me, and now bid you all a goodnight." The prolonged cheering of his audience followed Buchanan all the way back into the White House on his way to bed.

Some days later, Tyler wrote his son, "We begin to have more numerous calls by visitors to this region, and I become daily better informed of the status of public opinion . . . . I have much doubt whether any harmony can be brought about. The consequences of Lincoln's selection I cannot foretell. Neither Virginia, nor North Carolina, nor Maryland (to which you may add Kentucky, Tennessee and Missouri) will secede for that. My apprehension, however, is that South Carolina and others of the cotton states will do so, and any attempt to coerce such seceding states will most probably be resisted by all the south." He noted a "gloom which overspreads and enshrouds the country." As for Buchanan, "I may do him injustice in regarding him as a mere politician without heart." Nearly a month later, Tyler was more pessimistic, writing, "The country is undoubtedly in an alarming condition . . . Let things result as they may, I fear that the great republic has seen its last days."

On August 24, Tyler was the subject of an article in the *Baltimore Sun*. "This distinguished gentleman spends much of his time during the summer at Old Point, VA and is represented as the centre of the social circle at that popular place of resort. His country villa . . . is always open to strangers, who are entertained by himself and his accomplished lady in a handsome style." Tyler told the correspondent that he desired to once more visit the capital, to "see the vast improvements that have been made since the close of his own administration. But this, he says, is impossible. As he shall observe the imperative rule established by his predecessors—which is for an ex-President never to visit Washington after the close of his term of office."* On a trip to New York from Virginia Springs, as he transferred from the steamboat to train depot, Tyler told the journalist "he could plainly see the rapid strides the federal metropolis had made. He never expects to see Washington again." But Tyler was wrong, and in less than five months, he would make two fateful trips to the capital city. For now, when he was discussed at all, Tyler was an object of fun for much of the country. The *New York Daily Tribune*, weighing in on the mockery of an ex-congressman for taking a job as a pound keeper, offered "Did not John Tyler, though a poor president, make a first rate Virginia Road-master?"

Millard Fillmore had been mum about politics since his comments to the New York unity meeting a year earlier. The life of an ex-president had its advantages, and he was determined to make the most of it. That autumn he and his second wife traveled to New York City to meet the Prince of Wales. The crowd surrounding the 5th Avenue Hotel was so great that no one could enter or leave. Suffering from a head cold and ear infection that rendered him "almost deaf," Fillmore noted, "Every one seemed to regard

---

* Tyler had visited Washington once during his post-presidency to defend Daniel Webster against charges of malfeasance in office. It had been these extreme circumstances that had justified the unusual visit. That the newspaper erroneously believed the rule to be unbroken does reflect the widespread acceptance that former presidents were to stay out of public affairs.

it as his special business to talk to me, and I could not without difficulty understand what was said." Fillmore was content with his mostly private support of John Bell and the Constitutional Union Party, while the other ex-presidents were searching for last minute ways to derail Lincoln's candidacy.

⚬⚬

"A combination of all the [reactionary] forces is necessary to defeat Mr. Lincoln," Tyler wrote. Though he joined Pierce and Buchanan in supporting Breckinridge, Tyler believed he should withdraw from New York to give Douglas a chance for victory. "To detach New York from his [Lincoln's] support, or some other of the free states, is supposed to be the only 'open sesame' to the hopes of the other candidates." Tyler agreed to serve as a Virginia candidate for the Electoral College, pledged to Breckinridge. He engaged in a six-hour public debate with supporters of other candidates, and in his opinion, "knocked over four competitors at one and the same time." He accepted at least one invitation to campaign in Portsmouth on behalf of Breckinridge, who he believed would be chosen by the House of Representatives after an Electoral College deadlock. "The defeat of Lincoln was the great matter at issue," he stressed, "and that all others were subordinate."

Martin Van Buren agreed with Tyler. Though a Douglas supporter, he encouraged a strategy to support the strongest Democrat in every state, to cast the election into the House. Pierce, on the other hand, hoped for a clean victory through the nomination of a completely new slate. He wrote, "I fear the true danger to the Union to result from Mr. Lincoln's election are greater than any of us are willing to anticipate, and yet I have not seen, and do not now see, how the calamity is to be averted. My belief is that if Mr. Breckinridge and Mr. Douglas would voluntarily withdraw, and concur in the nomination of Mr. Guthrie and Gov. Seymour of New York, it is not too late to retrieve our fortunes and defeat sectionalism." Pierce surely agreed with one of his correspondents who preferred Douglas to Lincoln, writing "rather the 'Hair Splitter' than the 'Rail Splitter.'"

By the end, even Fillmore seemed to be regretting his reticence. In declining an invitation to address a group in Baltimore, he said, "Were it possible at this late period in the Presidential campaign to induce me to abandon the isolation which I formed at its commencement, and comply with your request . . . I should certainly yield to your solicitations." He was "with them in heart and soul, hoping for the best but fearing the worst. But come what may, I am for the Union and for the whole country, against all sectionalism, and sectional candidates."

Election Day was November 6. Abraham Lincoln waited for the least difficult time to cross the crowded courthouse square to the courthouse to vote. At 9:00 p.m. in the Springfield telegraph office, visitors were excluded.

John Nicolay and John Hay, Lincoln's private secretaries, would record, "There was never a closer calculator of political probability" than their boss. "All his political life he had scanned tables of returns with as much care and accuracy as he analyzed and scrutinized maxims of government and platforms of parties. Now, as formerly, he was familiar with all the turning-points in contested counties and 'close' districts, and knew by heart the value of each and every local loss or gain and its relation to the grand result." The telegraph operators handed him message after message, which Lincoln placed on his knee, "while he adjusted his spectacles, and then read and re-read several times with deliberation." The trickle of "encouraging local fragments" became a "shower of congratulatory telegrams." Above the clicking of the telegraph "he could hear the shouts and speeches of his Springfield followers, gathered in the great hall of the statehouse across the street." Abraham Lincoln processed the idea that he had been elected president of the United States. The immediate "pleasure and pride," quickly yielded before the "mighty task and responsibility" that he had inherited. "It seemed as if he suddenly bore the whole world upon his shoulders, and could not shake it off; and sitting there in the yet early watches of the night, he read the still coming telegrams in a sort of absentminded mechanical routine, while his inner man took up the crushing burden of his country's troubles, and traced out the laborious path of future duties."

Lincoln received 1,866,452 votes to Douglas's 1,376,957, Breckinridge's 849,781, and Bell's 588,879. Lincoln won 180 electoral votes; Breckinridge 72; Bell 39; Douglas, though closest to Lincoln in the popular vote, carried only the state of Missouri and a smattering of delegates from elsewhere adding up to 12. Despite the predictions and power plays of the former presidents, if all of Lincoln's opponents would have united, he still would have prevailed with 169 electors, a majority of 35.

"So all is over, and Lincoln elected," John Tyler wrote. "South Carolina will secede. What other states will do so remains to be seen. Virginia will abide developments . . . We shall see the result. For myself, I rest in quiet, and shall do so unless I see that my poor opinions have due weight."

"I have never desired to survive the wreck of the Union," said Franklin Pierce. "With submission to the Providence of God, I do not desire to live to see the day when the flag of my country, with all its stars in their places, will not float at home and abroad." He said that if he were a southerner, "after so many years of unrelenting aggression, I should probably be doing what they are doing . . . They see Mr. Lincoln elected and they take his election as an endorsement of his opinion that we cannot go on as we are but must in the end be all free or all slave states. Foolish absurd and groundless as this view is and will always stand. The south take his election as an endorsement of resistance" to the fugitive slave act.

A little boy standing in his father's gateway in Augusta, Georgia, recalled a man passing by and saying, "Mr. Lincoln was elected and there was to be war." The intensity of the statement forced Woodrow Wilson to ask his father what it meant. For the rest of his life, this incident would serve as his earliest memory.

Was war inevitable? America had been on the precipice before. Pierce believed that any act by Buchanan "in the way of coercion will drive out all the slave labor states, of that I entertain no doubt." This thinking was echoed in correspondence to the president, who heard from *Charleston Mercury* publisher Robert Rhett, the former senator from South Carolina and delegate to their upcoming secession convention. "I have truly sympathized with you in the difficulties which have surrounded your administration of a government tottering amidst the contending sections of the Union," Rhett wrote. But his condolences came wrapped in a warning. "South Carolina, I have not a doubt, will go out of the Union—and it is in your power to make this event peaceful or bloody. If you send any more troops into Charleston Bay, it will be bloody . . . If you have any hopes of reconstructing the Union, after South Carolina shall have seceded, they will, in my judgment, be utterly defeated by any demonstration of coercion in the Bay of Charleston."

Buchanan's cabinet met on November 9. The president, facing an unprecedented challenge, wanted to hold a convention under Article V of the Constitution to try to resolve the situation. "If this were done, and the north or non-slaveholding states should refuse it, the south would stand justified before the whole world for refusing longer to remain in a confederacy where her rights were so shamefully violated." Four members of the cabinet agreed, while two of them, Secretary of State Lewis Cass and Attorney General Jeremiah Black, favored coercion if necessary. Incredibly, two members of the cabinet, Howell Cobb of Georgia and John Floyd of Virginia, not only argued that the convention would achieve nothing, but that the Union was over, and that the president should accept it as fact. Joseph Holt of Kentucky opposed a convention, fearing that a failure to find a compromise would only embolden the secessionists. The following day, Buchanan proposed in cabinet a proclamation that called upon the South to accept the election results, and to declare secession unlawful, with a subtle reference to the possibility of force if necessary.

That November 10 cabinet meeting was a portrait in miniature of the dividing United States. Cobb believed that secession was not only a fait accompli but a good thing. Thompson of Mississippi shared his views. Floyd of Virginia, who had spoken out against secession in the past but believed in it in the abstract, acquiesced to his more militant colleagues. Cass, Black, Holt, and Isaac Toucey of Connecticut defended the president. The meeting broke up with no conclusion.

CHAPTER 14

The Gathering Storm

*It foreshadows such scenes of carnage as the world has not witnessed
for a thousand years.*

—Franklin Pierce

Buchanan ~ Lincoln ~ Fillmore ~ Pierce ~ Tyler ~ Van Buren

On November 17, Buchanan presented his attorney general, Jeremiah S. Black, with a list of questions. Is there any doubt that the federal government's laws are supreme? What are my powers if revenue collection is resisted by force? What right have I to defend public property? Can military force be used under the acts of 1795 and 1807? The response came three days later. According to *US v. Booth*, the chief executive must take care that the laws be faithfully executed, and Buchanan's powers were restricted by Congress. Black argued that the government could fight any force arrayed to stop them, but it could not fight against a state. His recommended language asserted the indivisibility of the Union, and a promise to "meet, repel, and subdue all those who rise against it."

Buchanan thought the language unduly hostile. He saw himself as the national mediator, not the advocate of one region over another. On December 4, 1860, Buchanan delivered his final annual message, which denied the right of secession but declared that he had no right to suppress it. Buchanan believed his speech would be "at first condemned in the north and the south." But he would "rely upon the sober second thought for justice," while bristling at accusations of inconsistency. The *New York Tribune* reported that secessionists were moving quickly: "They evidently calculate that our venerable president will remain perfectly inert, and that beyond a few empty words, rather of lamentation and regret than of admonition or warning, he will oppose no obstacles whatever to the operations which they have in hand."

On November 27, a message arrived from Major Robert Anderson in South Carolina, asking for two companies of troops to reinforce the forts at Charleston. Buchanan agreed, but then allowed his secretary of war John B. Floyd to talk him into waiting to consult with General Scott. It was a secessionist play for time, and a successful one, as Scott was ill in New York and unable to travel. Buchanan would soon reach a deal with commissioners from South Carolina to refrain from sending reinforcements while negotiations for a peaceful settlement continued.

On December 8, Lincoln wrote to William Seward to offer him the position as secretary of state. Five days later, the president-elect telegraphed to Edward Bates his appointment as attorney general. Salmon Chase would serve at Treasury, where his character would inspire confidence in national credit. His status as a former Democrat from the important state of Ohio also weighed in his favor. Simon Cameron of Pennsylvania was nominated as secretary of war; Gideon Welles of Connecticut would serve as secretary of the navy; Caleb Smith, Lincoln's old congressional colleague from Indiana, would helm the Interior, while Montgomery Blair of Missouri would oversee the Post Office.

In cabinet making, Lincoln hoped "to combine the experience of Seward, the integrity of Chase, the popularity of Cameron; to hold the west with Bates, attract New England with Welles, please the Whigs through Smith, and convince the Democrats through Blair." Cabinet making was a delicate balancing act, and Lincoln noted, "I suppose if the twelve apostles were to be chosen nowadays, the shrieks of locality would have to be heeded."

While Lincoln's cabinet was coming together, Buchanan's was coming apart. Cobb resigned, returning to Georgia to lead his state out of the Union; Cass quit over Buchanan's lack of firmness, replaced by Attorney General Jeremiah Black. Of the cabinet who remained, secretary of war Floyd engaged in the most serious treason at the highest level of government in American history. Floyd ordered the federal commander of Castle Pinckney in Charleston Harbor to return muskets he had acquired in Charleston, in response to complaints from South Carolina. While

Floyd was disarming soldiers in Charleston, he issued an order to ship forty-six cannon from Pennsylvania to Mississippi and seventy-nine cannon to Texas. Leaders in Pennsylvania physically prevented the mission from being carried out and were able to convince Buchanan to rescind the order the following day.

As the administration showed weakness, the public increasingly looked to the former presidents as peacemakers. One writer asked Fillmore to use his influence to repeal the personal liberty laws, since "Thousands of men who voted the Republican ticket hold you in the highest respect." A committee of New Yorkers was planning to head south "and endeavor to conciliate the people," inviting Fillmore to head the delegation.

"I am ready and willing to do any thing in my power to restore harmony to this distracted country," Fillmore replied, conceding "this is a contest from which the most humble has no right to shrink."

"Might not something still be done to preserve the Union?" Congressman Robert Mallory wrote Fillmore. "The expression at this time of your views might, I think would, materially aid those who are endeavoring to bring about such an adjustment." Stephen Douglas wrote Fillmore a list of constitutional amendments he was proposing. "The prospects of our country are indeed gloomy," he wrote, "but I do not yet despair of the Union."

On December 19, Supreme Court justice John Archibald Campbell wrote to Pierce, the man who had appointed him. The night before, Campbell had gone to the White House urging Buchanan to send commissioners to the states contemplating secession. "There is a wild and somewhat hysterical excitement in all the southern states," especially those from "South Carolina west to the Mississippi," which has "greatly increased" since "Lincoln's election has been announced." The Alabaman believed that nobody could rival Pierce's influence in his state, and urged him to attend the secession convention in person.

Pierce acknowledged to Campbell that in light of the wrongs "perpetrated against the people and institutions of the Southern States, I doubly honor the devotion with which you cling to the Union." If the Republicans would not compromise, "then there would seem to be no hope, except in the people, who are stronger than their servants.

THE GATHERING STORM

"I think our brethren of the south, warmhearted chivalrous men as they are, should remember in their highest exasperation how steady, true, and unfaltering has been the defense of their rights, on the part of hundreds of thousands of the people of the northern states." If the North does not redress the wrongs against the South, "bowing our heads in shame and sorrow, we will, if we must, bid farewell to the Union—farewell to those who have stood by us on so many fields in face of foreign foes—a final farewell to the dear friends and countrymen with whom we had believed our futures and the hopes of civil liberty were indissolubly linked. The very idea of dismemberment of the Union has always been to me one of terrible significance." But if we "cannot live together in peace, then in peace and on just terms let us separate—fearful will be the responsibility of those who would cast the last element of human woe—that of arms for fratricidal slaughter into the general chaos—the wisdom of man fails, may God in his mercy guide us."

Citing a cold and a "heavy and distressing cough," Pierce believed made it unsafe for him to travel, though "The clouds become more dense and dark" for the country. Pierce was especially disturbed by an editorial in Lincoln's hometown newspaper, arguing: "South Carolina will not go out of the Union unless she conquers the government." Pierce wondered, did the *Journal* "foreshadow the principles of Mr. Lincoln? If the sentence means anything, in the present state of affairs, it means civil war. It foreshadows such scenes of carnage as the world has not witnessed for a thousand years."

According to Campbell, Buchanan did not seem open to sending commissioners to Alabama. Worse, Campbell told Pierce that Buchanan's mind had lost the power to analyze "a complicated situation," describing him as "nervous and hysterical." Alabama, he wrote, has probably elected a majority of secessionists to their state convention, though "not a decisive one." If Alabama could be persuaded to stay, perhaps it could stem the tide.

Campbell was not the only southerner looking to an ex-president for assistance. J. E. Preston wrote Fillmore, "Your views . . . might prove so beneficial as to almost settle the minds of the people on present questions." Fillmore appeared to be better respected in the South than he realized. "I know of no one whose views I would" rather hear, wrote Rufus

Pollard of Ringgold, Georgia. From New Orleans came a letter: "In this sad night of our country's existence, I have looked over the land, to see if I could find someone who had the power to keep our glorious union from being broken into fragments. And sir my eyes have rested upon you, as the man having the power, and to whom belongs the duty of this great work." Fillmore, he argued, had "a work to do, and a destiny to fill."

Meanwhile, the only southerner of the ex-presidents weighed in: "Virginia looks on for the present with her arms folded, but she only bides her time. Despondency will be succeeded by action." Tyler believed that a conference of border states might find a solution.

On December 17, a South Carolina convention met to consider secession. The state legislature had, several weeks earlier, met and appointed a commission to prepare the financing and organization of a military force. Three days later there was the Washington marriage of John Bouligny, congressman from Louisiana, and Mary Parker. Her father, a successful grocer in the capital, filled his house with roses, lilies, fountains, and special light effects. No expense would be spared.

After the ceremony, Buchanan gave the couple his benediction, wishing them "a great deal of happiness." The congregation remained standing until he returned to his seat. The guests gradually made their way out of the drawing room to examine the gifts to the bride and groom.

Buchanan remained seated, receiving various well-wishers. Hearing a great commotion, Buchanan turned to Sara Pryor, wife of a congressman from Virginia, seated behind him. "Madam," he said, "do you suppose the house is on fire?"

"I will inquire the cause, Mr. President," she said. In the entrance hall she found Lawrence Keitt, congressman from South Carolina, jumping up and down and waving a piece of paper over his head and shouting "Thank God! Oh, thank God!"

"Mr. Keitt," she said, "are you crazy? The President hears you and wants to know what's the matter."

"Oh!" he responded. "South Carolina has seceded! Here's the telegram. I feel like a boy let out from school."

Returning to Buchanan, Pryor said quietly, "It appears, Mr. President, that South Carolina has seceded from the Union." Buchanan looked at her, stunned, grabbing the arms of his chair and falling back into it. "Madam," he said, "might I beg you to have my carriage called?" Pryor remembered "there were no more thoughts of bride, bridegroom, wedding-cake, or wedding breakfast."

That evening, President Buchanan met with Colonel Hamilton— who carried the message of the South Carolina governor, Francis Pickens, and who was escorted by Assistant Secretary of State William Trescot.

Pickens wrote that his message came "With a sincere desire to prevent a collision of force." He asked Buchanan to allow him to take Fort Sumter, which then only had a small handful of men, in order to quiet the concerns of the city that some kind of violence would come from those federal soldiers. If Buchanan declined, Pickens wrote, "I cannot answer for the consequences." Finished reading, Buchanan asked Hamilton when he planned on returning to South Carolina.

"The next morning," he replied.

Buchanan asked for more time.

"Yes," Hamilton agreed, "until the next evening."

Very well, Buchanan answered, he would have his response by then.

"Mr. President," Hamilton added, "I am aware of the contents of that letter, and think that if you would accept them, it would greatly facilitate the negotiations between my government and the United States."

Trescot, a South Carolinian who favored secession, was asked to stay behind and advise the president. After doing so, he reported to Louisiana senator John Slidell and Jefferson Davis, who wanted the governor to back down. As historian Allan Nevins points out, they knew the demand could never be satisfied, but that it might relieve Buchanan of his pledge not to reinforce Charleston. By the end of the day, Governor Pickens telegraphed Trescot and gave him permission to withdraw the letter. Trescot went in to see the president the next morning. Greatly relieved, Buchanan reiterated his wishes to avoid violence and his willingness to meet with commissioners from South Carolina, as well as his position not to make any decisions regarding the forts until negotiations were held.

But then on Christmas Eve, South Carolina gave the world its Declaration of Secession. Their theory for dissolution was simple and focused.

The Constitution was a contract between states. An essential provision of that agreement was the Fugitive Slave Clause, "so material to the compact, that without it that compact would not have been made." The convention pointed to the personal liberty laws of fourteen states as violations of that compact and decried the election of a political party hostile to the fugitive slave provision. The breach permitted South Carolina, they argued, to walk away.

The ticking time bomb of secession, which had begun with South Carolina's challenge to President Jackson in 1832, had been passed from one of his successors to the next—Van Buren, Harrison, Tyler, Polk, Taylor, Fillmore, and Pierce. Now it had exploded in the lap of James Buchanan. He now faced the greatest crisis of them all. What could he do? What should he do?

Buchanan would spend much of the Civil War at work on the very first presidential memoir. *The Administration on the Eve of the Rebellion* served as a defense for what he did, and did not do, during this critical time. "Under these circumstances it became the plain duty of the President, destitute as he was of military force, not only to refrain from any act which might provoke or encourage the cotton states into secession, but to smooth the way for such a Congressional compromise as had in times past happily averted danger from the Union."

For nearly eighty-five years America had been sustained by compromise. The Constitution itself, including the Fugitive Slave Clause, serves as evidence; one chamber of Congress determined by population, another where states have equality. Thomas Jefferson, James Madison, and Alexander Hamilton had formed a deal to place the capital on the Potomac in exchange for southern support for Hamilton's plan to have the national government assume state debt; the famous Missouri Compromise; the Compromise of 1833; the Compromise of 1850, which extinguished so many fires at once.

Even if hopes for compromise were unrealistic, and they were not, President Buchanan had fewer than sixteen thousand troops at his command, most of whom were stationed west of the Mississippi protecting settlers. The remainder were scattered throughout the country. Any attempt to muster these forces or raise more would have closed the door on compromise. In the meantime, despite large harvests and manufactures, "the price of all public securities fell in the market."

Whether Buchanan can be said to have risen to the challenge or not, no one can disagree with his assertion that "No public man was ever placed in a more trying and responsible position."

Buchanan believed that his hands were tied, with no legal authority to act against secession, even if he practically could. Bills to further empower the president went nowhere in Congress. A measure to raise troops and accept volunteers to recover stolen federal property attracted little support. "Had the President attempted . . . to exercise these high powers," Buchanan argued, "whilst Congress were at the very time deliberating whether to grant them to him or not, he would have made himself justly liable to impeachment." Even Jackson, with his expansive belief in executive power, at the height of the nullification crisis had asked for congressional authorization to use force against South Carolina.

The *Boston Courier* said it well: "If he does anything, he is a malignant traitor endeavoring to destroy the country: if he does nothing . . . he is an imbecile traitor. He is at the same time the most crafty of political rogues and the most stupid of political fools, an old bully, and an old Betty. . . ." Buchanan was days from his most decisive action, but as the paper predicted, it would not be well received.

John Tyler applauded Buchanan's conduct. "I am deeply concerned by the condition of public affairs," he wrote. "No ray of light yet appears to dispel the gloom which has settled upon the country. In the meantime, the president pursues a wise and statesmanlike course . . . . A blow struck would be the signal for united action with all the slave states." While Tyler watched, his namesake son had made up his mind. Speaking to a large crowd in Norfolk, he urged "let the Union go to Hell." He was "received with loud and repeated cheers," in an incident widely reported throughout the North.

As the crisis worsened, many throughout the country wondered about Buchanan's successor. Who *was* Abraham Lincoln? He had last held office twelve years earlier, a single term in the House of Representatives. This question was the subject of conversation at a New York dinner party where one very important guest had an answer. Martin Van Buren regaled the crowd with the story of his encounter with Lincoln in Rochester, Illinois, now eighteen years ago. He was "so forcibly struck by the intelligence and high toned sentiments of the man, his rare and pleasing conversational powers, that he often wondered, when he afterwards mentally reviewed his western tour, what had become of this man whom he remembered as one of the most remarkable he ever met." The frontier was a dangerous place, and Van Buren assumed the worst. "For years he heard no more from him, but frequently recalled to his mind the marked ability he then displayed." Coming from Van Buren, whose involvement in politics stretched back to the previous century and included acquaintance with the greatest leaders on both sides of the Atlantic Ocean, a more remarkable compliment would be hard to come by.

The day after Christmas, Jefferson Davis and Senator Robert Hunter of Virginia arrived at the White House to see the president.

"Have you received any intelligence from Charleston in the last few hours?" Davis asked.

"None," Buchanan said.

"Then I have a great calamity to announce to you," Davis said, reporting that Major Anderson and his men had relocated from Fort Moultrie to the more defensible Fort Sumter. "And now, Mr. President, you are surrounded with blood and dishonor on all sides."

"My God!" Buchanan said. "Are misfortunes never to come singly? I call God to witness, you gentlemen, better than anybody, *know* that this is not only without but against my orders. It is against my policy."

For his part, Anderson would argue, "I abandoned Fort Moultrie because I was certain that if attacked my men must have been sacrificed and the command of the harbor lost." Davis and Hunter advised the president to order Anderson back to Moultrie. Buchanan was inclined to do so, but waited to convene with his cabinet. Floyd argued that Anderson had disobeyed orders. Black proclaimed his actions not only justifiable but commendable. Floyd had actually shown up to cabinet uninvited. Buchanan, using Vice President Breckinridge as an intermediary, had demanded Floyd's resignation four days earlier, for improperly using the government's credit to assist faltering government contractors. Now it was clear he was looking to base his resignation on some higher purpose than personal indiscretions. He would resign two days later.

Black told Floyd that "no English minister who supinely surrendered a fortified place to an enemy would have failed to reach the block." Edwin Stanton, a prominent lawyer who had replaced Black as attorney general, argued that abandoning Sumter would be a crime on par with Benedict Arnold's, and any president who issued such an order would be guilty of treason.

"Oh, no!" Buchanan said, raising his hands, "Not so bad as that, my friend—not so bad as that!" But the decision would soon become not whether to surrender the fort, but whether to defend it, as an increasingly bellicose South Carolina seized the customs house, the arsenal, Fort Moultrie, and Castle Pinckney. Federal officials in the state had resigned their appointments, from the customs collector to the postmaster. The arsenal alone held $500,000 in public property.

The next day, Buchanan met with South Carolina's commissioners, whom he received as private citizens, not as representatives of a sovereign state. They formally protested Anderson's move, and in a follow-up letter demanded that Fort Sumter be abandoned.

A heated cabinet meeting considered the president's response. Buchanan showed a draft reply to the commissioners that nobody liked. While he had begun the crisis timidly and relied on secessionists for advice and counsel, he increasingly depended upon the Unionists in his cabinet. Stanton and Black were tasked with revising the response to the commissioners, and furiously went about it.

On the final day of 1860, President Buchanan dispatched a firm response, declaring "It is my duty to defend Fort Sumter, as a portion of the public property of the United States, against hostile attacks from whatever quarter they may come, by such means as I may possess for this purpose," adding, "I do not perceive how such a defense can be construed into a menace against the city of Charleston." As for giving up the fort, he wrote, "This I cannot do; this I will not do."

The commissioners' reply was so vituperative that Buchanan refused to receive it. The president realized, "It is all now over and reinforcements must be sent." The reinvigorated president issued the order the following day.

CHAPTER 15

The Tug Has to Come

Peace and harmony and union in a great nation were never purchased at so cheap a rate as we now have it in our power to do. It is a scruple only, a scruple of as little value as a barleycorn, that stands between us and peace, and reconciliation, and union; and we stand here pausing and hesitating about that little atom which is to be sacrificed.

—JOHN CRITTENDEN

If I live till the 4th of March I will ride to the Capitol with Old Abe whether I am assassinated or not.

—JAMES BUCHANAN

Buchanan ~ Van Buren ~ Fillmore ~ Tyler ~ Lincoln ~ Pierce

On January 5, the *Star of the West* sailed from New York, headed to reinforce Fort Sumter. Americans observed a national fast day, with "immense crowds at the churches." Public offices were closed, as the newspapers covered all kinds of religious services and sermons. Jacob Thompson, secretary of the interior from Mississippi, left the cabinet over the plans to reinforce Sumter. Unionist John Dix came in as secretary of the treasury, replacing a short-term failure who had himself replaced Howell Cobb.

All during Buchanan's back-and-forth with South Carolina, Congress, as it had successfully done so often in the past, had tried to meet the crisis with compromise. In the Senate, this task devolved upon "The Committee of Thirteen," including giants from different political stripes and all quarters of the country. There was Jefferson Davis of Mississippi and Robert Toombs of Georgia, John Crittenden of Kentucky, Stephen Douglas of Illinois, and William Seward of New York, among others.

Among the many plans that were put forward was Jefferson Davis's proposed amendment: to place slaves on equal footing with all other property, preempting the local laws of any state or territory, effectively turning every state into a slave state. Toombs's plan was to permit slave property in all the territories, abolish due process for fugitive slaves, and prohibit national legislation on slavery without the agreement of most slaveholding states, and ensconcing that amendment firmly in the Constitution by requiring every single slave state to agree in order to change it.

But it was the "Crittenden Compromise" that would form the most popular basis for settlement, a proposal made up of six constitutional amendments.

The most crucial provision would extend the Missouri Compromise line to the Pacific, with slaves in territories below 36' 30" but not above. Of particular appeal to the South, which had for years been attempting to annex parts of Mexico, Latin America, and Cuba, was that Crittenden's plan guaranteed slavery for those potential future acquisitions.

Any state could enter the Union free or slave based on its constitution once it received the requisite population. Congress would also be forbidden to abolish slavery where it had jurisdiction within a slave state (e.g., on federal property). Slavery would be legal in the District of Columbia, so long as Virginia or Maryland had slavery, and in either event no slave would be freed without compensation to the owner. Fourth, interstate transportation of slaves would be guaranteed. Fifth, Congress would pay for fugitive slaves rescued by force from a tax on the county responsible. Finally, Congress would be prevented from tampering with slavery, putting this issue on a constitutional shelf where no future policymakers could reach.

"The sacrifice to be made for its preservation is comparatively worthless," Crittenden argued. "Peace and harmony and union in a great nation were never purchased at so cheap a rate as we now have it in our power to do. It is a scruple only, a scruple of as little value as a barleycorn, that stands between us and peace, and reconciliation, and union; and we stand here pausing and hesitating about that little atom which is to be sacrificed."

Buchanan firmly supported Crittenden's plan, pointing out that slavery could never practically exist in New Mexico, the only present territory that would be impacted by extending the Missouri Compromise line. A "barren abstraction," he argued, was all the North would have to yield. But would the South have accepted a "barleycorn?" According to Stephen Douglas, the answer was "yes." Though they ultimately voted "no" on the Crittenden Compromise, Davis and Toombs were prepared to support it, so long as the Republican majority would join them.

Van Buren, like his fellow former presidents, received mail from anxious citizens desperately seeking advice. "We have certainly fallen on evil times," wrote congressman-elect John Law of Evansville, Indiana. "Can a state under our present form of government secede?" he asked. "If she cannot, what is the remedy?" If Congress ever meets again, Law said, "I shall be called on not only to discuss but to act on this great question." Van Buren responded optimistically, with hopes that a peaceful solution could still be achieved. To that end, he drafted a series of resolutions for the New York legislature to adopt, namely that the Union was "perpetual and irrevocable," and always understood to be so, arguing that no state could withdraw without using the Article V amendment process. Van Buren endorsed the Crittenden Compromise, which he believed would satisfactorily adjust the current troubles. Van Buren had spent the winter in New York City, and while there had met with Crittenden for a "free exchange" of "feelings and opinions." Shortly after, Van Buren wrote him, "I cannot but think that your suggestion," could not "fail to be acceptable to all who sincerely desire to see friendly relations between the different sections restored."

In addition to Buchanan and Van Buren, Fillmore agreed, "Mr. Crittenden's proposal ought to be made the basis of a settlement." Fillmore had sent a number of friends a copy of the "Causes and Remedies of the Present Convulsions," a sermon delivered by a minister in Buffalo on the recent day of fasting. This sermon blamed both sides for the current state of affairs, abolitionists in the North and slaveholders in the South, a sentiment very much in keeping with Fillmore's philosophy.

Tyler wanted something stronger than what Crittenden proposed, believing the only measure that could save the Union was a constitutional amendment codifying the *Dred Scott* plurality decision.

Van Buren was optimistic that the Republicans would support the Crittenden Compromise. Entering office "under circumstances more difficult and embarrassing than were ever before presented to an incoming administration," he was confident that they would "rejoice in an opportunity to secure in advance" a resolution. And after all, the president had always been a peacemaker-in-chief, ready to resolve any crisis with compromise, and to give the South what it demanded to stay in the Union. But even before taking office, Lincoln was revealing himself to be a different kind of president. The *New York Tribune* reported him "utterly opposed to any concession or compromise that shall yield one iota of the position occupied by the Republican Party on the question of slavery in the territories," adding for emphasis the "Federal Union must be preserved." Lincoln had read the Crittenden Compromise several times. He believed it would temporarily adjust the country's problems, but that as it always had, the South would be back for more. After all, it was four years after the Compromise of 1850 that the South successfully repealed the Missouri Compromise. There was persistent talk of new American conquests to spread slavery. Most ominously, there was a proposal gathering steam to reopen the African slave trade, which had been closed since 1808. Lincoln wrote Lyman Trumbull, perhaps his closest friend in the Senate, "Let there be no compromise on the question of extending slavery. If there be, all our labor is lost, and ere long, must be done again ... Stand firm. The tug has to come, and better now than at any time hereafter."

But the House would not give up, forming a committee of thirty-three to find a compromise, chaired by Ohio congressman Thomas Corwin. Corwin introduced five measures of his own: a full repeal of the personal liberty laws and enforcement of the Fugitive Slave Act; immediate admission of New Mexico as a state; fugitive slaves would be given a jury trial, but in the states from which they were accused of fleeing; a streamlined extradition process for fugitive slaves; and finally, a constitutional amendment guaranteeing that no future amendments could outlaw slavery.

On January 8, Buchanan sent Congress his final annual message. "The right and the duty to use military force defensively against those who resist the Federal officers in the execution of their legal functions, and against those who assail the property of the Federal Government, is clear and undeniable," he wrote. However, "A common ground on which conciliation and harmony can be produced is not unattainable. The prop-osition to compromise by letting the north have exclusive control of the territory above a certain line, and to give southern institutions protection below that line, ought to receive universal approbation . . . when the alter-native is between a reasonable concession on both sides and a destruction of the Union, it is an imputation upon the patriotism of Congress to assert that its members will hesitate for a moment."

The following day Mississippi became the second state to leave the Union, declaring "Our position is thoroughly identified with the insti-tution of slavery—the greatest material interest in the world . . . There was no choice left us but submission to the mandates of abolition, or a dissolution of the Union." That night the *Star of the West* was fired on in Charleston Harbor, hit three times but not seriously damaged. The cap-tain determined it was unsafe to proceed and returned to New York.

Franklin Pierce was mortified by Buchanan's action. "I cannot con-ceive of a more idle, foolish, ill motived if not criminal thing, than the sending of the *Star of the West* to Charleston under exciting circumstances . . . The gathering storm has not taken me by surprise. I have seen its approach and am prepared." The following two days saw the departure of Florida and Alabama.* As state after state seceded, letters poured in to the ex-presidents, seeking some kind of assurance, entreating them to do something. But at least one of them was as hopeless as anyone.

Millard Fillmore faulted Buchanan for his weakness and Lincoln for his unwillingness to meet southern demands. "My mind has been engrossed . . . by the startling revolutionary events of the south, which have seceded each other so rapidly as to keep the mind in a constant state of anxiety. It was a maxim of the Romans 'never to despair of the Republic,' and I have endeavored to feel so in regard to ours, but as state after state secedes, and congress seems paralyzed, my hopes fail me, and I give it all as

---

* The Alabama Convention declared: "Whereas, the election of Abraham Lincoln and Hannibal Hamlin to the offices of President and Vice-President of the United States of America by a sectional party avowedly hostile to the domestic institutions and to the peace and security of the State of Alabama, preceded by many and dangerous infractions of the Constitution of the United States by many of the States and people of the Northern section, is a political wrong of so insulting and menac-ing a character as to justify the people of the State of Alabama in the adoption of prompt and decided measures for their future peace and security." Florida did not prepare a declaration.

lost. It seems to me that if the President had acted with becoming vigor in the first instance, and the Republicans had shown a willingness to . . . grant reasonable concessions to the south, that the combined influences would have staid this treasonable torrent that is now sweeping away the pillars of the constitution. But there is no man of the dominant party who has the patriotism or courage to propose any practical form of adjustment."

As Jefferson Davis prepared to leave the Senate and return to Mississippi, he wrote to Pierce, "I have often and sadly turned my thoughts to you during the troublous times through which we have been passing and now I come to the hard task of announcing to you that the hour is at hand which closes my connection with the United States." His home state, he continued, "not as a matter of choice but of necessity has resolved to enter on the trial of secession." Davis believed that "When Lincoln comes in he will have but to continue in the path of his predecessor to inaugurate a civil war" and blame the Democratic administration.

"I leave immediately for Mississippi and know not what may devolve upon me after my return. Civil war has only horror for me, but whatever circumstances demand shall be met as a duty and I trust be so discharged that you will not be ashamed of our former connection or cease to be my friend." Davis closed with the sad reflection of a modest dream that would not be realized, for he "had hoped this summer to have had an opportunity to see you and Mrs. Pierce and to have shown to you our children."

It was Franklin Pierce who, years earlier, had helped convince Jefferson Davis that the South could secede without penalty. In a speech before the Mississippi legislature in 1858, Davis revealed that after a tour of the North, "I heard in many places what previously I had only heard from the late President Pierce, the declaration that whenever a northern army should be assembled to march for the subjugation of the south, they would have a battle to fight at home before they passed the limits of their own state, and one in which our friends claim that the victory will at least be doubtful." Pierce's prediction was soon to be tested.

Pierce, though prevailed upon from across the country for some kind of action, was in Boston seeking medical treatment as the secession crisis continued, regretting "that I am too seriously ill to take counsel with them in this most critical and alarming condition of our country."

"There are two people who can save this country and you are one of them," wrote one Pierce correspondent, omitting his other choice of savior. "Your name is already on the page of history, but if you would render it immortal, if you would place it high above America's greatest names, you must now act as a man for the good of your country. I want you to volunteer on a holy mission," asking him to speak to the people of Alabama and Georgia.

Tyler wrote in the *Richmond Enquirer,* "I will not despair of the good sense of my countrymen. The hope will linger with me to the last, that there is enough wisdom and patriotism among us to adjust these difficulties, although I frankly confess my doubts and fears." Virginia's "destiny for good or evil is with the South," Tyler believed. He argued for a convention of the border states without delay.

The Virginia General Assembly from the earliest hours of its current session had been hard at work. On the day Georgia seceded,* Virginia called for a peace conference in Washington on the fourth day of February. It would not be limited to border states, as Tyler wished, but extended to every state willing to send delegates. This olive branch was tempered by Virginia's decision, five days earlier, to schedule a conference to consider secession.

John Tyler was appointed a commissioner from Virginia to President Buchanan, while a second commissioner was sent to South Carolina and the seceded states. Both were instructed to urge caution pending a conference. The Virginia General Assembly then endorsed the Crittenden Compromise. John Tyler had been marginalized in his presidency, mocked and isolated in retirement. His grand expectations for elder

* Georgia argued, "For the last ten years we have had numerous and serious causes of complaint against our non-slaveholding confederate States with reference to the subject of African slavery . . . Because by their declared principles and policy they have outlawed $3,000,000,000 of our property in the common territories of the Union; put it under the ban of the Republic in the States where it exists and out of the protection of Federal law everywhere; because they give sanctuary to thieves and incendiaries who assail it to the whole extent of their power, in spite of their most solemn obligations and covenants; because their avowed purpose is to subvert our society and subject us not only to the loss of our property but the destruction of ourselves, our wives, and our children, and the desolation of our homes, our altars, and our firesides. To avoid these evils we resume the powers which our fathers delegated to the Government of the United States, and henceforth will seek new safeguards for our liberty, equality, security, and tranquility."

statesmanship, of traveling the world and mediating great conflicts like the Crimean War, had been unmet. But now a grave concern at home called for his immediate attention. Upon hearing of his appointment, Tyler raced to Richmond where he met with Governor John Letcher and Judge John Robertson, the commissioner to the seceded states. Months earlier, Tyler had despaired of ever seeing Washington again. But the current state of affairs rendered old rules obsolete. On the next morning's train, John Tyler was headed back to the White House.

Upon his arrival in Washington, Tyler settled into the Indian Queen Hotel, where he had quietly taken the oath of office as president after Harrison's death. He sent a note to President Buchanan asking for an early morning appointment the following day. Buchanan responded quickly, and at 10:00 a.m. the next morning Tyler walked again through the White House doors. Coming in from the cold, Tyler was warmed by Millard Fillmore's gravity-powered heating system. His old home had changed, in some ways unrecognizable from the splendid prison of his nearly four tumultuous years. The doorman would have led him up the stairs to President Buchanan's office on the second floor. Due to the importance of his guest and the excitement of the hour, Buchanan would have likely greeted Tyler in the "Reception Room," before heading to the adjacent presidential office. The office suite was a large room with little headspace, shortened to accommodate the high-ceilinged East Room below. The papers of state were piled high upon "several simple desks," and the room was warmed by a "wood stove in front of a marble mantelpiece, over which hung a portrait of Andrew Jackson." Light came in through the windows and from the gas chandelier, illuminating the many maps that adorned the walls. It was here on January 24, 1861, that the two presidents met to try and keep the Union together.

Tyler felt "a warm and cordial reception." As though the emissary of a foreign country, rather than a neighboring state still within the Union, Tyler presented his credentials to the president, as well as the resolutions of the Virginia General Assembly. Buchanan read them carefully, deeming their contents "very important." In fact, he promised Tyler that he would make them the subject of a message to Congress.

Tyler was pleased to find Buchanan "frank, and entirely confiding in his language and whole manner." Virginia was "almost universally inclined toward peace and reconciliation," Tyler informed the president. He reminded his host of Virginia's role in the revolution and founding of the country. Tyler believed his state was ready to do its part once again.

Buchanan stood by his annual message, saying that while he must enforce the laws, the power rested with Congress. He complained to Tyler of the actions of South Carolina, seizing the arsenal and the customs house. Tyler admitted that this had been done to inflame, but that it reflected popular sentiment in the state, and that in the end there was no harm. The two presidents met for an hour and a half. Buchanan made no promises, except to send a message to Congress urging the body to avoid any hostile actions. Tyler asked to preview the message, and Buchanan agreed.

The following morning, the 25th, Tyler returned to the White House, where President Buchanan read him the message he intended to send to Congress. Tyler had no suggestions, deeming it "amply sufficient." In the afternoon, Tyler was called on by Secretary of State Black and Attorney General Stanton. They apologized, letting him know that Congress had adjourned for the weekend before the message could be submitted, but that it would be done on Monday. While discussing the state of affairs, Tyler received a telegram. It was from Judge Robertson, asking about a rumor that the USS *Brooklyn* had been sent from Norfolk with troops. Tyler read it and handed it over to his guests. Stanton said, "You know sir, that I am attached to the law department and not in the way of knowing anything about it." Black said "he had heard and believed that the *Brooklyn* had sailed with some troops," but knew nothing further.

"I hope that she has not received her orders since my arrival in Washington," Tyler said. His guests urged him to ask the president directly.

Excusing himself, Tyler withdrew to an adjoining room and composed a letter to Buchanan. Stanton volunteered to deliver it personally. Tyler received his answer a half hour before midnight. The *Brooklyn* had been sent before his arrival, on a mission of "mercy and relief," and it was not bound for South Carolina. The next day Tyler wrote Virginia legislator Wyndham Robertson, the brother of commissioner Judge Robertson. "I doubt not [it] is designed for Pensacola, the troops for Fort Pickens."

As Tyler tried his hand at mediation, many others believed the ex-presidents should join him. Amos Lawrence, a leading abolitionist and relative of Pierce, wrote, "There is a desire here that all the ex-Presidents of the U. States should come to Washington by the 4th of February to exert their influence in favor of the Union. It is said that Mr. Van Buren will come and Mr. Tyler is here. Mr. Fillmore has been written to."

"The leading active men," as Lawrence referred to Douglas, Crittenden, Seward, and others who were attempting a compromise, "desire all the outside influence that can be obtained." Lawrence believed, "There is no one whose opinions would be more favorably received and would be more effective than yours." While the former presidents had been actively consulted from the first hour of danger, this call by Lawrence may have represented the inaugural attempt to bring them together. It would not be the last. John O'Sullivan, the newspaper editor who coined the phrase "Manifest Destiny," wrote to Pierce, "Has there even in history been such a dismal and disgraceful failure as that of Buchanan's presidency . . . Is not this occasion worthy of your direct intervention?" Meanwhile, the crisis worsened as Louisiana departed the Union.*

The Senate had changed since the days when Tyler had served, moving to its spacious new chambers in the new northern wing of the Capitol. Sitting in the visitors gallery to hear the president's message, Tyler "listened to its reading with pleasure." Buchanan explained that these resolutions had been delivered by "ex-President Tyler, who has left his dignified and honored retirement in the hope that he may render service to his country in this its hour of peril." The invitation was to all states, "slaveholding or non-slaveholding, as are willing to unite with Virginia in an earnest effort to adjust the present unhappy controversies in the spirit in which the Constitution was originally formed," to appoint commissioners to the meeting on February 4. But Virginia's resolutions were not even ordered to be printed, which would have been customary, nor were they referred to a committee. Rather they were left to lie on the table.

On his way out of town, Tyler wrote Buchanan to thank him for his reception and for his message to Congress. "I feel but one regret in all that

---

* Louisiana did not offer a declaration of causes.

has occurred," he said, "and that is the sailing of the *Brooklyn* under orders issued before my arrival in this city . . . There is nothing I more sincerely desire than that your administration may close amidst the rejoicings of a great people at the consummation of the work of a renewed and more harmonious confederacy." He pledged to return in a few days' time for the peace conference. The *New York Tribune* reported regarding "John Tyler of Virginia, whose recent visit to Washington, if it has not saved the Union, has, at least, produced a correspondence enlivened by the united abilities of himself and Mr. James Buchanan."

As John Tyler returned to Virginia, a nation that was rapidly losing states gained one. The *New York Times* on January 29 cheerfully announced KANSAS ADMITTED! Six years after the first elections in Kansas, she joined the Union as a free state, reflecting the will of her people.

Back at Sherwood Forest, Tyler learned of an alarming rumor, circulating in the Virginia press. Was Fortress Monroe, at Hampton, Virginia, turning its cannon toward the land, away from the sea? "If this be so, Mr. President," Tyler wrote, "is such a proceeding either appropriate or well-timed . . . when Virginia is making every possible effort to redeem and save the Union, it is seemingly ungenerous to have cannon leveled at her bosom." Buchanan responded quickly that evening, promising to inquire into the situation and wishing him safe travels on his return for the peace conference. "I shall then hope to see more of you," Buchanan said.

CHAPTER 16

The Last Winter of Peace

... a buzz of excitement here today in anticipation of the session of the Peace Convention. Numerous arrivals of delegates and spectators took place yesterday, and still continue.
—*ALBANY JOURNAL*, FEBRUARY 5, 1861

All political circles at Washington seem to coincide in the conclusion that unless this conference effects something, the fifteen southern states will be out before the middle of March.
—*NEW HAMPSHIRE SENTINEL*, FEBRUARY 7, 1861

Fillmore ~ Buchanan ~ Tyler ~ Lincoln ~ Pierce

On February 1, 1861, Texas, which had entered the Union after so much struggle and turmoil, whose maintenance in that Union had come at such a high cost, decided to leave. The twenty-eighth state cited violations of the fugitive slave law, the threat of the abolition movement, and the success of the Republican Party.*

---

* The Texas declaration clauses read: "We hold as undeniable truths that the governments of the various States, and of the confederacy itself, were established exclusively by the white race, for themselves and their posterity; that the African race had no agency in their establishment; that they were rightfully held and regarded as an inferior and dependent race, and in that condition only could their existence in this country be rendered beneficial or tolerable.

"That in this free government all white men are and of right ought to be entitled to equal civil and political rights; that the servitude of the African race, as existing in these States, is mutually beneficial to both bond and free, and is abundantly authorized and justified by the experience of mankind, and the revealed will of the Almighty Creator, as recognized by all Christian nations; while the destruction of the existing relations between the two races, as advocated by our sectional enemies, would bring inevitable calamities upon both and desolation upon the fifteen slave-holding states.

"By the secession of six of the slave-holding States, and the certainty that others will speedily do likewise, Texas has no alternative but to remain in an isolated connection with the North, or unite her destinies with the South."

The following day, Congressman Elbridge Spaulding wrote his most famous constituent, Millard Fillmore, to let him know that the petition signed by him and twenty-three thousand citizens in favor of the Crittenden Compromise had been introduced in the House. "Much depends on the vote of the people of Virginia on Monday next," he wrote, referring to the elections for the Secession Convention. But in any event, Spaulding cautioned, "our people ought to prepare for the worst."

That day Charles Sumner, recovered and returned to the Senate, visited the White House. "What, Mr. President, can Massachusetts do for the good of the country?"

"Much," Buchanan said, "no state more."

"What is that?"

"Adopt the Crittenden proposition."

"Is that necessary?" Sumner asked.

"Yes."

"Mr. President, Massachusetts has not yet spoken directly on these propositions. But I feel authorized to say—at least I give it as my opinion—that such are the unalterable convictions of the people, they would see their state sunk below the sea and become a sandbank before they would adopt these propositions."

On February 3, John Tyler returned to Washington to attend the Peace Conference. The next day, he was elected to Virginia's secession convention from the district covering James City County, Charles City County, and New Kent. Of 76 electors present, all but 11 gave Tyler one of their votes. Buchanan was encouraged by the results, noting that a very large majority of those elected to consider secession were "in favor of remaining in the Union."

The *New York Herald* took note of these results, but pointed out that Unionists had won their votes upon the hope of compromise from the Peace Conference. The paper predicted that the first fact presented to the secession convention would be the failure of the Peace Conference, which could revolutionize Virginians in a single day.

To Washington Tyler brought with him Julia, his son Alex, age twelve, and his baby daughter Pearl, who had arrived two months after her father's seventieth birthday. Visitors surrounded the old president and his young family. The most coveted dinner invitations arrived, but Tyler chose to rest instead, taking a dose of mercury and going to sleep. He was "quite tired out with the fatigues of the day," Julia wrote, "but he is in stronger condition to bear up than for many a day, and looks well. They are all looking to him in the settlement of the vexed question. His superiority over everybody else is felt and admitted by all."

The night they arrived, Julia wrote to her mother in Staten Island of her excitement "to be on hand at such a trying and exciting time to the President, and observe and listen to the doings of the convention, which has for me the most intense interest. Perhaps I am here during the last days of the Republic." It was always "the President" to Julia, even when writing to her closest family member, never "John," as if a reminder that in her youth, she had won over the most eligible man in the country. After their years in exile at Sherwood Forest, she reveled in their newfound status, as if she were once again the first lady. Julia wrote her mother of their impressive accommodations and private parlors. "The President's center table is loaded with correspondence from every quarter. There seems to be a general looking to him by those anxious to save the Union. I wish it might be possible for him to succeed in overcoming all obstacles. They all say, if through him it cannot be accomplished, it could not be through any one else." One former governor attending the conference told her of "the immortality he [Tyler] would achieve . . . if he could bring all the discordant elements together." Daniel Barringer told her "President Tyler has had the great happiness accorded him of living to see himself fully appreciated. All party feelings have faded away, and his old enemies are among his warmest friends."

The Peace Conference of 1861, upon which rested the best and final hope to avoid war, opened at the same time of another meeting in Montgomery, Alabama. Delegates from the seceded states gathered to form the Confederate States of America, and elect Jefferson Davis as president. Peace Conference delegates were badly divided, with those from the North and South required to use different entrances. But on their second day, in the hall of the Willard Hotel, the convention was unanimous in choosing a president. John Tyler assumed the chair to great fanfare and spoke to the delegates. He talked of the Founding Fathers and the difficult origins of the government under the Constitution. "You have before you, gentlemen, a task equally grand, equally sublime, quite as full of glory and immortality. You have to snatch from ruin a great and glorious Confederation, to preserve the government, and to renew and invigorate the Constitution. If you reach the height of this great occasion, your children's children will rise up and call you blessed. I confess myself to be ambitious of sharing in the glory of accomplishing this grand and magnificent result. To have our names enrolled in the Capitol, to be repeated by future generations with grateful applause—this is an honor higher than the mountains, more enduring than the monumental alabaster."

Tyler went through the roll of states, listing with each its contributions to the Union, along with the names of its great citizens. While heeding Tyler's inspiring call to meet the demands of the occasion, the delegates knew their efforts would be vanity if they could not convince President-elect Lincoln, who would soon be joining them to learn of their findings.

Meanwhile, events outside the Willard were proceeding badly. Congressional attempts at compromise had failed. Senator William Latham of California wrote Franklin Pierce of his exasperation. "I cannot tell you how blind the Republican leaders are in this body. Secession seems to them 'a grand joke.'" Latham continued, stating that he was "not without hope, and if the border states remain firm, and we can get the question before the people, I believe permanent guarantees will be conceded to the south, after which, a party will spring up in the states now gone, which I hope will eventually bring them back."

Despite Latham's hope, the negotiations over Fort Sumter were getting worse. The new secretary of war, Joseph Holt, answered South Carolina's proposal to buy the fort from the United States. Holt explained the title "is complete and incontestable. If, with all the multiplied proofs which exist of the President's anxiety for peace, and of the earnestness with which he has pursued it, the authorities of that state shall assault Fort Sumter, and peril the lives of the handful of brave and loyal men shut up within its walls, and thus plunge our common country into the horrors of civil war, then upon them and those they represent must rest the responsibility."

———

At 3:00 p.m. on February 8, John and Julia Tyler called on the president. Tyler explained that Isaac Hayne, South Carolina's attorney general, considered Holt's letter insulting. Buchanan assumed this to be a pretext, for the letter itself contained nothing to give offense. Buchanan added that Hayne's letter to him was "one of the most outrageous and insulting letters" ever addressed to any head of government. Tyler promised to ask him to withdraw the letter. Could he telegraph Governor Pickens to relay what Buchanan said about Holt's letter to Hayne? He was at perfect liberty to do so, Buchanan said, believing the letter would speak for itself. Tyler had another request. Let him tell Governor Pickens that the president would not reinforce the garrison at Sumter if Pickens would promise not to attack it. This would be "impossible," Buchanan said. "I could not agree to bind myself not to reinforce the garrison in case I deemed it necessary." Tyler asked Buchanan to remove all but an orderly sergeant and a guard at Fort Sumter to continue peaceful negotiations. Buchanan said if he did he would be burnt in effigy throughout the North.

"What of that, Sir?" Tyler replied. "In times as trying as these, have I not been burnt in effigy all over the land; and have I not seen through this window these grounds illuminated by the fires? But the light of those fires enabled me only the more clearly to pursue the path of duty."

CHAPTER 17

That All Will Yet Be Well

In your hands, my dissatisfied fellow-countrymen, and not in mine, is the momentous issue of civil war.

—ABRAHAM LINCOLN

Lincoln ~ Fillmore ~ Tyler ~ Buchanan

In the Law Offices of Lincoln and Herndon, the two longtime partners reviewed their outstanding files. Lincoln had ideas about how to handle certain cases and clients, and Herndon patiently heard him out. When they were through, Lincoln spread his large frame across the old sofa, propped up against the wall to keep it from falling apart, laying for a moment in silence, staring at the ceiling of his office. "Billy," he said, "how long have we been together?"

"Over sixteen years," Herndon answered.

"We've never had a cross word during all that time, have we?" Lincoln asked.

"No, indeed we have not."

Lincoln fondly remembered the colorful controversies that had made their way through their office. Herndon later said that he "never saw him in a more cheerful mood."

On his way out, Lincoln asked Herndon to keep the old sign that swayed outside on rusty hinges. "Let it hang there undisturbed," Lincoln said in a hushed tone. "Give our clients to understand that the election of a President makes no change in the form of Lincoln and Herndon. If I live I'm coming back some time, and then we'll go right on practicing law as if nothing had ever happened." With that, Lincoln took one last look at the office, and headed downstairs, accompanied by Herndon. On the way down, Lincoln confessed that leaving Springfield was affecting him more deeply than anyone could imagine, a sadness felt more acutely because of a stubborn premonition that he would never return alive. As the two left the building, a number of people clamored for Lincoln's attention. Turning toward Herndon, Lincoln grasped his hand warmly. "Goodbye," he said, disappearing into the crowd.

The following morning, February 11, Lincoln, his family, and his friends gathered at the railway station. For the next half hour, Lincoln shook the hands of the people he had known for so many years, the people whose mail he had sorted as a postmaster, who lived on plots that he had surveyed, customers who had come to his general store. They were the people who had sent him to the Illinois General Assembly and to Congress, people whom he had represented in the courts of law, jurors that he had addressed, as well as his dearest friends. Those who knew him best had never seen him so emotional. In the rain and the snow they had gathered by the thousands to send him off, and his breast heaved as he said farewell to as many as he could, trying hard to avoid being overwhelmed by his feelings. With the presidential party finally on board the train, the crowd, despite the rough winter weather, refused to part until they heard from their friend one last time. What could he say, Lincoln must have wondered. He had nothing prepared. How could he possibly explain what he was feeling? Obliging the crowd, who stood silently while whipped by wind and snow, Lincoln stepped out on the rear platform. "My friends," he began, "no one, not in my situation, can appreciate my feeling of sadness at this parting. To this place, and the kindness of these people, I owe everything. Here I have lived a quarter of a century, and have passed from a young to an old man. Here my children have been born, and one is buried. I now leave, not knowing when or whether ever I may return, with a task before me greater than that which rested upon Washington. Without the assistance of that Divine Being who ever attended him, I cannot succeed. With that assistance, I cannot fail. Trusting in Him who can go with me, and remain with you, and be everywhere for good, let us confidently hope that all will yet be well. To His care commending you, as I hope in your prayers you will commend me, I bid you an affectionate farewell." The crowd cheered as the door closed behind Lincoln, as the engine of the train geared up, the smokestack puffed, and the wheels began to roll. Abraham Lincoln looked upon Springfield for the final time, heading east toward an uncertain future.

Lincoln had been circumspect during the transition, knowing the power his words would have to impact the situation. The following day in Indianapolis, he argued that the government "should merely hold and retake its own forts and other property." He denied that the South could leave at their pleasure, as if the Union were some "free-love arrangement, to be maintained on passionate attraction."

Congress met on February 13 and certified the returns of the Electoral College. Lincoln was in Ohio that day, and learned the news late that afternoon. Under the Constitution, this special meeting of Congress was presided over by John C. Breckinridge, the vice president. "It was evidently an exceedingly unpleasant duty to Mr. B," reported the *Salem Register*.

Millard Fillmore, preparing to host Lincoln in western New York, had received multiple letters attesting to Lincoln's opinions of him. "He speaks of thee and the administration in the warmest terms," said one, while another said he was "gratified to learn that Mr. Lincoln has, on several occasions of late, expressed very emphatically his respect for you." These, it would seem, were too many to be accidental. Fillmore, a figure of national stature who was popular in the border states and the South, was the target of courtship by the president-elect.

At 4:00 p.m. on February 16, Lincoln arrived in Buffalo to absolute chaos. Ten thousand people were present at the depot. Lincoln stepped off the train and exchanged "a hearty grip of the hand" with Millard Fillmore. The "most terrific shouts were uttered," and the crowd rushed the train. Soldiers stationed at the depot "were tossed about as though they had been so many small boys" amid "indescribable" confusion. Cannon greeted the presidential party on both sides of the depot, but the brass band could not be heard over the "wild shouts" of a crowd that encircled the president in a "whirlpool."

"A little path had been kept open through the crowd, through which we got Mr. Lincoln," wrote John Nicolay, one of Lincoln's private secretaries. "The crowd closed up immediately after his passage, and the rest of the party only got through by dint of the most strenuous and persevering elbowing. Major Hunter [a member of the President's party] had his arm so badly sprained that it is doubtful tonight whether he can continue his journey." The president took two hours to traverse one mile to the hotel, only to find a crowd similar to that at the depot.

At 7:30 that evening Lincoln held a reception at the American Hotel, where "for over two hours a dense mass of people passed him, all eager to catch a glimpse of the countenance of 'honest old Abe.'" Lincoln briefly addressed the crowd, too hoarse to give much of a speech, before attempting some badly needed rest. From Lincoln's window, he could see the Young Men's Christian Union across the street, which had displayed a banner, promising WE WILL PRAY FOR YOU.

The next day was Sunday, and the weather "cold and blustering." Lincoln and Fillmore attended the 10:00 a.m. services at the Unitarian Church, presided over by Reverend George W. Hosmer. Afterwards the two had lunch. Later in the day, Lincoln went to see Father Beason, a famed Indian preacher.

Lincoln's pre-dawn departure the following morning was attended by hundreds of Buffalonians, determined to give him a proper send-off.

After Lincoln had taken his leave, Fillmore worried "everything looks dark and gloomy. The party which has elected Mr. Lincoln is already hopelessly divided, and perhaps after all this is the best symptom of the times. But every thing now depends upon the wisdom, discretion, and firmness of the incoming administration. If we can retain the border states, avoid a civil war, and offer an apology for the seceding states to come back, after they have tired of the folly of secession, I do not utterly despair of seeing the Union again restored." While he professed to know nothing of Lincoln's administrative ability, he thought that Seward and Bates would be capable advisers.

On February 22, troops paraded through the capital in celebration of Washington's Birthday. Tyler had protested what he deemed the unnecessary show of force. Buchanan responded, "I find it impossible to prevent two or three companies of the Federal troops here from joining the procession today with the volunteers of the district, without giving serious offense to the tens of thousands of the people who have assembled to witness the parade." Buchanan, of course, had more in mind than honoring his predecessor. He was determined to see an uneventful inaugural and to pass on a capital as secure as possible—if the president-elect could make it safely to Washington.

Fearful of an attempt on Lincoln's life in Maryland, his handlers changed his travel schedule, and Lincoln arrived in Washington early on February 23. His transition headquarters were in the "spacious parlors" of the Willard Hotel, where the Peace Conference was hard at work. Lincoln's secretaries recalled "the principal hotel, was never in its history more busy nor more brilliant."

Lincoln called on President Buchanan, and spent a few minutes with him in general conversation. Lincoln also visited the House and Senate, as well as the Supreme Court, where he had argued a case twelve years earlier. Buchanan and his cabinet later came to see him at the Willard. The Peace Conference, Douglas, and Breckinridge all paid their respects.

From the moment of his arrival to his swearing-in, "every moment of the day and many hours of the night were occupied." Meeting with the Peace Conference, Lincoln "created quite a sensation." One southern member muttered, "How in the mischief did he get through Baltimore?" The delegates formed a receiving line in the hall, led by Tyler and Chase. The latter introduced the former president to the president-elect, who "received him with all the respect due to his position." The members were introduced to Lincoln by their last names, but "in nine cases out of ten, Mr. Lincoln would promptly recall their entire name, no matter how many initials it contained," wowing the room with his "most wonderful memory." To James Brown Clay, son of America's greatest compromiser, he said, "I was a friend of your father." There was playful give-and-take. To William Rives, he said, "I always had an idea you were a much taller man." The southern delegates "freely expressed their gratification at his affability and easy manner, and all joined in expressing agreeable disappointment at his good looks in contrast to his pictures. Nothing was said to any one in regard to the condition of the country or the national troubles."

On February 24, Tyler wrote from Brown's Hotel to President Buchanan. "I think you may rely upon tranquility at the south. Since you left me I have made particular inquiries. General Davis has been written to and will be written to. He is advised to send a commissioner, and to go to Charleston himself to represent and quiet all things." Tyler believed that nothing would happen until a Confederate commissioner arrived in Washington.

On February 27, the Peace Conference concluded proposing a constitutional amendment, reminiscent of the Crittenden Compromise, which was referred to the House and Senate. Slavery would be prohibited above 36' 30" and permitted in the South; questions involving slave property in the territory would be resolved by common law. New states carved out of territory north or south would be free or slave as their constitutions provided at the time of statehood. John Tyler believed the slave interest was on the losing end. Through James Seddon of Virginia, Tyler introduced a measure to radically alter the Senate, requiring a majority of slave state senators before any action could be taken; for a majority of slave state senators to remove any officer of the executive branch; and for a method for states to formally leave the Union. As the conference drew to a close, Tyler urged the delegates to give his measures their support. When they declined, Tyler rejected the work of the conference entirely.

Despite Tyler's dissent, newspapers greeted the proposal with tremendous but ultimately unwarranted fanfare. The *Philadelphia Inquirer* reported "much rejoicing here in consequence of the favorable termination of the action of the Peace Congress." Headlines blared THE SKIES BRIGHT, GOOD NEWS FROM WASHINGTON, and THE PEACE CONFERENCE AGREE. One hundred guns were fired in Washington in celebration. But the *New Orleans Daily Picayune* realized "they cannot pass the Senate."

Crittenden wasted no time in bringing the Peace Conference's amendment before the Senate. But for all the work of the delegates, for all the high hopes invested in the conference, there was never even a vote. Crittenden attempted to strike out his own amendment and substitute the language of the conference, but was defeated 28–7. On final passage of his own resolutions, the count was 20–19, barely a majority and not nearly enough for a constitutional amendment.

The Peace Conference's work met a similar fate in the House. Thaddeus Stevens of Pennsylvania joked, "I object on behalf of John Tyler who does not want them in." Tyler, bemoaning the results, said he had to "address 'stocks and stones' who had neither ears nor hearts to understand." The day after the Peace Conference concluded, Tyler was back in Richmond speaking to an anxious crowd of Virginians from the steps of the Exchange Hotel. Tyler defended what he believed he had done for peace. Now, he was confident that no compromise could be made, "that every hour's delay was perilous, and that nothing remained but to act promptly and boldly in the exercise of state sovereignty." It was after eight o'clock in the evening when Tyler could hear a band outside his suite. Stepping onto his balcony, Tyler called the compromise proposed by the conference "A miserable, rickety affair," one that did nothing for the South. He called for its rejection.

Tyler had enjoyed a brief resurgence in the North, which this speech brought to an end. The *Albany Journal* reported "John Tyler is doing all he can to drive Virginia out of the Union, and it is believed that he will succeed in case Lincoln's Inaugural suggests a coercive policy." The *Cincinnati Gazette* jabbed, "John Tyler—The old reprobate!" With his initial speech at the Peace Conference, they assumed he "had risen from the grave of political infamy in which he had slept for so many years, that he might have an opportunity to reinstate himself somewhat in the estimation of the American people, by rendering service to a country once disgraced by his official trickery. But it is now plain it was for a different purpose altogether that he was called forth."

On March 1, John Tyler arrived to take his seat in the Virginia secession convention.

In the minutes leading to Lincoln's inauguration, the cabinet of James Buchanan met for the final time in the president's room of the Capitol. Secretary of War Holt received a dispatch from Major Anderson, saying that without twenty or thirty thousand men to capture the batteries pointed at Sumter, the fort could not be sustained. The "dark and rainy" weather on the morning of March 4 matched the mood. Under the headline JAMES BUCHANAN A HAPPY MAN, one newspaper speculated, "We do not suppose there is a happier man on the American Continent than is James Buchanan today.... However much his enemies may be disposed to attribute of trouble to him and his policy, it cannot be denied that his Administration has been during a time of extraordinary difficulty and trial."

Buchanan and the Committee of the Senate arrived at the Willard and walked with Lincoln to his carriage. Buchanan and Lincoln rode side by side. Winfield Scott had mustered every available soldier into the city. So many guards clustered around the carriage that one newspaper complained they hid its occupants from view. Platoons of soldiers, mounted and on foot, were there to preserve the peace. Marksmen adorned the rooftops. At the north entrance to the Capitol, Lincoln found a board tunnel created especially for the occasion, to shield him as he alighted from the carriage. Buchanan was not much for words on the ride, but is reported to have said, "My dear sir, if you are as happy in entering the White House as I shall feel on returning to Wheatland, you are a happy man indeed."

"Mr. President," Lincoln is said to have responded, "I cannot say that I shall enter it with much pleasure, but I assure you that I shall do what I can to maintain the high standards set by my illustrious predecessors who have occupied it."

Shortly after noon, two presidents walked through the tunnel and into the Capitol. For a time they waited in the President's Room. Buchanan took Lincoln aside to a corner where John Hay was standing. Hay waited with "boyish wonder and credulity to see what momentous counsels were to come from that gray and weather-beaten head." In a moment like this, every "word must have its value," Hay supposed.

"I think you will find the water of the right-hand well at the White House better than that at the left," Buchanan told his successor, before moving on to "many intimate details of the kitchen and pantry." Lincoln "listened with that weary, introverted look of his, not answering." The next day he would admit to Hay that he "had not heard a word of it."

They entered a crowded Senate chamber to watch the vice president sworn in. One observer noted, "Buchanan was so withered and bowed with age, that in contrast with the towering form of Mr. Lincoln he seemed little more than half a man." Guests in the chamber "crowded and pushed [Buchanan] rudely by, without a word or bow, and all through the awfully trying two hours he bravely and manfully bore himself by the side of his overshadowing, unshapely successor." From there, the party proceeded to a platform erected over the East Portico for the inauguration. "In a firm, clear voice," Lincoln delivered his address.

He acknowledged his predecessors and the tumultuous times over which they presided. "It is seventy-two years since the first inauguration of a President under our National Constitution. During that period fifteen different and greatly distinguished citizens have, in succession, administered the Executive branch of the government. They have conducted it through many perils, and generally with great success." Originally, this line was "on the whole, with great success." At Seward's recommendation, Lincoln changed it to "generally."

"Yet, with all this scope of precedent, I now enter upon the same task for the brief constitutional term of four years, under great and peculiar difficulty. A disruption of the Federal Union, heretofore only menaced, is now formidably attempted."

If its hearers in the South were within the reach of reason, Lincoln's inaugural could not have failed. "Before entering upon so grave a matter as the destruction of our national fabric, with all its benefits, its memories, and its hopes, would it not be wise to ascertain precisely why we do it? Will you hazard so desperate a step while there is any possibility that any portion of the ills you fly from have no real existence? Will you, while the certain ills you fly to are greater than all the real ones you fly from, will you risk the commission of so fearful a mistake?

"In *your* hands, my dissatisfied fellow-countrymen, and not in *mine*, is the momentous issue of civil war. The Government will not assail *you*. You can have no conflict without being yourselves the aggressors. *You* have no oath registered in heaven to destroy the Government, while I shall have the most solemn one to 'preserve, protect, and defend it.'

"I am loath to close. We are not enemies, but friends. We must not be enemies. Though passion may have strained it must not break our bonds of affection. The mystic chords of memory, stretching from every battlefield and patriot grave to every living heart and hearthstone all over this broad land, will yet swell the chorus of the Union, when again touched, as surely they will be, by the better angels of our nature."

Chief Justice Roger Taney, appointed by Jackson, had sworn in every president since Van Buren. He arose to perform this task one final time. "The clerk opened his Bible, and Mr. Lincoln, laying his hand upon it, with deliberation pronounced the oath."

With an artillery salute, Lincoln and Buchanan returned to their carriage, and back to the White House. At the threshold, "Mr. Buchanan warmly shook the hand of his successor, with cordial good wishes for his personal happiness and the national peace and prosperity." At 1:00 a.m., returning from the inaugural ball, Lincoln was handed a telegram regarding Fort Sumter—which would have to be "strongly reinforced or summarily abandoned" within "a few weeks at most."

The new administration was buried in work from the minute they opened their doors. Lincoln's secretaries would process two to three hundred letters in a given week, ranging from critical and time-sensitive missives to complete nonsense. There were two "big wicker waste-basket[s]" on either side of a desk where half the mail went. The other half were given "more or less respectful treatment," generally sent to one department or another, perhaps with or without remarks. "It is lightning work, necessarily." The rest, however, were "wildest, the fiercest and the most obscene ravings of utter insanity." Many had advice for the president. One of his clerks remembered, "It is marvelous how they can, theoretically, swing troops back and forth about the country. It is plain that they all have played the game of checkers, and have learned how to 'jump' the Confederate forces and forts with their men." Lincoln also saw visitors; well-wishers, job applicants, politicians, anyone concerned about an issue—all were able to access the president of the United States. Nicolay wrote, "some of us have work and annoyance enough to make almost anybody sick."

On the evening of March 6, the new cabinet met, "for introduction and acquaintance," a group of people who were mostly strangers to one another, who now had the biggest task before them of any cabinet in history. Gideon Welles recorded "doubts and uncertainty on every hand as to who could be trusted." Lincoln wanted no southerners thrown out of office on account of party, and especially no one from Virginia. "A strange state of things existed at that time in Washington. The atmosphere was thick with treason," Welles remembered.

On March 9, Lincoln wrote to Winfield Scott, asking him how long Anderson could remain at Sumter, if he could relieve him in that time with what he had, and what additional resources would make such relief possible. Scott responded that Anderson had provisions for forty days, but that "a single real assault" could take the fort. Scott argued that to resupply would require "a fleet of war vessels and transports which it would take four months to collect," along with "5,000 regulars and 20,000 volunteers," which Congress would need to approve and "from six to eight months to raise, organize, and discipline."

For those reasons, Scott recommended shifting focus to moving Anderson and his men safely from South Carolina. Lincoln, whose military service was limited to a militia captaincy in the Black Hawk War, who had never seen combat, had been told by the senior soldier in his command that he would have to abandon Fort Sumter.

CHAPTER 18

Home Again

Home again, home again,
From a foreign shore;
And O, it fills my soul with joy,
To meet my friends once more.
Here I dropped the parting tear,
To cross the ocean's foam;
But now I'm once again with those
Who kindly greet me home.

—Nineteenth-century song

Lincoln ~ Buchanan ~ Tyler ~ Fillmore

As newly installed president Abraham Lincoln assessed his situation, former president James Buchanan headed for Wheatland with Harriet Lane and a delegation of Pennsylvanians who had come to escort him home. Buchanan arrived to the friendliest crowd he had seen for some time. In Columbia, cannon were fired, church bells were rung, and he was paraded through the streets and public square in an open carriage drawn by four gray horses. A band assembled, playing the song "Home Again."

"Your fathers took me up when a young man," Buchanan said to the crowd, "fostered and cherished me through many long years. All of them have passed away, and I stand before you today in the midst of a new generation." A member of the crowd shouted his recollection of Buchanan's leaving to fight in the War of 1812. Now he had returned, to complete the final act of his life. "I have come to lay my bones among you, and during the brief, intermediate period which Heaven may allot me, I shall endeavor to perform the duties of a good citizen and a kind friend and neighbor. All political aspirations have departed. What I have done . . . has passed into history." He closed with his final remaining aspiration, that God would preserve the Constitution and the Union, "and in His good providence dispel the shadows, clouds, and darkness which have now cast a gloom over the land!

"May all our troubles end in a peaceful solution, and may the good old times return to bless us and our posterity!"

The audience responded with loud and sustained applause. From there, the carriage conveyed Buchanan along the road to Wheatland. City guards were assembled in front of his house, and a band played "Home, Sweet Home." Thanking them for the welcome, Buchanan entered his house, a private citizen. A week after leaving office, he wrote to Holt hoping to "hear often" from members of his cabinet. Indeed, the former presidents, though out of Washington, would be kept well informed by their former colleagues in the capital. "Pray enlighten me as to what is going on in Washington." His first reactions to Lincoln's administration were positive. "I am glad with all my heart that its policy seems to be pacific; because I believe that no other policy can preserve and restore the Union. Mr. Lincoln may now make an enviable name for himself and perhaps restore the Union."

To John Dix, his treasury secretary, he wrote, "You might envy me the quiet of Wheatland were my thoughts not constantly disturbed by the unfortunate condition of my country. It is probable an attempt will be made . . . to cast the responsibility on me. But I always refused to surrender the Fort and was ever ready to send reinforcements on the request of Major Anderson." Buchanan, however, would find little interest in history when the present was so very much alive.

The Virginia Secession Convention, meanwhile, was treated to a debate between Tyler and another delegate regarding the merits of the Peace Conference report. Tyler criticized the restraints on acquiring new land and the hardship faced by a slaveholder transporting his property to the west. One participant recalled, "He had the entire trust and confidence of every member of the Virginia convention, and exercised and wielded more influence and control over its deliberations and acts than any man in it. He won its confidence . . . His influence, and I may say, control, over the convention, during its whole term, was irresistible." Jefferson Davis would remember his great esteem and admiration for Tyler, and, "As an extemporaneous speaker, I regard him as the most felicitous among the orators I have known." It is a compounded tragedy, then, that Tyler had determined to tear Virginia from the Union. With his outsized authority and the solid Unionist presence in the convention, his concerted efforts may well have prevented secession and so much of the misery that followed.

On March 13, 1861, Tyler described himself "an old man wearied overmuch with a long course of public service." He asked the convention, "Whither are you going? You have to choose your association. Will you find it among the icebergs of the North or the cotton fields of the South?"

An article in the *Richmond Examiner* described Tyler as "An old Eagle, from Charles City," who "had lately flown over the enemy's camp, and had done his best to avert the calamity of war, but it was of no avail—they would listen to no compromise . . . Our only hope is stern resistance. He was old, but ready to fight, and if necessary, to lead the van."

Like Buchanan, Fillmore stayed on top of events through members of his cabinet. "I am gratified to hear that your state will stand by the union," Fillmore wrote his former secretary of the navy, John Pendleton Kennedy of Maryland. "It would indeed be most mortifying to me to hear the only state which cast its vote for me in 1856 turn traitor to the government." But not everyone shared Kennedy's optimism for the Old Line State. Stanton wrote to Buchanan on March 12 that Forts Sumter and Pickens would have to be surrendered. "It would not surprise me to see Virginia out in less than 90 days," he said, "and Maryland will be close at her heels." Stanton was bullish about Buchanan's future rehabilitation, writing two days later that "You will not have to live long to witness the entombment of the last of the falsehoods by which your patriotic career has been assailed. If you are not spared until then, you need have no fear but that history will do you justice." Dix agreed, writing the same day that the disappointment in losing Sumter "will be very great, and it will go far to turn the current against the new administration. Your record will brighten in proportion."

But Lincoln was not prepared to lose Sumter without a fight. Gustavus Fox, a former navy captain with a plan to reinforce the fort, was invited to make his case to the cabinet. He envisioned troops on a steamer with several tugboats loaded with provisions. The batteries of Charleston, he argued, could not "hit a small object moving rapidly at right angles to their line of fire at a distance of thirteen hundred yards, especially at night."

Lincoln asked his advisers in writing whether the attempt should be made to reinforce Fort Sumter. Chase and Blair agreed, but the rest said "no." The decided opinion of the cabinet was that Fort Sumter could not and should not be provisioned, that so doing would involve the unnecessary loss of human life. Seward was concerned about provoking war. Cameron argued that Fox's plan delayed the inevitable for perhaps one or two months. Multiple officers pointed out that Sumter was not valuable, that other military assets outranked it, and that a failed mission would deflate the already demoralized North.

Blair threatened to resign, but held off at the urging of his father, Francis Blair, who had been a Washington insider since the days of Jackson. The younger Blair met with the president and argued that giving up Sumter "would be justly considered by the people, by the world, by history, as treason to the country." He believed that abandoning Sumter would convince the rebels of what they already suspected; that the national government was weak. According to Welles, Lincoln "decided from that moment to convey supplies to Major Anderson, and that he would reinforce Sumter."

Fox arrived at Fort Sumter on a fact-finding mission for the president on the evening of March 21. He had traveled to Charleston, connecting with a former navy shipmate, a Captain Hartstene who had gone over to the Confederates. After meeting with Governor Pickens, he was permitted to travel with Hartstene to the fort. Speaking with Major Anderson, he learned the commander's opinion that it was impossible to reinforce the fort without an army landing at Morris Island. But looking out at the water from the parapet, Fox became more convinced than ever that his plan would work. He agreed to report back that April 15 was the ultimate deadline, after which Anderson would be forced to abandon the fort.

Gideon Welles was at dinner at the Willard on April 1 when John Nicolay brought him a package from the president. It concerned orders sending the reinforcements to Fort Pickens in Pensacola, not Sumter. Welles ran to the Executive Mansion "without delay" and found Lincoln in his office, writing at his desk. Looking up at his secretary, the president said, "What have I done wrong?" Welles explained. Lincoln was just as surprised as Welles. He had entrusted the drafting of the orders to Seward and his clerks and signed the papers without reading them for the sake of time. If he could not trust his secretary of state, Lincoln mused, who could he trust? Lincoln cancelled the order.

"The preparations for the Sumter expedition were carried forward with all the energy which the Department could command," Welles wrote. The plan was to rendezvous on April 11 ten miles east of the Charleston lighthouse, with Captain Samuel Mercer of the *Powhatan* in command. The *Powhatan, Pawnee, Pocahontas,* and the *Harriet Lane* would comprise the mission. If South Carolina resisted, Mercer was ordered to repel "by force if necessary all obstructions toward provisioning the fort and reinforcing it."

Feeling good about the situation, Welles returned to his rooms, assuming the ships were even then on their way to the rendezvous point. Late at night, Seward and his son, who was serving as assistant secretary of state, came to Welles's room with a telegram suggesting that the mission had been delayed due to his own conflicting orders. The group headed to the Executive Mansion in the dead of night to find the president.

Lincoln was awake, surprised at the late-night call and even more so at the news the men brought with them. Lincoln ordered that "on no account must the Sumter expedition fail or be interfered with." Seward made the case for intervention at Fort Pickens, Pensacola, pointing out that detaching the *Powhatan* would cause that mission to fail, one he regarded as at least equally important. Lincoln ordered Seward to return the *Powhatan* to Mercer immediately, then explained to Welles that he and Seward had, at his urging, simultaneously planned to reinforce Pickens, but in no way sought to interfere with the mission to Sumter. Lincoln took the blame. Welles remembered that his commander-in-chief "never shunned any responsibility and often declared that he, and not his Cabinet, was in fault for errors imputed to them, when I sometimes thought otherwise." Seward sent the telegram, but the *Powhatan* had already left for Pensacola. Another boat was hurriedly put out to sea to catch up with the Florida-bound vessel. When the message was successfully delivered, the *Powhatan*'s captain declined to obey, noting that this dispatch had come from Seward, whereas his previous orders had come directly from the president. Seward remarked to Welles that the lesson he had learned from this was to "attend to his own business and confine his labors to his own Department." To this, Welles wrote, "I cordially assented."

There would be many battles fought for Virginia, though the first of these was a political one, with Union forces led by Abraham Lincoln, and those of the secessionists led by John Tyler. Gideon Welles remembered, "For more than a month after his inauguration President Lincoln indulged the hope, I may say felt a strong confidence, that Virginia would not, when the decisive stand finally to be taken, secede, but adhere to the Union." Tyler had declared an end to compromise months earlier, and was now leveraging his high standing to push his state out of the Union. The stakes for these two presidents could not have been higher. Virginia was the most populous state in the South. Her border with Washington ensured that Virginia would offer a protective barrier or pose an imminent threat to the capital, depending on her decision. The secession movement had been arrested since February 1; Virginia's departure could bring with it the secession of Kentucky, Maryland, Tennessee, North Carolina, Missouri, and Arkansas.

On April 4 came the initial engagement, as the Virginia Convention cast its first votes on the question of leaving the Union. Under consideration was a resolution to pursue reconciliation efforts with the federal government. An amendment was offered by one member to strike that language, and instead adopt an ordinance of secession. Only 45 members voted "yes," to more than 90 opposed, a testament to the strong Union sentiment existing in Virginia. Among the 45 secessionists, however, was the former president of the United States, John Tyler.

Lincoln had sent a messenger to Richmond to retrieve George Summers, a Unionist leader in the Virginia Convention, who had sparred with Tyler earlier in the session, and with whom Lincoln had served in

Congress. In his place, regrettably, Summers sent John Baldwin, who did not arrive until April 5, some seven to ten days after Lincoln's invitation.

"Ah! Mr. Baldwin," Lincoln said, "why did you not come sooner? I have been expecting you gentlemen to come to me for more than a week past. I had a most important proposition to make to you. I am afraid that you have come too late. However, I will make the proposition now." Lincoln wanted the Virginia Convention to know that he had written Governor Pickens, offering that if Major Anderson could obtain provisions in Charleston, or if the governor would send them himself, that he would make no effort to resupply the fort. But now Lincoln was prepared to go even further. "Your convention in Richmond, Mr. Baldwin, has been sitting now nearly two months, and all it has done has been to shake the rod over my head." Lincoln took note that two-thirds of the convention had just voted down the secession ordinance. "If you will go back to Richmond and get that Union majority to adjourn and go home without passing the ordinance of secession, so anxious am I for the preservation of the peace of this country, and to save Virginia and the other border states from going out, that I will take the responsibility of evacuating Fort Sumter, and take the chance of negotiating with the cotton states which have already gone out."

Baldwin refused to listen, barely treating Lincoln with civility. Lincoln ordered the Sumter expedition that day, resolved to "send bread to Anderson." Lincoln telegraphed his message to Governor Pickens. "An attempt will be made to supply Fort Sumter with provisions only, and that, if such attempt be not resisted, no effort to throw in men, arms or supplies will be made, without further notice, or in case of an attack upon the Fort." As his secretaries noted, "If the rebels fired on that, they would not be able to convince the world that he had begun civil war." The Confederates could allow the fort to be resupplied, or fire the first shots of war against an unarmed humanitarian mission. Lincoln may have been a novice commander-in-chief. But he was a veteran politician.

Two days later, Lincoln sent for John Minor Botts, a Virginian and former congressional colleague who was in Washington. They sat together for four hours, and Lincoln told him of his conversation with Baldwin. Botts was horrified that the discussion had not become known in Virginia, and offered to take the message back personally. "I will guarantee, with my head," Botts said, "that they will adopt your proposition, and adopt it willingly and cheerfully."

Lincoln surely felt deflated. The fleet was on its way to Sumter. He had no means of stopping them, only a well-placed assurance that a better-timed offer to a more honorable party than Baldwin might have prevented all that was about to happen. Lincoln's gambit to save Virginia, willingness to suffer the public fallout, and desire for peace, remained a secret for years, coming out publicly in congressional testimony in 1866.

The Confederate government was in serious danger. Lincoln's election had been five months earlier and his inauguration a month past. No state had left the Union since Texas on February 1. Tempers had calmed, and people throughout the South were second-guessing what had been done. A delegation from Alabama told Jefferson Davis and his cabinet, "Unless you sprinkle blood in the face of the people of Alabama, they will be back in the old Union in less than ten days."

On April 10, Confederate general P. G. T. Beauregard, commanding the batteries at Charleston, received his orders. "You will at once demand its evacuation, and, if this is refused, proceed in such manner as you may determine to reduce it."

CHAPTER 19

Breakfast at Fort Sumter

The Confederate states have deliberately commenced the civil war, and God knows where it may end.

—JAMES BUCHANAN

Buchanan ~ Tyler ~ Lincoln ~ Fillmore ~ Pierce

On April 11, 1861, at 2:00 p.m., General P. G. T. Beauregard demanded that Major Robert Anderson, his former professor at West Point, surrender Fort Sumter. Anderson would decline this and another such demand made that day.

While the two commanders debated control of Charleston Harbor, Stanton wrote Buchanan of the dire situation in Washington. "The feeling of loyalty to the government has greatly diminished in this city," he said. There was trouble filling militia spots to guard the capital. No members of the cabinet had yet purchased homes or relocated their families. They were ready to "cut and run," he observed, "their tenure is like that of a Bedouin on the sands of the desert."

Hours after this letter was written, at 4:30 a.m. on April 12, the batteries of Charleston opened fire on Fort Sumter. Major Anderson raised the American flag, and settled in as the moment he had been anticipating for months was finally here. Sumter was operating at low capacity of men and munitions, and so Anderson would wait before returning fire. At 6:30 a.m. the men at Fort Sumter had a relaxed breakfast, as though the batteries were not raining hell itself upon them. Four thousand shots and shells were fired on Sumter over the next thirty-three hours.

As Sumter was being shelled, Stanton wrote Buchanan, "We have the war upon us. The impression here is held by many 1st that the effort to reinforce will be a failure. 2nd that in less than 24 hours from this time Anderson will have surrendered. 3rd. that in less than 30 days Davis will be in possession of Washington."

Stanton's first two predictions were correct. When his men could no longer offer any opposition, Anderson yielded to the inevitable and surrendered. Determined to leave with dignity, he ordered his men to formation for a one-hundred-gun salute, where a cartridge explosion took the life of the only person to die at Fort Sumter.

Buchanan wrote his nephew, "The Confederate states have deliberately commenced the civil war, and God knows where it may end." To General Dix, who was chairing the Union meeting in New York City to be held on April 24, he wrote, "Nobody seems to understand the course pursued by the late administration." He believed that South Carolina had been warned against attacking Fort Sumter. If the world knew this, he argued that it would help Lincoln. It would certainly help Buchanan. "The present administration had no alternative but to accept the war initiated by South Carolina or the Southern Confederacy. The north will sustain the administration almost to a man; and it ought to be sustained at all hazards."

The commencement of war would make Virginia's alliance with the Union, as it proved, nearly impossible. Tyler felt that Lincoln had made a serious mistake, "having weighed in the scales the value of a mere local fort against the value of the Union itself." Tyler questioned Lincoln's motives, arguing that his position on Sumter was taken to consolidate Republicans. "If the Confederate states have their own flag is anyone so stupid as to suppose that they will suffer the flag of England or France or of the northern states to float over their ramparts in place of their own?"

On April 15, 1861, Lincoln called for seventy-five thousand volunteers who would commit for ninety days. Two weeks later he would supplement this with a request for forty-two thousand three-year volunteers, twenty-three thousand additional regulars, and eighteen thousand sailors. Nicolay, who was charged with copying the initial call, wrote, "All these things will make stirring times, and I hardly realize that they are so, even as I write them."

And so a generation of Americans would trade their plans and hopes for the future for the opportunity to discover what they were made of.

Young men left farms and factories and families in response to calls from the North and South for the great coming conflict. Men who in an earlier or later generation would have passed their lives anonymously teaching at a university or tending a general store would find their countenances enshrined in marble, their deeds studied, celebrated, and reviled by millions yet unborn.

Historian James McPherson detailed the shocking state of ill-preparedness: "Most of the tiny 16,000-man army was scattered in seventy-nine frontier outposts west of the Mississippi. Near a third of its officers were resigning to go with the South . . . All but one of the heads of the eight army bureaus had been in service since the War of 1812 . . . Only two officers had commanded as much as a brigade in combat, and both were over seventy." Lincoln's administration would complete one of the greatest logistical feats in history, as their small and scattered forces increased to seven hundred thousand soldiers by the early days of 1862. But the Confederates had a significant head start. Nearly a month before Lincoln's initial request for volunteers, the Confederacy had called for one hundred thousand volunteers for twelve months. By mid-April 1861, they had achieved 60 percent of their goal.

In a matter of months, the administration would build an army greater than that which ever served Napoleon. Lincoln took great care to appoint generals from different political factions, ethnic groups, and regions. As a member of Congress, he had watched President Polk go to war with two prominent Whig generals, with whom he constantly fought, undermined, and tried to embarrass, which in turn helped cost him the support of the Whigs in Congress and throughout the country. Lincoln believed, "the Democrats must vote to hold the Union now, without bothering whether we or the Southern men got things where they are; and we must make it easy for them to do this, for we cannot live through the case without them." If Lincoln could hold the border states and maintain the unity of the North, he had a chance of winning the war. Similarly, he knew that if the support for the war collapsed, the Union itself would be over. Appointing generals from different constituency groups would help solidify their support for his administration.

Benjamin Butler never expected to be in a position of calling on a Republican president to give thanks for his appointment as a major-general in the army.

"I do not know whether I ought to accept this," Butler said. The Massachusetts lawyer pointed out that when the commission arrived, he was in trial, which was continued so that he might come to Washington.

"I guess we both wish we were back trying cases," Lincoln said.

"Besides, Mr. President, you may not be aware that I was the Breckinridge candidate for governor of my state in the last campaign, and did all I could to prevent your election."

"All the better," Lincoln said. "I hope your example will bring many of the same sort with you."

Butler was astonished. "But, I do not think that I can support the measures of your administration, Mr. President."

"I do not care whether you do or not, if you will fight for the country."

While assembling his army, Lincoln ordered a naval blockade to squeeze the South, preventing their lucrative exports or badly needed industrial imports from assisting the rebellion.

To accomplish this task Lincoln began with forty-two ships, a majority of which were "thousands of miles from the United States." Fewer than twelve warships were presently available on the eastern seaboard. McPherson calculated that five of every six Confederate blockade runners succeeded, a number he reaches by noting that nine out of ten attempts were successful in 1861 but by 1865 it was reduced to one out of every two. He further points out the deterrent effect of the blockade; eight thousand ships traveled to southern harbors during four years of Civil War, but twenty thousand had done the same in the previous four years. This reduction in trade, he argues, to less than a third of normal, coincided with a dramatic increase in the South's need for consumption.

While John Tyler was exhausting himself to undermine Lincoln, the president was receiving support from another of his predecessors. In response to Lincoln's call for volunteers, the Unionists of Buffalo gathered on the evening of April 16 at the Metropolitan Theater, selecting Millard

Fillmore as chairman. In addressing them, Fillmore publicly made clear not only to the audience in the seats, but also to the nation where he stood. It had been his first political event in some time, he noted, and he had never planned on another. But, "We have reached a crisis in the history of this country when no man, however humble his rank or limited his influence, has a right to stand neutral. Civil War has been inaugurated, and we must meet it. Our Government calls for aid, and we must give it. Our Constitution is in danger, and we must defend it. It is no time now to inquire by whose fault or folly this state of things has been produced. The ship of state is in the breakers, the muttering thunder and darkened sky indicate the coming storm, and if she sinks we must go down with her. We have a common lot and must meet a common fate. Let every man therefore stand to his post, and like the Roman sentinel at the gate of Pompeii, let posterity, when the storm is over, find our skeleton and armor on the spot where duty required us to stand."

Fillmore had hoped for compromise, or for a voluntary division of the Union, but in the face of "aggressive warfare, we have no alternative but to rally around the constituted authorities and defend the government." Buffalo applied its characteristic energy to the task of raising funds for the war, putting together $50,000 in private donations to secure enlistments. States and towns throughout the country had, even before Lincoln's call, begun putting together the resources necessary for war. Buffalo's figure was impressive, dwarfing that of much larger cities.

Fillmore was attacked following his speech, with critics dredging up the now infamous 1856 Albany address in which he warned against the election of the Republican Party, and argued that as the North would never accept an all-southern ticket, nor should the South accept a president and vice president from the North. "The position now taken by Mr. Fillmore has greatly wounded the feelings, destroyed the confidence, and outraged the high appreciation entertained for him by that majority of conservative Union men of our country who so zealously supported him," read one anonymous editorial.

One former southern supporter wrote him with "pain and sorrow ... I expected when you spoke, it would be for peace, that your voice would be heard calling upon your fellow citizens everywhere to put forth their efforts in favor of peace." He continued, "The southern people do not want war. They have been trying all the time to avoid it. The entire south (excepting, perhaps, South Carolina) would have gladly accepted Mr. Crittenden's proposition at one time as a basis of adjustment. My dear sir, I have for these many years loved you, as I have scarcely ever loved any other man, residing north of Mason's and Dixon's line, because I believed you to be a pure and genuine patriot—a true man in every sense of the word. It is to such men that we must look in times like these, to save us from the evils and horrors of civil war . . . So make an effort and then become the second Washington (Father) to your country."

Fillmore's speech also disappointed "A friend of peace" in Virginia, who wrote of his surprise to "find you in sympathy with the prevailing sentiment at the North that Mr. Lincoln must be sustained in his wicked war upon the South." Why not let the South go in peace? The South "inaugurated the Peace Conference, the results of which were rejected by the North."

"Mr. Lincoln's policy," he continued, "is coercion, under the guise of retaking the fort." If "you insist on prosecuting this wicked course, you will find the south just as ready to meet it as you are, and being in the right and fighting for their homes and families, they will not" be conquered.

—◦—

"The prospects are that we shall have war, and a trying one," John Tyler wrote to his wife. "The battle at Charleston has aroused the whole north. I fear that division no longer exists in their ranks, and that they will break upon the south with an immense force." Meanwhile the Virginia Secession Convention was lurching toward a vote, meeting in closed session. "Another day may decide our course."

On April 17, Virginia seceded from the Union, passing "An ordinance to repeal the ratification of the Constitution of the United States." The initial balloting was 88–55, nearly a total reversal of the vote against secession less than two weeks earlier. Once secession was accomplished, some delegates changed their votes and those who were absent (or hiding) appeared, changing the total to 103–46.

A shadow convention of secessionists had been meeting nearby, attempting to put pressure on the sanctioned convention. After the vote, a party visited the shadow convention to break the news. "Ex-President Tyler and [former] Governor Wise were conducted arm-in-arm," one witness remembered, "and bareheaded, down the center aisle amid a din of cheers, while every member rose to his feet. They were led to the platform, and called upon to address the convention. The venerable ex-President of the United States first rose responsive to the call, but remarked that the exhaustion incident to his recent incessant labors, and the nature of his emotions at such a momentous crisis, superadded to the feebleness of age, rendered him physically unable to utter what he felt and thought on such an occasion. Nevertheless, he seemed to acquire supernatural strength as he proceeded, and he spoke most effectively for the space of fifteen minutes.

"He gave a brief history of all the struggles of our race for freedom, from Magna Carta to the present day; and he concluded with a solemn declaration that at no period of our history were we engaged in a more just and holy effort for the maintenance of liberty and independence than at that present moment . . . He said that he might not survive to witness the consummation of the work begun that day; but generations yet unborn would bless those who had the high privilege of being participators in it."

To Julia, Tyler wrote, "Virginia has severed her connection with the north hive of abolitionists, and takes her stand as a sovereign and independent state . . . the die is thus cast, and her future is in the hands of the God of Battle . . . Do, dearest, live as frugally as possible in the household—trying times are before us." Writing to his concerned mother-in-law in New York, who had requested he send the kids to her, "The vaunts and terrible boasts of the north are one thing, the execution of them another. All are well at Sherwood Forest." Not only would he defend Virginia, but Tyler planned on taking the fight north, and "urged that a strong body of cavalry should be immediately sent to Washington to seize the capital."

The North was certainly not the safest place for at least one of Tyler's children. Robert Tyler, a prominent Philadelphian and prothonotary [clerk] of the Pennsylvania Supreme Court, had grand designs for his political future. Instead, he barely escaped being lynched by his neighbors, resigned his position, and fled south. After his hasty retreat, his neighbors "cut his carpets, defaced the pictures, broke the statues, and made kindling wood of the piano, sofas, etc." Robert Tyler was burned in effigy in his former home, and dummies representing him were hung from trees.

John Tyler, having overcome Lincoln's best efforts in Virginia, was now appointed by the convention to meet with Alexander Stephens, vice president of the Confederacy, to work out an alliance between their two governments. On April 25, Virginia formally joined the Provisional Confederate States of America. Tyler gleefully telegraphed Governor Pickens of South Carolina, "We are fellow citizens once more by an ordinance passed this day."

The abolitionist newspaper the *Liberator* declared that "John Tyler has put the finishing touch to the peculiar reputation he acquired while in the Presidential chair" by sending the telegraph to Pickens. The *Philadelphia Inquirer*, beneath the headline TYLER ALWAYS A TRAITOR, opined that he was "born to be a traitor, and this is by no means his first exhibition of the cloven foot," while the *New Hampshire Sentinel* pointed out "All of our ex-Presidents, except John Tyler, sustain the Union and oppose secession."

***

Within four days of Lincoln's call, The 6th Massachusetts Regiment was "the first fully equipped unit to respond." Arriving by rail in Baltimore, they had to cross town on foot to a different depot on their way to Washington. They had not left the train before an angry mob confronted them. "Taunts clothed in the most outrageous language were hurled at them by the panting crowd, who, almost breathless with running, pressed up to the car windows, presenting knives and revolvers, and cursed up into the faces of the soldiers." As police attempted to restore order, the troops began switching trains, "many of them cocking their muskets as they stepped on the platform." There were "loose paving stones which they hurled at the car, smashing in the windows and blinds, and adding to this method of assault an occasional shot from a pistol or gun." Four young soldiers, who left their homes expecting danger at a more southerly latitude, instead lost their lives in Baltimore.

Stanton wrote to Buchanan that "no description could convey to you the panic that prevailed" in the days after the riot. The situation was made worse by Baltimore's response, destroying railroad bridges to keep north-ern troops out of the city, and tearing down telegraph lines, leaving Wash-ington unable to communicate with the outside world. "Almost every family [in Washington] packed up their effects," Stanton noted. "Women and children were sent away in great numbers; provisions advanced to famine prices . . . there is still a deep apprehension that before long this city is doomed to the scene of battle and carnage."

Hay recorded that "The White House is turned into barracks." To protect the capital only two thousand people could be counted on, with three thousand District Militia who were unreliable or even traitors. "But with the city perfectly demoralized with secession feeling, no man could know whom of the residents to trust . . . We were not only surrounded by the enemy, but in the midst of traitors." One reporter remembered, "At night the campfires of the Confederates, who were assembling in force, could be seen on the southern bank of the Potomac, and it was not uncommon to meet on Pennsylvania Avenue a defiant Southerner openly wearing a large Virginia or South Carolina secession badge." Various gov-ernment clerks who quit their posts refused to say "goodbye," insisting on "au revoir," expecting to be in possession of the capital within a month. One Washington preacher left his favorite cat behind with three weeks food and water.

Lincoln, in less than two months as president, was seriously threat-ened with losing the capital. Casting a forlorn look out the White House window, he desperately waited for troops. "Why don't they come?"

—◦—

"What is to become of us as a people?" asked one correspondent of Frank-lin Pierce. "What is the duty of the citizen who cannot see any civil neces-sity for the impending fraternal war? What is your duty and mine?"

Millard Fillmore and John Tyler had both been outspoken on oppo-site sides of the conflict. Franklin Pierce, back in New Hampshire and sufficiently restored to health, was now prepared to break his silence. Pierce would answer the letter writer's question in a Concord address to a Union rally, whose members asked him for remarks. Speaking from the balcony of the Eagle Hotel, he said, "You call for me, my friends, as lovers of our country and of the blessed Union which our forefathers transmitted to us, on an occasion more grave, more momentous, and more deeply fraught with painful emotion than any under which I have ever addressed you. But I rejoice that that flag," he said, motioning to the Stars and Stripes above the hotel, "floats there," he said to cheering. He referenced his father's service in the Revolutionary War, at the Battle of Bunker Hill, and that of his brothers in the War of 1812, and his own in Mexico. "Never can we forget the gallant men of the North and South moved together like a band of brothers and mingled their blood on many a field in the common cause. Can I, if I would, feel other than the proudest sadness when I see that those who so often stood shoulder to shoulder in the face of foreign foes, and now in imminent danger of standing face to face as the foes of each other.

"I do not believe aggression by arms is a suitable or possible remedy for the existing evils ... [if] a war of aggression is to be waged against the National Capital and the north, then there is no way for us, as citizens of the old Thirteen States, but to stand together and uphold the flag to the last, with all the rights which pertain to it, and with the fidelity and endurance of brave men, I would counsel you to stand together with one mind and one heart, calm, faithful, and determined. But give no countenance to passion and violence, which are really unjust, and often in periods like these are the harbingers of domestic strife. Be just to yourselves, just to others, true to your country, and may God, who has so greatly blessed our fathers, graciously interpose in this hour of clouds and darkness, and save both extremities of the country, and to cause the old flag to be upheld by all hands and all hearts."

In response, Carlton Chase wrote, "How I wish I could take you by the hand and thank you for your noble and truly patriotic address delivered the other day at Concord!"

A soldier stationed in Missouri loved the speech, as well. "It is not easy to say if we will lift our hand against those whom we have so long here been enabled to call brothers. I can entertain no deep feeling of hostility to the South as taken at large, but I must feel that the time has come to punish without abatement those of the spirits who have struck at our institutions and made efforts to dissolve the Union ... While officers of the army are quitting by the score the flag they have so long followed . . . I hold it to be my duty, to the best of my ability, to stand by, and if it be so willed by Providence, to see the noble old ship of our Union, safely through the peril."

And so another of Lincoln's predecessors opposed his plans for a military response. Pierce would not support the president, unless the North itself were invaded. If the South would not return willingly, they must be permitted to depart peacefully. Pierce responded to a supporter of his Eagle Hotel speech, condemning the "moral aggression of the north" as well as "the arrogant rashness of the south," noting, "We cannot subjugate the Southern states, if we would." His wife Jane sent him a speech by General Robert Patterson supporting the war, indicating that the Pierces may have been a house divided. Pierce replied, "I know him, and know that he can do, what I cannot do—bow to the storm. My purpose, dearest, is irrevocably taken. I will never justify, sustain, or in any way or to any extent uphold this cruel, heartless, aimless, unnecessary war. Madness and imbecility are in the ascendant, I shall not succumb to them. Come what may, I have no opinion to retract—no line of action to change."

CHAPTER 20

The Meeting That Never Was

If there be five men on earth, whose voices, united in an appeal to stay strife and to awaken a purpose to calm the troubled and heaving sea may succeed, you are those men.
— SAMUEL LECOMPTE TO MARTIN VAN BUREN

Pierce - Van Buren - Tyler - Fillmore - Buchanan - Lincoln

Americans have viewed their former presidents almost like a fourth branch of government. These men have a distinct vantage point but, presumably free of political considerations, can provide unvarnished guidance to the country. At this critical hour, the American people had more former presidents to turn to than at any other time before. The American Civil War had begun. It had happened because of a failure of the three official branches of government. Congress had repealed the Missouri Compromise and failed to adopt measures to keep the peace in its place. The Supreme Court had gone far beyond what was needed to resolve a case, attempting to remove the most controversial issues in the country from the political arena, while siding with the most extreme position. Antebellum presidents had too often been inert when action was required. But in this "fourth branch" of government, the people were to be again disappointed. Former presidents, then as in the twenty-first century, tended toward a policy of staying out of politics. Ex-presidents of the nineteenth century would go so far as to stay away from Washington forever. But during the Civil War, this notion of post-presidential neutrality was discarded almost entirely.

In the wake of Sumter, not knowing that Virginia was leaving the Union that very day—April 17—the clerk of the US District Court in

Pennsylvania wrote a letter to every former president. The sections are "on the eve of a fearful deadly collision," he noted. "Can nothing be done to prevent this? The hostile parties have reached a point at which it seems impossible for them to propose or initiate negotiations.

"I propose that all the Ex-Presidents shall meet together at Washington City on the 1st day of May or sooner if possible. Apart from the weight and influence which such a body would carry with it the very novelty of the measures would attract the universal attention of the country and it would cause their countrymen to pause before" embarking on "the unfathomable horrors of a civil war." The letter proposed a cessation of hostilities for twelve months. "The Ex-Presidents should not shrink at the idea of being a self-constituted body. They would hold their commission from the hearts of all men of reflection and intelligence. The country demands from every man, and especially from her most eminent citizens, their best efforts to save it from destruction." Little did the writer know that at least one of the former presidents was very much of the same mind. The day before, Franklin Pierce wrote a letter to Martin Van Buren.

"The present unparalleled crisis in the affairs of our country is, I have no doubt filling you, as it is me with the profoundest sorrow," Pierce began. "Is there any human power which can arrest the conflict of arms now apparently near at hand, between the two sections of the Union? The news tonight would seem to indicate that the central and border states (at least Virginia, Kentucky, and Tennessee) will, in view of the military movements of the North, cast their lot with the states already seceded.

"There is no time for effective assemblages of the people. No time for conventions or protracted discussion. But it has occurred to me that you may take measures to suspend active military operations, secure opportunity for further reflection in the face of present dangers, and save the most fearful calamity which has ever suspended over a nation. If the five retired presidents of the United States, still living, were to meet at the earliest practicable day, at the city where the Constitution was formed, might not their consultation, if it would result in the concurrence of judgment reach the administration and the country with some degree of power? No man can with propriety summon such a meeting but yourself. I feel that we ought not omit at least an effort.

"Should this suggestion commend itself to your judgment will you communicate with Mr. Tyler, Mr. Fillmore, and Mr. Buchanan and advise me of the result?"

Only four days elapsed between Pierce's dating the letter and Van Buren posting his response (and during that time, Virginia went out of the Union with Tyler leading the charge). Van Buren chose his words carefully, and a practice copy of the letter can be found in his papers.

"I have received your friendly letter suggesting for my consideration the propriety of summoning a meeting of the Ex Presidents at Philadelphia, to consult on the present alarming condition of public affairs, and adopt such action in the premises as they may think, might be useful, and have given the subject all the consideration to which it is entitled, as well on the ground of its importance, as of the sincere respect I entertain for your opinions. Neither in regard to the extent of the danger, with which the country is menaced, nor to our duty to do all in our power to arrest the present adverse course of things, can there, I am very confident, be any difference in feeling or opinion between us. I regret however, to be obliged to say, that after the most careful consideration of the subject in all its bearings, I have not been able to repress the serious doubts I entertain in regard to the practicability of making a volunteer movement of that description on our party, with such action in the matter as we might think allowable.

"Sincerely entertaining such doubts, I have not been able to bring my mind to the execution of the plan for bringing them together, to which you refer. But it does not follow, my Dear Sir, that views of the subject imbibed by one, who, like myself, have been longest out of public life, and more completely excluded from all connection with public affairs than any of his associates, will also prove to be those of the rest of the Ex Presidents, nor would the exercise of the privilege of taking the initiative to bring about such a meeting, be more appropriate in me, than it would be in any one of them. The belief that such is the case, can only have arisen from the erroneous supposition that I was entitled to precedence in such matters, on account of my being the senior Ex President—while in truth, that distinction, as far as it goes, is, according to the opinions of those most conversant in such matters, accorded to the individual of the days, who was the latest incumbent of the principal office. But this is a matter which may, I think, had better be entirely laid out of view, and all the Ex Presidents regarded, in that respect, as standing on the same footing. If then you, who entertain more hopeful expectations upon the point, continue to think the proposed call, free from the embarrassments under which I labor, or either of our associates who entertain similar views to your own, shall deem such a call expedient, and ask my attendance, I will accept the invitation without hesitation, and comply with the request it contains, if it be in my power to do so." Van Buren had been canny and diplomatic in his response. It was not a refusal. He encouraged Pierce to pursue this course if he really believed in it. He also left himself an out if Pierce somehow managed to wrangle the others. Van Buren approved of the current president's course; perhaps he knew that Pierce would be disinclined to do so. Therefore, the meeting could only succeed in hamstringing Lincoln at a time when he needed maximum public support, which was likely Pierce's purpose.

But things did not end there. Former Pennsylvania congressman Charles Jared Ingersoll traveled in person to Kinderhook to try to win Van Buren's support for a meeting, with Pierce on his way. Ingersoll telegraphed Fillmore, "Pray meet Mr. Pierce and me there immediately." While there, Ingersoll obtained what he believed to be an agreement to a meeting of the ex-presidents as proposed by Pierce's letter. Van Buren insisted, however, "that we Ex-Presidents, whilst we held ourselves ready to exert whatever influence our past positions are supposed to have conferred upon us, to promote pacification, should take no important step without communicating our intention to the administration at Washington in advance, and receiving satisfactory assurance of their acquiescence." Summarizing these views in a subsequent letter to Ingersoll, Van Buren wrote, "The disposition to give [the administration] an earnest and rigorous support in the difficult struggle in which they are engaged, already become general in this state, is even now becoming more and more intense, and those who participate in it, every where would be liable to regard with distrust any steps which might, by possibility, embarrass the government, however differently they were intended."

Five days later, Ingersoll wrote again to Fillmore, on the eve of a second meeting with Van Buren. "I have come here to meet General Pierce and as I hoped Mr. Van Buren and possibly yourself with a view to a conference among the Ex Presidents. The idea of this conference of Ex Presidents originated in Philadelphia and has been much approved. But it will be nothing without your concurrence and approbation."

But Fillmore's sentiments might best be summarized in a response to a similar request from a correspondent in Brooklyn Heights. "No person deprecates, more than I do, the fratricidal war, now commencing between the north and the south. I have done all I could to prevent it, and am willing to do all I can to put an end to it. But unsolicited advice is often deemed officious if not offensive, and therefore is quite as likely to do harm as good."

On Tuesday, April 30, Ingersoll and Pierce arrived at Lindenhurst, the home of Martin Van Buren. A visitor once wrote that Lindenhurst, surrounded by willow trees, was "a sweet, secluded place, whither the hum of life at the village comes, faintly audible, like the music of a dream." Van Buren, famous for his hospitality, would have greeted his guests warmly. Which is not to say that they would get what they wanted. Van Buren regretted that he was no longer open to the idea of the ex-presidents meeting. Ingersoll was surprised. Hadn't their conversation been different just last week? Van Buren assured him that he had "correctly understood and reported his views—but subsequent reflection had satisfied him that the proposed meeting could do no good." One thing Van Buren and Pierce did agree upon, was that "neither could see anything hopeful or indicating a prospect of an immediate settlement of our national difficulties."

As the three were meeting in Kinderhook, Fillmore wrote to Ingersoll, joining his voice with Van Buren's in rejecting a conference. "Much as I wish to stop the effusion of blood," he said, "I fear that the time of compromise without it has passed, and that if it is to be prevented, it will be by the north showing as bold and united a front as the south."

Van Buren had resisted Pierce's proposal but was not content to remain silent. Writing Ingersoll after their meeting, he said "The disposition to give them an earnest and vigorous support in the difficult struggle in which they are engaged is every hour becoming more and more intense." A Union meeting was called at Stranahan's Hotel in Kinderhook, to support the president's request for troops. Van Buren remembered "a portion of my townsmen, who had been instrumental in making the call, gentlemen who differed from me in their general political views, did me the honor to ask me to advise with them in regards to its proceedings. My opinion and feelings upon the subject to be acted on were freely communicated to them. These were, in substance, that the attack upon our flag and the capture of Fort Sumter by the secessionists could be regarded in no other light than as the commencement of a treasonable attempt to overthrow the Federal Government by military force—that I approved of the call which had been made by the President upon the loyal states for the necessary means to enable him to suppress the Rebellion and rejoiced at the manner in which that call had been responded to, & was in favor of the earnest & vigorous support of the Federal Government in the prosecution of the war for its own maintenance & for the maintenance of the Union and the Constitution which had been forced upon it." Van Buren had now joined Fillmore in his public support of Lincoln and his war policy.

The meeting resolved: "While deploring the advent of civil war, which the madness of secession has precipitated upon us, we believe that policy and humanity alike demand the most vigorous and energetic measures to crush out treason now & forever; and that we will fully sustain the Government in such policy."

From Wheatland, James Buchanan became the last of the former presidents to publicly break his silence. In response to an article in the *National Intelligencer* about military personnel who had joined the Confederates, he wrote, "A military oath has ever been held sacred in all ages and in all countries. Besides the solemn sanctions of religion, there is superadded the highest appeal to personal honor. Each military officer swears that he will bear true allegiance to the United States, and serve them honestly and faithfully against all their enemies and oppressors whatsoever. They do not swear to support the Constitution of any State. Educated by the United States, they belong to the Federal Government in a peculiar sense. Whilst I can imagine why an officer might resign rather than shed the blood of citizens of his native State in war, yet it is difficult to excuse or palliate the next step, which is to go over to the enemy and make war upon the time-honored flag of the country. Maj. Beauregard, when he discharged the first gun against Fort Sumter, lighted a flame which it will require a long time to extinguish. The people of the North at present are enthusiastically unanimous. They never were aroused until that shot was fired. I often warned Southern gentlemen that this would be the inevitable result." He closed by recording that he enjoyed "good health and as tranquil a spirit as the evils impending over my country will permit."

Thus Buchanan began a familiar theme through the war years; he would receive a torrent of abuse at every attempt to speak out. "Would it not have been far more apropos for JB to have discoursed upon the nature of a Presidential oath?" asked the *Liberator*. The *Philadelphia Inquirer* felt it was far too little and late. "For him now to come forward and attempt, with his weak and imbecile utterances, to acquire tolerance for himself by branding the Southern traitors, is a mean and hopeless work . . . the only doubt which exists in the public mind is as to whether he was their abettor or accomplice, or their tool and dupe." In any event, whatever his opinion, "the commonest of all common sense should teach him to avoid thrusting his name before the people."

"Those who were in the Federal capitol on that Thursday, April 25, will never, during their lives, forget the event," remembered Lincoln's secretaries, Nicolay and Hay. "An indescribable gloom had hung over Washington nearly a week, paralyzing its traffic and crushing out its life." It all changed when the Seventh New York marched down Pennsylvania Avenue to the White House, with other regiments to follow. They had found an alternate route through Annapolis, and quick-thinking General Benjamin Butler had worked fast to repair the railway. Troops would continue to fill the city of Washington.

To "encourage a martial spirit," Millard Fillmore agreed to serve as commander of the Buffalo Union Continentals, a group of prominent citizens who, because of age, could not participate in combat. They did however "stir up enthusiasm" for the Union effort and escorted troops headed to the war. The Continentals took their responsibility seriously, drilling in the Buffalo arsenal on Saturday nights, and taking in the occasional target practice. To make sure they were properly trained, Fillmore requested "two or three copies of the General Regulations for the Militia of the State." All over forty-five years old, they were described by one observer as "large portly grandfathers with gray beards." On May 3, Fillmore led the Continentals in escorting four companies of young men to the train station, the first to depart from Buffalo. "The venerable and honored commander, ex-President Fillmore, marched stately and erect, at the head of the column, wearing a sword and plume, and looking like an emperor," wrote one reporter. An admirer would later write that he wished to come observe Fillmore and his men in action, saying "I would specially like to see you in your military costume, which seems to fit you no less than the civic robes which you have worn with much eminent dignity and renown." At the station, Fillmore raised his stately hat, stood erect, and commanded "Old Guard, attention! Three cheers for the Buffalo Volunteers!" Everyone lifted their hats and raised their arms, shouting "hurrah, hurrah, hurrah!" The few departing soldiers who did not respond in kind were attending to their goodbyes, to girlfriends, wives, family, and friends, the things familiar to them, so many of whom knew nothing of the world outside of Buffalo, now filled with anxiety on their way to the war. The Union Continentals had a somber corollary duty, which they would perform before long, to accompany some of these soldiers back from the train station, on their way to be buried.

As feared, Virginia's departure breathed new life into a moribund secession movement. On May 6, both Arkansas and Tennessee left the Union.

The governor of Tennessee, Nicolay and Hay recorded, "may almost be said" to have "carried the state into rebellion single-handed." On February 9, Tennessee voters had gone to the polls to consider two questions: whether to have a secession convention, and if so, who would serve as its delegates. By a majority of 11,875, the voters declined to have a convention; and the pro-Union delegates—though now unnecessary—crushed their secessionist opponents by 65,114. But Tennessee, like other border and southern states, began the war with an elected government determined to drag the state out of the Union regardless of public sentiment. On May 1, the legislature empowered the governor to appoint "commissioners to enter into a military league with the authorities of the Confederate states," a task he wasted little time in carrying into effect. By the time voters were asked to revisit the issue, secession was already accomplished.

North Carolina seceded on May 21. Two days later was Virginia's referendum on secession. Twenty-three citizens of Alexandria wrote John Tyler for his advice on how to vote. "It is a fallacy to suppose that the question to be voted on is Union or no Union," Tyler wrote, acknowledging that a popular vote held a month after the ordinance had already been passed, after the state had raised armed forces and signed a treaty joining the Confederacy, was a sham. "The union is gone forever, and the Constitution which ordained the Union has been torn up and trampled in the dust, and the real question is, shall we form another Union in which our liberties and our rights will be respected and secured, or shall we tamely submit to arbitrary power?" In light of the fait accompli, and the secession fever that permeated the state, it is a testament to the conviction of Virginia's Unionists, who mustered roughly 25 percent of the vote, losing 128,884–32,134.

Lincoln wrote, "The people of Virginia have thus allowed this giant insurrection to make its nest within her borders; and this government has no choice left but to deal with it where it finds it." At 2:00 a.m. on May 24, their movements lit by a bright moon, Union forces crossed into Virginia from the capital, seizing possession of the bridges leading into the city.

The Confederate States of America were now twice the size of any nation in Europe (Russia excepted), made up of nine million people, including three and a half million slaves. As General Beauregard put it, "No people ever warred for independence with more relative advantages than the Confederates," citing the well-organized central government, existing state governments, mountains, rivers, and other natural defenses. The administration's task would be a difficult one; the question now became whether events would make it an impossible one.

CHAPTER 21

The Border States

In vain does the victim of oppression demand, in the language of our Bill of Rights and of the Constitution, a fair and impartial trial . . . In vain that he appeals to the judges and the courts.

—JOHN TYLER

Lincoln ~ Pierce ~ Tyler ~ Van Buren

The border states had a decision to make. Delaware, Maryland, Kentucky, and Missouri had white populations of roughly 2.6 million. In the recent presidential election, Lincoln had lost Maryland with 2,294 votes to 89,848 for other candidates; received 1,364 in his birth state of Kentucky to 143,703 for others; and in his neighboring state of Missouri 17,028 to 148,490, while in Delaware, 3,815 to 12,224.

No states were more conflicted than Missouri and Kentucky. Lincoln knew it well. In St. Louis alone "There were Union speeches and rebel speeches; cheers for Lincoln and cheers for Davis; Union headquarters and rebel headquarters." Lincoln ordered Missouri Unionists to raise four regiments as quickly as possible and sent three Illinois regiments to St. Louis to protect the arsenal. A relatively junior officer, Captain Nathaniel Lyon, expertly managed the Union interest there. Lincoln authorized him to raise an army of ten thousand to maintain the authority of the United States, a force which Lyon would need to fight his own state government. Missouri governor Claiborne Jackson wrote to Jefferson Davis requesting support. Davis responded, "We look anxiously and hopefully for the day when the star of Missouri shall be added to the constellation of the Confederate States of America." But the Union forces won the race to mobilize. Governor Jackson saw his state militia forces largely disbanded.

When Captain Lyon moved on the capital, Jackson and his legislature fled Jefferson City, after passing a bill giving the governor dictatorial powers, burning the telegraph and bridges on their retreat.

Missouri was held by force; Kentucky would be a matter of finesse. Lincoln delayed recruiting soldiers in Kentucky and took no immediate steps to interfere with its residents who did business with Confederate states. Meanwhile, he quietly shipped five thousand guns to Union forces in the state, while appointing Major Anderson, a native and already a Union celebrity, commander of the Department of Kentucky, to open recruiting offices just outside of the state.

This pressing need for political sensitivity did not mean Lincoln lost his sense of humor. When a Kentucky state senator complained about the presence of troops in Cairo, Illinois, Lincoln responded "that he would certainly never have ordered the movement of troops, complained of, had he known that Cairo was in your Senatorial district." Hay noted, "It will take the quiet satire of the note about a half an hour to get through the thick skull of this Kentucky Senator, and then he will think it a damned poor joke."

One of Lincoln's greatest challenges would be to fight the insurrection while balancing the constitutional protections of its citizens. After the attack on federal troops in Baltimore, and the subsequent closure of transportation and communication lines, Lincoln issued a limited suspension of habeas corpus. Simply put, habeas corpus means that if the government holds someone against his will, it must demonstrate cause to judicial authorities. The constitution provides that "The privilege of the Writ of Habeas Corpus shall not be suspended, unless when in cases of rebellion or invasion the public safety may require it."

Lincoln's order to Winfield Scott read, "You are engaged in repressing an insurrection against the laws of the United States." If the army were to encounter resistance along the rail route from Philadelphia to Washington, "which renders it necessary to suspend the writ of Habeas Corpus for the public safety, you, personally, or through the officer in command at the point where the resistance occurs, are authorized to suspend the writ."

Though it may have seemed a nightmare, it was no dream when John Merryman was awoken in the dead of night. Rustled from bed by federal troops and removed to the confines of Fort McHenry, he was brought before the commandant, General George Cadwallader. Merryman was part of an organized conspiracy supportive of the Confederacy, one that had damaged railroad and telegraph wires. His friends enlisted lawyers, who prevailed upon none other than Roger Taney, chief justice of the United States Supreme Court, who issued a writ of habeas corpus ordering Cadwallader to appear in front of him at the United States Court room in Baltimore's Masonic Hall.

The courtroom was "filled with a dense crowd," eager to see what would happen. Taney, who likely entertained visions of embarrassing Cadwallader, would not get his chance. For fifteen minutes the chief justice and his audience waited. Finally, Cadwallader's aide appeared, bearing a response from his commanding officer. Merryman had been arrested on the orders of the military on a charge of treason, for holding the position of a lieutenant in a secessionist company possessing arms that belonged to the United States, "and avowing his purpose of armed hostilities against the government," and "in readiness to co-operate with those engaged in the present rebellion against the government of the United States." Cadwallader's communication further said that President Lincoln had authorized him to suspend the writ of habeas corpus.

The chief justice, as if he had not heard a word of the letter, interrupted the aide as he was leaving. "Have you brought with you the body of John Merryman?"*

"I have no instructions except to deliver this response to the Court," the aide replied.

"The commanding officer then declines to obey the writ?" Taney asked.

"After making that communication, my duty is ended," the aide said, rising and leaving the room.

The chief justice then gave his marshal the unenviable order to arrest General Cadwallader at a fortress he commanded, no less, and bring him before the court at noon the next day.

---

* In Latin, habeas corpus effectively, if not literally, means "bring the body with you."

The following day, the courthouse "was besieged by an immense crowd." Taney assumed the bench at one o'clock and asked his marshal to explain the situation. The marshal had indeed gone to Fort McHenry the previous day, identifying himself at the outer gate. The sentinel "returned with the reply, 'that there was no answer to my card.'"

An angered Taney then announced from the bench that he had so ordered the marshal because, firstly, the president of the United States does not have the right to suspend habeas corpus, nor can he authorize a military officer to do so, and secondly, a military officer cannot arrest and detain a person for crimes against the United States.

Taney further said that the marshal could not practically arrest Cadwallader, and would not require him to attempt it further. If Cadwallader were present, however, Taney indicated that he would be fined and imprisoned. He would file a written opinion by the end of the week and call upon President Lincoln "to perform his Constitutional duty—to enforce the laws, by compelling obedience to the civil process."

Franklin Pierce wrote to Taney commending him on his decisions. Taney thanked him, saying the ex-president's letter gave him "sincere pleasure. In the present state of the public mind inflamed with passion and seeking to accomplish its object by force of arms, I was sensible of the grave responsibility which the case of John Merryman cast upon me. But my duty was plain—and that duty required me to meet the question . . . without evasion, whatever might be the consequences to myself." The chief justice revealed himself an opponent of Lincoln's war policy and supporter of secession. He hoped "the north as well as the south will see that a peaceful separation with free institutions in each section is far better than the union of all the present states under a military government and reign of terror—preceded too by a civil war with all its horrors," which "may well prove ruinous to the traitors as well as the reconquered—but at present I grieve to say, passion and hate sweep every thing before us."

John Tyler, who had been unanimously chosen by the Virginia Convention to serve in the Provisional Confederate Congress, campaigned for a seat in the permanent Congress. In his address to the people, he spoke out against Lincoln's habeas corpus suspension. He charged, "In vain does the victim of oppression demand, in the language of our Bill of

Rights and of the Constitution, a fair and impartial trial . . . In vain that he appeals to the judges and the courts. The venerable Chief-Justice, in his attempt to restore the reign of the law and the Constitution, is mocked at, and his authority despised . . . Equally vain that the citizen claims his house to be his castle. Armed men, without authority of law, arouse him from his slumbers at midnight."

In Lincoln's April 15 proclamation, he had called Congress into special session to meet on July 4. When they convened, he addressed his habeas corpus suspension, pointing out that it had been "exercised but very sparingly." He asked, "Are all the laws but one to go unexecuted, and the government itself go to pieces, lest that one be violated? Even in such a case would not the official oath be broken, if I allow the government to be overthrown, when it was believed that disregarding the single law would tend to preserve it?" Habeas corpus could be suspended in cases of "rebellion or invasion," if required by "public safety." As the "provision was made for a dangerous emergency, it cannot be believed that the framers of that instrument intended that in every case the danger should run its course until Congress could be called together, the very assembling of which might be prevented, as was intended in this case, by the rebellion."

Once frighteningly empty, Washington soon swelled with soldiers, and a camp of one hundred thousand amassed. Nicolay recorded "the everywhere-ness of uniforms and muskets." Francis Blair wrote to Van Buren, "what you would feel to see daily great masses of troops passing the northern pillars of the White House . . . many of the public buildings are filled with soldiers as also the public squares."

One reporter remembered, "Washington was a vast citadel," with regiments "constantly on the march through the city." There was the Sixth Massachusetts in the Senate; the Eighth Massachusetts under the dome; the Seventh New York in the House. The basement of the Capitol was a bakery for the army, the crypt a storage space for flour. Inspecting the Sixth Massachusetts, Hay wrote, "The contrast was very painful between the grey haired dignity that filled the Senate Chamber when I saw it last and the present throng of bright-looking Yankee boys . . . scattered over the desks chairs and galleries, some loafing, many writing letters, slowly and with plough hardened hands . . . while [a Congressman] stood patient by the desk and franked for every body."

Cities North and South were growing accustomed to the presence of soldiers. "It is a thrilling, melting sight to see the entrances into the city of troops by the trains from all parts of the southern country, coming, as they appear to feel, to the rescue of old Virginia," wrote Julia Tyler from Richmond to her mother on June 16. She continued to revel in her husband's, and by extension her own, reentry to prominence. Julia gushed about the two men to whom she had been introduced at church that morning—Jefferson Davis and General Robert E. Lee.

With the Union capital increasingly secure and the military coming together, the administration turned their attention toward offensive action. To General James Fry, who became an active history writer after the war, it seemed "the capitals of the Union and of the Confederacy stood defiantly confronting each other."

On June 29 a special meeting of the cabinet was to discuss an attack on Manassas, Virginia, an important railroad junction on the way to Richmond. Winfield Scott opposed the plan entirely. He believed the priority should be advancing south along the Mississippi, cutting the Confederacy in two, and squeezing them with the naval blockade. General Irvin McDowell, who would lead the movement against Manassas, expected to encounter twenty-five thousand Confederates. That number could not be reinforced by more than ten thousand men, provided Union generals in northwestern Virginia could pin down Confederate general Joseph Johnston and his men.

As the army prepared for its first major battle, Lincoln was focused on his July 4 message to Congress. Thinking seriously about the war, he determined that the Union cause was "whether a free and representative government had the right and power to protect and maintain itself."

The night before the special session, Lincoln visited with Orville Browning, senator from Illinois and longtime friend. "Browning," he confided, "of all the trials I have had since I came here, none begin to compare with those I had between the inauguration and the fall of Fort Sumter. They were so great that could I have anticipated them, I would not have believed it possible to survive them." By the end of the special session, Congress had authorized one million men and five million dollars for the war effort, more than Lincoln had asked for.

On July 4, John Tyler addressed Confederate volunteers near Jamestown, offering that if young enough he would join and fight. Meanwhile on that very night, there was a splendid party at Tyler's summer home, Villa Margaret in Hampton, only he had not been invited. The *New York Herald* reported Ex-President Tyler's House the Scene of Novel Enjoyment.

The home "contains all the luxurious furniture as Mr. Tyler left it, mostly of a magnificent description." One item, his Confederate Flag, was removed, shipped to New York, and replaced with the Stars and Stripes. Rank and file Union soldiers camped in rows of tents on his lawn. "What must the venerable traitor Tyler's sensations be," the paper wondered, as the Union army relaxed in his easy chair and velvet sofas, enjoying his books and tobacco. Another newspaper crowed that Tyler would soon be forced "from his winter quarters at the ancient little city of Williamsburg. There is no rest for the wicked."

CHAPTER 22

Twilight at Wheatland, Dawn at Manassas

Upon re-examination of the whole course of my administration from the 6th November, 1860, I can find nothing to regret. I shall at all times be prepared to defend it.
—James Buchanan to Edwin Stanton

Buchanan ~ Lincoln ~ Pierce ~ Tyler ~ Fillmore ~ Van Buren

While the world outside Wheatland worried about more pressing affairs, James Buchanan was obsessed with clearing his name. Buchanan's sense of immediacy was driven by several factors. First was the severe degree to which he had fallen in the public estimate. He noted that he received, "almost every day . . . violent, insulting, and threatening anonymous letters . . . I should like to know whether I am in danger of a personal attack . . . so that I may be prepared to meet it. They know not what they would do; because when my record is presented to the world, all will be clear as light." If the attack on Fort Sumter had happened under his watch, Buchanan protested, he would have responded the same as Lincoln. Another reason for Buchanan's urgency was his precarious health during this time. From his perspective, he could not afford the luxury of waiting until after the war to ensure his legacy. Perhaps Buchanan could have focused on other things if he had another outlet, but as he noted, "All social visiting is at an end. Men, women, and children are all engaged in warlike pursuits."

A soldier stationed at nearby Camp Curtin left on a recruiting expedition and decided to visit Wheatland, to pay his respects to Buchanan. The house, he noted, "stands in a cluster of fine old pines, oaks, willows, and maples, about one hundred yards from the road." He walked past the "dilapidated black wooden gate, with an old fashioned iron latch," and pulled the bell to signal his arrival. While he waited, he took note of a flag atop a pine pole, and hickory armchairs on the portico, one with the "seat broken through." Generally, he felt the home had a "discarded, broken-down and hopeless appearance." After ringing the bell, he heard "shutting doors and hasty footfalls." The well-wisher might have done him good, but Buchanan was increasingly isolated, sick, and concerned for his safety. The soldier left without getting any response.

Buchanan believed that he must quickly reduce to writing a defense of his administration. He asked an intermediary to sound out an influential publisher. "Although nearly all upon record, the public seem to have forgotten it," he noted. "It has become necessary now to revive the public memory, and I know of no journal in the country so proper to do this as the Journal of Commerce."

Buchanan complained "the whole force at my command was just five companies, and neither of them full [referring to forces in proximity to the capital, rather than the 16,000 spread throughout the country]. They did not exceed in the whole 300 men. The *Herald*, however, from a spirit of malignity, and supposing that the world may have forgotten the circumstances, takes every occasion to blame me for my supineness. It will soon arrive at the point of denouncing me for not crushing out the rebellion at once, and thus try to make me the author of the war. Whenever it reaches that point, it is my purpose to indict [the publisher] for libel." Buchanan called it "an attempt to bring not only my character but my life into danger by malignant falsehood." A man who had been at the center of American life for four decades bemoaned "To be sick, while the whole world is alive."

He wrote to Joseph Holt, his secretary of war, "The time has certainly arrived when in justice to myself and to the members of my cabinet I must prepare, or have prepared under my immediate direction, an authentic statement of the events of the administration . . . If Providence were to call me away from this world before such a statement, the truth in its full extent might never be known." He asked Holt to come to Wheatland to help him prepare a defense, and to bring documents about Fort Pickens and the plans to save

Sumter. "We are not a gay household, but we will give you a cheerful welcome," he explained.

Holt responded, "The country is so completely occupied by the fearful and absorbing events occurring and impending, that you could not hope at present to engage its attention. While the country will accord to you a high patriotic purpose in the forbearing course you pursued, it has also, I am satisfied, arrived at the conclusion, from current events, that the policy was a mistaken one." Holt referenced the traitors in Buchanan's cabinet, and argued that if Buchanan had done in Charleston what Lincoln had done to secure St. Louis the rebellion would have "been dead as any antediluvian."

Jeremiah Black was a visitor to Wheatland around this time. He later wrote to Buchanan, "I think you owe it to your friends and to your country to give them a full and clear vindication of your conduct and character. If this be not done, you will continue to be slandered for half a century to come." No one would read a droll recitation of facts, Black argued. Rather, it should be "a compact narrative, readable, attractive, and interesting to all." He advised that Buchanan publish what he needed to convey right away, but to take time with the fuller explanation he suggested. Black was willing to be hired for this purpose, in exchange for $1,500 up front, $2,500 in Buchanan's will, and $3,500 to his family. "If you agree to this I will immediately move to York or Lancaster."

It seemed that Black and Buchanan would have conflicting recollections of the ex-president's time in office, however, and Black would end up departing Wheatland early, "very much to my surprise and regret," Buchanan noted. "I presume the biography is all over. I shall now depend upon myself with God's assistance."

The western counties of Virginia, possessing few slaves and strong Union sentiment, met in convention to form their own state government. Not yet proclaiming themselves a separate state, they rather held themselves out as the legitimate government of all of Virginia. The Confederates were determined to hold the disputed territory, just as the Union was committed to driving them out.

It was 4:00 a.m. on July 12, the sixth time that night Lincoln was awoken by a knock on the door from Colonel Daniel Butterfield, his military secretary.* Wearing nothing but a red flannel shirt, which he struggled to hold down in front of him, Lincoln answered the door. "Colonel, do you ever sleep?"

"Mr. President," he replied, "I was about to ask you the same question."

"I have not slept much since this civil war began," he admitted.

The colonel apologized for yet another disturbance, but he was there under orders from General Scott. Lincoln explained that his dressing gown was twisted around his wife's feet and, not wanting to wake her, he came out in this shirt instead. "Either I have grown too long or the shirt has grown too short, I know not which," he said, still struggling to hold the shirt down in front of him.

"Mr. President," said Butterfield, "the telegram I hold in my hand will give you the greatest pleasure; it is the announcement of the first victory of the Union Army."

But Lincoln, whose hands remained holding his shirt, asked, "What am I to do?"

"If you will allow me for once in my life to turn my back on the President of the United States, you can let go and I can pass the telegram over my shoulder."

"Do so, Colonel."

Butterfield turned around, handing him the dispatch over his shoulder.

Lincoln read over the news of Union victory at Rich Mountain, Virginia, then read it out loud, asking Butterfield if this had been corroborated, to which he answered affirmatively.

"Colonel," Lincoln said joyfully, "if you will come to me every night with such telegrams as that, I will come out not only in my red shirt, but without any shirt at all. Tell General Scott so." Handing back to him the first good news of the war, the president wished Butterfield goodnight and went back to bed for the sixth time. Lincoln's guards

---

* Butterfield's lasting legacy is as the composer of the song "Taps," played most often at military funerals.

would remember his getting but little sleep, but when it happened, his fearful moans "seemed to betray his real sentiments and it was frightful to hear him then."

—◦—

In the memory of one general, the battle to come was "the climax of a campaign undertaken at the dictation of a clique in the press led by the *New York Tribune*," and the excited state of the country "was enough to override the President, the Secretaries, and the General-in-Chief." This cry of "On to Richmond," the general recalled, "forced the Bull Run campaign on the country, with all its sequence of disaster and depression." The only good effect, he believed, was to teach the public "to be a little patient."

On the eve of Bull Run, Franklin Pierce reflected that he had always believed "aggression by arms is neither a suitable nor possible remedy for existing evils . . . I cannot find my way through the thick darkness. May God grant that light break up us with some unexpected quarter." Bureaucratic wrangling had delayed General Irvin McDowell and his army's departure by eight days. The unseasoned troops took three days to cover what veterans would cover in one. The slog caused the Union forces to run out of food, and they were forced to wait in Centreville to be replenished from the 18th through the 21st. Many spectators passed through the Union ranks during this time—members of Congress, members of the cabinet, and ordinary citizens. They would stay and watch the battle, "as they would have gone to see a horse race or to witness a Fourth of July procession."

The Union idling also permitted Confederate general Joseph Johnston's army in western Virginia to evade General Robert Patterson, and join Beauregard on the 20th and 21st, swelling his ranks by nine thousand soldiers. The soldiers who fought lacked any consistency with their uniforms, underscoring the amateur nature of the early war. The multicolored forces' garments varied by militia or state, "according to the aesthetic taste of place." Some regiments were in plain clothes.

The Confederates, led by General Beauregard, McDowell's West Point classmate and bombarder of Fort Sumter, were arrayed south of the Bull Run, "a sluggish, tree choked river a few miles north of Manassas." Beauregard positioned guards on the bridge to his right, on a turnpike bridge to his left six miles upstream, and at six fords in between. At 2:00 a.m. on July 21, McDowell's men crossed miles north of where they were anticipated, seeking to turn the Confederate left flank. The Confederates got the worst of it that morning, and fell back as the battle continued in front of Henry House Hill. The sun was scorching that day, and men's faces were blackened by "powder, smoke, and dust." Union artillery were "the prime features of the fight," according to one general. The Confederate line may have broken here, were it not for the bravery of Thomas Jackson, now practicing what months ago he taught as a professor at the Virginia Military Institute. By standing firm and keeping his forces in line, he earned the nickname "Stonewall," and a piece of martial immortality. Shot in the hand but dismissing it as "a mere scratch," Jackson told another officer, "My religious belief teaches me to feel as safe in battle as in bed. God has fixed the time for my death. I do not concern myself about *that*, but to be always ready, no matter when it may overtake me."

In the heat of the late afternoon, to the right of the Union artillery there emerged from the woods an infantry unit. About to open fire, the commander was dissuaded by his chief of artillery, certain that the new troops were Union reinforcements. The unit revealed themselves by firing a deadly volley at the batteries, killing or wounding every cannon operator and many of their horses, rendering the massive Union guns silent.

His major artillery gone, McDowell attempted to retreat back across Bull Run Creek. The Union forces slowly lost cohesion, as men set aside their muskets and began to walk, and finally to run away. The first arrived in Washington close to midnight. Two hours later, Winfield Scott called on the White House and asked that Mary Lincoln and the children leave the city. Mary turned to her husband and asked, "Will you go with us?" certain of his response.

"Most assuredly I will not leave at this juncture," he replied.

"Then I will not leave you at this juncture," she answered.

When morning came, Lincoln was still meeting with eyewitnesses, taking notes, planning his next move.

John Tyler was bedridden, but when he learned of the victory at Manassas, he called for champagne and made others drink to the health of Confederate generals.

Stanton wrote to Buchanan, "The dreadful disaster of Sunday can scarcely be mentioned. The imbecility of this administration culminated in that catastrophe—an irretrievable misfortune and national disgrace never to be forgotten are to be added to the ruin of all peaceful pursuits and national bankruptcy, as the result of Lincoln's 'running the machine' for five months. The capture of Washington now seems inevitable—during the whole of Monday and Tuesday it might have been taken without any resistance. The rout, overthrow, and utter demoralization of the whole army is complete. Even now I doubt whether any serious opposition to the entrance of the Confederate forces could be offered."

On July 23, Millard Fillmore received a letter from his stockbrokers, with bad news about his portfolio, noting "the times have interfered with their business very badly."

In terms of losses, the first major battle of the Civil War was more evenly distributed than suggested by its chaotic conclusion. The Union lost sixteen officers, 444 enlisted men with 1,046 wounded; the Confederates, twenty-five officers and 362 enlisted, with 1,519 wounded. Otherwise it was an embarrassing defeat for the North. As Beauregard put it, "It established as an accomplished fact [the Confederacy] . . . which before was but a political assertion." The three-month Union enlistees went home, their time having expired. The Civil War would not be the short, decisive conflict that both sides anticipated. Virginia's interior would not be invaded for eight more months.

After the battle, one resident remembered, "Washington seemed to me to be utterly demoralized. I did not see one really cheerful face, nor did I hear one encouraging word. The President was criticized; the manner in which the battle was fought was criticized; criticism was the order of the day." This visitor was also shocked at the vulnerability of Washington, saying that if the Confederates had known, "they might have captured the city and placed their banners upon its public buildings."

Buchanan believed that "nothing but a vigorous prosecution of the war can now determine the question between the north and south. It is vain to talk of peace at the present moment. The Confederate States, flushed with their success at Bull's Run, would consent to nothing less than a recognition of their independence, and this it is impossible to grant under any conceivable circumstances." He resisted allowing its publication, but by the fall was willing to publish a letter to a Union meeting of Chester and Lancaster Counties. "Our recent military reverses," Buchanan wrote, "so far from producing despondency in the minds of a loyal and powerful people, will only animate them to more mighty exertions in sustaining a war which became inevitable by the assault upon Fort Sumter.

"This is the moment for action, prompt, energetic, united action, and not for discussion of peace propositions. These would be rejected by the states that have seceded, unless we should offer to recognize their independence, which is entirely out of the question." Buchanan made "a solemn and earnest appeal to my countrymen, and especially those without families, to volunteer for the war and join the many thousands of brave and patriotic volunteers who are already in the field." Widely republished, the letter even led to some rare praise for Buchanan, such as that which came from the *Hartford Daily Courant*, pronouncing "'Old Buck' Sound at the Core!" But one friend did not think his remarks were wise. "Your endorsement of Lincoln's policy," Black wrote, "will be a very serious drawback upon the defense of your own." The January 9, 1861, firing on the *Star of the West* was as serious as against Fort Sumter, he argued, and the taking of Forts Moultrie and Pinckney "was worse than either ... if this war is right and politic and wise and Constitutional, I cannot but think you ought to have made it."

Martin Van Buren, in his final statement on the war, reaffirmed his earlier support for Lincoln, despite the initial setbacks. His positions "have, at no time, undergone the slightest change and have been freely repeated in conversation to my friends and neighbors and to all others who have asked to be informed of them."

If Washington was downtrodden, the North responded to this defeat with overwhelming support for the war effort. As late as November

Lincoln would write that there were more soldiers than guns. "The plain matter-of-fact is, our good people have rushed to the rescue of the government, faster than the government can find arms to put into their hands."

To equip, train, and lead these new men, General George McClellan was put in command, bringing badly needed professionalism and discipline, turning raw recruits into a professional fighting force. The son of a Philadelphia doctor and a graduate of West Point who had served with the Corps of Engineers in the Mexican War, he was one of three officers sent to Europe to study the logistics of organizing an army. Three years earlier he had resigned his commission to accept a position with the Illinois Central Railroad Company, first as chief-engineer, then vice president, and then president of the Eastern Division of the Ohio and Mississippi Railroad Company. As for so many others, the war meant a change of plans. After leading Union forces in Western Virginia, McClellan was brought to Washington in the wake of Bull Run and placed in charge of the Army of the Potomac.

"I feel that God has placed a great work in my hands," he wrote, and "I was called to it; my previous life seems to have been unwittingly directed to this great end; and I know that God can accomplish the greatest results with the weakest instruments."

CHAPTER 23

To Lose Kentucky Is Nearly the Same as to Lose the Whole Game

Thirty noted thieves and pickpockets of New York have sent a formal protest to the metropolitan police board against the disgrace inflicted upon them by placing the pictures of Davis, Cobb, Toucey, Floyd, and other public villains alongside of their own in the rogues gallery.
—SPRINGFIELD *WEEKLY REPUBLICAN*, AUGUST 3, 1861

Lincoln ~ Tyler ~ Buchanan ~ Pierce ~ Fillmore

Abraham Lincoln was fighting a war to preserve the Union. His success depended on the status of the border states, where the Union now had tenuous control. Any agitation over the slavery question could easily turn the tide, and so the president preferred to avoid it, for now. But the question could not be skirted entirely. American military forces operating in the South were encountering slaves and being forced to decide: Should they be freed or returned to their masters? Could they be put to work for the Union in some way?

The summer session of Congress had passed the First Confiscation Act, divesting owners of their slaves when used to assist the rebellion. Shortly thereafter, General John C. Fremont, Republican nominee for president in 1856, took it upon himself to emancipate all of the slaves in Missouri belonging to owners who supported the Confederates. Lincoln responded quickly, writing to Fremont that parts of his proclamation "give me some anxiety." He calmly explained, "I think there is great danger ... in relation to the confiscation of property, and the liberating slaves of traitorous owners, will alarm our Southern Union friends, and turn them

THE PRESIDENTS' WAR

against us—perhaps ruin our rather fair prospect for Kentucky." He asked Fremont to modify his order to conform to the Confiscation Act. "The Kentucky legislature would not budge till that proclamation was modified," Lincoln noted, and "a whole company of our [Kentucky] Volunteers threw down their arms and disbanded. I think to lose Kentucky is nearly the same as to lose the whole game. Kentucky gone, we can not hold Missouri, nor as I think, Maryland. These all against us, and the job on our hands is too large for us."

On August 1, 1861, John Tyler arrived in Richmond to take his seat as a delegate in the Provisional Confederate Congress. Going about his business with the vigor of a much younger man, he presented petitions from his constituents and focused on the issue of Confederate coinage, weights, and measures. Tyler also proposed and chaired a committee "to drive Union forces from Virginia waters." Their findings were sent to the secretary of war and the commander of the navy.

Late that summer a messenger arrived on horseback at Sherwood Forest. "Mr. President, you are elected, sir! You are elected!" Tyler, who had last been before the people as a candidate for vice president, had won his race for a seat in the permanent Congress of the Confederate States of America. The *Richmond Examiner* noted, "John Tyler, the patriot sage and statesman of Virginia, receives a majority of three hundred and eight-five votes over his principal competitor . . . and a majority of sixty-six over the combined vote" of his opponents. "The vote in Richmond is indeed a triumph. The friends of Mr. Tyler resorted to no unusual effort or appliances in his behalf. They were content to trust his claims to the good sense and intelligence of the people."

It made headlines around the country, the news that a former president had been elected to continue his service to the Confederacy. Meanwhile, other former presidents took a shot from the press when a Vermont couple had triplets and wrote to the sitting president to name them. Lincoln forwarded the request to the War Department. The names that came back were Abraham Lincoln, Gideon Welles, and Simon Cameron. One newspaper printed that it was in bad taste to

198

name babies after the living. After all, "How many innocent young chaps have been disgraced by the odium of such names as James Buchanan and Frank Pierce?"

— —

On September 16, Millard Fillmore responded to a request that he republish his presidential letters ordering troops to Charleston Harbor, especially his curt dismissal of South Carolina's governor. "Those who have succeeded me in the administration, and who have pursued a different course, might infer that I intended to censure them for not nipping rebellion in the bud as I did, instead of leaving it to bear fruit, and scatter its baneful seeds throughout the land," he said, a thinly veiled attack on Buchanan. But "knowing the embarrassments under which the administration is laboring and feeling that for the sake of our common country nothing should be done to weaken the confidence of the public in its wisdom . . . I must respectfully advise against it."

While Fillmore was careful not to undermine the war effort, Franklin Pierce arrived in Kentucky on a supposed mission of the opposite purpose. Henry McFarland, a newspaper editor in Concord, New Hampshire, wrote Secretary of War Cameron about Pierce's trip. "There is very general suspicion here that his mission there is not one friendly to the government. If the government has any way to observe his motions I hope it will do so." Cameron brought it to the president.

"I think it will be well that P. is away from the N.H. people," Lincoln responded. "He will do less harm anywhere else; and, by *when* he has gone, his neighbors will understand him better." In the fall, Pierce arrived in Michigan, in "the fulfillment of a long and cherished purpose to visit the Great West." While Lincoln dismissed Pierce's journey, not every member of the administration would be so sanguine.

For now, the president had greater worries than Franklin Pierce's travel schedule. As he told Nicolay, Fremont was ready to rebel, Salmon Chase was despairing, Simon Cameron "utterly ignorant," totally incompetent, and "openly discourteous." Financially, credit had been exhausted at St. Louis, Cincinnati, and Springfield, that day's overdraft being $12 million. Chase advised that the government's latest line of credit would be exhausted in eleven days, and there were "immense" numbers of claims that required congressional auditing. Militarily, Kentucky had been invaded by the Confederates, Missouri "virtually seized," and instead of preparing to conquer along the Mississippi, the Army of the West seemed more likely to be forced to defend St. Louis.

One of Fillmore's most faithful Washington correspondents was Isaac Newton, commissioner of agriculture. On October 14 Newton wrote, "We are very quiet here today but looking for a battle. Every hour the Rebels as drawn-up in a line for battle . . . our forces are ready to meet them at any moment."

A poorly planned operation in northern Virginia resulted in the Battle of Ball's Bluff, which claimed the life of Oregon senator Edward Baker, one of Lincoln's closest friends. The president would be far from immune from the horrors of a war that would claim 2.5 percent of all Americans. Newton wrote Fillmore, "The loss of General Baker has cast a gloom over the people of this place."

On October 26, Newton wrote to Fillmore again, saying "things look gloomy here . . . the loss of life . . . in the late battle was dreadful. The slaughter of our men is greater than we have had any account of yet." Newton was losing confidence in the Union commanders, and he was not alone.

Nicolay, who had been sent to monitor General Fremont, wrote Lincoln: "The universal opinion is that he has entirely failed, and that he ought to be removed." Lincoln promptly transferred his problematic general.

But when Lincoln had solved a problem with one commander, there would soon be something wrong with another. George McClellan was ascendant. Winfield Scott, who had entered the army during Washington's presidency, had been elbowed aside, retiring for "health reasons." McClellan had channeled the northern feeling into an incredible fighting force. By November, the southern head start was erased, and McClellan had three times the men and artillery as his opponents.

But success did not wear well on McClellan. He increasingly felt contempt for political leaders and developed unhealthy beliefs about himself. "I find myself in a new and strange position here," he wrote to his wife, "President, Cabinet . . . all deferring to me. By some strange operation of magic I seem to have become the power of the land . . . who would have thought when we were married that I should so soon be called upon to save my country?"

In another letter he wrote, "I must save it, and cannot respect anything that is in the way . . . the President cannot or will not see the true state of affairs." But McClellan, with such a massive advantage over the Confederates, kept his distance, refusing to take his forces into battle. Lincoln, he wrote, was "nothing more than a well meaning baboon" and an "idiot."

To prod his reluctant general, Lincoln, Seward, and Hay went to McClellan's house. McClellan was at a wedding, his servant explained, but would return shortly. After around an hour, McClellan came home, ignored the porter who told him of his guests, and passed the room where they were sitting. A half hour later, they sent a servant to remind the general that they were there. The servant returned, telling them that McClellan had gone to bed. On the way home Hay spoke to the president about it, "but he seemed not to have noticed it specially, saying it was better at this time not to be making points of etiquette and personal dignity." Lincoln would later add, "I will hold McClellan's horse if he will only bring us success."

Lincoln would, now and for some time, have to look away from the Army of the Potomac for Union victories. The navy was charged with blockading ten deep sea ports throughout the South, as well as "180 inlets, bays, and river mouths navigable by smaller vessels" across thirty-five hundred miles of coast. With only two southern naval bases, Key West and Hampton Roads, the navy required another. Port Royal, South Carolina, strategically positioned between Savannah and Charleston, was targeted.

Admiral Samuel du Pont ordered his steamships to maneuver in an oval in front of the two fortresses guarding the landing, "pounding them with heavy broadsides while presenting moving targets in return." Both forts surrendered four hours later. Inadvertently, the Union army that occupied the sea islands in Port Royal Sound found themselves at the head of a great new experiment. The plantation owners had fled, leaving thousands of slaves behind. What would become of them? Eventually, it was decided to put the slaves in charge of the land. Aid workers and missionaries soon found their way to Port Royal, with hopes of preparing the slaves for freedom.

Fillmore was encouraged by these naval successes, "and I trust that when General McClellan moves, he will win such a victory as will break the backbone of the rebellion. I shall wait patiently and anxiously for his first blow."

CHAPTER 24

Capture on the High Seas

I have never, under any circumstances, presumed to offer any advice as to men or measures to those who have succeeded me in the administration of the government.

—MILLARD FILLMORE

Buchanan ~ Lincoln ~ Fillmore

Richard Cobden, a prominent British manufacturer and member of Parliament, had written James Buchanan about the strain between the United States and his country. "The subject is so distressing to my feelings that I avoid as much as possible all correspondence with my American friends," he explained.

Cobden believed the war should be arbitrated, and that "The subject of the blockade is becoming more and more serious . . . I feel very anxious that nothing should arise to put in jeopardy the relations between England and your country." His nervousness would not be without reason.

The USS *San Jacinto* had passed an uneventful autumn in search of Confederate privateers. At Cienfuegos, Cuba, it was learned that Confederate diplomats James Mason and John Slidell had broken the blockade and arrived in Havana, bound for Europe, where they would seek recognition for the Confederacy. The officers went to shore in street clothes to gather intelligence. Mason and Slidell were still in the city, scheduled to depart aboard the *Trent*, a British steamer, to the island of St. Thomas and from there to Southampton, England. Shortly before noon on November 8, the smoke of the *Trent* appeared in view. Captain Charles Wilkes called Lieutenant Donald Fairfax into his cabin, giving him orders to prepare the *San Jacinto* for a confrontation; to board the *Trent*, and if

Mason and Slidell were to be found, to arrest them. Wilkes and Slidell had known each other as boys in New York, and had even fought over a girl. Their lives were about to intersect once again.

The *San Jacinto* fired a shot over the *Trent*'s bow, and when the plain meaning was not understood, another. Passengers could be seen running around on her deck.

"What do you mean by stopping my ship?" shouted the captain of the *Trent*.

"We are going to send a boat on board of you," said Lieutenant Breese of the *San Jacinto*, "Lay to."

Crossing the water in a small cutter ship, Fairfax boarded the *Trent* by himself. Captain Moir of the *Trent* demanded to see Fairfax's own captain, saying, "How dare you come on board of my ship? What right have you here? This is an outrage the flag there will make you pay for," he said, pointing to the St. George's Cross.

Fairfax courteously bowed and explained his mission.

Moir likened him to a "damned impertinent, outrageous puppy," telling him to return to his ship. "I deny your right of search. D'ye understand that?", upon which the captain was cheered by forty or fifty passengers now surrounding them. Fairfax declined, summoning to this ship his thirty men—including ten marines—from the cutters below.

"Do you wish to see me?" Slidell said, stepping forward. "To see me?" Mason asked.

Fairfax told them that they would join him aboard the *San Jacinto* "peaceably if you want to, but by force if necessary," with the result the same.

The Confederate diplomats returned to their staterooms with Fairfax in pursuit. Slidell's daughter stood in the doorway, pledging "I swear to heaven you shall not go into this cabin to my father."

Fairfax held his ground and watched Slidell try to leave his cabin through a window. Mason came outside and Fairfax ordered his men to seize him. When Slidell repeated his refusal, Fairfax grabbed him by the collar and with two others walked him down the gangplank. One of their clerks did not come as easily, punching one of his captors. On November 24, the *San Jacinto* arrived at Fort Warren, Massachusetts, with prisoners aboard.

When the news reached the telegraph office, a meeting between Lincoln, the cabinet, and some members of the Senate was held immediately. The consensus was that Wilkes had acted appropriately. Lincoln felt differently, aware of the potential unwanted consequences.

Buchanan was fearful of British public opinion. "We shall probably receive a terrible broadside from the English journals," he wrote. But he argued that America was in the right, writing to Cobden, "A neutral nation is the common friend of both belligerents, and has no right to aid the one to the injury of the other." Therefore, "a neutral vessel has no right to . . . transport his troops or his despatches."

"I fear the traitors will prove to be white elephants," Lincoln said. "We must stick to American principles concerning the rights of neutrals. We fought Great Britain for insisting, by theory and practice, on the right to do precisely what Captain Wilkes has done. If Great Britain shall now protest against the act, and demand their release, we must give them up, apologize for the act as a violation of our doctrines."

Britain's entry to the war would have brought about its conclusion. Their navy, the world's most renowned, could have smashed the Union blockade. British India was the principal supplier of saltpeter, necessary for making gunpowder; twenty-three hundred tons on five ships waited in Britain as a consequence of the *Trent* affair. Nicolay and Hay remembered, "There seemed little possibility that a war could be avoided." Eight thousand British soldiers were sent to Canada. Additional ships were sent to American waters. Seven months after the firing on Fort Sumter, four months after Bull Run, the South by itself was proving more than a match for the Union—aided by a global military power and the war was as good as lost.

Lord Palmerston, the British prime minister, penned a formal response to the United States, a draft of which he submitted to Queen Victoria and Prince Albert. Albert, in his last political memorandum, softened its wording, giving the administration possible outs, asking whether Wilkes was acting under orders, or whether he misunderstood those orders, and making clear that her Majesty was unwilling to believe that the United States would purposely insult the country.

"I'm not getting much sleep out of that exploit of Wilkes's," Lincoln told Attorney General Bates, "and I suppose we must look up the law of the case. I am not much of a prize [admiralty] lawyer, but it seems to me pretty clear that if Wilkes saw fit to make that capture on the high seas he had no right to turn his quarter-deck into a prize court."

Bates thought the more he saw of Lincoln, the more "he was impressed with the clearness and vigor of his intellect and the breadth and sagacity of his views," adding, "He is beyond question the master-mind of the cabinet."

Finessing this particular task would take all of Lincoln's skill. Keeping the prisoners would mean war with Britain. But on December 2, when the 37th Congress met, they unanimously passed a resolution commending Wilkes for "his brave, adroit, and patriotic conduct," and urging Lincoln to put the two would-be emissaries in solitary confinement.

Millard Fillmore, mindful of the strictures of former presidents, could not resist penning Lincoln a six-page letter. "I have never," he began, "under any circumstances, presumed to offer any advice as to men or measures to those who have succeeded me in the administration of the government. And I beg of you to consider the few candid suggestions which I am now about to make." Fillmore appreciated the difficulties that Lincoln must be feeling in handling this "unholy rebellion." He had "heard the threatening thunder, and viewed the gathering storm at a distance in 1850; and while I approve most cordially of the firm stand which you have taken in support of the Constitution as it is, against insane abolitionism on one side and rebellious secessionism on the other, and hope and trust that you will remain firm; yet it was not to speak of this that I took up my pen, but of a new danger which threatens more immediately our Northern frontier, but in its consequences, most fatally, the whole country." In a war with England, Fillmore argued, "the last hope of restoring the Union will vanish." Fillmore had heard that Britain had demanded the release of the prisoners and an apology. He hoped it was not true, but if it were, "one of two things must happen; the government must submit, or engage in a war to settle a point of international law."

Fillmore argued for a "firm but conciliatory" response, acknowledging that the two nations disagreed on the law—"this is a purely legal question"—and that no insult was intended to Great Britain. He suggested that Lincoln offer to submit to binding arbitration by one of the

European monarchs. Fillmore believed that England "can not refuse so fair a proposition. But if she does, and insists on an unconditional compliance with her demand or war, all Christendom will then hold her responsible for the consequences." No response from Lincoln has ever been found, but there can be little doubt that he knew of the letter. The two presidents were of similar minds. Weeks earlier, Lincoln had responded favorably to Fillmore's request to grant his nephew a commission in the army.

On December 23, the British minister presented Secretary of State Seward with a formal demand for the release of the prisoners and an apology. Privately, he told Seward that he was instructed to close the embassy and withdraw from Washington. With time running out, the cabinet met for four hours on Christmas. Charles Sumner, as chairman of the Senate Foreign Affairs Committee, was included. "All of us were impressed with the magnitude of the subject," Bates recalled, "and believed that upon our decision depended the dearest interest, probably the existence, of the nation." The next day the cabinet unanimously resolved to release the prisoners and accept the fallout in public opinion.

Meanwhile, Buchanan recorded "a very sober, quiet and contented Christmas." Just a year earlier he had been president of the United States, five days removed from South Carolina's secession. Now his day consisted of morning church services and a pleasant dinner with his housekeeper.

Buchanan believed that "under all the circumstances, the administration acted wisely in surrendering Mason and Slidell." But he regretted Seward's blustery letter of release. "When we determined to swallow the bitter pill, which I think was right," Buchanan wrote, "we ought to have done it gracefully and without pettifogging."

If war broke out with Britain, the city of Buffalo, on the Canadian border, would instantly find itself on the front lines, threatened with the kind of destruction it had met in the War of 1812. On January 2, 1862, 350 of the leading citizens of Buffalo received a printed circular from

Millard Fillmore. "There will be a meeting of the citizens of Buffalo, at the old Court House, on Friday evening, January 3d, at 8 o'clock, to take into consideration the subject of the defense of our city and frontier." At this first meeting, Fillmore was elected permanent chair of the Buffalo Committee of Public Defense, promising to do everything possible and necessary to defend the city against attack.

CHAPTER 25

The Bottom Is Out of the Tub

No terms except unconditional and immediate surrender can be accepted

—Ulysses Grant

Fillmore ~ Buchanan ~ Lincoln ~ Tyler ~ Pierce

With the *Trent* crisis averted, Millard Fillmore recorded himself "very happy, as myself and my family are all enjoying health." To Dorothea Dix, a frequent correspondent and friend, who had asked him for reassurance, he wrote, "I regret to say that I have never been as confident as many seem to be of this restoration of the union. I thought some concession had been made last winter, that would have given truly loyal men of the south a firm ground to stand upon." When this did not happen, Fillmore wrote, "I lost all hope for the Union and greatly feared that the government of the Northern states would be overthrown, and that the country" would end up in a "military despotism." The "unauthorized and despotic imprisonments in the loyal states, where the courts of justice are in full operation," led Fillmore to believe that the nation was more or less already there. "Will try to hope for the best," he concluded.

James Buchanan wrote to Horatio King, his postmaster general, "I do most earnestly hope that our army may be able to do something effective before the 1st of April. If not, there is great danger not merely of British but of European interference. There will then be such a clamor for cotton among the millions of operatives dependent upon it for bread, both in England and on the Continent, that I fear for the blockade."

Menaced at home and abroad, Lincoln had to have the very best men around him. Simon Cameron, who had been chosen as secretary of war for political and geographic considerations, simply could not do the job. Cameron made a move to stay by submitting his annual report directly to the newspapers, calling for the freeing and arming of slaves. He hoped the tactic would rally abolitionists behind him and protect his position. Lincoln rescinded the report and wrote Cameron that his time in the cabinet was at an end. Cameron cried when he read it, believing he would be personally and professionally ruined. Lincoln agreed to withdraw his own letter, allowing Cameron to resign.

Edwin Stanton, who had been Buchanan's last attorney general, a highly organized and forceful war Democrat who had done so much to provide backbone to that dying administration, would now be secretary of war. "Although you now belong to an administration which has manifested intense hostility to myself," Buchanan wrote, "I wish you all the success and glory in your efforts to conquer the rebellion and restore the Union which your heart can desire."

Fillmore seemed to agree, saving a newspaper article calling the switch "a stroke of policy of the gravest character, and one which cannot fail to produce great and, we trust, happy results." Lincoln's secretaries remembered, "Both the War Department and the army instantly felt the quickening influence of his rare organizing power, combined with a will which nothing but unquestioning obedience would satisfy."

Nearly six months after the defeat at Bull Run, the Army of the Potomac had not made another attempt at Richmond, McClellan was sick, and the country's credit and patience were being sorely tested—as was its president's confidence. Lincoln walked into the office of General Montgomery Meigs "in great distress." Sitting in front of the open fire, he said, "General, what shall I do? The people are impatient; Chase has no money and he tells me he can raise no more; the General of the Army has typhoid fever. The bottom is out of the tub. What shall I do?"

A "council of war" met over several nights at the White House. At one such meeting, Meigs moved his chair near McClellan and said, "The President evidently expects you to speak; can you not promise some movement toward Manassas? You are strong."

"I cannot move on them with as great a force as they have," he replied. "Why, you have near 200,000 men, how many have they?" Meigs said. "Not less than 175,000, according to my devices." (McClellan had four times the forces under his command as did the Confederates, who knew that they had less than a third of the Union's men).

"Do you think so? The President expects something from you."

"If I tell him my plans, they will be in the *New York Herald* tomorrow morning. He can't keep a secret, he will tell them to Tadd."

"That is a pity, but he is the President—the Commander-in-Chief; he has a right to know; it is not respectful to sit mute when he so clearly requires you to speak. He is superior to all."

When McClellan finally spoke, he declined to explain his plans in detail, but "thought it best to press the movement" in the west.

"Well, on this assurance of the General that he will press the advance in Kentucky, I will be satisfied," Lincoln said, "and will adjourn this council." Which was not to say he would defer to McClellan indefinitely. Lincoln worked tirelessly to learn about military strategy and tactics, so that in a short time generals and admirals were "astonished . . . by the extent of [Lincoln's] special knowledge and the keen intelligence of his questions." Lincoln could now take a more forceful role in military affairs. On the last day of January, Lincoln ordered McClellan that "all the disposable force of the Army of the Potomac, after providing safely for the defense of Washington, be formed into an expedition, for the immediate object of seizing and occupying a point upon the rail road south westward of what is known of Manassas Junction." Lincoln was careful to leave the details to McClellan, but on account of his extreme reticence to act, mandated that this occur on or before February 22. On January 27, Lincoln had read it to the cabinet, "not for their sanction but for their information." Hay recorded, "From that time he influenced actively the operations of the campaign. He stopped going to McClellan's and sent for the General to come to him."

McClellan responded with a twenty-two-page explanation to Stanton, the first time he had deigned to reveal his plans to the administration. On February 3, Lincoln wrote McClellan acknowledging their differences of opinion. Lincoln wanted to move on Manassas, McClellan down the Chesapeake, up the Rappahannock, and then across land to the railroad terminus on the York River. Lincoln asked whether his plan was more economical, more certain of victory, promised a more valuable victory, would actually break the enemy's line of communications, and made it easier to retreat if necessary. If McClellan answered satisfactorily, Lincoln promised, "I shall gladly yield my plan to yours."

Ultimately, Lincoln did yield. He could force his general into an action the officer did not think would work, remove the popular general from command without any obvious replacement, or accept his judgment. He chose the last.

Julia Tyler awoke from a terrible dream. "I thought I had risen to dress, but on looking back to the bed, observed Mr. Tyler lying there, looking pale and ill." She hastened to Richmond, where Tyler was serving in the Provisional Confederate Congress,* to check on her husband's health.

Julia arrived at the Exchange Hotel unexpected and after dark. Tyler was summoned. Their baby girl clapped her hands when she saw him. "I really believe she knows me," he delighted.

The next day they mingled with visitors, and "all were remarking on the health and cheerfulness of the President." One man complimented his new suit. Tyler "laughed heartily," replying "I wear it in honor of my wife's arrival; but I had always thought until now that there was no use in my having a new suit of clothes, for no one ever noticed it."

That night it was Julia who awoke with a headache. Tyler laughed at the irony; she had come out of concern for him and here he was taking care of her. Tyler gave her some morphine to ease the pain and help her sleep, telling her the dream was wrong. But when Julia awoke the next morning, her husband was standing by the fire fully clothed. He had arisen that morning with a chill, gone downstairs to have tea, and upon leaving the table, "staggered and fell." He was moved to another room and placed on the sofa where he woke up. He insisted on coming back alone so as not to alarm his wife.

---

* The First Confederate Congress, to which Tyler had been elected in November, would not meet until February 18, 1862.

Physicians were rushed to the hotel, where they found Tyler in bed. "Doctor, I am dying," he reported.

"I hope not, sir," said one doctor.

"Perhaps, it is best."

John Tyler, the tenth president of the United States, would lie in Congress Hall, the Capitol of the Confederacy. Plans were quickly made for a state funeral, flags were lowered to half staff, businesses closed, bells were tolled, and arrangements were made to bury him next to James Monroe.

The procession of 150 carriages included President Jefferson Davis, Vice President Alexander Stephens, the cabinet, the Congress, the judiciary, and the Virginia legislature. The military who accompanied Tyler's coffin to St. Paul's Church marched to the tune of "a solemn dirge."

The *Richmond Examiner* recorded, "We have never seen the evidence of sorrow for the loss of the great and good more universal than it was on the occasion alluded to," leading to a "never-ceasing throng pouring into the room to catch a last glimpse of the departed statesman." Reaction in the North was vastly different. "In ordinary times," the *Albany Evening Journal* reported, "the death of an Ex-President of the United States would arrest public attention for a brief hour," but Tyler's death "hardly adds a ripple to the rushing current of events." The *New York Herald* called him "empty-minded and hollow hearted," and pointed out that the annexation of Texas "commenced the long train of slavery aggressions which are beginning to bear fruit.

"Under other circumstances, a feeling of regret might have pervaded the entire country, but his treachery to the Union and its laws will prevent those persons in the North . . . from experiencing sorrow at his demise.

"He had been Chief Magistrate of the glorious Union, to the destruction of which he devoted the last ill-spent hours of his life."

On February 9, Newton wrote to Fillmore, "I believe every thing is ready for a movement upon Manassas . . . I think we shall be successful this time." McClellan, whom Newton had seen recently at the president's party, "looks very badly . . . I think the little man has more upon him than his physical strength will be able to bear him through in this great struggle in our country." On February 10, Buffalo's Union Continentals advertised weekly drills in Kremlin Hall. "We have a neat and convenient Armory fitted up in Room No. 8, on the first floor," the announcement read. "We now have about fifty muskets, purchased by individual owners, and the necessary accoutrements to accompany the same." On Washington's Birthday, Fillmore led the Union Continentals to the Presbyterian Church where he read the first president's famous Farewell Address. With war against Britain still a viable prospect, Buffalo would do their best to be ready.

To settle the competing strategies of Lincoln and McClellan, the latter convened a war council, presented his plan, and left his generals to debate. General Franklin remembered the vote being 9–3 in favor of McClellan's amphibious landing, although it was reported as 8–4. After the vote, the generals were summoned to the White House where Lincoln and Stanton awaited them. The president wanted their opinions on timetables, transportation, and organization. He concluded by asking them to use all of their energy to rescue the country, promising, "If you are faithful to me, I, on my part, will be faithful to you."

Where Lincoln lost patience with McClellan, Fillmore was brimming with confidence. Fillmore sent a letter to John Pendleton Kennedy, his navy secretary, expressing his confidence in McClellan. Kennedy shared the letter with the general, who thanked Fillmore for "The comforting assurance of your confidence at a moment when he is the target for fanatical malevolence." Fillmore replied that if he had known the letter would be shared, he would have been more effusive, and "expressed more fully and freely not merely my confidence in the General's patriotism and ability, but" his "military qualities" that make him "the best man to lead our armies to victory."

In the meantime, the man who was truly the best man to lead the Union armies to victory had launched a successful attack on Fort Henry. Ulysses Grant was a clerk in his younger brother's store, in Galena, Illinois, when the Civil War began. A West Point graduate and Mexican War veteran, he had struggled to find his footing in the civilian world. Grant rejoined as a colonel, but promotions were abundant in the rapidly expanding army, and he was now a general. He and his men had moved south to Paducah during the failed Confederate invasion of Kentucky. The Union now prepared to go on offense. The target was Fort Donelson, Tennessee, which protected the city of Nashville, scene of the first major engagement of the Western Theater. With roughly twenty thousand men, Grant approached a well-fortified structure protected by fifteen thousand troops. The defenders knew that they could not long withstand a siege, but they failed to drive away the Union forces. On the evening of February 15, as the Confederate commanders debated surrender, General Floyd, Buchanan's secretary of war, decided to flee rather than be taken captive, knowing that he might be held to answer for his actions in the previous administration.

Grant received a note on February 16 from Fort Donelson asking for terms. "No terms except unconditional and immediate surrender can be accepted," Grant replied, in words that would arrest the nation. "I propose to move immediately upon your works." Surrender came the following day, news enthusiastically received in the White House. It was a pleasant scene in the Cabinet Room when Stanton presented Lincoln with a nomination promoting Grant to Major General of Volunteers, which Lincoln signed "at once."

Floyd's escape was the only source of lament. "I am sorry he got away," Stanton said of his former cabinet colleague. "I want to catch and hang him. The last I saw of Floyd was in this room," Stanton remembered, "lying on the sofa which then stood between the windows yonder. I remember well—it was on the night of 19th of last December—we had had high words, and almost come to blows in our discussions over Fort Sumter."

The path was clear to Nashville, but good news was never to last long. As one correspondent wrote to Fillmore, "We have a rejoicing in this place today with our recent victories mingled with sorrow at the White House the loss of the President's son, is a severe stroke upon him." Willie Lincoln had died at age eleven of typhoid fever.

Franklin Pierce, who knew the devastation of losing a son, looked past his differences with Lincoln to their shared roles as fathers, forced to govern the nation in times of great personal tragedy, and shared his sentiments with the president. "The impulse to write you, the moment I heard of your great domestic affliction was very strong, but it brought back the crushing sorrow which befell me just before I went to Washington in 1853, with such power that I felt your grief to be too sacred for intrusion.

"Even in this hour, so full of danger to our country, and of trial and anxiety to all good men, your thoughts will be, of your cherished boy, who will nestle at your heart, until you meet him in that new life, when tears and toils and conflict will be unknown.

"I realize fully how vain it would be, to suggest sources of consolation. There can be but one refuge in such an hour, but one remedy for smitten hearts, which, is to trust in Him 'who doeth all things well,' and leave the rest to 'Time comforter and only healer when the heart hath bled.'" For whatever reason, Lincoln never acknowledged this timely and thoughtful note.

CHAPTER 26

Greenbacks and Ironclads

*Your administration has fallen upon times which will be remembered
as long as human events find a record.*
—George Bancroft to Abraham Lincoln

Lincoln ~ Buchanan

The Civil War would require unprecedented efforts in the field of
finance. On February 25, 1862, the Legal Tender Act was passed,
allowing the federal government to print $150 million in paper notes,
not backed by precious metal. This radical alteration to monetary policy
generated a great deal of criticism, but with the war ongoing and low
deposits of specie, the government had little choice. In discussing a
possible quotation to place on the notes, Lincoln offered a verse from
the New Testament, "'Silver and gold have I none, but such as I have
give I thee.'"

The administration's untried policy was not without detractors. "I
never expected to see the day when the federal government would assume
the power of issuing a paper currency, much less of making it a legal tender," Buchanan wrote.

Treasury Secretary Chase stormed in to see the president and placed
before him an offensive cartoon, which showed Chase feeding gold to a
goose while the goose was laying greenbacks. Chase complained that the
cartoon would be harmful to the credit of the United States and that the
author should be punished. "I would myself give a thousand dollars to
make an example of its author!" he exclaimed.

Lincoln fixed the secretary with "a look of mingled humor, sagacity, wisdom, and esteem," and "gently said, 'From which end would you pay, Chase?'"

Lincoln was hoping to spend these new federal funds on a measure other than war, one that could eliminate the very cause of the conflict.

George Bancroft, historian and member of the Polk cabinet, had written Lincoln, "If slavery and the Union are incompatible, listen to the words that come to you from the tomb of Andrew Jackson, 'The Union must be preserved at all hazards' . . . Your administration has fallen upon times which will be remembered as long as human events find a record," arguing that the Civil War was an instrument of God to destroy slavery. Lincoln responded, "The main thought in the closing paragraph of your letter is one which does not escape my attention, and with which I must deal in all due caution, and with the best judgment I can bring to it."

Lincoln shared this judgment in a White House meeting with Charles Sumner. Lincoln would ask Congress to adopt a simple resolution: If states were willing to create a program for compensated emancipation for slaves, then the federal government would commit the necessary resources. Delaware, with only 1,798 slaves, was the perfect place to experiment, Lincoln thought. The United States would pay Delaware $400 per slave, for a total of $719,200. If it worked there, perhaps Maryland could be next. The cost of the war was $2 million a day. Fewer than eighty-seven days of war could similarly pay for all of the slaves in Delaware, Maryland, Kentucky, Missouri, and the District of Columbia. Sumner disagreed with Lincoln's graduated approach, and thought one particular passage in the president's proposed resolution too easy to misconstrue. Lincoln offered to strike it out. Sumner reviewed the document again, finally saying that he did not want to delay the message.

Lincoln had this resolution back on his desk in a little over a month, after it passed by 3–1 margins in the Senate and House, along with another measure that he had long championed. As a congressman, Lincoln had introduced a bill for emancipation in the District of Columbia. Now as president, he would have the opportunity to sign such a bill into law. "I have ever desired to see the national capital freed from the institution in some satisfactory way," Lincoln said.

———

The Confederate vessel *Virginia*, commonly known by its former name, the *Merrimac*, and fitted with iron plates, steamed out of Norfolk on March 8. Its opponents watched as their shells bounced off of the armor, waiting in horror for the *Merrimac* to come for them. In its debut the newly armored vessel had "sunk the *Cumberland*, burned the *Congress*, and run the *Minnesota* aground." Nathaniel Hawthorne, writing for the *Atlantic*, was present to witness the aftermath. Only a "few sticks" were left of the *Congress*, and the masts of the *Cumberland* rose out of the water, "a tattered rag of a pennant fluttering from one of them ... A remnant of the dead crew still man the sunken ship, and sometimes a drowned body floats up to the surface."

The implications for the new weapon of war were terrifying. It could break up the blockade. It could terrorize northern cities and their commerce. It could steam up the Potomac and force the government to give up the capital.

News of the *Merrimac* arrived the following morning, a Sunday "of swiftly succeeding emotions at the Executive Mansion." Nicolay and Hay remembered Lincoln, "as usual in trying moments, composed but eagerly inquisitive, critically scanned the despatches ... joining scrap to scrap of information, applying his searching analysis and clear logic to read the danger and find the remedy." The emergency cabinet meeting might have been "the most excited and impressive of the whole war," his secretaries recalled. Stanton paced the floors. McClellan sat silently. The military scrambled to protect Washington, creating obstructions in the Potomac to prevent passage of the *Merrimac*.

Fortunately, the Union had been conducting ironclad experiments of its own, for which Congress had appropriated $1.5 million. The result was the *Monitor*, twice the size and displacing four times as much water as the *Merrimac*, it also had five times as many guns. The *Monitor* had, unbeknownst to the worried administration, already arrived to confront the *Merrimac*. The first battle of ironclads, which rendered obsolete all the navies of the earth, lasted three hours, as nine- and eleven-inch shells bounced off the sides of each ship. Unable to harm the other, the ships withdrew from the scene.

Meanwhile, McClellan's long awaited movement was underway. The expeditionary force left on March 17, arriving at Fort Monroe on the Virginia Peninsula on April 5. The logistical feat was impressive, as "121,500 men, 14,592 animals, 1,150 wagons, 44 batteries, 74 ambulances," and a substantial amount of material for building bridges, telegraph lines, and equipment, made the journey. Lost along the way were only eight mules and nine barges, whose contents were saved. An estimated fifty-five thousand troops were needed to secure Washington. McClellan left nineteen thousand.

CHAPTER 27

Any Explanations Which You May Offer Would Be Acceptable

I enclose an extract from a letter received at this department from which it would appear that you are a member of a secret league, the object of which is to overthrow the government. Any explanations upon the subject which you may offer would be acceptable.
—WILLIAM SEWARD TO FRANKLIN PIERCE,
DECEMBER 20, 1861

Pierce ~ Lincoln ~ Van Buren

As the Army of the Potomac headed for the Virginia Peninsula, Milton Latham of California took the Senate floor and revealed an explosive exchange of letters between the secretary of state and a former president. The first was drafted by a State Department clerk and signed by William Seward, addressed to Franklin Pierce on December 20, 1861. Enclosed was a copy of an anonymous letter dated North Branch, October 5, 1861. "President P—in his passage has drawn many brave and influential men to the league." The writer suggested that "the league" was working to undermine the Union, "preparing the minds of the people for a great change."

On Christmas Eve, 1861, Pierce responded, "Sir: A package indorsed Department of State, U.S.A., franked by W. Hunter, chief clerk, and addressed to Franklin Pierce, esq., Concord N.H. was received by me today, having been forwarded to the place of my residence." If he were not familiar with Mr. Hunter, Pierce said, he would have assumed it was some kind of prank. "I must I suppose, though I do so reluctantly, now view it in a different light.

"It is not easy to conceive how any person could give credence to or entertain for a moment the idea that I am now or have ever been connected with a secret league or with any league the object of which was or is to overthrow the government of my country.

"Nothing but the gravity of the insinuation, the high official source whence it emanates and the distracted condition of our recently united, prosperous and happy country could possibly lift this matter above ridicule and contempt." Pierce was especially put off that a clerk had been the one to request an answer, rather than Seward himself. Pierce distributed the letters among his associates for comment. Word made its way to Martin Van Buren, who believed Pierce firmly in the right. "All condemn Seward and pronounce your letter *perfect*," one friend replied.

On December 30 came Seward's defiant reply. In the meantime, he had learned the note had been written by someone attempting to play a joke on the Detroit press. "An injurious aspersion on your fair fame and loyalty came into my hands. Although it was in an anonymous letter the writer was detected and subsequently avowed the authorship."

Seward acknowledged he had given Pierce offense. "I regret it and apologize for it with the only excuse I can make, namely, the necessity of employing another head to do what ought to be done and yet which I had not the time to do personally."

Seward went on to explain that he was doing Pierce a favor by giving him a chance to place his answer in the State Department files along with the anonymous note, and "the unkindness of that answer does not in the least diminish the satisfaction with which I have performed in the best way I was able a public duty with a desire to render you a service."

On January 7, Pierce wrote, "It could hardly have surprised you to learn that I failed to discover in your official note, a desire to render me a service. You will excuse me if I regard even the suggestion from a source so eminent that I am 'a member of a secret league, the object of which is to overthrow the government,' as rather too grave to have been sent off with as little consideration as a note of rebuke might have been addressed to a delinquent clerk of one of the departments.

"I think you will upon reflection arrive at the conclusion that the whole ground upon which the allegation is repeated should as a simple act of justice been placed before me."

One of Pierce's friends urged him to take this "most impudent, insulting, and atrocious charge" public, "not merely for your own sake to settle the vile slander of others, but because the interests of the people would be served by the exposure of the contemptible knavery of this political mountebank."

Pierce was increasingly concerned with the state of civil liberties. He followed "with unusual interest and satisfaction" debates in the Senate on military arrests and detention and the suspension of habeas corpus. "The power," Pierce noted, "without charge, without examination, without opportunity of reply, at the click of a telegraph, to arrest a man in a peaceable portion of the country and impression him" is "the essence of despotism." He was shocked that the public did not seem to share his outrage. "When history shall be written up, that at this period of the Republic, the constitutional safeguards of personal liberty could have been so easily and with so little apparent concern, swept away." The letter of Seward demonstrated for him "the slight grounds, or the groundless suspicions, upon which, in these times, citizens are . . . to suffer in reputation, if not in loss of liberty."

Pierce further argued that a Union without personal liberty "is not the Union, which they have cherished and to the restoration of which they look, with earnest desire and hope," and that they cannot "without danger, suffer any breach of the Constitution to pass unnoticed."

For his part, Pierce seemed content to let his correspondence with Seward lie "in quietness upon the files of the Department." That was until the *Detroit Tribune* printed the anonymous letter. The Republican press fanned the flames, and Pierce now felt it necessary to correct the record.

As word of the exchange with Seward became public, Pierce wrote Latham in asking him to introduce a resolution calling for the entire correspondence to be published. He followed up by advising Latham on how to handle the matter, urging him to ask which "official source" placed it in the *Detroit Tribune*, and in light of press censorship, who authorized the publication of the letter.

Unsurprisingly, Pierce would get the better of Seward. Letters arrived praising Pierce's "dignified and manly" response, and condemning the administration. One asked, "When suspicions, no better founded, can reach you, what security has the private citizen who has no public record to disarm them? I will not express the pleasure which I felt as he [Seward] winced under your hands."

The *Pittsfield Sun* reported that the incident "Exploded ... in a manner that does not reflect credit on the administration of that Department during the past year. It seems that a Mr. Hopkins wrote an anonymous letter, for the purpose of playing a practical joke on a Detroit or other paper, and inducing the editors to believe that they had discovered a secession plot.

"An anonymous letter, written in joke, finds its way to the State Department, and is ground sufficient for what cannot but be regarded as a very offensive letter to an Ex-President of the United States."

In the court of public opinion, in his ongoing battle against the administration, Franklin Pierce had the upper hand—for now.

CHAPTER 28

West and East

Until recently the nations of the earth didn't know our power. We didn't know it ourselves. We don't know it yet. One half of it has not been put forth.

—*MACON DAILY TELEGRAPH*, JANUARY 20, 1862

Lincoln - Fillmore

General George McClellan and his men successfully carried out the largest amphibious invasion in world history, landing at Old Point Comfort, Virginia.* The Peninsula Campaign would be a dark and deadly walk through the young history of America, writing a new chapter for sacred sites from Jamestown to Yorktown. Christopher Newport's flagship, the *Susan Constant*, had landed here in 1607 on the voyage that birthed the Jamestown Colony. Marching into Hampton, McClellan's army saw a once "beautiful and aristocratic village" now "charred and blackened" in "ruins." At St. John's Episcopal Church, founded in 1610 with a current building dating to 1725, where George Washington had worshipped, the tombstones had been broken and overthrown, the graves robbed for whatever they might yield.

Despite "poor and muddy" roads, the army began its march on a sunny, "perfect Virginia day," accented by chirping birds and blossoming flowers, nature providing a welcome they would not receive from man. Eighty-one years earlier, George Washington had won a war for American independence after a siege at Yorktown. Now George McClellan would seek to further hallow the ground, by preserving the Union. Many of his men

---

* This record would remain intact until the Allied invasion of Normandy in World War II.

believed they were close to ending the war, writing their parents with big plans for the following season. Not everyone was convinced. One private who sought food at a house along the way was promised by the mother of a Confederate soldier that the Union men "would drink hot blood" before laying eyes on Richmond.

As McClellan's army sat before Yorktown, Union forces in the west believed they were on an offensive mission. They were collected at several points along the Tennessee River, including Pittsburg Landing, on their way to the critical railroad junction at Corinth, Mississippi. On April 6, General William Tecumseh Sherman wrote Ulysses Grant, "I have no doubt that nothing will occur today more than some picket firing." There had been skirmishes in the days before, and the Union forces did not believe today would be any different.

The Confederates were less than two miles away, preparing for an all-out assault.

Grant's breakfast was interrupted by the sounds of heavy firing in the direction of Pittsburg Landing. Summoning his diffused forces, the general acted quickly to bring reinforcements to the field of battle. "The Confederate assaults were made with such a disregard of losses on their own side that our line of tents soon fell into their hands," Grant remembered. The battle was fought over uneven land, with trees and "scattered clearings," giving each side a small measure of protection.

Throughout the first day, Confederates threw themselves at the Union lines, "first at one point, then at another," Grant wrote, "sometimes at several points at once." The heavily wooded area and close combat prevented the Union navy from assisting. After nightfall, however, weary Confederates were treated to a shell in their camp, every fifteen minutes until sunlight.

Several days before the battle, Grant had fallen with his horse, bruising his ankle so badly that his boot needed to be cut off. The throbbing pain kept him from sleeping, which the torrential rain may have done anyway. Around midnight, Grant entered the Shiloh Church, a one-room log meeting house. Shiloh, Hebrew for "peace," was being used as a hospital, where the wounded were being treated, and arms and legs amputated. At this grisly sight, Grant returned outside to the rain.

As sunlight broke on that second day, Grant observed "it would have been possible to walk across the clearing, in any direction, stepping on dead bodies, without a foot touching the ground." With his army finally concentrated in one place, the Union offensive drove the Confederates backward until the late afternoon, when a final "Charge!" command from Grant sent them to flight.

Union losses at the Battle of Shiloh were reported as 1,754 killed, 8,408 wounded, and 2,885 missing; the Confederates, 1,728 killed, 8,012 wounded, 959 missing. Among the Confederate dead was Lincoln's brother-in-law, Samuel Todd.

Fillmore was no doubt glad for the Union triumph at Shiloh, if shocked by the death toll. Isaac Newton had written him with the news. "People are rejoicing over their recent victory." Newton had shown Lincoln a complimentary message from Fillmore, to which Lincoln replied, "I have a very high opinion of Mr. Fillmore's judgment. He was a good president." Newton recorded that Lincoln was in "good spirits now and looks much better than he has for some time."

On April 9, Lincoln wrote to McClellan, who had persisted that he was not properly supported. These messages, "while they do not offend me," Lincoln said, "do pain me very much." The president pointed out that McClellan had stripped the capital region bare, leaving "20,000 unorganized men without a single field battery." The secretary of war listed 108,000 men with McClellan or on their way, but the general now said that he would have eighty-five thousand once everyone arrived. "How can the discrepancy of 23,000 be accounted for?"

"I think this is the precise time for you to strike a blow. By delay the enemy will relatively gain upon you—that is, he will gain faster, by fortifications and reinforcements, than you can by reinforcements alone.

"And once more let me tell you, it is indispensible to you that you strike a blow. I am powerless to help this." Lincoln reminded McClellan that he had yielded to his battle plans over his own objections.

"I beg to assure you that I have never written you, or spoken to you in greater kindness of feeling than now, nor with a fuller purpose to sustain you, so far as in my most anxious judgment I consistently can. But you must act," Lincoln concluded.

Meanwhile, McClellan received telegraphs from the chairman of the National Democratic Committee, among others, urging him to disregard the administration and to do what he thought best.

On May 1 the most populous city in the Confederacy, the crucial port of New Orleans, fell to the Union navy. Another of Lincoln's brothers-in-law, Alexander Todd, died from wounds received in a subsequent Confederate attempt to retake Louisiana.

On the third and fourth days of May, Yorktown was evacuated. A month of critical time was lost as McClellan refused to send fifty-five thousand men into battle against thirteen thousand Confederates. The next day, the forces reengaged outside Williamsburg, Virginia's colonial capital. McClellan stationed a guard at Sherwood Forest for the protection of Julia Tyler and her children. The Confederates withdrew the following day. Surveying the scene, one young private saw a comrade aiming a rifle over a fallen tree. Calling to him, he heard nothing. Grasping his shoulder, he realized, "He was dead! Shot through the brain; and so suddenly had the end come that his rigid hand grasped his musket, and he still preserved the attitude of watchfulness, literally occupying his post after death." Another man nearby had died holding a picture of his wife and children. On May 7, Union forces walked through "quaint, old fashioned Williamsburg," past the buildings of the College of William and Mary. Now used as a Union hospital, in an earlier time it had educated sixteen signers of the Declaration of Independence, and Presidents Jefferson, Monroe, and Tyler.

While the Peninsula Campaign was underway to the south, "Stonewall" Jackson and seventeen thousand Confederates moved quickly throughout northern Virginia. His incredible speed and devastating attacks "diverted 60,000 Union soldiers" and "disrupted two major strategic movements"—Fremont's campaign to liberate east Tennessee and McDowell's plan to join McClellan before Richmond. As one of his men put it, in thirty-five days, Jackson had traveled "245 miles, fighting in the meantime four desperate battles, and winning them all."

On May 25, Lincoln messaged McClellan that Confederate forces were driving northward in a way in which they could not if Richmond were actually being threatened. "I think the time is near when you must either attack Richmond or give up the job and come to the defense of Washington. Let me hear from you instantly." McClellan's forces were crossing the Chickahominy River at month's end, and arrived at Seven Pines, Virginia, seven miles from the Confederate capital. The outmatched Confederates went on offense, inflicting heavy losses in the first day of fighting; the second day they endured them. In the words of one Confederate colonel, now "the two armies lay passively watching each other in front of Richmond." Confederate general J. E. B. Stuart led his cavalry around McClellan's right flank, pursued unsuccessfully by Union forces led by his own father-in-law. His daring maneuver complete, he reported back to General Robert E. Lee, who had assumed command of the Army of Northern Virginia after General Johnston was wounded. McClellan, Stuart had learned, had no geographic defenses on his right flank.

On June 26, Lee's first attempt at striking McClellan's right flank failed terribly, exchanging two thousand men for 250. Throughout the night, the "moans of the dying and shrieks of the wounded" could be heard in the Union camp. With Lee amassing his army on McClellan's right, the latter could have moved straight ahead to Richmond, but he seems to have contemplated no such thing. Lee had left behind a remainder of his forces between McClellan and the capital, but merely to distract and deter. It worked.

On May 27, Lee attacked again, breaking the Union lines at Gaines's Mill. Though McClellan was driven back, the Confederates had again taken the worst of it. The same day, Confederates attacked McClellan's forces south of the Chickahominy and were repulsed. McClellan, despite superiority in numbers, having withstood two days of attacks, completely lost his nerve. That night, he decided to abandon the entire campaign and retreat.

"I have lost this battle because my force was too small," McClellan telegraphed Washington. "The government has not sustained this army . . . If I save this army now, I tell you plainly that I owe no thanks to you or to any other persons in Washington. You have done your best to sacrifice this army." An officer in the telegraph office decided to omit the last two lines before relaying the message to Secretary of War Stanton. McClellan's insubordination, elevated to a new level, with his inexplicable abandonment of the entire Peninsula Campaign, would surely have resulted in his removal.

"McClellan, if not always great in the advance, was masterly in retreat," according to one Confederate general. McClellan fell down to Harrison's Landing, the ancestral homeland of the family of President Harrison, where gunboats could protect his forces. McClellan's troops met him there, after winning a decisive battle against Lee at Malvern Hill. Despite this, they were ordered to abandon an impregnable position on the heels of another victory. The Peninsula Campaign, which had begun with such promise, had now ended. No Union soldier would stand as close to Richmond for three years.

"The suspense was dreadful whilst the fight was proceeding near Richmond," Buchanan wrote, feeling "greatly relieved when I learned that General McClellan and our brave army had escaped destruction. His strategy was admirable, but I am at a loss to know why he did not occupy his present position from the beginning. Mystery hangs over the whole affair, though I feel very confident that when all is unraveled McClellan will be justified."

The war was now well into its second year, with a massive loss of life but little indication of how it would end. Lincoln was determined to stay the course. He expressed this in a message to the Union governors, meeting in New York. After an update on recent happenings and his plans going forward, he asserted, "I expect to maintain this contest until successful, or till I die, or am conquered, or my term expires, or Congress or the country forsakes me."

This resoluteness was pulsing through Lincoln as he wrote to Quintin Campbell, a relative of his wife who had just entered West Point but finding it not to his liking, was ready to quit. "Allow me to assure you," the commander-in-chief wrote the cadet, "it is a perfect certainty that you will, very soon, feel better—quite happy—if you only stick to the resolution that you have taken to procure a military education. I am older than you, have felt badly myself, and *know*, what I tell you is true. Adhere to your purpose and you will soon feel as well as you ever did. On the contrary, if you falter and give up, you will lose the power of keeping any resolution, and will regret it all your life. Take the advice of a friend, who, though he never saw you, deeply sympathizes with you, and stick to your purpose."

Three days later, Lincoln issued a call for three hundred thousand volunteers.

CHAPTER 29

The Very Vortex of Hell

Mr. Hay, what is the use of growing old? You learn something of men and things but never until too late to use it.

—WILLIAM SEWARD

Lincoln ~ Fillmore ~ Van Buren

As the long awaited and expensive adventure of General George McClellan drew to an ignominious close, Lincoln began working on a confidential project in the War Department's telegraph office. One morning he sat at a desk and asked Major Eckert for some paper, on which "to write something special." During the first full day, as with each new day he worked at this, Lincoln never filled a complete piece of paper with his writing. When finished for the day, he asked Major Eckert to entrust the work to his care, to be locked up and not shown to anyone. He returned in the morning, a routine he would follow for weeks. Eckert remembered that "Sometimes he would not write more than a line or two, and once I observed that he had put question-marks on the margin of what he had written. He would read over each day all the matter he had previously written and revise it, studying carefully each sentence."

In Buffalo, meanwhile, undeterred by recent disappointments, the leading citizens of the city came together to form the Historical Society. Millard Fillmore, its first president, saved a newspaper article announcing, "the new organization . . . has been formed for the purpose of rescuing from oblivion the past and contemporaneous affairs of Buffalo . . . We shall expect to see a large and interested audience."

On July 1, 1862, at American Hall, Fillmore gave his inaugural address to the new organization. He acknowledged that Buffalo was scarcely older than its oldest living resident, but made clear that the Historical Society's objective was to collect and preserve information for posterity. He noted his own recent research into the origin of the town's name, which could not be positively identified.

"However it may sound to foreign ears, to me it signifies everything which I love and admire in a city, beautiful, clean, healthy, warm in winter [*sic*] and cool in summer; but above all, it is my home, and the home of the friends I love best, where my days have been spent, and my bones shall repose.

"Let our citizens unite heart and hand in building up this society, which, while it does justice to the dead, reflects honor upon the living." To start what he hoped would be a valuable collection, Fillmore donated the last letter ever written by Daniel Webster. But Fillmore was not insensitive to the history being made all around him.

For some months past, he had been especially concerned about the issue of emancipation, collecting a number of articles on the subject. One from the *Buffalo Commercial Advertiser* read, "we see that an African element is interposed between us and our design . . . We hear no more of treason, but much of emancipation and a war against slavery. Regiments march to the battlefield shouting hoarsely, 'the soul of John Brown is marching on' . . . We of the north should make this no more a part of our design, than any other necessary result of war." Another article from the same paper intoned, "Northern fanatics can now see that all our woe has proceeded from their foolishness." But what if such a thing came to pass? Fillmore also saved an editorial from the *World*, calling for an "experiment in practical emancipation." Citing the example of Port Royal, it argued that the purpose should be to demonstrate for the country and its political leaders "a practical demonstration of the capacity of the average mass of the plantation slaves of the south for regulated freedom."

Shortly after launching the Historical Society, Fillmore met a visitor to Buffalo. "He did not hesitate to express his views upon the present state of affairs of our country," the man remembered, while also recalling that Fillmore complained "abolitionists in Congress had undone what the army had done." Fillmore believed Lincoln had done well under the circumstances. But this approval was given with no knowledge of Lincoln's project in the telegraph office.

Lincoln met with a congressional delegation from the border states, who were adamantly opposed to any scheme of emancipation. From the beginning, Lincoln had been incredibly sensitive to the temperature in that region. Once again fears of driving them from the Union were brought up.

Shortly thereafter, Seward and Welles accompanied Lincoln in a carriage to the funeral of Stanton's son. The navy secretary remembered, "He dwelt earnestly on the gravity, importance, and delicacy of the movement, said he had given it much thought and had about come to the conclusion that it was a military necessity absolutely essential for the salvation of the Union, that we must free the slaves or be ourselves subdued." Lincoln said that he had never mentioned it to anyone and wanted their candid views. Seward replied that given the significance, he should like to think it over, but his initial impression was to agree with Lincoln. Welles concurred.

Lincoln became impressed that now was not the right time. Any movement against slavery would look desperate on the heels of so many military reversals. But as the president wrote to his friend Reverdy Johnson, senator from Maryland, "it may as well be understood, once for all, that I shall not surrender this game leaving any available card unplayed."

Despite increasing illness, Martin Van Buren took a deep interest in the movements of the army of the Union. Upon waking from frequent bouts of unconsciousness, Van Buren asked "for the details of military news since his indisposition."

Van Buren was often "insensible and unable to recognize friends or relatives." But during periods of lucidity he "evinced the most lively and patriotic interest in the affairs of the country," said one witness, "and expressed all faith in the ultimate triumph of our arms and cause. He has continually denounced the course of Mr. Buchanan's administration from the first, but has expressed the utmost confidence in that of Mr. Lincoln."

According to the *New York Tribune*, "A few hours before his death he motioned his grand-children to his side, when he bade them a final adieu.

His dying words are said to have been . . . 'there is but one Reliance.'"
The *Albany Evening Journal* reported, "Another pillar of the Republic has
fallen. Another Statesman has departed for the Silent land." The *Milwaukee Morning Sentinel* noted, "He dies in the fullness of years and with a
fame undimmed."

In contrast to the silence in Washington upon John Tyler's death,
Lincoln issued a glowing tribute to the first president he had ever met,
"his honored predecessor." Lincoln ordered that the White House and
non-military buildings be "placed in mourning," and civilian government
functions suspended the following day. As Lincoln wrote, "The grief of
his patriotic friends will measurably be assuaged by the consciousness
that while suffering with disease and seeing his end approaching, his
prayers were for the restoration of the authority of the government of
which he had been head, and for peace and good will among his fellow citizens." Van Buren biographer John Niven put it best: "Van Buren
would have approved the sentiment, one imagines, with a smile. After
all, a crucial election campaign was going on in the Empire State; the
race would be close. The Magician, whenever possible, had always offered
proper respects for the departed with an eye on the election returns."

The funeral at Kinderhook was conducted in a "plain unostentatious
manner most in keeping with the principles of republican institutions."
Reverend Berry of the Dutch Reformed Church held a brief afternoon
ceremony at Lindenwold. "The building was filled to its utmost capacity" with members of the community and many distinguished guests. The
pallbearers who conducted Van Buren to the church were older residents
of the town, the people who had grown up with him and who had made
up his society before, between, and after his time on the world stage.

The church entrance was draped in mourning, "as were also the ceil-
ings, balconies, organ, and altar inside. Over the altar was suspended the
National emblem hung with crape." Reverend Berry's sermon was a call
to action, something Van Buren could not have helped but appreciate.
"Before us lies the lifeless body of one of the Presidents of our Union,"
he said. "We bury him amid such circumstances as never attended the
burial of a President of the people's choice before," he said, in an unmistakable reference to John Tyler. "While we are engaged in these solemn

rites at the very hour an atrocious rebellion is warring for that Union's utter destruction. Shall it succeed? Shall it be said that the life of this Republic was measured only by the life of one of its rulers? Are you ready to lay the Union beside him in his grave?" Will you "pledge to our country now, in the hour of its stupendous danger, what true patriots pledged it at the hour of its birth—our lives, our fortunes, and our sacred honor?"

Lincoln and his cabinet were about to ask just such a pledge of General John Pope, who had been serving in the west. McClellan was asking for "much over rather than under" one hundred thousand troops to reinforce him on the peninsula, something that was impossible. The administration planned to create a new army under Pope and proceed south toward Richmond. Pope assented, on one condition: that McClellan be ordered in advance to "make a vigorous attack on the enemy with his whole force the moment he heard I was engaged." To this they agreed, and to this McClellan would follow with his usual scrupulousness, writing his wife, "Pope will be badly trashed within two days and . . . they will be very glad to turn over the redemption of their affairs to me. I won't take it unless I have full and entire control." Meanwhile, Lee determined to defeat Union forces in northern Virginia before McClellan could rejoin them.

On the peninsula, a team of McClellan's engineers were doing reconnaissance near the James River when a teenaged boy "came dashing out of a deep belt of woods, mounted on a superb charger. The lad at first was somewhat abashed, but soon recovered his presence of mind to such an extent that he repeated questions but few satisfactory answers were received." The engineers learned that his father was John Tyler, "that his mother was at the mansion . . . and sick, and that she had sent him to a neighboring plantation for medicine. The beauty and elegance of the general appearance of both bridle and saddle in use by the youngster, induced the party to make a closer examination. When they found them to be not only mounted with solid silver of the best material, stitched in every part with trappings to correspond, but upon the pommel of the saddle was found a silver plate, bearing the inscription: 'Santa Anna's saddle, presented to General John Tyler by General Winfield Scott.'"

Julia Tyler had seven children, ranging from age sixteen to two, and for the past seven months, had been raising them in the midst of a war and without her husband, and now she was bedridden. Weeks later, she and her six youngest arrived on Staten Island to live with her brother, having sailed from Harrison's Landing (her oldest son, future congressman David Tyler, remained to attend Washington College). True to form, Julia Tyler ran the blockade with five cotton bales, which she was easily able to sell upon her arrival.

———

From the 18th of August until the 26th, General Pope's new Army of Virginia engaged in skirmishes and minor engagements with Lee's Army of Northern Virginia. As the Confederate army converged on Manassas Junction, the frightening realization came over Pope that none of the promised reinforcements would arrive.

On August 30, Lincoln considered a report—prepared by Stanton and signed by Chase, Smith, and Bates—calling for McClellan's resignation. On a ride with Hay, Lincoln said he really believed that McClellan wanted Pope defeated. "The President seemed to think him a little crazy," Hay recalled. They went to bed that night "expecting glad tidings at sunrise."

At eight in the morning, Hay was dressing when the president came into his room. "Well John we are whipped again, I am afraid. The enemy reinforced on Pope and drove back his left wing and he has retired to Centerville where he says he will be able to hold his men." Throughout that day, the wounded straggled into Washington "in large numbers."

The fields near Manassas, for the second time the scene of incredible violence, would bear the scars for years, in the form of "mangled trees, rows of depressions from disinterred graves, the bleached bones of dead horses." One soldier remembered, "War has been designated as Hell, and I assure you that this was the very vortex of Hell."

Yet McClellan, who had left the Army of Virginia to be slaughtered, was beloved by his men, certainly more popular than the administration. For his faults, McClellan made certain that his men were properly provisioned. Upon their return to the capital, twenty to thirty thousand soldiers led a respectful review past McClellan's home. "It is painful to entertain the idea that the country is in the hands of such men," Welles wrote in his diary. "I hope I mistake them."

On a moonlight walk, Seward reflected for Hay on the terrible cost a man pays for acquiring wisdom. "Mr. Hay, what is the use of growing old? You learn something of men and things but never until too late to use it. I have only just now found out what military jealousy is. I have been wishing for some months to go home to my people but could not while our armies were scattered and in danger. The other day I went down to Alexandria and found General McClellan's army landing. I considered our armies united virtually and thought them invincible. I went home and the first news I received was that each had been attacked and each in effect, beaten. It never had occurred to me that any jealousy could prevent these generals from acting for their common fame and the welfare of the country."

Another forward movement was checked. Another slaughter on the fields around Bull Run had gained the Union nothing. In these dark days Lincoln wrote, "The will of God prevails. In great contests each party claims to act in accordance with the will of God. Both *may* be, and one *must* be wrong. God can not be *for*, and *against* the same thing at the same time. In the present civil war it is quite possible that God's purpose is something different from the purpose of either party . . . God wills this contest, and wills that it shall not end yet." God, Lincoln noted, could have prevented the conflict from happening at all. "Yet the contest began. And having begun He could give the final victory to either side any day. Yet the contest proceeds."

CHAPTER 30

Destroy the Rebel Army, If Possible

Washington is full of exciting, vague, and absurd rumors . . . We have information that the Rebels have crossed the Potomac in considerable force, with a view of invading Maryland and pushing on into Pennsylvania. The War Department is bewildered, knows but little, does nothing, proposes nothing.

—GIDEON WELLES

Lincoln

Emboldened by another victory at Manassas, Confederate forces crossed the Potomac singing "Maryland, My Maryland."* Their hopes were manifold: to live off the farms of the North, to "liberate" Maryland and bring her into the Confederacy, to reduce support for the northern war effort, and to help secure foreign recognition for the Confederacy. Lee expected the federal garrison at Harper's Ferry to pursue him, opening up his supply lines to the Shenandoah Valley. When they stayed put, he sent three-fourths of his army under Jackson to dislodge them.

On September 13, Union forces were near Frederick, Maryland, in search of Lee. One private noticed something out of the ordinary: three cigars wrapped in paper, lying on the ground. It was an order from Lee's adjutant-general, detailing the planned movement of his army. Lee, who badly needed time to reunite with Jackson, was in great peril.

McClellan caught up with Confederate forces the following day and fought them for control of three mountain passes. The Confederates had

---

* This Confederate battle hymn remains the state song of Maryland.

lost them by the evening, but had gained another day's delay. The following morning, Jackson forced the largest Union surrender of the entire war, 12,500 troops at Harper's Ferry.

Late that afternoon, McClellan found his adversary near the town of Sharpsburg, west of Antietam Creek. When all of Jackson's men returned, Lee would still have no more than thirty-eight thousand men; McClellan could bring seventy-five thousand to the fight.

At dawn on the 17th, one reporter remembered cannons "reverberating from cloud to mountain and from mountain to cloud . . . a continuous roar, like the unbroken roll of a thunder storm." He was seven miles away.

At first light Union general Joseph Hooker crossed the creek and came down against Lee's left flank. Separated by thirty acres of David Miller's corn, the two forces eventually crashed, with "men firing into each other's faces, the Confederate line breaking, the ground strewn with prostrate forms." In the "sunken road," a trench worn into the ground by wagon use, the reporter witnessed "a ghastly spectacle . . . resolution and energy still lingered in the pallid cheeks, in the set teeth, in the gripping hand" of the dead. "A young lieutenant had fallen while trying to rally his men; his hand was still firmly grasping his sword, and determination was visible in every line of his face." Bodies lay together "in a heap amid the corn rows . . . the broad, green leaves were sprinkled and stained with blood." Thirteen thousand died or were injured in the first four hours. Later that morning, Union forces were thrown against the center of Lee's men. In the late afternoon, Union general Ambrose Burnside finally found and battled his way across a bridge to the south, hitting Lee to the right. As the Confederate army faced annihilation, a division of Jackson's men crashed into Burnside's forces, pushing them back across the bridge. McClellan's delay had allowed Lee to reunite his army. Such were the state of things when the sun set on the bloodiest day of battle in the history of the United States. Among the killed, injured, or missing were 22,700 men, 12,400 Union and 10,300 Confederates.

Lincoln spent the day at the Soldiers' Home,* completing his second draft of the preliminary Emancipation Proclamation. He had resolved to wait for a victory. The carnage at Antietam would have to do.

----

* Lincoln's presidential retreat, now known as "President Lincoln's Cottage," is open to the public, as is the room where he worked on the Emancipation Proclamation.

The next day, McClellan refused to give battle again. McClellan believed that Lee had 120,000 men, though in fact he outnumbered Lee by better than two to one. McClellan had twenty-nine thousand fresh troops that had not been used the first day, two-thirds of Lee's entire force. But the battle was not made. That night, Lee began his retreat toward Virginia. When Lincoln heard the news, he wrote McClellan, "God bless you, and all with you. Destroy the rebel army, if possible."

But McClellan would not give chase. Lee's men, who had sung "Maryland, My Maryland" on the way in, sang "Carry Me Back to Old Virginny" as they left.

Shortly thereafter, representatives from the Woman's Council called on the president. One woman remembered, "Not more ghastly or rigid was his dead face, as he lay in his coffin, than on that never to be forgotten night." His appearance and the way he moved reminded her of a man sleepwalking. He briefly perked up when he learned that two of his guests were from Chicago. "You are not scared by Washington mud, then," he said sitting between them, "for you can beat us all to pieces in that."

The two ladies asked Lincoln for some words of encouragement, but he responded, "I have no word of encouragement to give!" He continued, "The fact is, the people haven't yet made up their minds that we are at war with the South. They haven't buckled down to the determination to fight this war through.

"They think there is a royal road to peace, and that General McClellan is to find it." Furloughs and desertions outnumbered new recruits. Lincoln, who famously stretched for any reason to pardon soldiers, was asked, why not enforce the death penalty for desertion?

Lincoln protested, calling it "unmerciful, barbarous." And the public would never stand for people executed by the dozens, "and they ought not to stand it." Things would have to change a different way. In this Lincoln was correct. Nothing short of total war against the Confederacy could give the Union victory.

❧

On September 22, Stanton was surprised to find himself summoned to a cabinet meeting. In light of managing his massive department, his attendance was not generally required. Lincoln read a story from Artemus Ward, and his cabinet laughed along, Stanton excepted. Lincoln then reached for his stove-pipe hat and withdrew what he called "a little paper of much significance."

In a "graver tone," he said, "Gentlemen, I have, as you are aware, thought a great deal about the relation of this war to slavery; and you all remember that, several weeks ago, I read to you an order I had prepared on this subject, which, on account of objections made by some of you, was not issued. Ever since then, my mind has been much occupied with this subject, and I have thought all along that the time for acting on it might very probably come. I think the time has come now. I wish it were a better time. I wish that we were in a better condition. The action of the army against the rebels has not been quite what I should have liked. But they have been driven out of Maryland, and Pennsylvania is no longer in danger of invasion. When the rebel army was at Frederick, I determined, as soon as it should be driven out of Maryland, to issue a Proclamation of Emancipation such as I thought most likely to be useful. I said nothing to any one; but I made the promise to myself, and," he paused, "to my Maker. The rebel army is now driven out, and I am going to fulfill that promise."

Stanton remembered Lincoln saying that "the question was finally decided, the act and the consequences were his, but that he felt it due to us to make us acquainted with the fact and to invite criticism on the paper which he had prepared." Lincoln told his cabinet that he had made "a vow, a covenant, that if God gave us the victory in the approaching battle, he would consider it an indication of Divine will, and that it was his duty to move forward in the cause of emancipation. It might be thought strange," he acknowledged, but "God had decided this question in favor of the slaves." Lincoln then read his proclamation to the cabinet. Pursuant to his powers as commander-in-chief of the army and navy, to seize the property of the enemy, he would declare, as of "January 1, 1863, all persons held as slaves within any state or designated part of a state, the people whereof shall be in rebellion against the United States, shall be then, thenceforward, and forever free."

Montgomery Blair of Maryland, voice of the border states in the cabinet, worried that the Unionist sentiment in the region would be jeopardized, and that throughout the North partisans would have a new weapon against the administration. Lincoln responded that the first was indeed a great danger, but no greater a danger than inaction, and did not worry about the second. At the end, only Bates and Blair dissented.

After the meeting, there was a gathering hosted by Chase where the guests drank wine "in a glorious humor." Chase laughed, "this was a most wonderful history of an insanity of a class that the world had ever seen. If the slaveholders had stayed in the Union they might have kept the life in their institution for many years to come. That what no party and no public feeling in the north could ever have hoped to touch they had madly placed in the very path of destruction." Hay noted, "They all seemed to feel a sort of new and exhilarated life; they breathed freer; the President's Proclamation had freed them as well as the slaves. They gleefully and merrily called each other and themselves abolitionists, and seemed to enjoy the novel sensation of appropriating that horrible name."

While many celebrated the September 22 issuing of the preliminary Emancipation Proclamation, Lincoln's challenges with McClellan were ongoing. "Are you not over-cautious when you assume that you can not do what the enemy is constantly doing?" Lincoln asked. "Should you not claim to be at least his equal in prowess, and act upon the claim?" When Lee invaded, Lincoln believed he tendered "us an advantage which we should not waive. We should not so operate as to merely drive him away. If we can not beat the enemy where he now is, we never can, he again being within the entrenchments of Richmond." Reading about McClellan's sore and fatigued horses, Lincoln wrote, "Will you pardon me for asking what the horses of your army have done since the battle of Antietam that fatigue anything?"

On October 3, Lincoln, joined by his friend Ward Hill Lamon, who had come with him to the White House from Illinois, surveyed the army, which he referred to as "General McClellan's bodyguard." While traveling from one corps to another, Lincoln, reflecting on the enormous loss of life in a war clearly far from finished, asked Lamon to sing one of his "little sad songs." Lamon chose his friend's favorite, "Twenty Years Ago":

I've wandered to the village, Tom; I've sat beneath the tree
Upon the schoolhouse play-ground, that sheltered you and me:
But none were left to greet me, Tom, and few were left to know
Who played with us upon the green, some twenty years ago.

CHAPTER 31

A Continuation of War by Other Means

I feel it to be my duty to put down this rabid abolition party at the north, which in my opinion is not only aiding the rebels to destroy the Union, but is violating the Constitution by its attempts to abolish slavery, and to establish a military despotism over the loyal states.

—MILLARD FILLMORE

Lincoln - Fillmore - Buchanan

It has been famously observed that war is a continuation of politics by other means. The converse is also true. In a democratic society, it is politics, itself a sublimation of war, that ultimately determines the initiation, objectives, and termination of armed conflict. Lincoln relied heavily on Republican support in Congress. He also depended on Union governors and state legislatures for the raising and delivery of troops. Now, in state and federal elections throughout the country, the public would render a verdict on the policies of the administration. The results reflected the public's unease with a costly, bloody, and inconclusive war.

On October 16, 1862, John Nicolay wrote, "We are all blue here today on account of the election news. We have lost almost everything in Pennsylvania, Ohio and Indiana. We have not yet heard from Iowa, but expect that that too will be swallowed up by the general drift. It never rains but it pours." Elections in different states were held on different days. As one after another brought bad news for the administration, all eyes turned toward the November 4 contest in New York. Democrat Horatio Seymour, the former governor, was seeking his old office on a platform hostile to the administration, opposed to the Emancipation Proclamation, or any war fought on the basis of limiting slavery, calling Lincoln's expansion of the war objective "a violation of public faith," while condemning the administration's "criminal" acts against civil liberties.

Martin Van Buren had died before this critical election in his home state. Would he have maintained his steadfast support of Lincoln? Would he have fallen out with him over the Emancipation Proclamation? The answers can only be speculated. His son and longtime political ally, John Van Buren, gave a speech at Cooper Institute supporting Seymour.

What of the other former president from New York? Millard Fill-more, too, had begun the war as a strong supporter of Lincoln. But he had long been concerned about what he perceived as threats to civil liberties, and even more opposed to broadening the war aims. While Fillmore kept his views out of the newspapers, he gave the Seymour effort his considerable support. Seymour prevailed with 306,649, to 295,897 for the Republican.

A professor from Columbia wrote to Fillmore, noting that "from the vote of Erie County, that your influence, in the late election, was given for Governor Seymour." Later that winter, Fillmore responded to a former Whig who had voted for Lincoln, asking for political advice in the upcoming New York state elections for the legislature and other statewide offices. Intending "nothing for publication," Fillmore wrote, "I voted the Democratic ticket at our last election, not because I was a Democrat but because I was not a Republican. I feel it to be my duty," he said, to put down "this rabid abolition party at the north, which in my opinion is not only aiding the rebels to destroy the Union, but is violating the Constitution by its attempts to abolish slavery, and to establish a military despotism over the loyal states. I care not for names—they have no charm for me. I go for the Union and Constitutional freedom, and oppose all those who violate it."

When the elections of 1862 were said and done, the Democrats gained thirty-four seats in the US House of Representatives. Democrats won control of the state legislatures in New Jersey, Indiana, and even Lincoln's Illinois, meaning a new Democrat would be joining the US Senate from all three states in 1863.

On November 5, a messenger called at the tent of General McClellan. With him was General Ambrose Burnside. McClellan was removed as commander of the Army of the Potomac, with Burnside to assume his place. When Lee heard the news, he said, "We always understood each other so well. I fear they may continue to make these changes till they find some one whom I don't understand." Burnside would waste no time making a move against Richmond. His plan would take the Army of the Potomac across the Rappahannock River near Fredericksburg, and from there to the capital of the Confederacy.

The Bank of Pottsville, Pennsylvania, was having a problem with its five-dollar notes. The picture of James Buchanan in one corner led to their chronic defacement. Representative drawings included red ink over his eyes, a rope around his neck, and the word "Judas" on his forehead. Hundreds of bills evinced the creative backlash of their holders.

Cornell Jewett of the Colorado Territory had traveled as a private citizen throughout Europe to advocate for the Union cause. Upon his return he paid a visit to Wheatland. Buchanan told him of his plans to someday publish a "vindication before the world, placing his loyalty, integrity of purpose and public acts beyond question . . . With my hand upon my heart, before the Almighty, I acquit myself of any wrong to my country or to the Union."

Jewett would write, "I will never forget . . . how forcibly I was reminded of the ingratitude of Republics, the severe, unjust criticisms of the mass, with the after all only reliable tribunal, a clear conscience, under sense of responsibility to the Almighty." Jewett wrote of his visit to the *New York Tribune*. The paper printed his letter, which it followed with a severe editorial, arguing "Blacker than that of Arnold, of Judas, is the treason of James Buchanan, and fearful must be the verdict which history must pronounce on the pusillanimous, perfidious close of his inglorious public career."

Jeremiah Black, his former secretary of state, encouraged Buchanan in his temporary silence, saying he had "no cause for low spirits. Your fame will be taken care of by history; though the passions or the interests of the hour may cloud it for the present." Buchanan was right to wait for peace to publicly make his case.

Lincoln's success, Buchanan believed, would vindicate him, as the president was simply following his own policies. "As to my course since the wicked bombardment of Fort Sumter—it is but a regular consequence of my whole policy towards the seceding states. They had been informed over and over again by me what would be the consequence of an attack upon it. They chose to commence civil war, and Mr. Lincoln had no alternative but to defend the country against dismemberment. I certainly should have done the same thing had they begun the war in my time; and this they well knew."

But in the fall of 1862 came a public assault from the former general-in-chief of the army, Winfield Scott. With that, all the ex-president's considerations of waiting were temporarily set aside. Buchanan wrote to the *National Intelligencer* to dispute Scott's charges. First, he pointed out that no troops were available to fortify the nine garrisons that Scott proposed, quoting Scott's report of October 30, 1860. To secure Washington during the inauguration, Buchanan could only muster 650 men, some of them engineers and cadets from West Point. To garrison these nine forts even his army of sixteen thousand would not have been enough. As for Fort Pickens, he pointed out that a Florida senator offered him assurance that no attack would be made if the fort were not reinforced. With the Peace Conference about to meet, Buchanan felt it was a worthy gamble. The fort, he pointed out, never fell to the Confederates. He asserted that he had always refused to surrender Fort Sumter, and that he had dispatched the *Star of the West* for the purpose of sustaining it one day after Scott requested it.

The *Philadelphia Press* reported that Buchanan should discontinue his efforts at rehabilitation. "He had better burn his sheets and say no more. His last defense has only dragged him deeper in the slough of shame."

The *Albany Evening Journal* laughed, "James Buchanan makes another pitiable exhibition of himself in the papers. Is there no one to protect him against his own folly?" As for Buchanan's argument that none of the national arsenal had been strategically moved by his secessionist secretary of war, the journal asked, "But what will the OPF [Old Public Functionary] say to the fact that the latter confessed the larceny and bragged of it?"

Buchanan seemed satisfied, particularly with the "letters and papers" he received indicating approval of his conduct against Scott. But it should have been increasingly apparent that the public was not now, nor would they ever be, receptive to his defenses.

CHAPTER 32

A Storm of Lead

What will the civilized world say when they read these words sent forth by the President of the United States . . . they will say justly that a crime so fearful as that proposed was never before contemplated by any nation, civilized or barborous.

—FRANKLIN PIERCE

Lincoln

On December 11, 1862, at 3:00 a.m., Union engineers went quickly to work building bridges across the icy Rappahannock near Fredericksburg. When daylight came, they found themselves under fire and fled, their work incomplete. The response by General Burnside, now in charge of the Army of the Potomac, came in eight thousand pieces, courtesy of 150 cannon, which Longstreet observed was "a perfect storm of shot and shell, crushing the houses with a cyclone of fiery metal." The city burst into flames in several places, and "solid shot rained like hail." When the engineers resumed their work, the sniper fire was renewed, and Burnside sent soldiers across in pontoon boats to clear the area. He and his men marched into Fredericksburg the next day.

The Confederates, now sixty-five thousand strong, were expecting him, and for more than twenty days had been preparing their welcome. Watching one hundred thousand men under Burnside prepare for combat, Jackson "grimly awaited the onslaught."

To the Confederate left was Marye's Heights, and at its base a sunken road, at the end of which was a shoulder-high wall. Behind this wall Longstreet placed twenty-five hundred men. The night before, at least some of Burnside's commanders believed he was making a terrible mistake. "If you make the attack as contemplated," General Hawkins told him, "it will be the greatest slaughter of the war; there isn't infantry enough in our whole army to carry those heights if they are well defended." A colonel advised, "The carrying out of your plan will be murder, not warfare." Burnside bristled at their eagerness to throw cold water on his plans, citing another general who had predicted victory in forty-eight hours. The next morning the attack on the raised and heavily fortified position began.

As the Union forces approached, "a storm of lead was poured into their advancing ranks and they were swept from the field like chaff before the wind. A cloud of smoke" concealed the scene for a moment when it was finished. Those who survived sought refuge in a railroad cut, only to be bombarded by artillery. Moments later came another attempt with the same results, as men would "melt like snow coming down on warm ground," according to a Union general. By the second charge, Longstreet noted, "the field in front ... was thickly strewn with the dead and dying Federals, but again they formed with desperate courage and renewed the attack and were driven off. At each attack the slaughter was so great that by the time the third attack was repulsed, the ground was so thickly strewn with dead that the bodies seriously impeded the approach of the Federals." The fourth wave finally saw a single man make it within one hundred feet of the Confederate position before being killed. They came a fifth time and a sixth time with the same results, "leaving the battlefield literally heaped with the bodies of their dead ... fallen like the steady dripping of rain from the eaves of a house," piled as high as three bodies deep in some places. The temperature dropped to zero overnight, with many wounded on the field dying of cold, freezing the bodies to the ground. For thirty minutes that evening the aurora borealis appeared in the sky above Fredericksburg, one of the southernmost instances in history of the northern lights. The battle was not renewed the following day, and finally on the 15th Burnside withdrew from Fredericksburg and back across the Rappahannock. It was such a tragic irony; Burnside's aggression might well have resulted in the taking of Richmond the previous year, or the destruction of Lee at Antietam, but McClellan's caution at Fredericksburg would have saved countless lives from a pointless and sudden end. The cover of *Harper's*

Weekly featured a cartoon of Columbia, the personification of America, commanding Lincoln and Stanton to explain to her, "Where are my 15,000 sons—murdered at Fredericksburg?" Lincoln was devastated by the news of yet another Union defeat. "Oh, if there is a man out of hell that suffers more than I do, I pity him!"

Martin Van Buren as president. Founder of the first statewide political machine and the national Democratic Party, this son of a tavern keeper ascended to the nation's highest office before the first national economic crisis cost him re-election.

LIBRARY OF CONGRESS

THE BUFFALO HUNT.

In 1848, Van Buren agreed to run as a Free Soil candidate for president, committed to the Wilmot Proviso. Here he pushes aside Lewis Cass and Zachary Taylor, his opponents.

LIBRARY OF CONGRESS

John Tyler as president. The first to ascend to the office, Tyler found himself bitterly at odds with the Whig Party. He would doggedly pursue the annexation of the Republic of Texas, leaving a legacy of challenge and opportunity for his successors.
LIBRARY OF CONGRESS

Congressman Abraham Lincoln, Whig of Illinois. Lincoln opposed the war in Mexico and the extension of slavery into the new territory. His bill to emancipate the slaves in Washington went nowhere.
LIBRARY OF CONGRESS

Henry Clay addresses the Senate on his proposals to diffuse a crisis that had brought America to the brink of civil war. Presiding in his role as vice president is Millard Fillmore, who will soon inherit the presidency and play the pivotal role in passing the Compromise of 1850.

Millard Fillmore, desperately poor and poorly educated, committed himself to overcoming his circumstances.

In the first days of the Civil War, Fillmore vigorously supported President Lincoln, raising a home guard unit and serving as its commander.

Franklin Pierce's career seemed limitless when his wife convinced him to leave the public stage. After service as a general in Mexico, Pierce returned to his quiet retirement. In 1852, a divided Democratic Party chose him as its nominee, sending him to the presidency.
LIBRARY OF CONGRESS

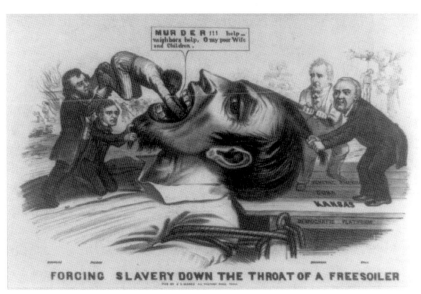

The Kansas-Nebraska Act, written by Senator Stephen Douglas and championed by President Pierce, opened vast new territory to the possibility of slavery and re-opened the fires that had been held in check since the Compromise of 1850.
LIBRARY OF CONGRESS

James Buchanan, perhaps the most experienced man to serve as president, surrounded himself with a similarly credentialed cabinet. When faced with an unprecedented crisis, Buchanan found himself surrounded by secessionists and beset by others who wanted him to take a more aggressive approach.

Abraham Lincoln, the surprise nominee of a new political party, had prevailed despite the efforts of five former presidents to stop him.

MAKING OF AMERICA, THE UNIVERSITY OF
MICHIGAN UNIVERSITY LIBRARY

As the nation slid toward civil war,
many believed the ex-presidents
should work together to arrange a
settlement. This *Vanity Fair* cartoon
mocks the idea, charging that the
presidents who caused the crisis
could do little to solve it. Ultimately,
Van Buren would thwart Pierce's
attempts to convene a meeting.

To win re-election in 1864, a feat
that had eluded his predecessors
for twenty-two years, Lincoln would
need to defeat his former commanding general, George McClellan.
Lincoln's triumph, over the opposition of three former presidents,
effectively sealed the fate of the
Confederacy.

LIBRARY OF CONGRESS

CHAPTER 33

If My Name Ever Goes into History, It Will Be for This Act

The last proclamation of the president caps the climax of folly and wickedness.

—FRANKLIN PIERCE

Lincoln ~ Pierce ~ Fillmore

As the dreadful year of 1862 drew to a close, Union efforts in the west focused on Vicksburg, Mississippi. That critical city occupied high ground above the Mississippi River. For as long as Vicksburg remained in Confederate hands, the Union could not control the great waterway. From Vicksburg the railroad ran east, connecting other railroads leading to every southern state. Across the river a railroad ran west to Shreveport, Louisiana. Vicksburg was the only junction connecting every part of the Confederacy.

"Vicksburg is the key," Lincoln said. "The war can never be brought to a close until the key is in our pocket." Jefferson Davis called Vicksburg "the nail head that holds the South's two halves together."

Ulysses Grant was determined to have it. Grant, now the highest-ranking general in the west, was discouraged by the elections of 1862. Northern enlistments had dried up, and now the Union resorted to the draft. Grant resolved, "There was nothing left to be done but to go forward to a decisive victory." But the path to Vicksburg, over land and water, was heavily fortified and protected, and filled with dangers, natural and otherwise.

The first day of 1863 brought with it, like every year, a levee at the White House. When it was done came the important business of the day. After Antietam, Lincoln had announced that he would issue the Emancipation Proclamation on January 1. Now that time had arrived. The Proclamation was brought to Lincoln on a scroll by Seward and his son Frederick, who served as his aide at the State Department. Lincoln dipped his pen in ink, but paused as he prepared to sign and dropped the pen. After a moment, Lincoln again picked up the pen, but hesitated and dropped it again. Looking at Seward, he said, "I have been shaking hands since nine o'clock this morning and my right arm is almost paralyzed. If my name ever goes into history it will be for this act, and my whole soul is in it. If my hand trembles when I sign the Proclamation, all who examine the document hereafter will say, 'He hesitated.'" Lincoln gripped the pen a third time and wrote "Abraham Lincoln" at the end. Looking up and smiling, he said, "That will do!"

In Beaufort, South Carolina, controlled by the Union forces after the landing at Port Royal, three thousand slaves arrived to hear a reading. They were treated to a fine barbecue and waited on by Union soldiers. For more than a year the emancipation experiment had thrived, as they demonstrated their ability to work the plantations and sustain themselves and one another. Even so, their legal status had been in doubt. But from a platform the Emancipation Proclamation was now read. The American flag was waved from the stage, by a man who recognized that "now for the first time, it meant anything to these people." The now former slaves in the audience spontaneously broke into song:

> My country 'tis of thee,
> Sweet land of liberty,
> Of thee I sing!

Franklin Pierce was livid. "The last proclamation of the president caps the climax of folly and wickedness . . . the most obvious dictates of humanity, honor, and common honesty, to say nothing of patriotism, commands the withdrawal of support promptly and irrevocably," he wrote his former law partner.

"Mr. Lincoln has been and is to what his limited ability and narrow intelligence [allow] their willing instrument for all the woe which has thus far been brought upon the country and for all the degradation, all the atrocity, all the desolation and ruin which is only too palpably before us."

Pierce argued that the Constitution had been "deliberately violated and defied by the national executive sworn to maintain it," that "five hundred thousand men have been induced to take their places in the ranks of the Army under false pretences," and "one hundred thousand of them at least have poured out their life and blood for the consummation of an object to which they never did give and never could have given their approbation.

"All of this would have been sufficiently replete with a degree of wrong, disgrace, and honor [*sic*] which admits of no expression. But what will the world say of a proclamation, emanating from the President of the United States, not only in defiance of the fundamental law of the country for the upholding of which he ought to have been willing to pour his own blood, but in defiance of all law human and Divine which invites the black race in six entire states and parts of several others to use and with all the barbaric features ... slay and devastate without regard to age or sex ... the homes of the descendants of men whose fathers fought with our fathers the battles of the Revolution, and whose fathers with our fathers formed and adopted the Constitution ... the women and children brutally violated and slaughtered shall be white women and children.

"What will the civilized world say when they read these words sent forth by the President of the United States ... they will say justly that a crime so fearful as that proposed was never before contemplated by any nation, civilized or barbarous.

"If it be not too late for the people of the United States to utter a voice which shall terrify duplicity and overcome fanaticism—if it be not too late to rescue the Republic from ruin financially and politically—is it too late to stay the restless march of barbarism, to save such remnants of honor as may warrant as to claim and deserve a place among the civilized peoples of the earth.

"But I will say no more now," Pierce concluded. "My heart is sick of the contemplation."

Millard Fillmore was similarly incensed, sending Pierce an article from the *Commercial Advertiser* critical of Lincoln's Proclamation. Pierce responded with thanks, arguing, "If this war is prosecuted to abolish slavery . . . what possible justification could be argued for it? A war prosecuted for these objects is itself treason.

"If Mr. Lincoln had decided at the outset that he was" to fight a war on this basis, "who would have sprung to arms for such objects?" He encouraged Fillmore to "continue to deliver your heavy blows, thick and fast" against these and all unconstitutional measures.

Had Lincoln gone too far? Not far enough? Had he acted rashly? Had he waited too long? The *Springfield Republican* may have said it best. "The President's action is timely—neither too soon nor too late. It is thorough—neither defeating itself by halfway measures nor by passionate excess. It is just and magnanimous—doing no wrong to any loyal man, and offering no exasperation to the disloyal. It is practical and effective—attempting neither too little nor too much. And it will be sustained by the great mass of loyal people, north and south; and thus, by the courage and prudence of the President, the greatest social and political revolution of the age will be triumphantly carried through the midst of a civil war."

The fears that the army would "disintegrate," in McClellan's words, over the freeing of slaves were wildly exaggerated, but not without foundation. Many of those serving had signed up to fight for the Union, and others, including General William Sherman, were supportive of or at least ambivalent toward slavery. Lincoln was prepared to respond generously toward those who protested. One of these was Major Alexander Montgomery, dismissed for allegedly saying that Lincoln "ought to have his damned black heart cut out." Lincoln noted that his dismissal "is doing the Union cause great harm in his neighborhood and country . . . he is a man of character, did good service in raising troops for us last fall, and still declares for the Union and his wish to fight for it." If upon further inquiry Montgomery still wished to fight for the Union, Lincoln asked that he be restored.

General Burnside followed Fredericksburg with an aborted march against Lee, called off due to the weather. His subordinate generals complained loudly of his leadership, and ultimately he was replaced as head of the Army of the Potomac. "Is it not strange that among a population so numerous and so intelligent and enterprising as ours, the war has not yet produced one great General?" Buchanan asked. "McClellan is best among them . . . During the French Revolution there sprang up, often from the ranks, Generals of the first order, possessing dash and strategy and capable of conducting a war of invasion in the most efficient manner."

Lincoln wrote to Burnside's replacement, Joseph Hooker, letting him know that he would be keeping a close watch on him. Lincoln liked that he was "brave and skillful," free of politics, confident, "a valuable, if not indispensable quality," ambitious, "which, within reasonable bounds, does good rather than harm." But Lincoln also accused him of undermining Burnside, and thus "did a great wrong to the country." He also said that he found credible rumors of Hooker saying that the army and country need a dictator. Lincoln reminded him, "Only those generals who gain successes, can set up dictators. What I now ask of you is military success, and I will risk the dictatorship." He closed with encouragement. "And now, beware of rashness. Beware of rashness, but with energy, and sleepless vigilance, go forward, and give us victories."

—⁘—

As the Army of the Potomac witnessed another leadership change, so did the tiny home guard unit known as the Union Continentals of Buffalo. The troops expressed their "high sense of the valuable and efficient services rendered by Captain Fillmore during his term of office, to put on record our appreciation of that . . . his knowledge of the duties of a soldier, his patience and perseverance as a military instructor, the great interest which he has evinced in forming from men of character and position in this community a body of soldiers, trained and disciplined for service in the preservation of order and the defense of the Union," praising his "esprit de corps." But Fillmore was not leaving civic life. He agreed to allow his name to be used as an incorporator of a hospital for invalid soldiers. He would donate personally, he said, but he had "exhausted my limited means, and I am not in the way of earning more."

Shortly thereafter, in the midst of a Civil War, Buffalo opened its Fine Arts Academy, one of the first art museums in the United States. The *Commercial Advertiser* noted that it "has taken its place among the recognized institutions of the city. The collection of paintings there grouped is a very superior one—indeed, a prominent New York artist who recently examined the pictures declared that it was rare to find as choice a collection even in the metropolis . . . . An hour or two can hardly be so pleasantly and profitably spent as in the art gallery. The very atmosphere of the place is refining." In the midst of so much brutality, the people of Buffalo would never lose sight of what was good about life.

Even in the most refined quarters the war was never far from the home front. A soldier from Buffalo in the 119th New York Volunteers wrote from Baton Rouge, "How much I would like to be with you," he said. "I feel now as if home and dear Buffalo would suit me very well, could I but be there. I have traveled in this direction long enough to suit me for a short period of time, at least, and I would be perfectly willing, as far as my own pleasure is concerned, to quit the sunny south, and pass the remainder of my days in peace up north."

On March 26, 1863, Lincoln wrote to Andrew Johnson after hearing of his thoughts about raising a black regiment. Johnson, the only senator to remain while his state seceded, was now serving as the military governor of Tennessee, over the parts occupied by Union forces. "In my opinion the country now needs no specific thing so much as some man of your ability, and position, to go to this work . . . The colored population is the great *available* and yet *unavailed* of force for restoring the Union. The bare sight of fifty thousand armed, and drilled black soldiers on the banks of the Mississippi would end the rebellion at once."

As Lincoln worked toward arming former slaves, the rest of the country was still processing the Emancipation Proclamation. Democrats saw a tremendous opportunity to capitalize on the fallout. Granite State voters would have the first word. One newspaper reported, "The coming state election in New Hampshire will be severely contested by the peace Democrats. Franklin Pierce, the Ex President, is the manager of the campaign, descending to the minutia of a town and district canvass. He is outspoken in his opposition to the war . . . The Republicans are certain, however, of carrying the state, if we have any military success to speak of before the election."

There would be no military victories before the election, with opposing armies camped across the Rappahannock from one another. But New Hampshire was unequivocal all the same. As the *New York Times* reported, "The people of that state are not willing to be misunderstood on the subject. They have elected a Republican member of Congress in every district, and a strong Republican majority in the legislature," which would in turn select a Republican governor. "It indicates . . . a firm and settled purpose to stand by the administration in its prosecution of the war."

CHAPTER 34

We Are Ruined

I would be very happy to oblige you, if my passes were respected; but the fact is, sir, I have, within the past two years given passes to 250,000 men to go to Richmond, and not one has got there yet.
—ABRAHAM LINCOLN, TO A MAN REQUESTING A PASS TO RICHMOND

Lincoln – Fillmore

It was daybreak on April 29, 1863. The peace that had existed throughout the winter and early spring was suddenly at an end when Hooker, taking advantage of a heavy fog, moved the Army of the Potomac across the Rappahannock. For two days, the Confederates retained their strong defenses around Fredericksburg, where they had been since December. After two disasters at Bull Run, the failed Peninsula Campaign, and the earlier slaughter of Fredericksburg, this moment seemed to be a great chance for a Union victory. It was the largest mismatch on any Civil War battlefield, 130,000 to sixty thousand, and one of Hooker's generals believed his chances of ending the war were 90 percent. But this conflict would prove the worth of military strategy and leadership, and place its victors in the pantheon of military history. Though terribly outnumbered, Lee divided his forces, leaving a contingent in Fredericksburg to tie down Union forces of a far greater number. Lee then took the initiative, attacking Hooker's superior numbers.

On May 1, Jackson beat back an advance detachment under Hooker and took control of the highest ground for miles at Zoan Church. Hooker withdrew to the simple country crossroad that gave the battle its grandiose name, near the isolated house of the Chancellor family.

That evening, Lee, Jackson, and Longstreet sat beneath a pine tree and rewrote the laws of war. The next morning, Lee divided his forces once again, giving Jackson twenty-five thousand men. Jackson led them on a long, circuitous western route, around the Union right flank, using the heavily wooded area to screen his movements. The march took nearly the entire day. At dusk, Jackson's men "swarmed out of the woods," a quarter of a mile in front of Union lines. For a half hour Jackson "had the Army of the Potomac at his mercy," until artillery fire sent them back into the woods.

That night, Jackson rode through the forest to plot out a second attack. Riding near his lines, a group of his own sentries fired at him, killing two of the men accompanying him and shooting the general twice in his left arm and through his right hand. Carried to the Chancellor house after midnight, Jackson had his left arm amputated and the ball removed from his right hand. Lee, horrified, delivered a note wishing he could have been wounded in his stead.

Jackson had lost his left arm; Lee believed that he was losing his right. Jackson would never fully recover, dying from pneumonia before the month was out. The morning after his injury, the Union line was broken. Against the overwhelming odds, Chancellorsville had been a complete Confederate victory. Jackson's attack, his last, had all but sealed its outcome.

———

It was late in the Telegraph Office when the news came in. "My God! Stanton," Lincoln said, "our cause is lost! We are ruined—we are ruined; and such a fearful loss of life. My God! This is more than I can endure." Lincoln stood up, "trembling visibly, his face of ghastly hue, the perspiration standing out in big spots on his brow." Putting on his coat and hat, he paced back and forth for five minutes. "If I am not about early tomorrow," Lincoln said, "do not send for me, nor allow anyone to disturb me. Defeated again, and so many of our noble countrymen killed. What will the people say?"

He returned to the White House to greet visitors still holding the telegram. "The sight of his face and figure was frightful," remembered one.

Lincoln "seemed stricken with death," and nearly tottered as he found his way to a chair. His complexion blended into the wall behind him, "not pale, not even sallow, but gray, like ashes." Handing the telegram to one of his guests, he asked, "What will the country say? Oh, what will the country say?" Lincoln's last visitors departed at 9:00 p.m. The president walked back and forth across the room the rest of the night. His secretary left at 3:00 a.m. Arriving back at the office at 8:00 a.m., he found Lincoln breakfasting by himself. He had not left the room. But his secretary noticed a "cheery, hopeful morning light on his face instead of the funeral battle cloud of Chancellorsville." Next to him he had written instructions urging Hooker to renew the fight again.

On May 16, Millard Fillmore wrote to Lincoln on behalf of his nephew, recently a first lieutenant serving in South Carolina, but who had been dismissed "for alleged intemperance and inefficiency."

"If I believed the charges true," Fillmore wrote, "I should not utter a word of complaint, but commend the act." His nephew, however, had presented him with a letter from his company commander refuting the charges. He asked Lincoln for a court of inquiry. Fillmore asked "as a matter of justice that he may have an opportunity to show his innocence."

Lincoln forwarded the letter to the judge advocate general, asking him to "please examine and report upon this case. The young man is nephew of Ex. President Fillmore, who writes the within letter."

Ambrose Burnside, shifted to command the Department of the Ohio, would now trouble the administration again. Pursuant to Lincoln's expanded order suspending habeas corpus, the general announced that anyone committing "express or implied treason" would be tried in a military court with execution or exile as possible punishments. Clement Vallandigham, Ohio congressman and the leader of the anti-war Democrats, accepted this invitation, making a speech attacking "King Lincoln" for freeing blacks and putting whites into slavery. He was promptly arrested and convicted under Burnside's order for "disloyal sentiments" calculated to weaken the government's war effort.

Welles recorded, "It was an error on the part of Burnside. All regretted the arrest, but, having been made, every one wished he had been sent over the lines to the Rebels with whom he sympathizes." Lincoln came under withering criticism; it was not just a rallying point for Democrats, but also from friendly quarters. The president ultimately commuted Vallandigham's sentence to exile in the Confederacy.

Lincoln defended the action as best he could, in his response to the "Albany Resolutions," adopted by a meeting of prominent members of that community, including Erastus Corning. This group was strongly pro-Union and supportive of the war, but had real concerns about civil liberties. Vallandigham's "arrest was made because he was laboring, with some effect, to prevent the raising of troops, to encourage desertions from the army, and to leave the rebellion without an adequate military force to suppress it. He was not arrested because he was damaging the political prospects of the administration, or the personal interests of the commanding general; but because he was damaging the army, upon the existence, and vigor of which, the life of the nation depends. He was warring upon the military; and this gave the military constitutional jurisdiction to lay hands upon him. If Mr. Vallandigham was not damaging the military power of the country, then his arrest was made on mistake of fact, which I would be glad to correct, on reasonably satisfactory evidence."

Ohio Democrats, eager to capitalize on the fallout, nominated Vallandigham for governor.

CHAPTER 35

The Brave Men, Living and Dead

Lancaster is in a state of agitation and alarm.

—James Buchanan

Lincoln ~ Buchanan

After gathering his forces, confronting heavily armed Confederates and swollen rivers, General Ulysses S. Grant had finally fought his way to Vicksburg. That mighty city and the Mississippi stood between him and his supply lines. "But," he said, "I was on dry ground on the same side of the river with the enemy. All the campaigns, labors, hardships, and exposures, from the month of December previous to this time, that had been made and endured, were for the accomplishment of this one object."

Grant's men had won five battles, including the capture of Jackson, the state capital, took control of four hundred miles of the Mississippi River, survived constant skirmishing, and had traversed an average of 180 miles to reunite at this place. The city was too powerful to attack head on, a lesson Grant initially learned the hard way. Instead, he and his forces dug in for a siege. Vicksburg would not fall until the city ran out of food.

Grant thought his greatest concern was a Confederate effort to lift the siege, but in fact, he had completely lost support in Congress, with persistent calls for his removal, including from his longtime friend and sponsor. But Grant had the confidence of the one man who mattered. A senator angrily told Lincoln that he was "the father of every military blunder that has been made during the war. You are on your road to hell, sir . . . and you are not a mile off this minute." Lincoln asked, "Senator, that is just about the distance from here to the Capitol, is it not?" Lincoln would stick by his general.

As the Union gained ground in the west, they would find themselves under an unprecedented threat in the east.

As the critical summer of 1863 began, James Buchanan noted that his life was "tranquil and monotonous," his "evenings are rather solitary," and that he was resigned "to the privations inseparable from old age." Soon the conflict that began during his presidency would find its way almost to his doorstep.

"Something of a panic pervades the city," Welles noted from Washington on June 15. "Singular rumors reach us of Rebel advances into Maryland. It is said they have reached Hagerstown, and some of them have penetrated as far as Chambersburg in Pennsylvania." There were no straight answers to be found from the War Department. Lincoln made an emergency call for one hundred thousand volunteers to be raised in Maryland, Pennsylvania, New York, Ohio, and West Virginia.

On June 26 Buchanan wrote to Harriet, his niece, "Lancaster is in a state of agitation and alarm," ordering her to remain at her Uncle Edward's and not to come home. Confederates marched on Wrightsville, intending to head east, putting them within miles of Wheatland. Union soldiers burned the bridge, marking the easternmost advance of the Confederate army. "They were within eleven miles of us," Buchanan wrote in horror.

General George Meade of the Army of the Potomac was asleep when destiny, in the form of a messenger, arrived at his tent. Seeing the War Department officer in front of him, Meade initially thought he was going to be arrested, though he was not sure for what. Instead, he was put in command. Meade attempted to protest. He was not familiar enough with the army and its positions. The men would prefer General Reynolds, a good friend of his. But the Army of the Potomac, which had passed through the hands of McDowell, McClellan, Burnside, and Hooker, was now his. His lofty task was to locate General Lee and defeat him.

The land around Gettysburg, Pennsylvania, can be said to have chosen its combatants rather than the reverse. It was a pastoral, tranquil town, as evidenced by the place-names in and around it that would later become famous: the peach orchard, the wheat field, Little

Round Top, Culp's Hill, Spangler's Spring. Neither army had intended to make their stand here. But throughout the day on June 30, unbeknownst to either, Union and Confederate forces were hurtling toward one another. When the sun set, the extreme left of Meade's line was several miles south of Gettysburg; the extreme right was thirty miles away in Maryland.

On the first of July, detachments of Confederate and Union forces encountered each other west of the city, quite inadvertently, and began fighting around 6:00 a.m. Each would send for reinforcements, until all of the fighting forces on both sides converged. The first reinforcements arrived around noon. Union forces were pushed back, beating a bloody withdrawal through the streets of Gettysburg and to the south. They concentrated on Cemetery Hill, final resting place of the town's founders.

General Lee arrived in the afternoon on the first day, establishing his base on Seminary Ridge, to the west of Union forces. He ordered General Ewell to attack Cemetery Hill "if practicable." Ewell decided to wait for reinforcements, despite superiority of numbers. Confederate chances of taking Cemetery Hill would never be greater.

Standing on the summit of Seminary Ridge, surveying the Union forces with Lee, Longstreet remarked that "All we have to do is throw our army around by their left, and we shall interpose between the Federal army and Washington." They could find a strong defensive position and wait for the attack.

"No," Lee responded, "the enemy is there, and I am going to attack him there."

Longstreet pushed back, arguing that his plan would give them control of the roads to Washington and Baltimore.

But Lee was firm. "They are in position, and I am going to whip them or they are going to whip me."

Meade arrived after midnight, inspecting his Union lines by the light of a full moon. Throughout the night, troops continued to arrive at Gettysburg.

At the beginning of July 2, Union forces were arrayed along the high ground south of town in a fishhook formation, which curved north and east before coming back south.

General Daniel Sickles, a former congressman who had murdered his wife's lover in front of the White House,* was ordered to hold a position on the Union left flank, near the base of the hook. Sickles moved his men west to a peach orchard, which he believed would be more defensible. In so doing, however, he created a bulge in the Union line and invited the thrust of the Confederate attack, which would ultimately cost him his right leg. Meade was forced to pour in men behind Sickles to prevent the line from being broken.

Little Round Top, a hill on the southernmost part of the battlefield, south of the Union lines, was undefended. Noticing Confederates about to seize this critical position, one Union general frantically searched for men to contest them. He succeeded without a second to lose, and the two forces met at the summit. Hundreds of Union soldiers were gunned down in their charge, and soon they had exhausted their sixty bullets. Colonel Joshua Chamberlain, formerly a rhetoric professor from Maine, gave the order, "Fix bayonets. Charge!" Many were killed on both sides, while others scattered "like a herd of wild cattle." But Little Round Top was secure.

At the end of July 2, the Union "hook" was intact, from Little Round Top in the south, north along Cemetery Ridge, and northeast along Cemetery Hill, until it curved south along Culp's Hill.

That evening, twelve Union generals gathered in a council of war at Meade's headquarters, most of whom had to stand due to a lack of seats. They decided to retain their defensive position and wait for an attack. As the meeting dispersed, Meade said to General John Gibbon, whose men occupied the center, "If Lee attacks tomorrow, it will be in your front." Meade said this was "Because he has made attacks on both our flanks and failed, and if he concludes to try it again it will be on our center." General Gibbon said he hoped so, and that if Lee did, he would defeat him.

———

Around 10:00 a.m. outside Vicksburg, white flags appeared along the Confederate works. Two officers, a general and a white-flag-wielding

---

* Sickles was acquitted after his lawyer, Edwin Stanton, made the first successful "temporary insanity" argument to the jury. Sickles was a favorite of then-president James Buchanan, who had written him a letter while in jail.

colonel, brought a letter to Grant from John Pemberton, their commander, proposing an armistice while negotiations could take place.
Grant responded that "The useless effusion of blood" cited by Pemberton
could abate at his discretion, with the surrender of his garrison and the
city. Declining to appoint commissioners, he said "I have no terms other
than those indicated above." While Grant was reaching the end of his
siege, the nation itself was fighting for its life in the east.

From Seminary Ridge, the heights opposite the Union lines occupied by
Lee's forces, 130 artillery pieces at midday announced the next movement
in the struggle for Gettysburg. Seventy Union cannon responded for the
next hour. One witness to the largest artillery battle in North America
described the hills "capped with crowns of flames and smoke," while the
guns "vomited their iron hail upon each other."

Half a mile across from the Union center of Cemetery Ridge, General Pickett's men appeared from where they had been hiding and formed
a column. Fifteen thousand men in all made the charge. If they succeeded,
they would break the Union lines, divide them in two, and crush the
Army of the Potomac. But such a great reward would not come without
tremendous risk. Longstreet had issued the command under protest. "I
have been a soldier," he told Lee, "I may say, from the ranks up to the
position I now hold. I have been in pretty much all kinds of skirmishes,
from those of two or three soldiers up to those of an army corps, and I
think I can safely say there was never a body of fifteen thousand men who
could make that attack successfully." Yet it fell to Longstreet to explain
to General Pickett that this charge, across fourteen hundred feet of open
field and up Cemetery Ridge, under artillery and musket fire against the
Union center, was his to make. "I could see the desperate and hopeless
nature of the charge and the cruel slaughter it would cause," Longstreet
remembered. "My heart was heavy when I left Pickett."

Pickett was once a young law student in Springfield, where Lincoln's
law partner had recommended him for his position at West Point. If
successful with his charge, he could cost Lincoln the war. The Confederates were exposed to heavy fire, but many made it to the low stone wall

protecting Union forces. Union soldiers now closed in on the right and left of the Confederates in a pincer movement, cutting them down on all sides. The Union lines had held; the "high water mark of the Confederacy" had receded.

At the end of the day—July 3, 1863—Lee and his army were back along Seminary Ridge, where tomorrow would bring a new battle or a retreat.

CHAPTER 36

The Fourth of July

The President announces to the country that news from the Army of the Potomac . . . is such as to cover that Army with the highest honor, to promise a great success to the cause of the Union, and to claim the condolence of all the many gallant fallen. And for this, he especially desires that on this day, He whose will, not ours, should ever be done, be everywhere remembered and reverenced with profoundest gratitude.
—WHITE HOUSE PRESS RELEASE, JULY 4, 1863

The glorious Fourth . . . was just in season to catch Franklin Pierce with his trousers down at Concord.
—*DAILY NATIONAL REPUBLICAN*, JULY 14, 1863

Lincoln ~ Pierce ~ Buchanan

Lincoln was euphoric over the news from Gettysburg. But he did not know what was happening that day in Vicksburg. On the morning of July 4, General Pemberton's men lined up outside of their works, deposited their guns, and marched back into the city. The anxious eyes of the Union army observed their surrender without visible celebration, and when it was finished, they entered the city. Grant's men, who had lived off the abundance of the Mississippi River Valley, generously shared food with their starving counterparts, who had resorted to eating rats and tree bark.

"The men of the two armies fraternized as if they had been fighting for the same cause," Grant noted.

The great mass of thirty-one thousand Confederates were paroled—released on a written promise not to take up arms against the Union. Sixty thousand muskets and 172 cannon were taken. Vicksburg had fallen, and the last remaining fort on the Mississippi surrendered in a matter of days. The Union controlled the great river from the source to the mouth. The Confederacy was cut in half. And the key was in Lincoln's pocket.

It was an inauspicious time for Franklin Pierce to make his next movement against the administration. The sequence of events would prove to be a political Pickett's Charge. A newspaper of July 3 announced that Franklin Pierce "will preside and speak at the Democratic Mass Convention which meets in this city [Concord] on July 4." The entire town was prepared for the occasion. The estimated crowd of twenty-five thousand began pouring into the city the night before, and gathered on the morning of the Fourth at 8:00 a.m. "Every foot of space within hearing distance of the stand, held its man," according to the *Sun,* with twenty people crowded into a single tree. It was suggested that this was the largest political meeting in New Hampshire history, and perhaps in all of New England.

In front of the Capitol there was an "exquisite arch decorated with shields and miniature flags," with the words LIBERTY AND LAW in gilt letters. Above was a large eagle holding "a profusion of radiating flags." The Columbian Hotel to the south was "gracefully and beautifully decorated," with an arch over the entrance proclaiming 1775–JULY 4, 1863. Banners and pennants were everywhere, and one newspaper reported "the street at this point seemed to be a field of waving flags." Representative slogans included THE CONSTITUTION AS IT IS; THE UNION AS IT WAS.

Pierce wasted no time in declaring where he stood. "Do we not know that the cause of our calamities is the vicious intermeddling of . . . the northern states with the constitutional rights of the southern states? And now, war! War, in its direst shape—war, such as it makes the blood run cold to read of . . . war, on a scale of a million men in arms—war, horrid as that of barbaric ages, rages in several of the states of the Union . . . and casts the lurid shadow of its death . . . into every nook and corner of our vast domain.

"Even here in the loyal states, the mailed hand of military usurpation strikes down the liberties of the people and its foot tramples on a desecrated Constitution.

"It is made criminal . . . for that noble martyr of free speech, Mr. Vallandigham, to discuss public affairs in Ohio." Here Pierce received a loud applause.

"This fearful, fruitless, fatal civil war has exhibited our amazing resources and vast military power," Pierce continued, condemning emancipation, which could only yield a "harvest of woe . . . ripening for what was once the peerless Republic."

Pierce argued that if he were president, his effort would be entirely invested in "moral power," rather than "the coercive instrumentalities of military power." He argued that the last two years had proven the conflict to be futile, and even if successful, that the nation could never be reconstructed by arms.

Pierce then painted a dark picture of America after the Constitution failed, when "the ballot box is sealed." What then? Pierce argued, "You will take care of yourselves; with or without arms, with or without leaders, we will, at least, in the effort to defend our rights as a free people, build up a great mausoleum of hearts, to which men who yearn for liberty will, in after years, with bowed heads and reverently resort, as Christian pilgrims to the sacred shrines of the Holy Land."

Pierce spent the rest of the day at his home with Nathaniel Hawthorne. By nightfall he had received word that his friend Colonel Cross of the 5th New Hampshire regiment had been killed at Gettysburg.

The *New Hampshire Patriot* called Pierce's speech "a most complete and triumphant success," with headlines such as FREE SPEECH VINDICATED AND EXERCISED, and IMMENSE DEMONSTRATION IN DEFENSE OF THE CONSTITUTION AND UNION. But reaction from throughout the north was almost universally devastating. The *Hartford Courant* editorialized "when his country is in peril, when an invading army is in Pennsylvania, this black-hearted copperhead reviles the men who have rallied to the defense of their country, and would build up a party on the ruins of every thing dear to patriots. Jefferson Davis is a saint compared with such a copperhead as Franklin Pierce." The *Vermont Phoenix* announced, under the headline REBEL INVASION OF NEW HAMPSHIRE, that "Gen. Pierce, with a force variously estimated at from ten to twenty thousand persons, occupied Concord, N.H., on the 4th of July." The *Boston Daily Advertiser* noted with understatement that "the news from Pennsylvania was some-what untimely," while the *Constitution* cracked that Pierce "stands up for the south now in the same way that some of the Pennsylvania Dutchmen in the back counties are said to vote every year for Gen. Jackson. The country ought to be spared the shame of being reminded that it ever had such a president."

On that same Independence Day, Lincoln appeared at an upper win-dow of the White House in response to a procession and bands serenad-ing him. Lincoln thanked "Almighty God" for the news that had brought them there. "How long ago is it?" he asked, "eighty odd years—since on the Fourth of July for the first time in the history of the world a nation by its representatives, assembled and declared a self-evident truth that 'all men are created equal.'" The crowd cheered. "That was the birthday of the United States of America. Since then the Fourth of July has had several peculiar recognitions." Lincoln pointed out how, fifty years to the day of the Declaration, the two men most responsible for it—its author and strongest defender—Thomas Jefferson and John Adams died. And five years later, James Monroe. Now, in the midst of "a gigantic Rebellion, at the bottom of which is an effort to overthrow the principle that all men are created equal, we have the surrender of a most powerful position and an army on that very day." There were "long and continued cheers" for the president. Lincoln confessed that he was not prepared to make a speech worthy of this great occasion. "Having said this much," he concluded, "I will now take the music."

The day had ended with Lincoln triumphant and Pierce at his nadir. But once again the Union army would fail to consolidate its success. With "sadness and despondency," the president announced to his cabinet that Meade lingered at Gettysburg, instead of intercepting the retreating rebel army. Lincoln believed that at this pace, Meade was "quite as likely to capture the Man-in-the-Moon as any part of Lee's Army."

Lincoln was with Treasury Secretary Chase and several others point-ing out Grant's movements on a map when Welles entered with a tele-gram. Vicksburg had fallen on the 4th. Lincoln put down the map, stood up, and picked up his hat, "His countenance beaming with joy." Grabbing Welles by the hand, he said, "What can we do for the Secretary of the

Navy for this glorious intelligence? He is always giving us good news. I cannot, in words, tell you my joy over this result. It is great, Mr. Welles, it is great!" Together they walked across the lawn to telegraph the news to General Meade.

As Lee retreated back to Virginia, after a long delay caused by the swollen Potomac, Lincoln lay on a sofa in Stanton's office. Thirty-one thousand soldiers at Vicksburg had been paroled. If Meade had pursued Lee, the war might well have ended. Lincoln was "absorbed, overwhelmed with the news." Though "subdued and sad," he was also "calm and resolute." He wrote to Meade, "Yet you stood and let the flood run down, bridges be built, and the enemy move away at his leisure, without attacking him . . . I do not believe you appreciate the magnitude of the misfortune involved in Lee's escape. He was within your easy grasp, and to have closed upon him would, in connection with our other late successes, have ended the war."

Lee had escaped with the remains of his army. "We had only to stretch forth our hands and they were ours," Lincoln said despondently. "And nothing I could say or do could make the army move . . . This is a dreadful reminiscence of McClellan. The same spirit that moved McClellan to claim a great victory because Pennsylvania and Maryland were safe . . . Will our generals never get that idea out of their heads? The whole country is our soil."

But after "A few days having passed," Lincoln recorded, "I am now profoundly grateful for what was done, without criticism for what was not done." And while the aftermath of July 4 was bittersweet for the president, the news continued to worsen for Franklin Pierce. The *New York Herald* was soon to announce an IMPORTANT CAPTURE, the DISCOVERY AND SEIZURE OF JEFF. DAVIS' PRIVATE LIBRARY AND CORRESPONDENCE. A former slave had directed Union soldiers to Brierfield, the home of Jefferson Davis, twenty miles south of Vicksburg. Nearly everything of value was stolen or destroyed. Above the door, Union soldiers painted THE HOUSE THAT JEFF BUILT. The home was then turned over to runaway slaves. Davis's personal "papers were brought into camp, and served as novel literature for our officers and men." They also discovered a walking cane from Pierce, inscribed, "from a soldier to a soldier's friend."

Initially, controversy came from uncovered Davis correspondence with Buchanan. In 1853, Buchanan had written Davis, "I heartily rejoice that you are in the cabinet." He recommended an applicant to federal office, adding, "You might perhaps be pleased to know that he even went ahead of myself in his opinions on the subject of southern rights." But these messages were innocent enough in their context.

As Davis's papers were examined further, and his correspondence with Pierce was discovered, there was "a great ado," in the words of one newspaper. At issue was Pierce's January 1860 letter, encouraging Davis to run for president and remarking on the current state of affairs. The *New York Daily Tribune* called it "a valuable contribution to the history of the Rebellion, and, though nobody will be surprised that Mr. Pierce should have written it, its publication will be a sore perplexity to those who insist that the Abolitionists were the instigators of the rebellion, that it was not premeditated by southern politicians, and that their plans were not known and approved of by their northern associates.

In the letter, Pierce emphasized the need to "overthrow abolitionism at the polls, and repeal unconstitutional and obnoxious laws [specifically the Liberty Laws]." The *Tribune* opined, "We doubt if Jeff Davis ever received from the most rampant of his Southern fellow-conspirators more unequivocal assurances of sympathy and aid than Franklin Pierce gives him in this letter."

After that summer's excitement, Buchanan traveled to Bedford Springs to relax, finding a warm reception there "as in the days of my power." There was a large dinner given in his honor, and many callers came to pay their respects, including "several naughty secession girls here from Baltimore—some of them very bright," he recorded. "My principal amusement has been with them." They told him stories of how they provoked the occupying federal troops, and he laughed. "They speak rather contemptuously of General Dix; but [General] Schenk is their abomination. I treat them playfully," he noted, "and tell them I love them so that it would be impossible for me ever to consent to part from them and that the shocking idea has never once entered my head of living in a separate confederacy from them."

Lincoln was busy ensuring that Buchanan would never have to do so. The idea of arming blacks was loaded with controversy, requiring Lincoln to tread carefully. The Second Confiscation Act of 1862 permitted blacks to enlist, but it was a much different thing in practice. In the final Emancipation Proclamation, Lincoln announced that blacks would be armed, but in defensive roles and aboard ships. Quietly, Stanton had permitted several generals to begin recruiting black soldiers. By the spring of 1863, Lincoln was directing a widespread recruiting drive for black soldiers and regiments. To that end, the president met on August 10 with Frederick Douglass at the White House. Douglass, an escaped slave who had inspired millions with his intellect and oratory in defense of freedom, was nervous at meeting the nation's leader on his first visit to the president's mansion. But the presence of Lincoln put him instantly at ease. Douglass first saw Lincoln "seated in a low chair, surrounded by a multitude of books and papers .... On my approach he slowly drew his feet in from the different parts of the room into which they had strayed, and he began to rise, and continued to rise until he looked down upon me, and extended his hand and gave me a welcome."

"You need not tell me who you are, Mr. Douglass," he said, inviting him to sit down next to him.

"Mr. Lincoln," Douglass said, "I have assisted in filling up two regiments in Massachusetts, and am now at work in the same way in Pennsylvania, and have come to say this to you, sir, if you wish to make this branch of the service successful." Douglass asked for equal pay, compulsion to force Confederates to treat captured black soldiers the same as whites.

"I assure you, Mr. Douglass, that in the end they shall have the same pay as white soldiers." Lincoln had already issued his Order of Retaliation, arguing that under the laws of war the Confederacy must treat black prisoners of war the same as whites, promising to retaliate against their prisoners should that not be the case. By the end of the year, one hundred thousand blacks were serving the Union cause in uniform.

Lincoln was not only executing his plan to include blacks in the war, but preparing for their success when it had concluded. With this in mind, Lincoln wrote Nathaniel Banks, the former Know Nothing Speaker of the House and the new commander of the Department of the Gulf. He recommended a new state constitution for Louisiana recognizing the Emancipation Proclamation. "And while she is at it, I think it would not be objectionable for her to adopt some practical system by which the two races could gradually live themselves out of their old relation to each other, and both come out better prepared for the new.

"As an anti-slavery man I have a motive to desire emancipation, which pro-slavery men do not have; but even they have strong enough reason to thus place themselves again under the shield of the Union; and to thus perpetually hedge against the recurrence of the scenes through which we are now passing."

CHAPTER 37

A New Birth of Freedom

Four score and seven years ago, our fathers brought forth on this continent a new nation, conceived in liberty, and dedicated to the proposition that all men are created equal.

—ABRAHAM LINCOLN

Lincoln ~ Fillmore

In October, the *New York Post* observed that the presidential election was "mingling itself more or less with nearly all other public questions. Its shadow is everywhere . . . You can hardly send a man to the United States Senate but he begins to think of being one day President. Make a soldier a General, and the tempter whispers in his ear.

"There is scarce any chapter in those ample records which illustrate the vanity of human wishes . . . than that which related the failures of distinguished men who have aspired to the Presidency of the United States."

The 1863 state elections would serve as a precursor. No race was perhaps more personal for Lincoln than Clement Vallandigham's campaign for governor of Ohio, being waged from his exile in Canada. When his wife left Dayton to join him, she bragged that when she returned, it would be as the wife of Ohio's governor.

Hearing of this, Lincoln said, "That reminds me of a pleasant little affair that occurred out in Illinois. A gentleman was nominated for Supervisor. On leaving home on the morning of election, he said: 'Wife, tonight you shall sleep with the Supervisor of this town.' The election passed, and the confident gentleman was defeated. The wife heard the news before her defeated spouse returned home. She immediately dressed for going out, and awaited her husband's return, when she met him at the door. 'Wife, where are you going at this time of night?' he exclaimed. 'Going?'" she replied. 'Why, you told me this morning that I should tonight sleep with the Supervisor of this town, and I was going to his house.'"

On October 14, Welles visited Lincoln to congratulate him on Union victories in Pennsylvania and Ohio, saying "the defeat of Vallandigham is emphatic." Lincoln told him that "he had more anxiety in regard to the election results of yesterday than he had in 1860 when he was chosen," Welles recorded. "He could not . . . have believed four years ago that one genuine American would, or could be induced to, vote for such a man as Vallandigham," he said, displaying "a good deal of emotion."

Army soldier J. H. Moore wrote to his uncle, Millard Fillmore, from Louisville, Kentucky, while in the largest hospital he had ever seen. He mentioned that one soldier there had voted for a Vallandigham ticket, "but he gets well paid for it." General Boyd had him arrested and court-martialed, and sentenced to lie in the guard house for twenty-one days. Every morning he was taken out and made to stand on a barrel for two hours.

From the outset of his presidency, Lincoln had been forced to confront the Democrats, but also carefully threaded the needle between moderate and radical Republicans. Salmon Chase, in the latter category, had been not so subtly campaigning for president. Governor Denison of Ohio confided in Lincoln that Chase was "working like a beaver," using his vast network of revenue collectors. Denison declined to talk to him, saying he was pledged to Lincoln. Lincoln replied that "it was in very bad taste, but that he had determined to shut his eyes to all these performances: that Chase made a good Secretary and that he would keep him where he is: if he becomes President, all right. I hope we may never have a worse man. I have all along clearly seen his plan of strengthening himself. Whenever he sees that an important matter is troubling me, if I am compelled to decide it in a way to give offense to a man of some influence he always ranges himself in opposition to me and persuades the victim that he has been hardly dealt by and that he would have arranged it very differently." He concluded, "I am entirely indifferent as to his success or failure in these schemes, so long as he does his duty as the head of the Treasury Department."

Lincoln's remarkable magnanimity surfaced again, days later, when he commuted the sentence of Stephen Douglas's brother-in-law, who was convicted of fighting a fellow soldier in the army. Lincoln told him to make the best of his reprieve, writing, "No man resolved to make the most of himself can spare time for personal contention."

If Lincoln could not spare time for quarreling, he could occasionally indulge one of his favorite loves, the theater. On November 9, he went with his wife and Hay to see *The Marble Heart* at Ford's Theatre. The star was John Wilkes Booth. And so for hours that evening, Lincoln was entertained by his murderer in the very place where he would be assassinated.

Lincoln was running late in departing for Gettysburg, where he had been invited to make "a few appropriate remarks" following the main speaker at the dedication of the Soldier's Cemetery. The general sent to conduct him there was attempting to rush him. Lincoln replied, "I feel about that as the convict did in Illinois, when he was going to the gallows. Passing along the road in custody of the sheriff, and seeing the people who were eager for the execution crowding and jostling one another past him, he at last called out, 'Boys! You needn't be in such a hurry to get ahead, for there won't be any fun till I get there.'"

Edward Everett spoke for two hours, followed by a "musical interlude." According to Nicolay, Lincoln held his draft of the speech but did not appear to read from it. In 272 words, Lincoln spelled out a mission statement for the United States, which was itself a restoration of the vision that prevailed at the nation's founding. He committed the country to "the unfinished work which they who fought here have thus far so nobly advanced." He resolved that "these dead shall not have died in vain." And pledged "that this nation, under God, shall have a new birth of freedom—and that government of the people, by the people, for the people, shall not perish from the earth."

Nobody had heard nor seen this speech before he delivered it. His audience was shocked by its brevity, perhaps none more so than the photographer who managed to take one hasty shot before the speaker returned to his seat. Sitting down, Lincoln confessed to his friend, Ward Hill Lamon, "It is a flat failure, and the people are disappointed."

Those who had accompanied him may not have shared his harsh assessment, but believed him capable of better. Hay's diary did not give the address its own sentence: ". . . and the President in a firm free way, with more grace than is his wont said his half dozen lines of consecration and the music wailed and we went home through crowded and cheering streets." More than twenty years later, the biography of Lincoln he wrote with Nicolay gave the address its own chapter and thirteen pages.

Many initial press accounts realized what has later come to be accepted as fact, that the speech represented something transformative. Biographer David Donald takes note of the criticism as well, which attacked Lincoln's definition of the war, presenting as evidence "that Lincoln had succeeded in broadening the aims of the war from Union to Equality and Union."

CHAPTER 38

Our Old Home

Three years of civil war have desolated the fairest portion of our land, loaded our country with an enormous debt that the sweat of millions yet unborn must be taxed to pay; arrayed brother against brother, and father against son in mortal combat; deluged our country with fraternal blood, whitened our battle-fields with the bones of the slain, and darkened the sky with the pall of mourning.

—MILLARD FILLMORE

Pierce ~ Lincoln ~ Buchanan ~ Fillmore

In autumn 1863, Nathaniel Hawthorne published his long awaited *Our Old Home,* a collection of travel essays from his seven years abroad, which had been serialized in the *Atlantic Monthly.* The author of *The Scarlet Letter* encountered an uncommon controversy, not for the content of the essays, but for their dedication:

TO
FRANKLIN PIERCE,
AS A SLIGHT MEMORIAL OF A COLLEGE FRIENDSHIP,
PROLONGED THROUGH MANHOOD, AND RETAINING
ALL ITS VITALITY
IN OUR AUTUMNAL YEARS,
THIS VOLUME IS INSCRIBED BY
NATHANIEL HAWTHORNE

Pierce was riding a long train of unpopularity, from the Kansas-Nebraska Act to his criticism of Lincoln and the war, and the recent discovery of his correspondence with Jefferson Davis, which had been printed widely throughout the country. Hawthorne fought his editor to keep the dedication as it was, writing him that it would be an act of cowardice to do otherwise, noting that Pierce's patronage by appointing him to the consulate at Liverpool made the entire book possible. For good measure, he pointed out, "if he is so exceedingly unpopular that his name is enough to sink the volume, there is so much the more need that an old friend should stand by him. I cannot, merely on account of pecuniary profit or literary reputation, go back from what I have deliberately thought and felt it was right to do." Hawthorne remarked that he would never be able to think of the book without "remorse and shame" if he gave in. The social cost was high to him, for he noted, "My friends have dropped off from me like autumn leaves." One large bookseller refused to order any copies, though his customers were very much fans of Hawthorne. Many friends still bought the book, and in the case of Ralph Waldo Emerson, cut out the dedication before reading. To paraphrase the old adage, when forced to choose between his friend and his country, Hawthorne had the courage to choose his friend.

Pierce was soon to need Hawthorne more than ever before. On December 2, 1863, he lost his wife. Hawthorne arrived immediately at his friend's side. After the funeral the two kept vigil at her graveside at the Old North Church in Concord. The Pierces had never been much of a fit for one another, the healthy convivial public figure, versus the sickly, reclusive woman who hated politics. Once asked why he married her, Pierce had said, "I could take better care of her than anyone else." As Pierce stood by Jane's grave throughout that day, he probably wondered whether he had done so, hoping that he had made her happy. At one point during the vigil, "though completely overcome with his own sorrow," Pierce "turned and drew up the collar of Hawthorne's coat to shield him from the bitter cold."

On December 8, the president released a controversial publication of his own. In a "Proclamation of Amnesty and Reconstruction," Lincoln promised that people wishing to return to the Union would receive "a full pardon," have their property restored, except for their slaves, after taking an oath to support the Constitution and laws of the United States, as well as those proclamations issued by Lincoln as president. High-ranking Confederate officers and government officials would be exempt. Whenever 10 percent of a state's population had sworn the oath, a state would be recognized as having resumed its former role in the Union.

Hay recorded, "Whatever may be the results or the verdict of history the immediate effect of this paper is something wonderful. I never have seen such an effect produced by a public document. Men acted as if the millennium had come. Chandler was delighted, Sumner was beaming, while at the other political pole Dixon and Reverdy Johnson said it was highly satisfactory." Senator Henry Wilson of Massachusetts placed his hands on Hay's shoulders and said, "The President has struck another great blow. Tell him from me God Bless him."

At Ford & Levett's Auction House, a crowd had gathered to bid on books, with some going as high as $1.50. The auctioneer announced the next volume for sale, "Here gentlemen, is the life of James Buchanan; how much am I offered?"

"A postage stamp," came the opening bid.

"Five cents," came another, to laughter.

"Ten cents."

"Twelve."

"Fifteen."

Sold for fifteen cents.

"And damned dear at that," someone said. The crowd cheered in agreement.

On February 8, 1864, Millard Fillmore contributed $24.81 to the Bounty Committee to recruit troops. Later that month he served as president of the committee of arrangements for the Buffalo Sanitary Fair. The United States Sanitary Commission had been formed to modernize the Army Medical Bureau. It was at that time the largest voluntary association in the history of the United States. Fillmore and his wife had worked hard to raise funds, and the event netted an incredible $25,000.

As the head organizer and the first citizen of Buffalo, Fillmore was asked to address the crowd at St. James Hall on February 22. He talked about the progress of Buffalo and of the nation, of revolutions in technology, travel, and communications. "But now, alas! All this changed. Three years of civil war have desolated the fairest portion of our land, loaded our country with an enormous debt that the sweat of millions yet unborn must be taxed to pay; arrayed brother against brother, and father against son in mortal combat; deluged our country with fraternal blood, whitened our battle-fields with the bones of the slain, and darkened the sky with the pall of mourning.

"The impartial historian will [decide who is at fault] when the passions engendered by the strife have cooled, and partisan prejudice, petty jealousies, malignant envy, and intriguing, selfish ambition shall be laid in the dust, and, it is hoped, buried in oblivion. And much less are we called upon to predict when or how this war will end. Let those who seek light on this subject, read General Jackson's Farewell Address." Fillmore pointed out that much must be forgiven, if not forgotten, for the country to truly reconcile. He argued "the administration must be supported in all constitutional efforts to conquer and disperse the rebel army." Nothing more could be done, Fillmore argued, than "to provide for the wants, physical and spiritual, of the sick and wounded soldier. Let him feel when he goes to the battlefield, that we appreciate the sacrifices he makes and the dangers he is to encounter." Fillmore took especial pains to praise the women who had served as nurses and otherwise aided soldiers in the war effort.

Fillmore, unlike Pierce in his summer speech, was not attempting to make news. And yet he did. It was in "Shocking bad taste," according to the *Buffalo Commercial Advertiser*. "The only thing that marred the harmony of the proceedings . . . was the speech of the venerable president, ex-President Fillmore. We give his remarks as *toned down*. We should have been glad to have placed upon record some words from Mr. Fillmore which would have identified him with the friends of . . . the Union, instead of being obliged to class him, as we now do, amongst the bitterest opponents of the war." One representative letter to Fillmore read, "I was pained to witness what to me seemed the favor of sympathy with rebellion and slavery."

But no matter what the former presidents did, or were perceived to have done, there was still talk of bringing them in as part of a negotiated peace. A resolution in the House called for just that. The *New York Daily Tribune* joked, "We have a dim recollection that persons of that name were buried some centuries ago. 22 living men [the number of Congressmen who supported the resolution] voted to hunt in the tombs for them—and there was whisper of the still more ghastly name of James Buchanan." This bizarre measure spurred a congressman to offer another: "Resolved, that the rebellion be and the same is hereby abolished." That motion, however, carried, "to much laughter."

Franklin Pierce, who throughout the war had taken a hands-on role in the Democratic fortunes in his state, was determined to defeat the administration. New Hampshire would cast the first ballots of 1864, offering critical momentum either to Lincoln or his opponents. The Democratic platform took credit for predicting "the consequences of abolition agitation," and supported negotiations with the South if they were willing to return to the Union. The platform attacked Lincoln's plan for reconstruction. They denounced Lincoln's expansion of the war's objective. By seeking to destroy slavery, they argued, Lincoln had forced the South to fight until they could fight no more. A vote for the Republicans, according to New Hampshire's Democratic nominee for governor, was for "perpetual war."

The Republican nominee for governor was an unconditional Unionist and "in favor of every effective measure for crushing out treason, whether it rears its head defiantly as in South Carolina or masks its hideous features with hypocritical smiles in New Hampshire."

A critical component of Civil War elections was the soldiers' vote. When the war began, the young men fighting it often could not participate, which made the difference in the reversals sustained by the Republicans in 1862. Generous furloughs were given near election time, but the vast majority of soldiers were consistently disenfranchised. The situation led to efforts in many states to permit absentee voting. In New Hampshire, such a measure had passed, but the state Supreme Court had ruled it unconstitutional. Still, the Thirteenth New Hampshire Volunteers would not be silenced. Together they had defended Washington, fought at Fredericksburg, and were now in Virginia. A letter drafted by them and signed by all but three regimental officers appeared in New Hampshire newspapers on February 25. "Great issues are at stake," they wrote "and upon their settlement depends the great question of liberty and self-government throughout the civilized world. Although it is upon the battlefield that these vital questions are to be fought out and settled . . . depends in a great measure upon the position taken by the voters of the North the present year.

"To New Hampshire all eyes are anxiously turned. The soldier fighting for the restoration of our once glorious Union expects you to sustain him by an expression at the polls that can not be mistaken.

"If you sustain the party that comes out boldly for a vigorous prosecution of the war until treason every where be put down, then will the soldier in the field go forth to fight with renewed energy, knowing well that the rebellion will be speedily ended; but if, on the contrary, the voice of New Hampshire is in favor of that party which has among its leaders Vallandigham, Fernando Wood, Franklin Pierce, and others of like character, then will the war be prolonged at the cost of countless treasure and many thousand valuable lives."

If the North had united from the beginning, they argued, the war would be over. "It is by the dissensions at the north that the leaders of the rebellion hope to achieve their independence.

"Fellow citizens, we are deprived of the right of suffrage, and is it presumption on our part to ask you to sustain us by your votes? Sustain those brave soldiers who have gone forth from the old Granite State, from the farm, from the workshop, and the desk, determined to do or die, men who have sealed their devotion to their country's cause on many a bloody field."

Franklin Pierce may have preferred his role in the state elections to be behind-the-scenes, if still very active. But the Republicans favored a very public role for him. Pierce's July 4, 1863, "Mausoleum of Hearts" speech was widely reprinted, and he was indicted in Republican campaign literature for treason. Republicans campaigned for the state legislature against the threat that the Democrats would send Pierce to the Senate. On Election Day, it was reported that Franklin Pierce was "shunned" at his polling place, and "skedaddled" by train after voting.

On March 8, as New Hampshire voters headed to the polls, "a considerable crowd" braved bad weather to be present at the White House reception. Around 9:30 p.m., the "buzz and the movement" indicated to Lincoln that his guest of honor had arrived. When he approached the president, Lincoln said, "This is General Grant, isn't it?"

"Yes!" Grant replied. He had been summoned to Washington for Lincoln to appoint him lieutenant general, head of all the army. During the reception, Nicolay received a message announcing that the New Hampshire Union ticket had prevailed by three thousand votes. Governor Gilmore, safely re-elected, wrote to the president, "The Granite State sends you greeting. New Hampshire stands fast by the country and your administration of the government. The spirit of liberty dwells among my people."

James Buchanan lamented the results. "The Democrats of New Hampshire, with General Pierce, have fought a noble battle worthy of a better fate."

The Republicans won the governorship with 54 percent, the biggest margin in eleven years, while carrying 63 percent of the state House and three-fourths of the Senate.

The *Hartford Courant* praised the results as an "Example for Connecticut," writing, "New Hampshire has spoken as a brave and loyal people should. She has just emerged from the smoke of a hotly-contested election, with streamers flying, and victory inscribed upon her banners." The paper noted "The copperheads put forth stupendous efforts to carry the state," but "The pro-slavery clique of New Hampshire, headed by Franklin Pierce, has nearly run its course. They have battled long and desperately against God and the right, but the current of events is overwhelmingly against them. In the election of Tuesday they are warned again that their bark is upon the breakers."

Pierce's portrait was removed from the Capitol Rotunda and "cast among the rubbish." Buchanan's smiling visage had suffered a similar fate earlier in the war. Pierce's political tragedy was about to be compounded by a personal one. Nathaniel Hawthorne had been unwell, and Pierce had hoped that vacationing in the White Mountains of New Hampshire would help restore him.

One night, Pierce recalled, "Hastening softly to his bedside, I could not perceive that he breathed, although no change had come over his features. I seized his wrist, but found no pulse; ran my hand down upon his bare side, but the great, generous, brave heart beat no more."

Collecting his things, Pierce looked inside a suitcase and found a pocketbook. It was empty, save for a picture of himself. Hawthorne, it seemed, had carried this image of his treasured friend wherever he went. The funeral was attended by Hawthorne's great contemporaries, such as Whittier, Longfellow, and Emerson. But those arranging the memorial excluded Pierce from the final honor of bearing his friend to the grave.

CHAPTER 39

Those Not Skinning Can Hold a Leg

Please tell these little people I am very glad their young hearts are so full of just and generous sympathy, and that, while I have not the power to grant all they ask, I trust they will remember that God has, and that, as it seems, He wills to do it.
— ABRAHAM LINCOLN, RESPONSE TO A PETITION FROM FREE
CHILDREN FOR THE EMANCIPATION OF SLAVE CHILDREN

Fillmore ~ Lincoln

Planning out the spring campaign from his headquarters at the Culpeper Courthouse, Lieutenant General Ulysses S. Grant noted that despite some of the greatest battles fought in the history of warfare, in the east "the opposing forces stood in substantially the same relations towards each other as . . . when the war began."

The Union efforts, which had from the beginning been disjointed, would now work in concert, and move, per Grant's orders to General Sherman, "somewhat towards a common center." Aside from Richmond, the greatest target was the army of Joseph Johnston, near Atlanta, Georgia. The fall of that city, entrusted to General William Sherman, would be crucial in bringing down the Confederacy. Sherman noted the enormity of the task. The Confederates were fighting on the defensive, in territory they knew, and where the population supported them. As the Union moved forward, they were required to leave forces behind to secure their gains. As the Confederates fell back, they gained reinforcements. The Union would have to rely on long supply lines through the hostile territory of a sorely deprived people; the Confederates could more easily be provisioned by railroads in their interior lines.

On March 24, 1864, Fillmore responded to George McClellan's wife, who wanted to auction his autograph for the New York Sanitary Fair. "The pleasure would be greatly increased—instead of the autograph I had the power for the sake of my bleeding country to send you an order restoring your gallant husband to the position of 'General Commander in Chief,'" Fillmore said. He felt his "blood boil with indignation at the injustice that has been done him," and prayed "that the people may do him justice by elevating him to be" president of the United States. Fillmore closed by saying, "I have long since ceased to be a politician, and have no other wish or desire than to see our Union restored and our distracted country once more enjoying the blessings of peace."

President Lincoln wrote Lieutenant General Grant on April 30, 1864, expressing his "entire satisfaction with what you have done up to this time, so far as I understand it.

"You are vigilant and self-reliant," he wrote. "If there is anything wanting which is within my power to give, do not fail to let me know. And now with a brave Army, and a just cause, may God sustain you."

Grant replied, "From my first entrance into the volunteer service of the country, to the present day, I have never had cause of complaint, have never expressed or implied a complaint, against the Administration, or the Sec. of War, for throwing any embarrassment in the way of my vigorously prosecuting what appeared to me my duty. Indeed since the promotion which placed me in command of all the Armies, and in view of the great responsibility, and importance of success, I have been astonished at the readiness with which every thing asked for has been yielded without even an explanation being asked. Should my success be less than I desire, and expect, the least I can say is, the fault is not with you."

While planning his movement into Virginia, Grant left his headquarters at Culpeper regularly for meetings with Lincoln and Stanton. On their final interview before departing, Grant explained that troops could hold territory and protect the North from invasion just as well by advancing as standing still.

From the beginning of the war, Lincoln had wanted to pressure the Confederacy on as many points as possible. Lincoln easily understood, offering a saying popular in the west. "Those not skinning can hold a leg."

On May 2, Confederate officers at the signal station on Clark's Mountain observed through their field glasses a Union force unlike any they had ever seen, amassing north of the Rapidan. The following day, Grant and his men crossed that river. Lee was headquartered near the courthouse in Orange, Virginia, where seventy-five years earlier James Madison and James Monroe, in their campaign against one another for Congress, had debated the merits of the Constitution.

Grant and Lee met near the Spotsylvania Wilderness, an "uneven [ground covered with] woods, thickets, and ravines right and left. Tangled thickets of pine, scrub oak, and cedar," which reduced Lee's numerical disadvantage. A Confederate general remembered "a desperate fight" at "close quarters." In the thick forest, "Officers could not see the whole length of their commands, and could tell whether the troops on their right and left were driving or being driven only by the sound of the firing."

The trees burned in every direction, and more than two hundred Union men died from fire alone. The wounded, unable to move from the no man's land were burned or suffocated. The second day of fighting was the same smoky, scorching hell as the tide "ebbed and flowed many times . . . strewing the Wilderness with human wrecks."

Lee's forces withdrew on the evening of May 6. Sherman, who was not present, would call Grant's next decision "the supreme moment of his life . . . Without stopping to count his numbers, he gave his orders calmly, specifically, and absolutely—'Forward to Spotsylvania.'"

Union casualties were 17,666, to 11,400 for the Confederates. "How near we have been to this thing before and failed," Lincoln said, receiving the news. "I believe if any other general had been at the head of that army it would have now been on this side of the Rapidan. It is the dogged pertinacity of Grant that wins." Meade reportedly told Grant that the enemy seemed ready to make it a cat fight, to which Grant responded "Our cat has the longest tail."

From the Wilderness Grant moved to Spotsylvania in an attempt to put himself between Lee's army and Richmond, and perhaps to bring him out into the open. Lee, arriving first, fortified the area, forcing Grant to attack him there. On May 11, Grant reported that for six days his men had engaged in "very hard fighting." He noted heavy losses, but determined that the enemy's must be more severe, promising to "fight it out on this line if it takes all summer." Actually, Grant had suffered 18,399 casualties to Lee's nine thousand in front of Spotsylvania. But again Grant moved forward, forcing Lee into the defenses around Richmond. For the next five days there was constant rain, leaving the wounded to die in ambulances trapped by washed-out roads.

Lincoln paced the floor of the Executive Chamber with his hands behind his back. When Speaker of the House Schuyler Colfax arrived to see him, Lincoln looked at him with the saddest face he had ever seen, "his dark features contracted still more with gloom." Lincoln said, "Why do we suffer reverses after reverses! Could we have avoided this terrible, bloody war! Was it not forced upon us! Is it ever to end!" But then "hope beamed on his face," and he said, "Grant will not fail us now; he says he will 'fight it out on that line,' and this is now the hope of our country."

On May 30, a convention met in Cleveland, seeking to nominate a more radical candidate than Lincoln and settling on John C. Fremont. But only four hundred delegates came, rather than the thousands expected. When word arrived in the telegraph office on June 1, Lincoln requested a Bible, and read from 1 Samuel 12:2. "And every one that was in distress, and every one that was in debt, and every one that was discontented, gathered themselves unto him; and he became a captain over them; and there were with him about four hundred men." But while Fremont fizzled, the radical Republican threat remained, in the form of Lincoln's rogue treasury secretary, Salmon Chase.

Throughout May and June, as Sherman pushed from Tennessee into Georgia, Johnston continued to fall back. Each time he did so expertly, leaving nothing behind, delaying Sherman. For the remainder of 1864, these three campaigns—Sherman's, Grant's, and Lincoln's—would determine the fate of the United States.

CHAPTER 40

Not Unworthy to Remain in My Present Position

The most reliable indication of public purpose in this country is derived through our popular elections.

—ABRAHAM LINCOLN

Lincoln ~ Pierce ~ Fillmore ~ Buchanan

"I always think of our arrival at Cold Harbor as marking a new phase of the war," remembered George Eggleston, a sergeant-major in the Confederate army. "I remember surprise and disappointment were the prevailing emotions in the ranks of the Army of Northern Virginia when we discovered, after the contest in the Wilderness, that General Grant was not going to retire behind the river," allowing Lee to menace Washington as he had before, and instead moving forward to Spotsylvania. "We had been accustomed to a program which began with a Federal advance, culminated in one great battle, and ended in the retirement of the Union army, the substitution of a new Federal commander for the one beaten, and the institution of a more or less offensive campaign on our part. This was the usual order of events, and this was what we confidently expected." Grant was "fresh from the west and so ill-informed as to the military customs in our part of the country that when the battle of the Wilderness was over . . . [he] had the temerity" to advance and fight Lee's forces again.

The movement against Cold Harbor would be costly. Hundreds of Grant's men wrote their names and addresses on pieces of paper, which they clipped to their uniforms. In the first eight minutes, "more men fell bleeding as they advanced than in any other like period of time throughout the war," remembered a Union general. Grant lost 14,931 dead or wounded to seventeen hundred for the Confederates. Welles noted, "The bodies of our brave men, slain or mutilated, are brought daily to Washington by hundreds."

In the last days of his life, Grant would write, "I have always regretted that the last assault at Cold Harbor was ever made. No advantage whatever was gained to compensate for the heavy loss we sustained." But retreat was never an option.

Lee would not engage Grant's superior numbers in an open field. Grant had watched for nearly two months as Lee fought from behind breastworks, staying on defense, refusing to risk his men. Forced to choose between two dangerous options—one, to fight straight to Richmond, over dangerous and defensible terrain against an entrenched army, or, two, to cross the James River and approach Richmond from the south—Grant opted for the latter.

For the 1864 election, Republicans branded themselves as the National Union Party, hoping to unite all supporters of the war. Lincoln was unanimously re-nominated, the first president since Van Buren in 1840, on a platform of unconditional Confederate surrender and amending the Constitution to abolish slavery. Entering the telegraph office to congratulations, Lincoln looked over the dispatches from the affair. "Send it right over to the Madam," he said, "She will be more interested than I am." Democrat Andrew Johnson, Tennessee's military governor, was chosen as his running mate. "I thought possibly he might be the man," Lincoln said. "Perhaps he is the best man, but—" without completing his thought, he rose and left the room.

Accepting the nomination, Lincoln said, "I will neither conceal my gratification, nor restrain the expression of my gratitude, that the Union people, through their convention, in their continued effort to save, and advance the nation, have deemed me not unworthy to remain in my present position.

"I approve the declaration in favor of so amending the Constitution as to prohibit slavery throughout the nation . . . Such alone can meet and cover all cavils. Now, the unconditional Union men, north and south, perceive its importance, and embrace it. In the joint names of Liberty and Union, let us labor to give it legal form, and practical effect."

To a Union League delegation from New York later that day, Lincoln confessed his unworthiness for the job, but was reminded of an old Dutch farmer who told a companion "it was not best to swap horses when crossing streams."

Franklin Pierce believed Lincoln's opponent would be none other than George McClellan, an anticipation shared by "All men in this region." He wrote, "In the present condition of affairs, no man can guess what changes in public sentiment or opinion are likely to take place" before the election. The country, he believed, "should be animated by a common object—just and above all—the restoration of the Union, if folly and madness ... have not placed it beyond hope."

Union private John Kick of Buffalo, New York, had marched with Grant's army throughout the Overland Campaign. On the road from Cold Harbor toward the James, he suffered heatstroke and nearly died. His fellow soldiers arranged to leave him at the nearest house, which happened to be Sherwood Forest. Anna Tyler, the former president's niece, who was "young, good looking, and withal strongly rebellious," lived there along with an older relative. Over a course of weeks she nursed him back to health. What was likely an icy beginning quickly changed and the two fell in love. A minister from a nearby town was summoned, and "they were united in the bonds of matrimony, more fortunate, in this respect, than the prototypical 'Romeo' and 'Juliet.'" Returning to his regiment, Kick asked for a thirty-day furlough to take his honeymoon. It was granted. Sherwood Forest was, throughout that stage of the war, near or within the lines of General Benjamin Butler's Army of the James. Butler, frequently pestered by letters from Julia Tyler on a variety of subjects, including her niece's well-being, responded with a note. Her niece should no longer give her anxiety, he wrote, now that she had "taken for her husband and lawful protector John Kick, a brave soldier of the army of the United States." And if she wanted to see the happy couple, or give them "such advice as a matronly relative only could bestow," he would finally grant her the pass she had been seeking to return. Kick would survive the war and live to take his bride back to Buffalo.

On June 14, Grant and his army reached the James. The general ordered boats to be sunk in the river to prevent the Confederate navy from interfering. Pontoon bridges were laid down, and the Army of the Potomac crossed, returning to the vicinity of Richmond. After days of skirmishing, Grant began a siege of the city of Petersburg, a vital source of supplies for the capital of Richmond and Lee's army. Since Grant set forth from Washington, sixty-five thousand northern men had been "killed, wounded, or missing."

On June 23, Lincoln arrived at the front, sunburned and exhausted, "but still refreshed and cheered." Grant told him "it may be a long summer's day before he does his work but that he is as sure of doing it as he is of anything in the world." Lincoln returned from his visit "in very good spirits." His "journey has done him good," thought Welles, "physically, and strengthened him mentally and inspired confidence in the general and army."

Meanwhile, tensions with the treasury secretary reached a breaking point. Chase's candidate to serve at an important post in New York was opposed by the congressional delegation. Lincoln thought he had diffused the situation by convincing the incumbent to remain. He was writing Chase a letter to that effect, when he received his resignation. This time Lincoln decided to accept. "I thought I could not stand it any longer," he said.

In the perennial chess match between Lincoln and Davis, a movement against Richmond meant a Confederate play for Washington. On July 11, Jubal Early was within five miles of the White House with fifteen thousand men. Grant countered by sending his own detachment, but believed that had Early arrived sooner he could have seized the capital.

Surveying the wreckage around Washington, Welles recorded "chimneys of the burnt houses, the still barricaded road, the trampled field." The home of Montgomery Blair had been put to the torch. In an orchard where fighting had taken place trees were "riddled to pieces with musketry."

Outside Atlanta, Jefferson Davis removed Johnston from command, replacing him with General John Hood. Johnston's policy of falling back and playing for time dissatisfied the Confederate president. The change in command was evident on July 20, when Hood directed a vicious assault where the lines commingled and a four-hour hand-to-hand fight ensued. Hooker lost 4,796 men to Sherman's 1,710. Sherman advanced again on Atlanta. Closing in, Hood sent half of his forces to attack Sherman's left flank. From noon till nightfall they battled, Hood losing 8,499 to 3,641. Six days later, the same attack cost Hood 4,632 men, to Sherman's seven hundred. With every hour it seemed Hood was vindicating Johnston's cautious, defensive strategy. It had been an expensive lesson for the Confederates. Sherman would not attack, but wait, "because soldiers, like other mortals, must have food." To that end, Sherman would carefully maneuver to destroy the railroad lines into the city.

As the Democratic Convention approached, there was a great deal of interest in Millard Fillmore and Franklin Pierce.

Senator George Read Riddle of Delaware wrote to Fillmore asking him to accept the nomination on a peace platform, or at least, "The Constitution as it is and the Union as it was."

"Pardon me for saying," Fillmore responded, "that I have no desire under any circumstances ever to be president again . . . That General McClellan would be nominated as the conservative Union candidate and in such a nomination I should most cordially concur." As for the platform, Fillmore said, he did not see any use for one "beyond the Constitution . . . the sole object."

Declining to be put forth as the nominee, Fillmore similarly refused to attend, referencing his oft cited retirement from politics, telling another supporter, "All I ask and all I hope for is that that convention will make a judicious nomination, which will unite all opposition elements against the present administration. For in my opinion if this administration (and its destructive, tyrannical policy is) continued for four years longer, our government will become a military despotism and this country be ruined." Strong language, but Fillmore insisted that the letter be kept private. That said, Fillmore was sharing his private views with a number of people. The same day he wrote, "all men who value their own liberty should unite to change the administration and if possible restore the Union and give peace to our bleeding country."

On August 25, James Buchanan wrote, "From all appearances, McClellan will be nominated. Whether for good or for evil time must determine." He was worried that the platform was too pacific: "We ought to commence negotiations with the South and offer them every reasonable guarantee for the security of their rights within the Union." He even supported a temporary cease-fire and a convention of the states. But as for a peace that recognized the independence of the South, "I confess I am far from being prepared."

Nor was Lincoln prepared. On August 17 he telegraphed Grant, "I have seen your dispatch expressing your unwillingness to break your hold where you are. Neither am I willing. Hold on with a bull-dog grip, and chew and choke as much as possible."

Nicolay wrote to Bates, "There is rather a bad state of feeling throughout the Union party about the political condition of things. The want of any decided military successes thus far, and the necessity of the new draft in the coming month, has materially discouraged many of our good friends, who are inclined to be a little weak kneed, and croakers are talking everywhere about the impossibility of re-electing Mr. Lincoln 'unless something is done.'"

The enormous death toll from Grant's Overland Campaign, with Richmond still standing strong, and with Sherman shut out of Atlanta, was depressing the president's fortunes with the war-weary public. On August 23, Lincoln gathered his cabinet and had them sign the back of a memorandum, sight unseen. "I am going to be beaten, and unless some great change takes place badly beaten," he wrote.

One week later, in one of the greatest acts of irony in the history of American politics, George McClellan was nominated by the

Democratic Party to defeat Lincoln for failing to successfully end the war.

"He would not have been my first choice," Buchanan said, "but I am satisfied. God grant that he may succeed! Peace would be a great, a very great blessing, but it would be purchased at too high a price at the expense of the Union."

Nicolay recorded that August 28 was "a sort of political Bull Run." The chairman of the Republican Executive Committee wrote the president that unless he sent commissioners with peace terms to the rebels, "we might as well quit and give up the contest." Meeting him in person with the cabinet, Lincoln argued that it would be worse to preemptively surrender the war than to lose the race.

On September 5, Fillmore declined an invitation to attend a McClellan rally in Union Square. He pointed out however that he would "with great pleasure cast my vote for General McClellan," on whose success "depends the salvation of our country." The recipients of the letter immediately asked permission to publish. Fillmore repeated again his desire to stay above the fray, "but you seem to think its publication might do good to the ... cause in which I confess I feel a very deep interest." This he had also heard from others, and therefore "reluctantly permit it to be published. The fact is, I can see no reasonable prospect of a restoration of this Union—the object nearest my heart—without a change of the avowed policy of this administration itself. Hence I am for a change and I look upon the election of General McClellan as the last hope for the restoration of the Union, and an honorable peace, and the security of personal liberty; and this you may publish to the world as my views on the pending crisis." Fillmore's letter and sentiments made major news throughout the country. If anything, it increased rather than abated the clamor for his time and attention. He resisted, retreating to his previous silence, his strong words in favor of McClellan and in opposition of Lincoln leaving no room for doubt. Toward the end of the 1860 election, he had expressed regret at not having taken a more public stand against Lincoln. Come what may, there would be no such recriminations this time.

The *Albany Evening Journal* remarked that Fillmore "is just the man out of which to make a first class Copperhead." The *Albany Journal* recorded that "The Copperhead press are rejoicing" over the endorsement, adding that "Fillmore, who stands about a shade worse than John Tyler, is quoted among the rebels in justification of their course."

Throughout the war, elections for state and federal offices alternatively constrained and strengthened the administration's efforts. But these elections were in great part influenced by the success of the war. The two were symbiotic; Union victories at the ballot box helped produce Union victories on the battlefield, which in turn lifted Union candidates. There is no better example of this than September 1, 1864, when General Sherman entered Atlanta. This, Grant believed, "probably had more effect in settling the election of the following November than all the speeches, all the bonfires, and all the parading with banners and bands of music in the north." Later in the month Hood would counterattack, driving around Sherman into Tennessee, hoping to cut him off from supplies and communications, trapping him and his army in Georgia. Detaching several divisions to deal with Hood, Sherman would drive into the heart of the Confederacy, to Savannah, before turning north with the objective of joining Grant before Richmond.

"Returns of the elections from Pennsylvania, Ohio, and Indiana come in today," wrote Welles on October 12. "They look very well, particularly the two latter." Chief justice Taney's death that day led one congressman to speculate, "The elections carried him off." Taney passed from the scene with his view of America as a stronghold for slavery thoroughly discredited, and the institution he had promoted so vigorously on the verge of destruction. The following day, in lieu of flowers, his home state of Maryland adopted a constitution that abolished slavery.

The former presidents were living in a world they did not recognize. The war policy they had criticized was working. The institution of slavery that they had conciliated was on the verge of destruction. With days to go in the election, Franklin Pierce reached out to Millard Fillmore. "I have been gratified by the attitude you have had from the commencement of the terrible civil war which has brought the Constitution to the dust and" the country "to the brink of utter ruin ... What have we to do but observe the march of events, thus far beyond the control of human wisdom and wait for returning reason and patriotism?"

November 8 was Election Day. Hay recorded, "The [White] House has been still and almost deserted today. Every body in Washington, not at home voting seems ashamed of it and stays away from the President." Lincoln told his secretary, "It is a little singular that I who am not a vindictive man, should have always been before the people for election in canvasses marked for their bitterness: always but once: When I came to Congress it was a quiet time: But always besides that the contests in which I have been prominent have been marked with great rancor."

Around 7:00 p.m., Lincoln went to the War Department to await the verdict. Major Eckert "came in shaking the rain from his cloak, with trousers very disreputably muddy," having fallen outside. "For such an awkward fellow," Lincoln said, "I am pretty sure-footed. It used to take a pretty dexterous man to throw me. I remember, the evening of the day in 1858, that decided the contest for the Senate between Mr. Douglas and myself, was something like this, dark, rainy, and gloomy. I had been reading the returns, and had ascertained that we had lost the legislature and started to go home. The path had been worn hog-backed and was slippering. My foot slipped from under me, knocking the other one out of the way, but I recovered myself and lit square: and I said to myself, 'It's a slip and not a fall.'" Lincoln had the first results sent to his wife, saying "She is more anxious than I." Abraham Lincoln had been the first president to win re-election since 1832. Conducted in the midst of a Civil War, the contest of 1864 brought over four million voters to the polls. Lincoln prevailed with 55 percent to 44 percent, winning every state but three— Kentucky, Delaware, and McClellan's home of New Jersey.

At the November 11 cabinet meeting, Lincoln revealed the secret document he had directed them to sign on August 23. "Gentlemen, do you remember last summer I asked you all to sign your names to the back of a paper of which I did not show you the inside? This is it." He directed Hay to open the letter without tearing it. The letter pledged their cooperation with the new president "as to save the Union between the election and the inauguration; as he will have secured his election on such ground that he cannot possibly save it afterwards."

"You will remember," Lincoln said, "that this was written at a time (6 days before the Chicago nominating convention) when as yet we had no adversary, and seemed to have no friends. I then solemnly resolved on the course of action indicated above. I resolved, in the case of election of General McClellan being certain that he would be the candidate, that I would see him and talk matters over with him." Lincoln intended to tell him "the election has demonstrated that you are stronger, have more influence with the American people than I. Now let us together, you with your influence and I with all the executive power of the government, try to save the country. You raise as many troops as you possibly can for this final trial, and I will devote all my energies to assisting and finishing the war."

Seward joked that McClellan would answer "'yes, yes,' and then when you saw him again and pressed these views upon him he would say 'yes-yes' and so on forever and would have done nothing at all."

"At least," Lincoln said, "I should have done my duty and have stood clear before my own conscience."

CHAPTER 41

The Last Full Measure

It seems to me that I have been dreaming a horrid dream for four years, and now the nightmare is gone. I want to see Richmond.
—ABRAHAM LINCOLN

Lincoln - Buchanan

The election of 1860 had ushered in a new America. After all the compromises, before and after the Constitution, the North would not yield another foot to slavery. So much had transpired in the four years since then. Now the election of 1864 had ratified that earlier verdict but also expanded it. The Marquis de Chambrun, a visiting French aristocrat who would come to know Lincoln well, put it best: "By Mr. Lincoln's re-election the American people had clearly signified its political intentions: the war was to be carried on to ultimate success and slavery to be abolished. Such were the solemn and decisive utterances of the national will." The former presidents, who had compromised and capitulated in the face of the slave power for so long, were living relics of an era that now was gone. Whatever compass they had followed that had led them to the presidency now failed to work in the new America. Nothing better reflected this disconnect than the words of James Buchanan after the election.

"Now would be the time for conciliation on the part of Mr. Lincoln," he wrote. "A frank and manly offer to the Confederates that they might return to the Union just as they were before they left it, leaving the slavery question to settle itself, might possibly be accepted. Should they return, he would have the glory of accomplishing the object of the war against the most formidable rebellion which has ever existed. He ought to desire nothing more." Somehow a traveling French marquis had discerned what was happening with the American people, while a former president did not.

On December 8, Lincoln took a major step in implementing the public's vision of a new America, nominating Salmon Chase to replace Roger Taney as chief justice. A leading and longtime abolitionist would now sit in the chair of the author of *Dred Scott*. Nicolay recorded, "Probably no other man than Lincoln would have had, in this age of the world, the degree of magnanimity to thus forgive and exalt a rival who had so deeply and so unjustifiably intrigued against him. It is however only another most marked illustration of the greatness of the President, in this age of little men."

Another example of Lincoln's generosity was soon to be found, for on Christmas Eve, Laura Jones, who had traveled north three years earlier to care for her sick mother, became stuck behind the lines, separated from her fiancée. She asked for a pass so that she could travel to Richmond to be married. Welles, who was helping Lincoln process his many visitors that day, warned that she was a secessionist. Welles remembered, "He said he would let her go; the war had depopulated the country and prevented marriages enough, and if he could do a kindness of this sort he was disposed to, unless I advised otherwise. He wrote a pass and handed it to me."

The day after Christmas, three hundred guns were fired on Vermont Avenue, announcing major news from Georgia. Lincoln wrote Sherman, "Many, many thanks for your Christmas gift, the capture of Savannah." Lincoln acknowledged that Sherman's strategy of dividing his forces and driving to the east received nothing but his acquiescence, and gave him all the credit for its success. It had indeed been successful; Hood's movements on Tennessee were a flat failure, and after attacks on Franklin and Nashville, his army was obliterated, removing them from the field of battle. Receiving Lincoln's letter, Sherman "experienced more satisfaction in giving to his overburdened and weary soul one gleam of satisfaction and happiness, than of selfish pride in an achievement which has given me among men a larger measure of fame than any single act of my life."

In his final annual message, Lincoln recommended a constitutional amendment abolishing slavery to the lame duck Congress that had rejected it. Lincoln had asked the National Union Convention that had nominated him to include it in the platform. Lincoln had run on that amendment, won on that amendment, and now urged Congress to enact the mandate of the people.

Lincoln was engaged in the legislative process as never before, working with congressional leaders, counting votes, lobbying members personally for passage. It was not long before this day that the massive patronage power of the president had been leveraged to try to force a pro-slavery Constitution on an unwilling people. Now it would be harnessed to effect passage of an amendment banning slavery throughout the country. No evidence exists for Lincoln specifically offering jobs in exchange for votes, but it appears he allowed the floor managers of the amendment to do so, promises that were later honored in a number of instances. Where votes could not be procured, absences during the vote were encouraged, since the 2/3 threshold necessary for passage was limited to members present. On the eve of the vote, the amendment was threatened by a rumor of Confederate peace commissioners on their way to Washington. With a substantial number of "yes" votes predicated on the argument that the amendment could bring about peace, a conclusion of hostilities was perhaps the worst news possible. To counteract it, Lincoln wrote Congressman James Ashley, the amendment's sponsor, "So far as I know, there are no peace commissioners in the city, or likely to be in it." The commissioners were, in fact, on their way to Hampton Roads, under a pass that Lincoln issued the day before.

All the efforts succeeded, by the narrow margin of 118–59. There was "loud and long applause" upon passage. The victory "filled [Lincoln's] heart with joy. He saw in it the complete consummation of his own great work, the Emancipation Proclamation."

On February 1, 1865, Lincoln transmitted the amendment to the states for ratification, while Sherman left Savannah on his way to the state where the crisis began. "The whole army is burning with an insatiable desire to wreak vengeance upon South Carolina," Sherman wrote. "I almost tremble at her fate, but feel that she deserves all that seems to be in store for her. This march was like the thrust of a sword toward the heart of the human body; each mile of advance swept aside all opposition, consumed the very food on which Lee's army depended for life, and demonstrated a power in the national government which was irresistible."

James Buchanan wrote, "I confess I was much gratified at the capture of Charleston. This city was the nest of all our troubles. For more than a quarter century the people were disunionists, and during this whole period have been persistently engaged in inoculating the other slave states with their virus. Alas! for poor Virginia, who has suffered so much, and who was so reluctantly dragged into their support."

March 4, 1865, began "rainy and unpleasant, and the streets and sidewalks were encrusted with from two to ten inches of muddy paste, through which men and horses plodded wearily." But as "Lincoln stepped forward to take the oath of office, the sun, which had been obscured by rain clouds, burst forth in splendor." In the crowd were freed blacks, now able to participate in a presidential inauguration. In his address, Lincoln succinctly explained what had led to this moment. "Both parties deprecated war, but one of them would make war rather than let the nation survive, and the other would accept war rather than let it perish, and the war came." From the ashes of the war, Lincoln articulated his vision for the future of America. "With malice toward none, with charity for all, with firmness in the right as God gives us to see the right, let us strive on to finish the work we are in, to bind up the nation's wounds, to care for him who shall have borne the battle and for his widow and his orphan, to do all which may achieve and cherish a just and lasting peace among ourselves and with all nations."

The president of the United States heard "subdued sobs, as if a number of people were weeping." He walked downstairs and traveled room to room but encountered no one. "Where were all the people who were grieving as if their hearts would break?" he wondered. He found the East Room filled with mourners, where he saw a coffin resting on a platform, guarded by soldiers. He asked one, "Who is dead in the White House?"

"The President," he answered. "He was killed by an assassin!" A scream from the crowd woke Lincoln from his dream. He "slept no more that night."

On April 2, "a strange agitation was perceptible on the streets of Richmond," wrote one Confederate captain. While attending church,

Jefferson Davis received a telegram from Lee. They could hold out no longer; Richmond must be evacuated. It was shortly thereafter announced that evening services would be cancelled.

Ulysses Grant awoke every day worried that he would find Lee had escaped him. One of his generals joked, "Grant had been sleeping with one eye open and one foot out of bed for many weeks." On April 3, the enemy was gone. Grant declined to use his artillery to destroy the retreating Confederates, believing he could force them to surrender before long.

Lincoln landed by boat in Virginia, and traveled to Petersburg to meet with Grant. As he did, "many of the dead and dying were still on the ground." Lincoln's companion, George Crook, wrote, "I can still see one man with a bullet hole through his forehead and another with both arms shot away." The previously high-spirited president's face "settled into its old lines of sadness." They were greeted at their destination by Captain Robert Lincoln, his oldest son, who had been serving on Grant's staff, and who led them through the ghostly streets of Petersburg to his commander.

"Do you know, General," Lincoln said to Grant, "that I have had a sort of a sneaking idea for some days that you intended to do something like this."

When Lincoln returned to City Point, news had arrived that Richmond had been taken at 8:15 that morning. The Third New Hampshire, who had spoken out so strongly against Pierce and his allies in the 1864 elections, had the honor to be the first to enter. "Thank God I have lived to see this," Lincoln said. "It seems to me that I have been dreaming a horrid dream for four years, and now the nightmare is gone. I want to see Richmond."

The James River narrowed as it approached Richmond, and Lincoln, along with his party, was tugged in by a little boat, the *Bat*, which was manned by Marines. They were pulled by a long rope, in case the *Bat* struck one of the many mines or torpedoes left in the water. "On either side dead horses, broken ordnance, wrecked boats floated near our boat," Crook remembered, "and we passed so close to torpedoes that we could have put out our hands and touched them."

Lincoln walked through the captured capital with six sailors in front of him, and six behind, armed with short rifles. Lincoln was silently scrutinized from a distance through windows, behind trees and telegraph poles. Crook, looking at Lincoln, saw "His face was set. It had the calm in it that comes over the face of a brave man when he is ready for whatever may come."

This trip to Richmond may well be considered the climax of the Lincoln story, for perhaps nothing he did thereafter was of greater moment. From his time as a little boy, Abraham Lincoln had dreamt of being president of the United States. His election, when it finally happened, had been resisted by arms, and he had assumed the presidency of a Union badly broken. But now, in the former capital of the Confederacy, with Grant and Sherman on the heels of their adversaries, his very presence was a powerful deposit on his promise, "malice toward none . . . charity for all."

The first residents of Richmond encountered by Lincoln were black workers who, dropping their tools, enveloped the president, fell to their knees, and attempted to kiss his feet.

"Don't kneel to me," Lincoln said, "That is not right. You must kneel to God only, and thank Him for the liberty you will hereafter enjoy. My poor friends, you are free—free as air. You can cast off the name of slave and trample upon it; it will come to you no more. Liberty is your birthright. God gave it to you as He gave it to others, and it is a sin that you have been deprived of it for so many years."

From there the party traveled to the Confederate White House. "This must have been President Davis's chair," Lincoln said. Lincoln crossed his legs and "looked far off with a serious, dreamy expression."

On April 6, Mary, members of the cabinet, and the Marquis de Chambrun joined Lincoln at City Point. Lincoln led his guests to the River Queen and discussed the positions of Grant's army, his recent communications with his general, and where he believed Lee would finally be compelled to surrender. Lincoln appeared "satisfied and at rest, but in spite of the manifest success of his policy it was impossible to detect in him the slightest feeling of pride, much less of vanity. He spoke with the modest accent of a man who realizes that success has crowned his persistent efforts, and who finds in that very success the end of a terrible responsibility."

On Sunday, Lincoln joined his wife, members of Congress and the cabinet, and the marquis on a steamer up the Potomac. The president entertained his guests with hours of recited Shakespeare. He paused during a reading from *Macbeth*, the soliloquy that follows the murder of the king. Lincoln explained that, "the dark deed achieved, its tortured perpetrator came to envy the sleep of his victim." Lincoln then read the scene again. Passing Mount Vernon, the marquis told him, "Mount Vernon and Springfield, the memories of Washington and your own, those of the revolutionary and civil wars; these are the spots and names America shall one day equally honor."

"Springfield!" Lincoln said. "How happy, four years hence, will I be to return there in peace and tranquility."

Arriving in Washington, the presidential party noticed, "The streets were alive with people, all very much excited. There were bonfires everywhere." They stopped a passing carriage to ask what had happened. Grant had cornered Lee near Appomattox Courthouse and accepted his surrender.

A senator traveling with Lincoln noticed, "His whole appearance, poise, and bearing had marvelously changed. He was, in fact, transfigured. That indescribable sadness which had previously seemed to be an adamantine element of his very being, had been suddenly changed for an equally indescribable expression of serene joy, as if conscious that the great purpose of his life had been achieved."

On April 14, Lincoln breakfasted with son Robert, before meeting with his cabinet and General Grant at 11:00 a.m. Lincoln predicted that good news would be soon in coming from Sherman in his movements against Johnston, for he had always experienced the same dream before such events.

Welles remembered Lincoln's vision. "He seemed to be in some singular, indescribable vessel, and that he was moving with great rapidity towards an indefinite shore; that he had this dream preceding Sumter, Bull Run, Antietam, Gettysburg, Stone River, Vicksburg, Wilmington, etc."

Grant pointed out that Stone River was certainly no victory.

The president said "however that might be, his dream preceded that fight."

"I had this strange dream again last night," he continued, "and we shall, judging from the past, have great news very soon. I think it must be from Sherman."

Lincoln spoke against "persecution" and "bloody work" now that war was done. There would be no hangings, not even for the leaders of the rebellion. "We must extinguish our resentment if we expect harmony and union." Stanton remembered him "more cheerful and happy than I had ever seen him."

On a carriage ride that afternoon, Mary remarked that she had only seen her husband this happy once before, right before Willie died. "And well may I feel so, Mary, for I consider that this day the war has come to a close."

"Mary," he said, "we have had a hard time of it since we came to Washington, but the war is over, and with God's blessing we may hope for four years of peace and happiness, and then we will go back to Illinois and pass the rest of our lives in quiet." Lincoln talked fondly of Springfield, the days of his youth, his law practice and time on the circuit. As the day came to an end, Washington was the scene of "torchlight processions" and music.

Lincoln received many callers throughout the day. At ten past eight he excused himself, for he and Mary had tickets to see *Our American Cousin* at Ford's Theatre. "Mother," he said to his wife, "I suppose it's time to go, though I would rather stay."

Do Not Despair of the Republic

*Let us buy one immense homestead for Fillmore, Pierce, and Buchanan
... the Republic certainly owes them a debt of gratitude for the neglect
to advocate in any hearty manner the cause of the Republic during its
late struggle for existence. If we had been cursed with the active assistance of such friends, we should surely have gone to ruin.*
—*SYRACUSE DAILY JOURNAL,* MAY 12, 1865

On the morning of April 15, Franklin Pierce waited at the Concord Post
Office for updates on Lincoln's condition. That evening a crowd gathered
outside Pierce's house, which displayed no signs of mourning, prepared
to cause trouble. The former president came outside to address them. "I
wish I could address to you words of solace. But that can hardly be done.
The magnitude of the calamity, in all its aspects, is overwhelming. If your
hearts are oppressed by events more calculated to awaken profound sorrow and regret than any which have hitherto occurred in our history, mine
mingles its deepest regrets and sorrows with yours.

"It is not necessary for me to show my devotion for the Stars and
Stripes by any special exhibition of any man or body of men . . . If the
period which I have served our state and country in various situations,
commencing more than thirty-five years ago, has left the question of my
devotion to the flag, the constitution and the Union in doubt, it is too
late now to resume it by any such exhibition as the enquiry suggests." The
crowd had listened to him silently. He bid them "Good night!" and they
responded with "three cheers" for Pierce.

After the war, Pierce would spend considerable time trying to secure
Jefferson Davis's release from prison. Pierce was Davis's first choice for an

attorney, but his friends, unaware of his preference, enlisted someone else. The ex-president reread the body of Hawthorne's work, knowing perhaps that an author can always be accessed through what he leaves behind. Famously secular, the only president who had affirmed rather than sworn the oath of office was baptized at St. Paul's Episcopal Church in Concord, on the two-year anniversary of his devout wife's death. "I have turned, I hope, with a submission of spirit to Him who is 'the resurrection and the life.'" What sins he may have atoned for remained between him and God.

On April 16, 1865, a group of young men visited Julia Tyler on Staten Island.

"Madame, I beg pardon for disturbing you," their leader said, "but we have called to ask for the Secession flag you have in your possession."

"There is no such flag here," replied Mrs. Tyler.

"I beg pardon again, but such a flag, if I am not mistaken, hangs over your parlor mantle-piece."

Tyler denied it again. "You can look for yourself." He did, and found it right where he was looking. The object in question, which bears a striking resemblance to the Confederate battle flag, was actually made by her sister ten years earlier. It was eventually returned.

Robert Tyler, the president's oldest son, Confederate Register of the Treasury, had fled Richmond with Jefferson Davis. Dismissed in Charlotte, he was left destitute. James Buchanan, whose ambitions he had served over many years, sent him a check for $1,000. "Although I could not approve your course in favor of the secessionists," Buchanan wrote, "yet I have never doubted the sincerity of your belief and the purity of your motives. Thank God! The war is over, and the Union has not been broken."

Tyler responded that he was "not originally a disunionist, as I had no intention of leaving Pennsylvania at the commencement of the war. I was forcibly expelled, and lost all in a day—office, home, friends, and property—for which I had toiled for years."

Ironically, in light of its multiple occupations during the war, Sherwood Forest remains the only home of any president occupied by his descendants.* President Andrew Johnson pardoned Julia Tyler, while John Tyler, never pardoned by name, was covered by a general amnesty for Confederate officials issued after the war. He remains the only president of the United States to die an enemy of his country.

James Buchanan believed Lincoln was "a man of kindly and benevolent heart," an impression that never changed. He wrote, "The ways of divine providence are inscrutable, and it is the duty of poor, frail man, whether he will or not, to submit to his mysterious dispensations. The war—the necessary war, forced upon us by the madness of the rebels—we all fondly hoped was drawing to a triumphant conclusion in the restoration of the Union with a return of friendly relations among all the states, under the auspices of Mr. Lincoln. At such a moment the terrible crime was committed, which hurried him into eternity; and God only knows what may be the direful consequences. I deeply mourn his loss from private feelings, but still more for the sake of the country. Heaven, I trust, will not suffer the perpetrators of the deed and their guilty accomplices to escape just punishment." But "we must not despair for the Republic," offering his encouragement at the presidency of Andrew Johnson, whom he had "known . . . for many years."

The war over, Buchanan could now attempt the overriding ambition of his post-presidency. "The world is at last favored with James Buchanan's book on the rebellion," quipped the *Lowell Daily Citizen.* But contrary to his expectations, Buchanan would find his reputation materially unchanged from the day he left office. The *Philadelphia Inquirer* wrote, "Nobody cares particularly what excuses Mr. Buchanan may offer for his official derelictions. We know what the effect of his vacillation was, and we have paid very dearly for the information . . . As a literary venture, Buchanan's 'last dying speech and confession' would not command as wide a sale as the recollections of the hero of the last sensational murder."

On the day Lincoln died, Millard Fillmore's house was splashed with black ink, in retaliation for the fact that it was the only one on his block without mourning drape. The lack of recognition was attributable to a less sinister motive than the vandals suspected—Fillmore was simply out of

---

* Two sons of his second youngest son, Tyler, are still alive at the time of this writing.

town. Writing his condolences to Mary Lincoln, Fillmore said, "Sympathizing most deeply with you in your affliction, and understanding from the papers that you may be expected in this city on Thursday next, Mrs. Fillmore and myself would esteem it a favor if you and your family would make our house your house during your time in the city." Robert Lincoln, on behalf of his mother, responded that they would not be in Buffalo on Thursday, and therefore unable to accept. "My mother is still confined to her room . . . and will not be able to travel for some weeks."

A debate began in the newspapers regarding Fillmore's role in the war. He saved some of these articles, positive and otherwise. One read, "Discussion of Mr. Fillmore's course in connection with the war has been opened by his friends and social satellites. We seem to have no choice left us but to allow the use of our columns to those who desire to oppose, in a dignified manner, the effort that is being made to puff up the patriotism and loyalty of an 'old public functionary.'" Another was from his neighbor of twenty years, who reminded the public of his loyalty, particularly his services at the outset of the war, reminding them that streets named after Fillmore in the South were changed to Davis and Beauregard and Lee.

On May 9, Fillmore spoke to the Buffalo Historical Society, formed in the midst of a Civil War, in the ultimate recognition that the past has value.

"Perhaps no member of this society appreciates more fully than I do, the difficult task which President Lincoln had to perform, and I am sure none can deplore his death more sincerely than I do.

"It is well known that I have not approved of all acts which have been done in his name during his administration, but I am happy to say that his recent course met my approbation, and I have looked forward with confident expectation that he would soon be able to end the war, and by his kind, conciliatory manner win back our erring and repentant brethren and restore the Union." He expressed sympathy for President Johnson, "in being thus suddenly called to the helm of state.

"While, therefore, we justly deplore the loss of President Lincoln, let us never despair of the republic . . . Let us remember amidst all our grief and disappointments that there is an unerring Providence that governs this world, and that no one man is indispensable to a nation's life; and let us look hopefully for the rainbow of peace that will surely succeed the storm if we do our own duty."

As Fillmore, Pierce, and Buchanan reacted to the death of their successor, it fell once again to the Marquis de Chambrun, who was far enough away, to describe the situation accurately. "Nothing revealed to me more clearly the true greatness of America," he wrote, than watching a nation, through its sorrow, invest its support in the new president. "Thus while I stood motionless and awed with sadness before Mr. Lincoln's bloody remains, his country had already recovered self-possession. I then understood and realized that a nation may place her confidence in a chief without giving herself wholly to him; and that room still is left for great characters and great virtues in a people proud enough to believe that however pure, honest, and noble those to whom it entrusts governmental honors may be, itself remains greater yet than they."

Abraham Lincoln assumed the presidency over the opposition of five of his predecessors, who feared that he would break the customs of the office that they had established and carefully cultivated. Their concerns were well founded. The American presidency is now a dynamic institution and powerful force for principle in the hands of the proper occupant. Enlarged to these new proportions, it could never again shrink to what it was before. In the last of the debates that made him famous, Lincoln argued that the cause for which he dedicated—and gave—his life was part of a struggle as ancient as humanity itself: whether a man had the right to control another man. The struggle continues to this day. The American people have often been governed by a chief executive who did not reflect their inherent wisdom, integrity, and exceptionalism. Often America has been bereft of the leadership it wanted. But we may find comfort in knowing that in hours of great crisis for the Republic, America has never failed to find the leader to match the moment.

ACKNOWLEDGMENTS

I begin, as with all my acknowledgments, by thanking God for the ability and opportunity to write yet another book. "A man can receive nothing unless it has been given him from heaven" (John 3:27 NAS).

I am thankful for my family, my mother Anna and sister Cathy, for their constant love and support.

I am indebted to Rob Peck for inspiring this book. I had never known of the former presidents who lived to see the Civil War until a visit to Seattle in 2012 and a conversation with my friend.

Trey Terry, combat veteran and Civil War expert, was invaluable in my understanding of tactics, troop movements, and the play by play of various critical battles, sometimes demonstrated with different-colored sweetener packets in Trey's unique pedagogical style.

James Slattery, my best friend, was critical in helping me identify the central thesis of the book: namely, that the former presidents represented an old America, the close of which was ushered in by Abraham Lincoln.

Nolan Davis, longtime mentor and friend, to whom this book is dedicated, who taught me whatever it is I know about chasing (and catching) dreams.

Amy Durbin, a great historian who read this book first and provided valuable feedback.

Keith Wallman, my superlative editor who makes my writing better. I am at a rare loss for words to properly express how grateful I am to have had him on this book. For Meredith Dias, my highly organized and supportive project manager, and all of the professionals at Globe Pequot/ Lyons Press. For Josh Rosenberg, who copyedited this manuscript with an extraordinary eye for detail. It has been a pure joy to collaborate with such high-caliber people, who clearly love this project and have worked so hard to make it successful.

For Adam Chromy, my outstanding agent at Movable Type Management, may this be the first of many successful projects together.

For my colleagues and students at Arizona Summit Law School, who have enriched my life immensely, especially McKay Cunningham, Dave Cole, Steve Gerst, Christine Ritland, Nancy Milar, Keith Swisher, and Stacey Dowdell.

Abraham Lincoln was right when he said, "The better part of one's life consists of their friendships." The better part of mine has included friends like Nahiyan Ahmed, Chris Ashby, Elliot Berke, Tim Bourcet, Ed Brookover. Josh Daniels, Jeremy Duda, Ashley Fickel, Megan Flickinger-Wojtulewicz, Meredith Glacken, James Green, Justin Herman, Eric Johnson, Gabby and Tom Kearney, Josh Kilroy, Adam Kwasman, Michael LaPidus, Heather Macre and Steven Kruczek, Danny and Bonnie Mazza, Pete and Theresa Nguyen, Mike Nimtz, Steve Orlando, Larry Pike, Katrina Shackelford, Jonathan Shuffield, Todd Sommers, David and Caroline Van Slyke and our entire small group, Vinnie Vernuccio, and Jim and Kitty Waring.

And finally, for all of my wonderful readers. It has meant the world to me to have such a dedicated, smart group of people who enjoy these books. Thank you for making possible this extraordinary new chapter in my life.

Sources

Prologue: In Jackson's Time

xi. *"unsurpassed for richness and variety, elegance and abundance.":* New-Hampshire Patriot, April 26, 1830.

xi. *occupied by the president of the United States.:* Parton, James. *The Life of Andrew Jackson.* New York: Houghton, Mifflin, and Company, 1888, 282.

xii. *stay at the dinner while others walked out.:* Benton, Thomas Hart. *Thirty Years' View,* Volumes I–III (New York: D. Appleton and Company, 1854), 148.

xii. *an exploded bomb!" as one biographer put it.:* Parton, *Life of Andrew Jackson,* 284.

xii. *emanated will forever sustain it.":* Van Buren, Martin. *The Autobiography of Martin Van Buren* (Washington, DC: Government Printing Office, 1920), 417.

xiii. *upon the first tree I can reach.":* This encounter with the congressman appears in Parton, *Life of Andrew Jackson,* 284–85.

xiii. *the staple question of his daily visitors.":* Nicolay, John, and Hay, John. *Abraham Lincoln: A History,* Volumes I–X (New York: The Century Company, 1914), 3:247.

xiv. *and maintain the existing government.":* Ibid., 3:248.

Chapter 1: I Met Nullification at Its Threshold

1. *faded along with his view of the coast.:* Van Buren, *Autobiography,* 446–47.

1. *by 200 votes out of 30,000 cast.:* Bancroft, George. *Martin Van Buren to the End of His Public Career* (New York: Harper and Brothers, 1889), 20.

1. *along with six slaves his mother had inherited.:* Sibley, Joel. *Martin Van Buren and the Emergence of American Popular Politics* (Lanham, MD: Rowman and Littlefield, 2002), 2.

2. *administrations of Jefferson and Madison.":* Ibid., 9.

2. *his employer's office to earn his place.:* Ibid., 4.

2. *a name for himself defending small landholders.:* Bancroft, *Van Buren,* 9.

2. *competing ideological and ethnic factions.:* Silbey, *Martin Van Buren,* 22.

2. *first true statewide political machine.:* Ibid., 25.

2. *concurrently with his state senate seat).:* Bancroft, *Van Buren,* Chapter 2, passim; 49.

2. *Van Buren a member of the US Senate.:* Silbey, *Martin Van Buren,* 35.

2. *led by Secretary of State John Quincy Adams.:* Ibid., 41.

3. *offered him an early endorsement in 1826.:* Ibid., 48.

3. *popularity," he believed they could unseat Adams.:* Martin Van Buren to Thomas Ritchie, January 13, 1827, Papers of Martin Van Buren.

3. *in the building of new party operations.:* Silbey, *Martin Van Buren,* 49.

3. *to winning a landslide across the country.:* Ibid., 54.

4. *disparaging the character of the government.":* Van Buren, *Autobiography,* 339.

4. *cabinet wives in ostracizing the Eatons.:* Meacham, Jon. *American Lion: Andrew Jackson in the White House* (New York: Random House, 2008), 71.

4. *caused the president "daily anguish.":* Van Buren, *Autobiography,* 339.

4. *joined Van Buren in supporting Margaret.:* Parton, *Life of Andrew Jackson,* 302.

4. *are becoming very jealous of each other.":* Silbey, *Martin Van Buren,* 69.

4. *mounting upon the shoulders of Mrs. Eaton.":* Meacham, *American Lion,* 124–25.

4. *by the British and Russian ministers.:* Parton, *Life of Andrew Jackson,* 289.

5. *say as much for Mr. Calhoun.":* Ibid., 295; Jackson to Judge Overton, December 31, 1829.

5. *humiliation of his friend by his enemies.":* Van Buren, *Autobiography,* 403.

5. *England would allow him a face-saving departure.:* Ibid., 405.

5. *the truth as I spread it before him.":* Ibid.

5. *who had failed to follow in kind.:* Parton, *Life of Andrew Jackson,* 345.

6. *warm a reception as ever a conqueror had.":* Letter from Churchill Cambreleng to Van Buren, January 27, 1832, reprinted in Van Buren, *Autobiography,* 454.

6. *experiencing the excesses of party spirit.":* Van Buren, *Autobiography,* 456.

6. *had come after two days of fiery debate.:* Remini, Robert. *Henry Clay, Statesman for the Union* (New York: W.W. Norton, 1991). 384.

6. *he predicted, "and elected a Vice President.":* Byrd, Robert. *The Senate 1789–1989* (Washington DC: 1991), 121.

6. *Calhoun is greatly injured.":* Tyler, Lyon Gardiner, ed. *The Letters and Times of the Tylers,* Volumes I–III (Richmond: Whittet & Shepperson, 1884), 1:438–39.

6. *and to select his running mate.:* Van Buren, *Autobiography,* 503.

7. *declining to yield to their wishes.":* Ibid., 510

7. *and establishing an independent nation.:* Parton, *Life of Andrew Jackson,* 457–58.

7. *with which he had been entrusted.":* Ibid., 461.

7. *and even sell cargo to satisfy the duty.:* Ibid.

8. *smashing his pipe to splinters on the table.:* The story of Dale's visit to the White House can be found in Parton, *Life of Andrew Jackson,* 462.

8. *the pages in order for them to dry.:* Ibid., 466.

8. *Palmetto State had gone over to the nullifiers.:* Somit, Albert. "Jackson as Administrator." *Public Administration Review,* Vol. 8, No. 3 (Summer, 1948), 195–96.

8. *preserved at all hazards and at any price.":* Jackson's proclamation, issued December 12, 1830.

9. *to obtain a mastery over his passions.":* Tyler, *Letters and Times, 1:531.*

9. *my nose must be there already.":* Ibid., 1:546.

9. *request to use the military in South Carolina.:* Ibid., 1:453.

9. *lose his seat in opposition if necessary.:* Ibid., 1:441.

10. *politically speaking, elsewhere than to my state.:* Senate Journal, February 6, 1833

10. *grow out of this measure, you are alone responsible.":* Ibid.

10. *in his reappointment by a wide margin.:* Tyler, *Letters and Times,* 1:454.

10. *whether this tact would resolve the crisis.:* Remini, *Clay,* 418.

10. *tariff existed simply to fund the government.:* Ibid., 425

10. *hands on the floor, congratulating one another.:* Tyler, *Letters and Times,* 1:596.

11. *in Washington on the 26th of February, 1833.":* Van Buren, *Autobiography*, 554.
11. *vice president, over friends and enemies alike.:* Ibid., 566.
11. *shall be troubled with them again shortly.":* Both Jackson's letter and Buchanan's response can be found in Buchanan, James. *The Works of James Buchanan*, Volumes I–XI (Philadelphia: J.B. Lippincott Company, 1911), 2:328.

Chapter 2: The Freshmen

12. *to backbreaking labor in western New York.:* Smith, Elbert. *The Presidencies of Zachary Taylor and Millard Fillmore* (Lawrence: University of Kansas Press, 1988), 43.
12. *and could then fix it in my memory.":* Rayback, Robert. *Millard Fillmore: Biography of a President* (Buffalo: Publications of the Buffalo Historical Society, 1959), 6.
12. *personal library of more than four thousand volumes.:* Ibid., 43.
13. *I enjoyed the reading very much.":* Autobiographical statement in the Millard Fillmore Papers. Severance, Frank, ed. *The Papers of Millard Fillmore*, Volumes I–II (Buffalo: Buffalo Historical Society, 1907).
13. *whom he persuaded to take on Fillmore as a law clerk.:* Rayback, *Fillmore*, 7.
13. *a sturdy home, one that stands to this day.:* Millard Fillmore Papers, autobiographical statement ("Fillmore Autobiography").
14. *that abolished imprisonment for debt.:* Rayback, *Fillmore*, 35, 39.
14. *become the best known of its citizens.:* Millard Fillmore Papers, 2:485.
14. *destruction by the British had been complete.":* Rayback, *Fillmore*, 11.
14. *Abigail were frequent guests and hosts.:* Ibid., 43, 47.
14. *had started, only wetter, colder, and more fatigued.:* Nichols, Roy. *Franklin Pierce: Young Hickory of the Granite Hills* (Philadelphia: University of Pennsylvania Press, 1969), 9.
14. *the most important friendship of his life.:* Ibid., 19.
14–15. *provide him a salary while studying law.:* Ibid., 28.
15. *New Hampshire's governor after two previous defeats.:* Ibid., 32.
15. *helped create the New Hampshire Democratic Party.:* Ibid., 34.
15. *committee to overhaul control of the local schools.:* Ibid., 44.
15. *New Hampshire's legislative body of 230 to serve as speaker.:* Ibid., 54.
15. *and beckons us on—to find what? Disappointment.":* Ibid., 55.
15. *giving an advantage to Pierce's party.:* Wallner, Peter. *Franklin Pierce*, Volumes I–II (Concord: Plaidswede Publishing, 2007), 1:45.
15. *and check the course of our ambition.":* Ibid., 1:45.
15. *for Washington and the next session of Congress.:* Ibid., 1:52.
15. *with 25 Anti-Masons and 9 Nullifiers.:* Party Divisions in the House of Representatives; www.House.gov.
16. *to be so constantly pressed with engagements.":* Wallner, *Pierce*, 150.
16. *later be known as "The Panic Session" of Congress.:* Remini, *Clay*, 447.
16. *new revenues were placed in various state banks.:* Ibid., 444.
16. *the deposit question seems to be interminable.":* Wallner, *Pierce*, 1:49.
16. *opposite sides of numerous votes on the bank.:* House Journal, February 18, 1835.
16. *his own pocket as easily as in the state banks.:* Tyler, *Letters and Times*, 1:485.

16. *whether the separation of powers would be preserved.:* Scarry, Robert. *Millard Fillmore* *(Jefferson, NC: McFarland and Company, 2001)*, 48; Tyler, *Letters and Times*, 1:487.

16. *another pinch of your aromatic Maccoboy [tobacco].":* Remini, *Clay*, 452–53.

17. *a new era of political parties was born.:* Ibid., 461.

17. *as he was tackled to the ground.:* Tyler, *Letters and Times*, 1:508.

17. *as much fearlessness as one could possibly have done.":* Ibid., 1:509.

17. *taken you for a young man of twenty-five.":* Ibid., 1:510.

17. *attempt to assassinate the president.":* Scarry, *Fillmore*, 50.

17. *was such that Fillmore chose not to run again.:* Millard Fillmore Papers, Millard Fillmore autobiographical statement.

17. *printed, read, or referred to a committee.:* Wallner, *Pierce*, 1:62–63.

18. *and denounced abolitionists on the House floor.:* Ibid., 1: Chapter 4 passim.

18. *to disturb occasionally the quiet of a village.":* Nichols, *Young Hickory*, 83.

18. *with nine years of spirited debate to follow.:* Wallner, *Pierce*, 1:63.

18. *realigned Jackson with his base of support in Virginia.:* Tyler, *Letters and Times*, 1:522.

18. *my walking papers from the legislature," Tyler wrote.:* Ibid., 1:531.

18. *not to let the legislature drive him from the Senate.:* Ibid., 1:528.

18. Perserverando, *and all difficulties will vanish.":* Ibid., 1:514.

18. *and Socrates was poisoned.":* Ibid., 1:547.

18. *offered a judgeship to go away quietly, he declined.:* Ibid., 1:524.

18. *attained or held at the sacrifice of honor.":* Ibid., 1:536.

Chapter 3: The Setting Sun

19. *be nominated by the Democratic Party as his successor.:* Silbey, *Martin Van Buren*, 101.

19. *this against badly divided opposition.:* Ibid., 107.

19. *the rising was eclipsed by the setting sun.":* Benton, *Thirty Years' View*, 1:735.

20. *special session of Congress, the first in twenty-four years.:* Niven, John. *Martin Van Buren:* *The Romantic Age of American Politics* (Newtown, CT: American Political Biography Press, 2000), 412, 414–16, 422.

20. *essentially making the government its own banker.:* Ibid., 417–18.

20. *it extorted the respect of his enemies.":* Buchanan, *Works*, 3:324.

20. *too small for him to mount" on his behalf.:* Rayback, *Fillmore*, 100.

20. *Clay supporters looking to be mollified.:* Chitwood, Oliver. *John Tyler: Champion of the* *Old South* (Newtown, CT: American Political Biography Press, 1990), 167.

21. *an increase from 1.5 million to 2.5 million voters.:* Silbey, *Martin Van Buren*, 153–54.

21. *coonskin-cap-wearing, hard-cider-drinking yeoman farmer.:* Niven, *Romantic Age*, 461.

21. *log cabin was in reality a mansion in Indiana.:* Millard Fillmore Papers, 1:403.

21. *financial crisis, and advocating federal public works.:* Niven, *Romantic Age* 461.

21. *47 percent nationally while losing his home state to Harrison.:* Silbey, *Martin Van Buren* 153–54.

Chapter 4: . . . And Tyler, Too

22. *he took the oath of office at Brown's Indian Queen.:* Chitwood, *Tyler,* 202–3.
22. *the same shall devolve on the Vice President.":* United States Constitution, Article II, s. 1.
22. *special election was required to complete Harrison's term.:* John Tyler, Tenth Vice President, www.senate.gov/artandhistory/history/common/generic/VP_John_Tyler.htm.
23. *otherwise, your resignations will be accepted.":* Chitwood, *Tyler,* 270.
23. *spirited fight from former president John Quincy Adams.:* Tyler, *Letters and Times,* 2:13.
23. *and now Tyler was very much in Clay's way.:* Chitwood, *Tyler,* 211.
23. *he thought "will be in the nature of a regency.":* Remini, *Clay,* 580.
23. *May 31, in response to a call by President Harrison.:* Chitwood, *Tyler,* 211.
24. *empowered to set up branches in states that agreed.:* Tyler, *Letters and Times,* 2:15.
24. *voices were raised and Clay would not yield.:* Remini, *Clay,* 583.
24. *at this end of it as I shall think proper.":* Tyler, *Letters and Times,* 2:33.
24. *obsessive desire to fashion a third national bank.":* Remini, *Clay,* 581
24. *"earnestly recommended" Tyler sign it into law.:* Chitwood, *Tyler,* 224.
24. *"he has found one of old Jackson's pens.":* Remini, *Clay,* 590.
25. *himself burned in effigy:* Chitwood, *Tyler,* 228–29.
25. *banks to discount notes without state concurrence.:* Remini, *Clay,* 591.
25. *not with the Whigs, but with the Democrats.:* Remini, *Clay,* 594.
25. *that Henry Clay is a doomed man.":* Chitwood, *Tyler,* 273.
25. *fallen out with Jackson for the same reasons as himself.:* Ibid., 280.
25. *kicked Tyler out of the Whig Party.:* Ibid., 249.
25. *both of these are applicants for office.":* Millard Fillmore Papers, 2:225.
26. *you shall have the best train on the road.":* Lamon, Ward Hill. *Recollections of Abraham Lincoln 1847–1865* (Washington, DC: Published by his daughter, Dorothy Lamon Teillard), 133.
26. *returned to New Hampshire and his family.:* Wallner, *Pierce,* 1: 154.
26. *sore from laughter for days afterward.:* Arnold, Isaac Newton. *The Life of Abraham Lincoln* (Chicago: Jansen, McClurg, & Co., 1885), 74.
26. *hungry to be somebody.":* DeRose, Chris. *Congressman Lincoln: The Making of America's Greatest President* (New York: Simon and Schuster/Threshold, 2013), 63.
27. *he backed a successful bankruptcy bill.:* Scarry, *Fillmore,* 72.
27. *feasibility of this revolutionary new technology.:* Ibid., 74.
27. *to the cargo of American versus foreign ships.:* Ibid., 76.
27. *emotion, in the words of one reporter.:* Ibid., 76–77.
27. *deficit had become a surplus of five million dollars.:* Ibid., 78.
27. *quiet enjoyments of my own family and fireside.":* Ibid., 78.
27. *the lawful representatives of the state.:* Chitwood, *Tyler,* 326.
28. *and to pardon the leaders of the convention.:* Ibid., 337–38.
28. *Connecticut militia to defend the state government.:* Tyler, *Letters and Times,* 2:196.
28. *amended the constitution to increase voting rights.:* Chitwood, *Tyler,* 328.
28. *to the Republic, giving them official recognition.:* Niven, *Romantic Age,* 445.
28. *Mexico, who refused to acknowledge that Texas was independent, threatened war.:* Ibid., 445.
28. *been burned by Van Buren's snubbing of Texas's overtures.:* Merry, Robert. *A Nation of Vast Designs: James K. Polk, the Mexican War, and the Conquest of the American Continent* (New York: Simon & Schuster, 2009), 63, 73.

29. *a toast, causing him to miss the demonstration.:* Written recollection of John J. Hardin, in his papers, Chicago Historical Society, March 1, 1844; Chitwood, *Tyler*, 398.

29. *she collapsed in the arms of John Tyler.:* Chitwood, *Tyler*, 401.

29. *that he hoped to be their nominee in 1844.:* Ibid., 284.

29. *maybe even war backed by a European power.:* Remini, *Clay*, 639.

29. *had been traversing back to the presidency.:* Niven, *Romantic Age*, 531–32.

29. *a treaty of annexation was sent to the Senate.:* Chitwood, *Tyler*, 352.

29. *by the lopsided margin of 16–35.:* Ibid., 355.

29. *went on a month-long honeymoon in July.:* Ibid., 405.

30. *remaining six did not commit to any candidate.:* Silbey, *Martin Van Buren*, 167.

30. *he was forced to withdraw after nine ballots.:* Ibid., 177, 179.

30. *he would be bound to support the nominee.:* Tyler, *Letters and Times*, 2:317.

30. *met in Baltimore and nominated him for another term.:* Ibid., 2:315.

30. *country which would forbid my doing so.":* Ibid., 2:318–21.

31. *remained to achieve was for Texas to give her assent.:* Ibid., 2:363.

31. *People's eyes were filled with tears.:* Ibid., 2:367.

31. *and fell, and trembled, and rose again.":* Ibid., 2:369.

31. *status after his expulsion from the Whigs.:* Chitwood, *Tyler*, 410.

31. *sixty to ninety slaves living in twenty cabins on the property.:* Crapol, Edward. *John Tyler, the Accidental President* (Chapel Hill: University of North Carolina Press, 2012), 249, 253.

31. *and an assortment of other necessities.:* Chitwood, *Tyler*, 409.

31. *actions properly vindicated," his son remembered.:* Tyler, *Letters and Times*, 2:463.

32. *visit him, a courtesy due even a stranger.:* Omohundro Institute of Early American History and Culture. "Edmund Ruffin's Visit to Sherwood Forest." *William and Mary Quarterly*, Vol. 14, No. 3 (January 1906), 198.

32. *as faithfully as he had all of his other offices.:* Ibid., 198.

32. *a solemn obligation to continue his duty.:* Tyler, *Letters and Times*, 2:465.

32. *that I would not accede to their wishes.":* Curtis, George Ticknor. *Life of James Buchanan* (New York: Harper and Brothers, 1883), 1:549.

Chapter 5: War in Mexico!

33. *with her children, sharpening their debating skills.:* Autobiographical account by James Buchanan printed in Curtis, *Buchanan*, 1:2–3.

34. *refrain from shenanigans if he could only be readmitted.:* Curtis, *Buchanan*, 1:4–5.

34. *to humble our pride and self-sufficiency.":* Ibid., 1:6.

34. *a British invasion of the city that never materialized.:* Ibid., 1:8

34. *argued for his acquittal before the Senate.:* Ibid., 1:16–17.

35. *expected reconciliation could come to pass:* Ibid., 1:17.

35. *was infinitely dearer to me than life.":* Ibid., 1:18–19.

35. *would experience to having a child of his own.:* Ibid., 1:531.

35. *December of 1821, during the presidency of James Monroe.:* Ibid., 1:22–23.

35. *efforts helped Old Hickory win Pennsylvania.:* Ibid., 1:94.

35. *being talked about for the vice presidency.:* Ibid., 1:126.

35. *he was confirmed by the Senate a month later.:* Ibid., 1:135.
36. *attempt to see his ailing mother one final time.:* Ibid., 1:217.
36. *as Van Buren's attorney general five years later.:* Ibid., 1:452.
36. *an open field and a fair start.":* Ibid., 1:519.
36. *had been made under the circumstances.:* Ibid., 1:524.
36. *that Van Buren would have lost to Clay.:* Ibid., 1:525.
36. *withdraw from the treaty after a one-year notice.:* Merry, *Vast Designs,* 168.
36. *the United States did not find a way to bring them in.:* Ibid., 164.
37. *to revisit the question when Congress convened in December.:* Quaife, Milton, ed. *The Diary of James K. Polk During His Presidency,* Volumes I–IV (Chicago: McClurg, 1910), September 29, 1845.
37. *stormy deep nearly a quarter of a century.":* Curtis, *Buchanan,* 1:561.
37. *to back his Supreme Court claim, unsuccessfully.:* Polk Diary, January 22, 23, 26, 1846.
37. *in administering the government without his aid.":* Ibid., January 31, 1846.
38. *were arrested or placed in slavery.:* Merry, *Vast Designs,* 183–84.
38. *a technicality to send him back to Washington.:* Ibid., 210.
38. *to protect Texas from Mexican aggression.:* Ibid., 240.
38. *drafted by Buchanan and sent to Congress.:* Polk Diary, April 25, 1846.
38. *the president in his message to Congress.:* Ibid., May 9, 1846.
39. *which is about to divide the American people.":* Remini, *Clay,* 181; Potter, David. *The Impending Crisis: America Before the Civil War* (New York: Harper and Row, 1976), 20–23.
39. *North, but a serious insult to the South.:* Tyler, *Letters and Times,* 2:477.
40. *elevated as his rival for the nomination.:* Meigs, Montgomery. *The Life of Thomas Hart Benton* (Philadelphia: J.B. Lippincott Company, 1904), 365.
40. *made him the most popular man in America.:* DeRose, *Congressman Lincoln,* 63.
40. *resolved that Jane would not deny him this.:* Wallner, *Pierce* 1:138.
40. *head while killing the horse next to him.:* Ibid., 1:140.
40. *together accomplished exactly that within three hours.:* Ibid., 1:141.
41. *marched toward their final destination.:* Ibid., 1:143.
41. *the field while attempting to find his men.:* Ibid., 1:146.
41. *some of the bloodiest fighting of the war ensued.:* Ibid., 1:148.
41. *a strategic outpost for the defense of the capital.:* Ibid., 1:150.
41. *while the rest of the army triumphantly entered Mexico City.:* Ibid., 1:152.
41. *in 1847, had more power than the governor.:* Scarry, *Fillmore,* 92; Rayback, *Fillmore,* 169.
42. *the largest margin of any Whig in state history,:* Rayback, *Fillmore,* 170.
42. *as the party took control of the House of Representatives.:* Nevin, *Romantic Age,* 576.

Chapter 6: The 30th Congress

43. *reducing the number Winthrop needed for a majority.:* DeRose, *Lincoln,* 93–94.
43. *who were eager to bring the war to a conclusion.:* Ibid., 97.
43. *more painful than all his mental perplexity!":* Ibid., 98.
44. *he now finds himself he knows not where.":* Ibid., 135.
44. *a subsequent attempt to reverse it failed 105–95.:* Ibid., 123.

44. *Hidalgo, and sent it to a furious president.:* Ibid., 117.

45. *for a party and a country divided over slavery.:* Ibid., 120.

45. *one of whom is sure to be elected, if he is not.":* Basler, Roy, ed. *The Collected Works of Abraham Lincoln* (Springfield, IL: Abraham Lincoln Association, 1953), 1:463–64.

45. *thoroughly refuting the Democratic arguments.:* Nevin, *Romantic Age*, 570.

45. *had resulted in the Barnburners walking out.:* Silbey, *Martin Van Buren*, 192–93.

45. *each claiming to be the official Democratic meeting.:* Ibid., 195.

45. *unlikely event that he was placed for re-nomination.:* Nevin, *Romantic Age*, 578–79.

46. *presumably go through Fillmore rather than them.:* Rayback, *Fillmore*, 185–86.

46. *and none of the conspirators will succeed.":* Tyler, *Letters and Times*, 2:460.

47. *one issue, slavery extending into the territories.":* Niven, *Romantic Age*, 582, 587.

47. *"the most fallen man I have ever known.":* Ibid., 586–89.

47. *member to interrupt, shouting, "We give it up!".:* DeRose, *Lincoln*, 192.

48. *few lessons in deportment," he would remember.:* Ibid., 203.

48. *Kinderhook and could only spoil the election.":* Ibid. 205.

48. *respects to Millard Fillmore at Delevan House in Albany.:* Scarry, *Fillmore*, 93.

48. *anybody can be elected but himself.":* Tyler, *Letters and Times*, 2:462.

48. *Julia, he noted, was a Taylor supporter.:* Chitwood, *Tyler*, 428.

48. *the North, helping tip the election to Taylor.:* Silbey, *Martin Van Buren*, 201.

49. *we are at a crisis of some importance.":* DeRose, *Lincoln*, 240.

50. *against only one member who wanted it vetoed.:* Ibid., 239–40.

50. *my duties as President of the U. States.":* DeRose, *Congressman Lincoln*, 39–40.

Chapter 7: A Final Settlement

51. *to save the Whig party, if possible.:* Holt, Michael. *The Rise and Fall of the American Whig Party* (New York: Oxford University Press, 2003).

51. *refusal of northern states to surrender fugitive slaves.:* Nevins, Allan. *Ordeal of the Union*, Volumes I–VIII (New York: Scribner's, 1947), 1:257.

52. *slave trade; and a stronger fugitive slave law.:* Ibid., 1:266.

52. *for the North to cease agitating the slavery issue.:* Ibid., 1:282–83.

52. *"It is too ultra, and his ultimata impracticable.":* Tyler, *Letters and Times*, 2:481.

52. *product of decades of opposition to slavery.:* Nevins, *Ordeal*, 1:289–90.

53. *document provided the surest protection for slavery.:* Ibid., 1:300.

53. *its head to put down any rebellion in the South.:* Nevins, *Ordeal*, 1:308.

53. *I deemed it for the interests of the country.":* Rayback, *Fillmore*, 237.

53. *from the White House—the president was deathly sick.:* Scarry, *Fillmore*, 135.

53. *responsibility that would now devolve on him.:* Millard Fillmore Papers, 2:491.

53. *resignations; Fillmore accepted them all.:* Rayback, *Fillmore*, 242.

53. *fulfilled the role of secretary of state for Harrison and Tyler.:* Millard Fillmore Papers, 2:492.

54. *stepped Stephen Douglas of Illinois.:* Scarry, *Fillmore*, 170.

54. *dispatching 750 additional troops to the region.:* Ibid., 171.

54. *regardless of all consequences to himself.":* Millard Fillmore to an autograph seeker, October 20, 1859, Papers of Millard Fillmore.

55. *a federal crime to interfere with a slave capture.*: Scarry, *Fillmore*, 172–73.

55. *contributing his own money to the project.*: Ibid., 172.

55. *him and sending him on his way to Canada.*: Nevins, *Ordeal*, 1:388–89.

55. *to the governor, the legislature, or anyone else.*: Rayback, *Fillmore*, 276.

56. *published in half of all known languages.*: Nevins, *Ordeal*, 1:404.

56. *which is overrunning with sorrow and with tears.*": Wallace, Warden William. *The Pen and Pencil* (Cincinnati: publisher unknown), 1:216–17.

57. *for me in view of all the circumstances.*": Wallner, *Pierce*, 1:192.

57. *government. She fainted at the news.*: Ibid., 1:202.

57. *thirty-fifth ballot, was the nominee on the forty-ninth.*: Ibid., 1:200–201.

57. *predicting Pierce's election "as next to certain."*: Tyler, *Letters and Times*, 2:497.

57. *support north and south for another bid.*: Rayback, *Fillmore*, 338.

57. *throughout the South nominated him for re-election.*: Nevins, *Ordeal*, 2:28.

57. *a deathbed endorsement from Henry Clay.*: Rayback, *Fillmore*, 350.

58. *help the Whigs win the upcoming state elections.*: Ibid., 348; Holt, *Rise and Fall*, 17280 (digital version).

58. *Scott prevailed on the fifty-third ballot.*: Nevins, *Ordeal*, 2:28–29; Holt, *Rise and Fall*, 17293.

58. *had a fair trial and have been fairly defeated.*": Tyler, *Letters and Times*, 2:498.

58. *without which no man is fit to be President.*": Curtis, *Buchanan*, 2:42.

58–59. *ranks! How preposterous!*": Ibid., 2:44.

59. *Free Soil dalliance, endorsed Pierce in a letter.*: Nevins, *Ordeal*, 2:32.

59. *Electoral College, and carrying twenty-seven states to Scott's four.*: Ibid., 2:36.

59. *Harriet was headed to dinner at Robert Tyler's.*: Buchanan, *Works*, 8:501.

59. *and reminding her to mind her social etiquette.*: Ibid., 8:504.

60. *of which removed the top part of his head.*: Litchfield (CT) *Republican*, January 13, 1853.

Chapter 8: A Hell of a Storm

61. *go into seclusion and perhaps poverty.*": New York Herald, September 16, 1873.

61. *his inaugural address without notes, a first.*: Nevins, *Ordeal*, 44.

61. *wore a black veil on her infrequent excursions.*: Wallner, *Pierce*, 2:14.

62. *the position of minister to England.*: Buchanan, *Works*, 8:504.

62. *any other Department of the Government," Buchanan thought.*: Ibid., 8:507–8.

62. *really permit him to handle these on his own?*: Wallner, *Pierce*, 2, Chapter 2 passim.

63. *minister as though nothing had ever happened.*: Buchanan, *Works*, 8:510.

63. *that he had succeeded in fending him off.*: Ibid., 9:6.

63. *Philadelphia, where Pierce was scheduled to appear.*: Ibid., 9:11.

64. *by some, and with gratification by all.*": Tyler, *Letters and Times*, 2:505.

64. *the last barrier to significant settlement.*: Nevins, *Ordeal*, 2:123; 2:91.

65. *though I know it will raise a hell of a storm.*": Wallner, *Pierce*, 2:93–94.

65. *an organization of these lands that outlawed slavery.*: Ibid., 2:97.

65. *be "directly involved" in securing passage of the bill.*: Ibid., 2:98.

65. *These agitations cannot end in good.*": Tyler, *Letters and Times*, 2:509.

65. *something found in the bedrock of the revolution.: Ibid.,* 2:510

66. *bitter feeling in Congress," wrote one reporter.: St. Louis Missouri Republican,* February 8, 1854; Nevins, 2:121.

66. *at 5:00 a.m., 37–14, to pass the Kansas-Nebraska Act.:* Wallner, *Pierce,* 2:102.

66. *the eighty-nine Democrats in the state House were eliminated.:* Nevins, *Ordeal,* 2:147.

66. *Every single northern Whig opposed the bill, 45 in all.:* Ibid., 2:157.

66. *and the judge ordered him returned to Virginia.:* Ibid., 2:150–52.

66. *"had converted to abolitionism in twenty years.":* Ibid., 2:154.

67. *"aroused him as he had never been before.":* Lincoln autobiographical statement, June 1860.

67. *"Oh Lincoln," said Dickey, "go to sleep!":* Whipple, Wayne. *The Story Life of Lincoln* (Philadelphia: John C. Winston, 1908), 237.

67. *"arguing against the extension of a bad thing.":* CW, 2:248–83.

67. *there would be more than eight thousand.:* Etcheson, Nicole. *Bleeding Kansas: Contested Liberty in the Civil War Era* (Lawrence: University Press of Kansas, 2004), 29.

68. *office, stores, hotel, and boarding houses.":* Nevins, *Ordeal,* 2:314.

68. *at Fort Leavenworth on October 7.:* Ibid., 2:312.

68. *had between fifteen hundred and two thousand adult males.:* Ibid., 2:313.

68. *concentrated in and around the town of Lawrence.:* Whipple, *Story Life,* 238.

68. *additional $1 million from the Massachusetts legislature.:* Etcheson, *Bleeding Kansas,* 36.

68. *discounted fares over rail and steam.:* Ibid., 37.

68. *1,114 were legal.:* Nevins, *Ordeal,* 2:313.

68. *of being in favor of any other candidate.":* Etcheson, *Bleeding Kansas,* 53.

68. *a dollar a day, and liquor" to vote in Kansas.:* Ibid., 32.

68. *Reeder allowed the results to stand.:* Ibid., 54.

68. *who opposed Catholicism and immigration.:* Nevins, *Ordeal,* 2:414.

69. *the pro-slavery faction had won all but three seats.:* Etcheson, *Bleeding Kansas,* 56.

69. *earlier had recorded just 2,905 legal voters.:* Ibid., 59.

69. *sold at a fake slave auction for a dollar.:* Ibid., 58.

69. *the legislature and of the actual fraud.:* Ibid., 61.

69. *territory where he intended to have new elections.:* Ibid., 61.

69. *issued vetoes but found himself overridden.:* Nevins, *Ordeal,* 2:387.

69. *seats to the candidates who had originally won.:* Etcheson, *Bleeding Kansas,* 62.

69. *legislature to convene on property that he owned.:* Ibid., 67.

69. *re-election there after his support for Kansas-Nebraska.:* Ibid., 69.

70. *the election scheduled by the legislature.:* Ibid., 73.

70. *Topeka to establish their own government.:* Ibid., 74.

70. *claimed self-defense and hastened to Missouri.:* Ibid., 79.

70. *arrested Branson in bed for "disturbing the peace.":* Ibid., 80.

70. *his custody and taking him to Lawrence.:* Ibid., 80.

70. *Shannon, who called up the territorial militia.:* Ibid., 81.

70. *Lawrence swelled with a similar number of defenders.:* Ibid., 83.

70. *outside the town seemed unlikely to disband.:* Ibid., 88.

71. *your support my chances would be reasonably good.":* CW, 2:290.

71. *and it would be a close fought thing.:* Ibid., 2:296–97.

71. *with the pro-slavery element boycotting the election.:* Etcheson, *Bleeding Kansas*, 75.

71. *elections were held for state officers.:* Ibid., 89.

71. *murdered me like cowards," he told them as he lay dying.:* Ibid., 91.

71. *"available forces of the United States.":* *Franklin Pierce Special Message to Congress*, January 24, 1856, accessed online at the American Presidency Project, www.presidency. ucsb.edu.

72. *crowned monarch on the surface of the globe.":* Millard Fillmore Papers, 1:445.

72. *which helped them fall back to sleep.:* Tyler, *Letters and Times*, 2:523.

72. *the longest election for Speaker in history.:* History.House.Gov, http://history.house. gov/HistoricalHighlight/Detail/36895?ret=True

72. *Giddings said. "I am satisfied.":* Nevins, *Ordeal*, 2:416; Julian, George. *The Life of Joshua R. Giddings* (Chicago: McClurg, 1892), 326.

73. *had been frustrated yet again.:* CW, 2:305–6.

73. *up and down the eastern seaboard.:* Rayback, *Fillmore*, 380.

73. *certainty with which it marches to victory.":* Tyler, *Letters and Times*, 2:513.

73. *he returned to the United States to campaign.:* Rayback, *Fillmore*, 395.

74. *the sheriff suffered the same result.:* Etcheson, *Bleeding Kansas*, 101.

74. *by the pro-slavery forces.:* Ibid.

74. *his status as a front-runner for president.:* Curtis, *Buchanan*, 2:169.

74. *to indict the entire free state government.:* Etcheson, *Bleeding Kansas*, 102.

74. *governor was arrested on his way out of town.:* Ibid., 104.

74. *burned, including that of the governor.:* Ibid., 104–5.

75. *by the Massachusetts legislature despite his absence.:* The attack and fallout are described in Nevins, *Ordeal*, 444–47.

75. *by "moaning, as if a person was dying.":* Howard Report, 1193.

Chapter 9: The Final Election of the Old America

77. *puts Lincoln on the track for the Presidency.":* Whipple, *Story Life*, 250–53.

77. *opinion my friends will succeed in Cincinnati.":* Tyler, *Letters and Times*, 2:526.

77. *but badly trailed Buchanan.":* Official Proceedings of the Democratic National Convention (Cincinnati: Enquirer Company Steam Printing Establishment, 1856).

77. *to abandon and disgust all reflecting men.":* Ibid., 2:527.

77. *helplessly on the waves of doubt and debt.":* Ibid., 2:527.

78. *who aspires to be Vice President of the United States.":* Whipple, *Story Life*, 254–55.

78. *bequeathed to us, a priceless inheritance.":* Millard Fillmore Papers, 2:19–22.

78. *he must "command you to disburse.":* Etcheson, *Bleeding Kansas*, 116.

79. *evacuating the town, which was burned and looted.:* John Brown to his wife, September 7, 1856; H. J. Strickler to Thomas Stinson, September 2, 1856. Available through Territorial Kansas Online, www.territorialkansasonline.org

79. *The Herald of Freedom. How do you like it?":* Bridgman, Edward Payson, and Parsons, Luke Fisher. *With John Brown in Kansas* (Madison, WI: J.N. Davidson, 1915).

79. *not suspend fratricidal strife?":* Etcheson, *Bleeding Kansas*, 131.

79. *who worked in his fields as they left.:* Ibid., 133.

79. *and bequeathed to us as a priceless inheritance.":* Buchanan, *Works,* 10:96.

80. *(carrying Maryland) and 43 percent in the South.:* Rayback, *Fillmore,* 413.

80. *the constitutional convention at Lecompton.:* Etcheson, *Bleeding Kansas,* 141.

80. *No polling place was established at Lawrence.:* Ibid., 142.

81. *that 'all* men *are created equal.'":* CW 2:383–85.

81. *satisfied no one and disgusted all.":* Boulard, Gary. *The Expatriation of Franklin Pierce* (Bloomington, IN: iUniverse, 2006), 250.

81. *will speak a single honest word about him.":* Ibid., 364.

81. *the president of the United States as a guest.:* Ibid., 144.

81. *presidential life that I can scarcely endure it.":* Ibid., 156.

81. *motives which have prompted your official action.":* Ibid., 375.

81. *four anxious years and never failed me.":* Ibid., 380.

81. *Brooks's funeral was held in the House.:* Nevins, *Ordeal,* 3:69.

82. *and insult upon the pale tenants of the grave.":* *Richmond Whig,* February 3, 1857.

82. *"What is there to do but drink?":* *Oxford Dictionary of American Quotes,* 542.

82. *Was this how Americans treated their ex-presidents?:* Mackay, Charles. *Through the Long Day* (London: W.H. Allen, 1887), 156–60.

Chapter 10: General Jackson Is Dead!

83. *removed by their owner to Missouri.:* Howard, Robert Lorenzo. *American State Trials,* Volume IX (St. Louis: Thomas Law Book Company, 1919), 13:249–50.

84. *no power to regulate slavery in the territories.:* Ibid., 253–55.

84. *slavery issue once and for all.:* Buchanan, *Works,* 10:106–8.

84. *where his three predecessors had failed.:* Etcheson, *Bleeding Kansas,* 143.

84. *with only an estimated 10 percent turnout.:* Ibid., 147.

84. *His protecting gaurdianship and care.":* Tyler, *Letters and Times,* 1:34.

85. *done before them, summering at Lake Geneva, Switzerland.:* Nichols, *Young Hickory,* 508.

85. *manage the affairs of state with no greater effect.:* Ibid., 509.

85. *nowhere to be found, "is quite notable.":* Wallner, *Pierce,* 2:320.

85. *(corresponding exactly to the Cincinnati Directory).:* Nevins, *Ordeal,* 3:174; *National Intelligencer,* November 5, 1857.

85. *who had allegedly come and gone.:* Etcheson, *Bleeding Kansas,* 153.

85. *that the choice was unacceptable.:* Ibid., 156.

85. *though now the mother of six children.":* "Edmund Ruffin's Visit to Sherwood Forest," *William and Mary Quarterly,* Vol. 14, No. 3 (January 1906), 194.

86. *because of his former place and power.":* Ibid., 196–97.

86. *expediency of a separation of the Union," Ruffin wrote in his diary.:* Ibid., 195.

86. *document, not just the slavery components.:* Etcheson, *Bleeding Kansas,* 157.

86. *and who had signed off on the measure.:* Ibid., 158.

86. *and I intend to prevent their doing either.":* Nevins, Allan. "Stephen A. Douglas: His Weaknesses and His Greatness." *Journal of the Illinois State Historical Society,* Vol. 42, No. 4 (Dec. 1949)

87. *remind you that General Jackson is dead.":* Nevins, *Ordeal,* 3:256.

87. *accusing the president of malfeasance.:* Etcheson, *Bleeding Kansas*, 160.
87. *and leave the future to take care of itself.":* Tyler, *Letters and Times*, 2:13–14.
87. *and the Lecompton Constitution and to start afresh.:* Etcheson, *Bleeding Kansas*, 161.
87. *winning 6,226 to 569 in an election boycotted by free staters.:* Curtis, *Buchanan*, 2:202.
87. *138 supported it without slavery and 24 with slavery.:* Nevins, *Ordeal*, 3:269.
87–88. *famous actor, Horace Greeley, and James Buchanan.:* Etcheson, *Bleeding Kansas*, 164.
88. *disappearance of polling books shortly after the election.:* Ibid., 165.
88. *three hundred forged ballots buried like treasure.:* Kansas State Historical Society. Retrieved online. www.kshs.org/kansapedia/cool-things-calhoun-s-candlebox/10180
88. *delegates to a new constitutional convention.:* Etcheson, *Bleeding Kansas*, 165.
88. *one vote in Congress and not a thousand outside.":* Nevins, *Ordeal*, 3:275.
88. *March 23, sustaining the administration 33–25.:* Ibid., 3:279.
88. *southern senators of either party voted "yes.":* Etcheson, *Bleeding Kansas*, 174.
88. *vote on the constitution, carried 120–112.:* Ibid., 176.
88. *the tactic prevented an embarrassing defeat.:* Ibid., 180.
88. *a fair election, the Lecompton Constitution was crushed, 11,812–1,926.:* Nevins, *Ordeal*, 3:301.
88. *anti-Douglas delegates to the national presidential convention.:* Milton, George Fort. "Stephen A. Douglas' Efforts for Peace." *Journal of Southern History*, Vol. 1, No. 3 (Aug. 1935), 269

Chapter 11: The First and Only Choice of the Republicans of Illinois

90. *choice of the Republicans of Illinois for the United States Senate.":* Whipple, *Story Life*, 258.
90. *instructing their delegates to the state meeting accordingly.:* Guelzo, Allen. *Lincoln and Douglas: The Debates that Defined America* (New York: Simon & Schuster, 2008), 54.
90. *578 delegates and fifteen hundred spectators at the State Capitol.:* Ibid., 55.
91. *old as well as new—north as well as south.":* CW, 2:461–69.
91. *both ambitious; I, perhaps, quite as much so as he.:* Ibid., 2:382–83.
91. *pressures forced Douglas as a young man to head west.:* Guelzo, *Debates*, 3.
91. *"On my way to Congress, Mother," he wrote at age twenty.:* Ibid., 4.
91. *sworn into the US Senate at thirty-three.:* Ibid., 6.
92. *trampled by the dark horse, Franklin Pierce.:* CW 2:382–83.
92. *a member of the lower house of Congress.":* Ibid., 2:459.
92. *not unknown, even, in foreign lands.":* Ibid., 2:382–83.
92. *He was intensely jealous of him.":* Lamon, *Lincoln*, Chapter XIV.
92. *stalwarts from top patronage jobs in Illinois.:* Guelzo, *Debates*, Chapter 2 passim.
93. *and if I beat him my victory will be hardly won.":* Ibid., 75.
93. *speaking after him as a pathetic ploy.:* Ibid., 91.
93. *the same audiences during the present canvass?":* CW, 2:522.
93. *districts where neither candidate had yet spoken.:* Guelzo, *Debates*, 92.
93. *accounts widely reprinted throughout the country.:* Donald, David Herbert. *Lincoln* (New York: Simon & Schuster, 1995), 214.
93. *Ten thousand people attended the first debate in Ottawa.:* Ibid., 215.

93. *between slave and free, as they had always done.:* Guelzo, *Debates,* 120.

93. *and prevent people who did not want it from disapproving it.:* Ibid., 122–23.

94. *as well as the position of many Democrats.:* Donald, *Lincoln,* 218–19.

94. *the Democrats, with 47 percent of the vote, won 53 percent.":* Ibid., 228.

94. *have met the enemy in Pennsylvania and we are theirs.":* Buchanan, *Works,* 10:229.

95. *and anti-Lecompton Democrats took twenty-nine of thirty-three seats.:* Nevins, *Ordeal,* 3:400–401.

95. *become too plain for the people to stand them.":* CW, 3:337, 3:339–40, 3:341, 3:346.

96. *Lincoln "disappeared into the darkness.":* Whipple, *Story Life,* 312–13.

Chapter 12: A Startling Tide of Reckless Fanaticism

97. *Great Lakes to celebrate the opening of a new route.:* Invitation to Millard Fillmore, August 9, 1859, Papers of Millard Fillmore.

97. *Nearly half our number have already.":* Julia Harris to Millard Fillmore, August 24, 1859, Papers of Millard Fillmore.

97. *and we will follow it and strike it boldly.":* John McGanley? to Millard Fillmore, September 9, 1859, Papers of Millard Fillmore.

98. *delighted that I have no responsibility.":* Millard Fillmore to Dorothea Dix, October 1859, Papers of Millard Fillmore.

98. *along with their slaves, brought to Harper's Ferry.:* Nevins, *Ordeals,* 4:79.

98. *putting Colonel Robert E. Lee in command.:* Ibid., 4:80–81.

98. *Tennessee and Alabama, would never happen.:* Ibid., 4:73.

98. *Brown was beaten unconscious.:* Ibid., 4:82–83.

99. *with John Tyler chosen as commander.:* Chitwood, *Tyler,* 430.

99. *expedition by the abolitionists of the north.":* Buchanan, James. *Mr. Buchanan's Administration on the Eve of the Rebellion* (New York: D. Appleton, 1866), 63.

99. *Brown "a man of lawless . . . disposition.":* Cole, Donald. *Martin Van Buren and the American Political System* (Fort Washington, PA: Eastern National, 2004), 424.

99. *"foolish and criminal invasion of Virginia.":* Millard Fillmore to Dorothea Dix, March 5, 1860, Papers of Millard Fillmore.

99. *was the mechanism for opposing slavery.:* CW, 3:496.

100. *as old John Brown has been dealt with.":* Ibid., 3:501–2.

100. *four thousand miles and delivered twenty-three speeches.:* Nevins, *Ordeal,* 4:240; Donald, *Lincoln,* 235.

100. *It was an instant bestseller.:* Donald, *Lincoln,* 237

100. *or sage was about to pass from Earth to Heaven.":* Franklin Pierce to a gathering in Binghamton, December 17, 1859, Papers of Franklin Pierce.

101. *to the peace and durability of this Union.":* Franklin Pierce to a Union gathering in Massachusetts, December 7, 1859, Papers of Franklin Pierce.

101. *in favor of freedom.":* Franklin Pierce to a Union gathering in Massachusetts, December 7, 1859, Papers of Franklin Pierce.

102. *country to sustain and defend it.":* Millard Fillmore to a public meeting, December 16, 1859.

102. *anything better said or in better time."*: Two letters addressed to Fillmore dated December 21, 1859, December 25, 1859, and February 1, 1860, Papers of Millard Fillmore.

103. *that it will eventually destroy this government."*: Millard Fillmore to Dorothea Dix, March 5, 1860, Papers of Millard Fillmore.

103. *dare to do our duty as we understand it."*: CW, 3:550.

103. *"the greatest man since St. Paul."*: Donald, 239.

103. *and Connecticut, eleven different cities in twelve days.*: The Lincoln Log, February and March 1860.

103. *a good work and made many warm friends."*: New York Tribune, March 12, 1860.

Chapter 13: Five against Lincoln

104. *'personal liberty' have been placed upon our statute-books."*: Franklin Pierce to Jefferson Davis, January 6, 1860, Papers of Franklin Pierce.

104. *a sentiment shared by many in Mississippi.*: Boulard, *Expatriation*, 1256.

105. *would not support the Republican nominee.*: Daily Confederation (Montgomery, AL), June 6, 1860.

105. *or whoever else the Republicans put forward.*: Correspondence dated May 18, 1860, Millard Fillmore Papers.

105. *at Chicago which I can support."*: J. M. Randolph to Millard Fillmore, May 15, 1860, Papers of Millard Fillmore.

105. *My voice is for war!"*: This article from the summer of 1860 is found in the Papers of Millard Fillmore.

105. *and vote for him with alacrity."*: Tyler, *Letters and Times,* 2:557.

105. *of at least three candidates."*: Ibid., 2:546.

105. *should there be a Democratic deadlock.*: Chitwood, *Tyler,* 431.

105. *"the whole south would rally with a shout."*: Tyler, *Letters and Times,* 3:546–47, 553; Chitwood, 432.

106. *abide by decisions of the Supreme Court.*: Buchanan, *Eve of the Rebellion,* 66.

106. *that night and then forty-five the following day.*: Nevins, *Ordeal,* 4:222.

106. *more than 152½, needing 202.*: Curtis, *Buchanan,* 2:288.

106. *"filled me with apprehension and regret."*: Tyler, *Letters and Times,* 2:558.

106. *concerned about the expansion of slavery.*: Donald, *Lincoln,* 247.

106. *from reaching any sort of agreement.*: Ibid., 248.

107. *you must excuse me until I inform her."*: Whipple, *Story Life,* 325–26.

107. *and no one can tell what is to be our future."*: Thomas Seymour to Franklin Pierce, May 19, 1860, Papers of Franklin Pierce.

107. *seem to be unconscious of the necessity."*: Jefferson Davis to Franklin Pierce, June 13, 1860, Papers of Franklin Pierce.

108. *nomination could be the sure harbinger of victory."*: Franklin Pierce to Caleb Cushing, June 7, 1860, Papers of Franklin Pierce.

108. *Only South Carolina boycotted.*: Glasgow Weekly Times, May 17, 1860; Nevins, *Ordeal,* 4:267.

108. *withdrawn substituted slates of pro-Douglas delegates.*: Nevins, *Ordeal,* 4:275.

108. *along with Maryland, California, and Oregon.:* Ibid., 4:276.

108. *they nominated Vice President John C. Breckinridge of Kentucky for president.:* Ibid., 4:271.

108. *has no coherence, no strength, no organization.":* The Constitution (Atlanta, GA), July 4, 1860.

108. *Douglas Repealers and Squatter sovereigntyites.":* Salem (MA) *Register,* August 20, 1860.

109. *but this cannot even be hoped for.":* Franklin Pierce to Benjamin Hallett, June 8, 1860, Papers of Franklin Pierce.

109. *Constitution which our fathers made and bequeathed to us.":* Nevins, "Stephen A. Douglas," 408.

109. *"if his were the only vote in the state.":* Wisconsin *Patriot,* June 9, 1860.

109. *cool evening twilight, at Washington Heights.":* Letter to the Editor of the *New York Herald,* July 17, 1860.

109. *seemed to be coalescing around Lincoln.:* New York *Tribune,* July 17, 1860.

110. *already "at work to form such a coalition.":* Columbian *Register,* July 21, 1860, reprinting a *New York Tribune* story.

110. *back into the White House on his way to bed.:* Buchanan, *Works,* 10:457–64.

111. *as a mere politician without heart.":* Tyler, *Letters and Times,* 2:559.

111. *the great republic has seen its last days.":* Ibid., 2:560.

111. *He never expects to see Washington again.":* Baltimore *Sun,* August 24, 1860.

111. *a poor president, make a first rate Virginia Road-master?":* New York Daily *Tribune,* September 15, 1860.

112. *not without difficulty understand what was said.":* Millard Fillmore to Dorothea Dix, October 18, 1860, Papers of Millard Fillmore.

112. *'open sesame' to the hopes of the other candidates.":* Tyler, *Letters and Times,* 2:560.

112. *House of Representatives after an Electoral College deadlock.:* Tyler to John Cook, October 3, 1860; *New York Times,* June 8, 1862.

112. *"and that all others were subordinate.":* Tyler, *Letter and Times,* 2:562.

112. *retrieve our fortunes and defeat sectionalism.":* Franklin Pierce to James Campbell, October 17, 1860, Papers of Franklin Pierce.

112. *'Hair Splitter' than the 'Rail Splitter.'":* Merritt to Franklin Pierce, August 24, 1860, Papers of Franklin Pierce.

113. *against all sectionalism, and sectional candidates.":* Millard Fillmore to a public meeting in Baltimore, October 30, 1860, Papers of Millard Fillmore.

113. *crowded courthouse square to the courthouse to vote.:* Burlingame, Michael, ed. *With Lincoln in the White House: Letters, Memoranda, and Other Writings of John G. Nicolay* (Carbondale: Southern Illinois University Press, 2000), November 6, 1860.

113. *and re-read several times with deliberation.":* Nicolay and Hay, *History,* 3:346.

113. *great hall of the statehouse across the street.":* Ibid., 3:346.

113. *and traced out the laborious path of future duties.":* Ibid., 3:346–47.

114. *prevailed with 169 electors, a majority of 35.:* Nevins, *Ordeals,* 4:313.

114. *I see that my poor opinions have due weight.":* Tyler, *Letters and Times,* 2:563.

114. *endorsement of resistance" to the fugitive slave act.:* Unaddressed and unsent correspondence, November 23, 1860, Papers of Franklin Pierce.

114. *and there was to be war.":* Georgia Encyclopedia online, www.georgiaencyclopedia
.org/history-archaeology/woodrow-wilson-georgia.
114. *labor states, of that I entertain no doubt.":* Correspondence of Franklin Pierce dated
November 28, 1860, Papers of Franklin Pierce.
115. *any demonstration of coercion in the Bay of Charleston.":* Buchanan, *Works*, 11:5.
115. *would only embolden the secessionists.:* Nevins, *Ordeal*, 4:342–43.
115. *The meeting broke up with no conclusion.:* Descriptions of the cabinet meetings on
November 9 and 10 can be found in Ibid., 4:342–44.

Chapter 14: The Gathering Storm

116. *not the advocate of one region over another.:* Nevins, *Ordeals*, 4:346.
116. *while bristling at accusations of inconsistency.:* Buchanan, *Works*, 11:55.
117. *operations which they have in hand.":* New York Daily Tribune, December 11, 1860.
117. *negotiations for a peaceful settlement continued.:* Nevins, *Ordeal*, 4:349.
117. *to offer him the position as secretary of state.:* Nicolay and Hay, *History*, 3:349.
117. *to Edward Bates his appointment as attorney general.:* Whipple, *Story Life*, 247.
117. *state of Ohio also weighed in his favor.:* Nicolay and Hay, *History*, 3:354.
117. *and convince the Democrats through Blair.":* Ibid., 3:373.
117. *shrieks of locality would have to be heeded.":* Hertz, Emanuel. *Lincoln Talks: An Oral
Biography* (New York: Viking Press, 1939), 198.
117. *replaced by Attorney General Jeremiah Black.:* Nevins, *Ordeal*, 4:358.
117. *in response to complaints from South Carolina.:* Ibid., 4:366.
118. *Buchanan to rescind the order the following day.:* Ibid., 4:375.
118. *Republican ticket hold you in the highest respect.":* Correspondence to Millard Fillmore, November 23, 1860, Papers of Millard Fillmore.
118. *the people," inviting Fillmore to head the delegation.:* V. W. Kingsley to Millard Fillmore, December 8, 1860, Papers of Millard Fillmore.
118. *the most humble has no right to shrink.":* Millard Fillmore to V. W. Kingsley,
December 10, 1860, Papers of Millard Fillmore.
118. *are endeavoring to bring about such an adjustment.":* Robert Mallory to Millard Fillmore, December 13, 1860, Papers of Millard Fillmore.
118. *I do not yet despair of the Union.":* Stephen Douglas to Millard Fillmore, December 29,
1860, Papers of Millard Fillmore.
118. *"Lincoln's election has been announced.":* John Campbell to Franklin Pierce, December 19,
1860, Papers of Franklin Pierce.
119. *fails, may God in his mercy guide us.":* Franklin Pierce to John Campbell, December 24,
1860, Papers of Franklin Pierce.
119. *world has not witnessed for a thousand years.":* Franklin Pierce to Colonel J. H.
George, December 22, 1860, Papers of Franklin Pierce.
119. *though "not a decisive one.":* John Campbell to Franklin Pierce, December 29, 1860,
Papers of Franklin Pierce.
119. *the minds of the people on present questions.":* J. E. Preston to Millard Fillmore,
December 14, 1860, Papers of Millard Fillmore.

119–120. *rather hear, wrote Rufus Pollard of Ringgold, Georgia.:* Rufus Pollard to Millard Fillmore, December 17, 1860, Papers of Millard Fillmore.

120. *had "a work to do, and a destiny to fill.":* Alfred Feunbush to Millard Fillmore, January 21, 1861, Papers of Millard Fillmore.

120. *that a conference of border states might find a solution.:* Tyler, *Letters and Times,* 2:577.

120. *and organization of a military force.:* *New York Times,* December 1, 1860.

121. *bridegroom, wedding-cake, or wedding breakfast.":* The account of the wedding and Buchanan's discovery can be found in Pryor, Sarah, *Reminiscences of Peace and War* ((New York: Macmillan, 1905), 110–12.

121. *decisions regarding the forts until negotiations were held.:* Trescot's version of this story is found in Crawford, Samuel Wylie. *The Genesis of the Civil War: the Story of Sumter, 1860–1861* (New York: Charles L. Webster, 1887), 81–86.

122. *permitted South Carolina, they argued, to walk away.:* Confederate States of America—Declaration of the Immediate Causes Which Induce and Justify the Secession of South Carolina from the Federal Union, December 24, 1860.

122. *happily averted danger from the Union.":* Buchanan, *Eve of the Rebellion,* 106.

123. *placed in a more trying and responsible position.":* Ibid., 109.

123. *to recover stolen federal property attracted little support.:* Ibid., 157.

123. *have made himself justly liable to impeachment.":* Ibid., 161.

123. *stupid of political fools, an old bully, and an old Betty. . . . ":* Boston Courier, December 31, 1860.

123. *the signal for united action with all the slave states.":* Tyler, *Letters and Times,* 2:578.

123. *incident widely reported throughout the North.:* *Daily Ohio Statesman*

124. *the marked ability he then displayed.":* This story was widely reprinted. For one example, see the *Fremont Journal,* December 28, 1860.

124. *against my orders. It is against my policy.":* The meeting at the White House and subsequent cabinet meeting are described in Rhodes, John Ford. *History of the United States from the Compromise of 1850 to the Restoration of Home Rule at the South in 1877,* Volume III (New York: Macmillan, 1907). 225–26.

124. *and the command of the harbor lost.":* Rhodes, *History,* 224.

125. *He would resign two days later.:* Rhodes, *History,* 225–26.

125. *my friend—not so bad as that!":* Nevins, *Ordeal,* 4:370.

125. *alone held $500,000 in public property.:* Curtis, *Buchanan,* 2:373.

125. *the commissioners, and furiously went about it.:* Nevins, *Ordeal,* 4:378.

125. *against the city of Charleston.":* Curtis, *Buchanan,* 2:390.

125. *and reinforcements must be sent.":* Ibid., 2:445–46.

Chapter 15: The Tug Has to Come

126. *religious services and sermons.:* *New York Herald,* January 5, 1861.

126. *who had himself replaced Howell Cobb.:* Nevins, *Ordeal,* 4:380.

126. *William Seward of New York, among others.:* Ibid., 4:390.

127. *no future policymakers could reach.:* Ibid., 4:391.

127. *little atom which is to be sacrificed.":* Curtis, *Buchanan,* 2:423.

127. *was all the North would have to yield.*: Buchanan, *Eve of the Rebellion,* 136.

128. *Douglas, the answer was "yes."*: Ibid., 137.

128. *discuss but to act on this great question."*: John Law to Martin Van Buren, January 7, 1861.

128. *a peaceful solution could still be achieved.*: John Law to Martin Van Buren, March 31, 1861, references Van Buren's sentiment from his reply, which is missing.

128. *relations between the different sections restored."*: Van Buren to Crittenden, December 24, 1860.

128. *to be made the basis of a settlement."*: Millard Fillmore to Dorothea Dix, January 17, 1860.

128. *codifying the* Dred Scott *plurality decision.*: Tyler, *Letters and Times,* 2:643.

129. *opportunity to secure in advance" a resolution.*: Resolutions of Martin Van Buren, in the Martin Van Buren Papers.

129. *and better now than at any time hereafter."*: Curtis, *Buchanan,* 2:426; CW, 4:149–50.

129. *no future amendments could outlaw slavery.*: Nevins, *Ordeal,* 4:409–10.

130. *members will hesitate for a moment."*: Curtis, *Buchanan,* 2:434–35.

130. *abolition, or a dissolution of the Union."*: *A Declaration of the Immediate Causes which Induce and Justify the Secession of the State of Mississippi from the Federal Union.*

130. *have seen its approach and am prepared."*: Franklin Pierce to Jane Pierce, January 1861.

131. *any practical form of adjustment."*: Millard Fillmore correspondence dated January 17, 1860, Papers of Millard Fillmore.

131. *and to have shown to you our children."*: Jefferson Davis to Franklin Pierce, January 20, 1861, Papers of Franklin Pierce.

131. *the victory will at least be doubtful."*: *Speeches of the Honorable Jefferson Davis,* 55.

131. *and alarming condition of our country."*: Franklin Pierce to John Campbell, January 7, 1861, Papers of Franklin Pierce.

132. *to speak to the people of Alabama and Georgia.*: George Miller to Franklin Pierce, January 13, 1861, Papers of Franklin Pierce.

132. *convention of the border states without delay.*: Tyler, *Letters and Times,* 2:579.

132. *then endorsed the Crittenden Compromise.*: Ibid., 2:580–81.

133. *John Tyler was headed back to the White House.*: Ibid., 2:582.

133. *the high-ceilinged East Room below.*: Seale, William. *The President's House* (Washington, DC: White House Historical Association, 2008), 1:338.

133. *which hung a portrait of Andrew Jackson."*: Ibid., 1:339.

133. *resolutions of the Virginia General Assembly.*: The story of Tyler's activities of the 24th and 25th of January can be found in Tyler, *Letters and Times,* 2:588–89.

134. *for Pensacola, the troops for Fort Pickens."*: Tyler, *Letters and Times,* 2:591.

135. *and would be more effective than yours."*: Amos Lawrence to Franklin Pierce, January 27, 1861, Papers of Franklin Pierce.

135. *occasion worthy of your direct intervention?"*: John O'Sullivan to Franklin Pierce, February 7, 1861, Papers of Franklin Pierce.

135. *they were left to lie on the table.*: Letters and Times, 2:591; Buchanan, *Works,* 11:116.

136. *of a renewed and more harmonious confederacy."*: Tyler, *Letters and Times,* 2:591.

136. *united abilities of himself and Mr. James Buchanan.*": *New York Tribune,* February 8, 1861.

136. "*I shall then hope to see more of you.*": Buchanan, *Works,* 11:121.

Chapter 16: The Last Winter of Peace

138. "*our people ought to prepare for the worst.*": E. G. Spaulding to Millard Fillmore, February 2, 1861, Papers of Millard Fillmore.

138. *sandbank before they would adopt these propositions.*": Nevins, *Ordeal,* 4:431.

138. *all but 11 gave Tyler one of their votes.*: Tyler, *Letters and Times,* 2:618–19.

138. "*in favor of remaining in the Union.*": Buchanan, *Eve of the Rebellion,* 163.

138. *which could revolutionize Virginians in a single day.*: *New York Herald,* February 6, 1861.

139. *it could not be through any one else.*": Tyler, *Letters and Times,* 2:596.

139. *all the discordant elements together.*": Ibid., 2:597.

139. *are among his warmest friends.*": Ibid.

140. "*more enduring than the monumental alabaster.*": Tyler, *Letters and Times,* 2:598.

140. *which I hope will eventually bring them back.*": William Latham to Franklin Pierce, February 6, 1861, Papers of Franklin Pierce.

141. *they represent must rest the responsibility.*": Buchanan, *Works,* 11:139–41.

141. *reinforce the garrison in case I deemed it necessary.*": Ibid., 11:141–43.

141. *more clearly to pursue the path of duty.*": Chitwood, *Tyler,* 447; Chitwood cites a letter written in 1883 as his source, which does not necessarily place this conversation at a specific meeting between the two. However, it is consistent with what we know of their discussion and I believe it happened at this encounter.

Chapter 17: That All Will Yet Be Well

142. *indeed we have not.*": Herndon, William, and Jesse Weik. *Herndon's Lincoln: The True Story of a Great Life* (New York: Da Capo, republished 2008), 390.

143. *I bid you an affectionate farewell.*": CW, 4:190.

144. *duty to Mr. B,*" *reported the* Salem Register.: *Salem* (MA) *Register,* February 18, 1861.

144. *emphatically his respect for you.*": Correspondence to Millard Fillmore dated February 10 and 12, 1861, Papers of Millard Fillmore.

144. *At 4:00 p.m.: New York Times,* February 18, 1861.

144. "*a hearty grip of the hand" with Millard Fillmore.: Philadelphia Inquirer,* February 18, 1861.

144. *encircled the president in a "whirlpool.*": *Philadelphia Inquirer,* February 20, 1861.

145. *whether he can continue on the journey*": Nicolay to Therena Bates, February 17, 1861.

145. *a crowd similar to that at the depot.*: Ibid.

145. *of the countenance of 'honest old Abe.'*": *Philadelphia Inquirer,* February 20, 1861.

145. *promising* WE WILL PRAY FOR YOU.: Ibid.

145. *the weather "cold and blustering.":* New York Times, February 17, 1861.

145. *despair of seeing the Union again restored.":* Millard Fillmore to Dorothea Dix, February 26, 1861, Papers of Millard Fillmore.

145–146. *who have assembled to witness the parade.":* Curtis, *Buchanan,* 2:495.

146. *history more busy nor more brilliant.":* Nicolay and Hay, *History,* 3:367.

146. *a few minutes with him in general conversation.:* Philadelphia Inquirer, February 26, 1861.

146. *Douglas, and Breckinridge all paid their respects.:* Nicolay and Hay, *History,* 3:317.

146. *many hours of the night were occupied.":* Ibid., 3:318.

146. *mischief did he get through Baltimore?":* Poore, Benjamin Perley. *Reminiscences of Sixty Years in the National Metropolis* (Philadelphia: Hubbard Brothers, 1886), 62.

146. *with all the respect due to his position.":* Ibid., 64

146. *with his "most wonderful memory.":* Ibid.

146. *"I was a friend of your father.":* Ibid., 65.

146. *condition of the country or the national troubles.":* Ibid., 65.

147. *a Confederate commissioner arrived in Washington.:* Buchanan, *Works,* 11:143.

147. *provided at the time of statehood.:* Chitwood, Tyler, 443.

147. *the work of the conference entirely.:* Ibid., 444.

147. *termination of the action of the Peace Congress.":* Philadelphia Inquirer, February 28, 1861.

147. *guns were fired in Washington in celebration.:* Nicolay and Hay, *History,* 3:232.

147. *realized "they cannot pass the Senate.":* Daily Picayune, February 28, 1861.

147. *not nearly enough for a constitutional amendment.:* Curtis, *Buchanan,* 2:443.

147. *work met a similar fate in the House.:* Ibid., 2:444.

147. *John Tyler who does not want them in.":* Chitwood, *Tyler,* 446.

148. *neither ears nor hearts to understand.":* Chitwood, *Tyler,* 446.

148. *and boldly in the exercise of state sovereignty.":* Tyler, *Letters and Times,* 2:616.

148. *He called for its rejection.:* Richmond Times Dispatch, March 1, 1861.

148. *Inaugural suggests a coercive policy.":* Albany Journal, March 2, 1861.

148. *purpose altogether that he was called forth.":* Milwaukee Daily Journal of March 6, 1861, quoting the *Cincinnati Gazette.*

148. *take his seat in the Virginia secession convention.:* Virginia Secession Convention, March 1, 1861.

148. *Sumter, the fort could not be sustained.:* Buchanan, *Works,* 11:156.

148. *on the morning of March 4 matched the mood.:* Riddle, Albert Gallatin, *Recollections of War Times* (New York: Putnam's Sons, 1895), 13.

148. *a time of extraordinary difficulty and trial.":* Daily Evening Bulletin (San Francisco, CA), March 4, 1861.

149. *Buchanan and Lincoln rode side by side.:* Nicolay and Hay, *History,* 3:326.

149. *predecessors who have occupied it.":* Holzer, Harold. *Lincoln President-Elect* (New York: Simon & Schuster, 2009), 450.

149. *"had not heard a word of it.":* Burlingame, Michael. *At Lincoln's Side: John Hay's Civil War Correspondence and Other Writings* (Carbondale: Southern Illinois University Press, 2006), 119.

149. *Lincoln he seemed little more than half a man. ":* Riddle, *Recollections*, 13; Whipple, *Story Life*, 384–86.

149. *his overshadowing, unshapely successor. ":* Riddle, *Recollections*, 14.

149. *clear voice," Lincoln delivered his address.:* Nicolay and Hay, *History*, 3:327.

150. *Lincoln changed it to "generally. ":* Ibid., 3:330, footnote 4.

150. *heretofore only menaced, is now formidably attempted. ":* Lincoln's First Inaugural Address.

150. *with deliberation pronounced the oath. ":* Nicolay and Hay, *History*, 3:344.

151. *happiness and the national peace and prosperity. ":* Ibid., 3:344.

151. *abandoned" within "a few weeks at most. ":* Ibid., 3:377.

151. *"It is lightning work, necessarily. ":* Stoddard, William, *Inside the White House in War Times* (New York: Ogilve, 1895), 29.

151. *obscene ravings of utter insanity. ":* Ibid., 31.

151. *Confederate forces and forts with their men. ":* Ibid., 33.

151. *annoyance enough to make almost anybody sick. ":* Nicolay to Bates, March 20, 1861.

151. *on every hand as to who could be trusted. ":* Welles, Gideon. *Diary of Gideon Welles: Secretary of the Navy Under Lincoln and Johnson* (New York: Houghton, Mifflin, 1911) 1:5.

151. *especially no one from Virginia.:* Ibid., 1:5.

151. *thick with treason," Welles remembered.:* Ibid., 1:10.

151–152. *additional resources would make such relief possible.:* Nicolay and Hay, *History*, 3:379

152. *and his men safely from South Carolina.:* Ibid., 3:382.

Chapter 18: Home Again

153. *had come to escort him home.:* Curtis, *Buchanan*, 2:506.

153. *playing the song "Home Again. ":* Buchanan, *Works*, 11:160.

154. *return to bless us and our posterity!":* Ibid., 11:161.

154. *Buchanan entered his house, a private citizen.:* Curtis, *Buchanan*, 2:510.

154. *me as to what is going on in Washington. ":* Buchanan, *Works*, 11:165.

154. *himself and perhaps restore the Union. ":* Ibid., 11:171–73.

154. *reinforcements on the request of Major Anderson. ":* Ibid., 11:174.

155. *during its whole term, was irresistible. ":* Tyler, *Letters and Times*, 2:668.

155. *most felicitous among the orators I have known. ":* Ibid., 3:130.

155. *if necessary, to lead the van. ":* Ibid., 2:659.

155. *in 1856 turn traitor to the government. ":* Millard Fillmore to John P. Kennedy, March 22, 1861, Papers of Millard Fillmore.

155. *"and Maryland will be close at her heels. ":* Buchanan, *Works*, 11:166.

155. *but that history will do you justice. ":* Ibid., 11:167.

155. *Your record will brighten in proportion. ":* Ibid., 11:168.

155–156. *was invited to make his case to the cabinet.:* Nicolay and Hay, *History*, 3:384.

156. *distance of thirteen hundred yards, especially at night. ":* Ibid., 3:385.

156. *and Blair agreed, but the rest said "no. ":* Ibid.

156. *deflate the already demoralized North.:* Nicolay and Hay, *History*, 3:388.

156. *by history, as treason to the country.":* Welles, *Diary,* 1:14.

156. *Major Anderson, and that he would reinforce Sumter.":* Ibid.

156. *Anderson would be forced to abandon the fort.:* Fox's official report, Nicolay and Hay, *History,* 3:389.

157. *could he trust? Lincoln cancelled the order.:* Welles, *Diary,* 1:17–18.

157. *the Department could command,"* Welles wrote.: Ibid., 1:21.

157. *provisioning the fort and reinforcing it.":* Ibid., 1:22.

157. *in the dead of night to find the president.:* Ibid., 1:23–24.

157. *when I sometimes thought otherwise.":* Ibid., 1:24–25.

158. *orders had come directly from the president.:* Nicolay and Hay, *History,* 4:6.

158. *Welles wrote, "I cordially assented.":* Welles, *Diary,* 1:23–24.

158. *secede, but adhere to the Union.":* Welles, *Diary,* 1:39.

158. *former president of the United States, John Tyler.:* Virginia Secession Convention, April 4, 1861.

159. *the world that he had begun civil war.":* Nicolay and Hay, *History,* 4:44.

159. *congressional colleague who was in Washington.:* Report of the Committee on Reconstruction, 114.

160. *have prevented all that was about to happen.:* Ibid., 115.

160. *back in the old Union in less than ten days.":* Nicolay and Hay, *History,* 4:45.

160. *as you may determine to reduce it.":* Ibid., 4:45–46.

Chapter 19: Breakfast at Fort Sumter

161. *and another such demand made that day.:* Nicolay and Hay, *History,* 4:46.

161. *of a Bedouin on the sands of the desert.":* Buchanan, *Works,* 11:179.

161. *fired on Sumter for the next thirty-three hours.:* McPherson, James. *Battle Cry of Freedom: The Civil War Era* (New York: Oxford University Press, 1988), 273.

161. *Davis will be in possession of Washington.":* Buchanan, *Works,* 11:180

162. *the life of the only person to die at Fort Sumter.:* Whipple, *Story Life,* 395–97.

162. *and God knows where it may end.":* Buchanan, *Works,* 11:181.

162. *and it ought to be sustained at all hazards.":* Ibid.

162. *Sumter was taken to consolidate Republicans.:* Chitwood, *Tyler,* 455.

162. *float over their ramparts in place of their own?":* Ibid.

162. *realize that they are so, even as I write them.":* Nicolay to Bates, April 14, 1861.

163. *in combat, and both were over seventy.":* McPherson, *Battle Cry,* 313.

163. *seven hundred thousand soldiers by the early days of 1862.:* Ibid., 322.

163. *1861, they had achieved 60 percent of their goal.:* Ibid., 318.

163. *cannot live through the case without them.":* Lamon, *Lincoln,* 137.

164. *if you will fight for the country.":* Whipple, *Story Life,* 411.

164. *available on the eastern seaboard.:* McPherson, *Battle Cry,* 313.

164. *by 1865 it was reduced to one out of every two.:* Ibid., 380.

164. *the same in the previous four years.:* Ibid., 382.

165. *constituted authorities and defend the government.":* Fillmore's speech can be found in *The Millard Fillmore Papers,* edited by Frank Severance, 2:62–63.

165. *impressive, dwarfing that of much larger cities.:* Nevins, *Ordeal,* 5:88.

165. *supported him," read one anonymous editorial.:* Newspaper editorial by "Amanuensis," Papers of Millard Fillmore.

166. *the second Washington (Father) to your country.":* J. Smithon to Millard Fillmore, April 18, 1861, Papers of Millard Fillmore.

166. *and families, they will not" be conquered.:* Anonymous letter to Millard Fillmore, April 18, 1861.

166. *"Another day may decide our course.":* Tyler, *Letters and Times,* 2:640.

166. *ratification of the Constitution of the United States.":* Nicolay and Hay, *History,* 4:91.

166. *appeared, changing the total to 103–46.:* McPherson, *Battle Cry,* 279.

167. *high privilege of being participators in it.":* Jones, J. B. *A Rebel War Clerk's Diary, Volumes I–II* (Philadelphia: J. B. Lippincott, 1866), 1:22–23.

167. *household—trying times are before us.":* Tyler, *Letters and Times,* 2:641–42.

167. *All are well at Sherwood Forest.":* Ibid., 2:643.

167. *sent to Washington to seize the capital.":* Ibid., 2:659.

168. *representing him were hung from trees.:* Crapol, *Accidental President,* 269–70.

168. *except John Tyler, sustain the Union and oppose secession.":* *Liberator* (Boston, MA), May 10, 1861; *Philadelphia Inquirer* May 13, 1861; *New Hampshire Sentinel,* May 9, 1861.

168. *their muskets as they stepped on the platform.":* Nicolay and Hay, *History,* 4:113.

168. *an occasional shot from a pistol or gun.":* Ibid., 4:113.

168. *that prevailed" in the days after the riot.:* Buchanan, *Works,* 11:190–91.

169. *unable to communicate with the outside world.:* McPherson, *Battle Cry,* 285.

169. *city is doomed to the scene of battle and carnage.":* Buchanan, *Works,* 11:190–91.

169. *"The White House is turned into barracks.":* *Inside Lincoln's White House: The Complete Civil War Diary of John Hay,* April 18, 1861.

169. *the enemy, but in the midst of traitors.":* Nicolay to Bates, April 29, 1861.

169. *behind with three weeks food and water.:* Poore, *Reminiscences,* 80.

169. *for troops. "Why don't they come?":* Donald, *Lincoln,* 298.

169. *What is your duty and mine?":* Sidney Webster to Franklin Pierce, April 19, 1861, Papers of Franklin Pierce.

170. *be upheld by all hands and all hearts.":* *New York Times,* April 23, 1861.

170. *patriotic address delivered the other day at Concord!":* Carleton Chase to Franklin Pierce, April 22, 1861, Papers of Franklin Pierce.

171. *old ship of our Union, safely through the peril.":* Albert Tracy to Franklin Pierce, April 30, 1861, Papers of Franklin Pierce.

171. *"We cannot subjugate the Southern states, if we would.":* Franklin Pierce to Carleton Chase, May 6, 1861, Papers of Franklin Pierce.

171. *retract—no line of action to change.":* Wallner, *Pierce,* 2:337.

Chapter 20: The Meeting That Never Was

173. *efforts to save it from destruction.":* This letter can be found in the papers of all five former presidents. April 17, 1861.

174. *and Mr. Buchanan and advise me of the result?".*: Pierce to Van Buren, April 16, 1861, Papers of Martin Van Buren.

175. *contains, if it be in my power to do so.".*: Martin Van Buren to Franklin Pierce, April 20, 1861, Papers of Martin Van Buren.

175. *Mr. Pierce and me there immediately.".*: Telegraph from James Ingersoll to Millard Fillmore, April 24, 1861, Papers of Millard Fillmore.

175. *government, however differently they were intended.".*: Martin Van Buren to Charles J. Ingersoll, April 27, 1861, Papers of Martin Van Buren.

176. *nothing without your concurrence and approbation.".*: James Ingersoll to Millard Fillmore, April 29, 1861, Papers of Millard Fillmore.

176. *is quite as likely to do harm as good.".*: Millard Fillmore to E. Merriam, April 25, 1861, Papers of Millard Fillmore.

176. *faintly audible, like the music of a dream.".*: *Wisconsin Patriot*, August 18, 1862.

176. *that the proposed meeting could do no good.".*: James Ingersoll to Millard Fillmore, May 2, 1861, Papers of Millard Fillmore.

176. *immediate settlement of our national difficulties.".*: *New York Times*, June 16, 1861, reprints the *Danbury Times* account of a visit of two people to Van Buren, whom he told about his meeting with Pierce.

176. *as bold and united a front as the south.".*: Millard Fillmore to James Ingersoll, April 30, 1861, Papers of Millard Fillmore.

176–177. *becoming more and more intense.".*: Niven, *Romantic Age*, 610–11.

177. *the Constitution which had been forced upon it.".*: Martin Van Buren to John Halberton, November 28, 1861, Papers of Martin Van Buren.

177. *will fully sustain the Government in such policy.".*: Collier, 200.

178. *evils impending over my country will permit.".*: *New York Times*, May 19, 1861, reprinting from the *Intelligencer*, a letter dated May 6, 1861.

178. *of a Presidential oath?" asked the* Liberator.: *Liberator*, June 7, 1861.

178. *avoid thrusting his name before the people.".*: *Philadelphia Inquirer*, May 21, 1861.

178. *to the White House, with other regiments to follow.*: Nicolay and Hay, *History*, 4:156.

178. *had worked fast to repair the railway.*: McPherson, *Battle Cry*, 286.

178. *because of age, could not participate in combat.*: Millard Fillmore autobiographical statement, Papers of Millard Fillmore.

178–179. *and escorted troops headed to the war.*: Millard Fillmore Papers 1:xxxii, introduction and editing by Frank Severance.

179. *and taking in the occasional target practice.*: Regimental Colonel to Millard Fillmore, May 25, 1861, Papers of Millard Fillmore.

179. *of the General Regulations for the Militia of the State.".*: Millard Fillmore correspondence dated May 28, 1861, Papers of Millard Fillmore.

179. *"large portly grandfathers with gray beards.".*: Rayback, *Fillmore*, 425; *Buffalo Morning Express*, September 9, 1862

179. *and looking like an emperor," wrote one reporter.*: *Buffalo Commercial Advertiser*, May 4, 1861, reprinted in Severance's *Papers of Millard Fillmore*, 1:xxxii.

179. *with much eminent dignity and renown.".*: Washington Hunt to Millard Fillmore, September 18, 1861, Papers of Millard Fillmore.

179. *now filled with anxiety on their way to the war.*: *Buffalo Commercial Advertiser,* May 4, 1861, reprinted in Severance's *Papers of Millard Fillmore,* 1:xxxii.

179. *"carried the state into rebellion single-handed."*: Nicolay and Hay, *History,* 4:250.

179. *crushed their secessionist opponents by 65,114.*: Ibid., 4:250.

180. *secession was already accomplished.*: Nevins, *Ordeal,* 5:105.

180. *his advice on how to vote.*: Chitwood, *Tyler,* 457.

180. *or shall we tamely submit to arbitrary power?"*: Ibid., 457–58.

180. *25 percent of the vote, losing 128,884–32,134.*: McPherson, *Battle Cry,* 280.

180. *but to deal with it where it finds it."*: Nicolay and Hay, *History,* 4:311.

180. *possession of the bridges leading into the city.*: Ibid., 4:312

180. *including three and a half million slaves.*: Nicolay and Hay, *History,* 4:253.

180. *mountains, rivers, and other natural defenses.*: Johnson, Robert Underwood, ed. *Battles and Leaders of the Civil War,* Volumes I–IV (New York: The Century Company, 1887), 1:222.

Chapter 21: The Border States

181. *white populations of roughly 2.6 million.*: Gineapp, William. "Abraham Lincoln and the Border States," *Journal of Abraham Lincoln Association,* Vol. 13, No. 1 (1992) 13.

181. *while in Delaware, 3,815 to 12,224.*: Ibid., 23.

181. *Union headquarters and rebel headquarters."*: Nicolay and Hay, *History,* 4:209.

181. *would need to fight his own state government.*: Ibid., 4:212.

181. *constellation of the Confederate States of America."*: Ibid., 4:210.

182. *burning the telegraph and bridges on their retreat.*: Ibid., 4:213, 219.

182. *to open recruiting offices just outside of the state.*: Donald, *Lincoln,* 300.

182. *and then he will think it a damned poor joke."*: Burlingame, *At Lincoln's Side,* May 6, 1861.

182. *or invasion the public safety may require it."*: Constitution, Article I, Section 9.

182. *occurs, are authorized to suspend the writ."*: CW, 4:348.

183. *before the commandant, General George Cadwallader.*: Howard, *American State Trials,* 9:880.

183. *damaged railroad and telegraph wires.*: McPherson, *Battle Cry,* 287.

183. *United States Court room in Baltimore's Masonic Hall.*: Taney, Roger. *The Merryman Habeas Corpus Case, Baltimore: The United States Government a Military Despotism* (Jackson, MS.: J. L. Power, 1861).

183. *to suspend the writ of habeas corpus.*: Howard, *American State Trials,* 9:880.

183. *bring him before the court at noon the next day.*: Taney, Roger. *The Proceedings in the case of John Merryman* (Baltimore: Lucas Brothers, 1861), 4.

184. *'that there was no answer to my card.'"*: Ibid.

184. *by compelling obedience to the civil process."*: Ibid., 5.

184. *and hate sweep every thing before us."*: Roger Taney to Franklin Pierce, June 12, 1861, Papers of Franklin Pierce.

185. *arouse him from his slumbers at midnight."*: Tyler, *Letters and Times,* 2:663.

185. *as was intended in this case, by the rebellion."*: Nicolay and Hay, *History,* 4:177.

185. *with soldiers, and a camp of one hundred thousand amassed.:* Nevins, *Ordeal,* 5:187.

185. *"the everywhere-ness of uniforms and muskets.":* Nicolay to Bates, April 29, 1861.

185. *are filled with soldiers as also the public squares.":* Francis Blair to Martin Van Buren, May 31, 1861, Papers of Martin Van Buren.

185. *"constantly on the march through the city.":* Poore, *Reminiscences,* 94.

185. *under the dome; the Seventh New York in the House.:* Nevins, *Ordeal,* 5:86.

185. *for the army, the crypt a storage space for flour.:* Ibid., 5:189.

186. *patient by the desk and franked for every body.":* Burlingame, *Inside Lincoln's White House,* April 20, 1861.

186. *Jefferson Davis and General Robert E. Lee.:* Tyler, *Letters and Times,* 2:652.

186. *stood defiantly confronting each other.":* BL, 1:171.

186. *could pin down Confederate general Joseph Johnston and his men.:* Nicolay and Hay, *History,* 4:323–24.

186. *and power to protect and maintain itself.":* Nicolay Memorandum, May 7, 1861.

187. *believed it possible to survive them.":* Nicolay correspondence to Bates and memorandum dated July 3, 1861.

187. *that if young enough he would join and fight.:* *Richmond Dispatch,* July 9, 1861; Chitwood, *Tyler,* 461.

187. *There is no rest for the wicked.":* *Wisconsin Daily Patriot,* November 27, 1861.

Chapter 22: Twilight at Wheatland, Dawn at Manassas

188. *would have responded the same as Lincoln.:* Buchanan, *Works,* 11:186.

188. *and children are all engaged in warlike pursuits.":* Ibid., 11:187.

189. *"shutting doors and hasty footfalls.":* *Philadelphia Inquirer,* June 17, 1861.

189. *"To be sick, while the whole world is alive.":* Buchanan, *Works,* 11:191–93.

190. *you a cheerful welcome," he explained.:* Ibid., 11:194–95.

190. *"been dead as any antediluvian.":* Ibid., 11:195–97.

190. *immediately move to York or Lancaster.":* Ibid., 11:198–203.

190. *depend upon myself with God's assistance.":* Ibid., 11:226.

190. *was committed to driving them out of it.:* Nicolay and Hay, *History,* 4:331.

191. *went back to bed for the sixth time.:* Hertz, *Lincoln Talks,* 377–78.

192. *sentiments and it was frightful to hear him then.":* Whipple, *Story Life,* 497.

192. *"to be a little patient.":* *Annals of War by Leading Participants North and South* (Philadelphia: Times Publishing Company, 1879), 73.

192. *break up us with some unexpected quarter.":* Franklin Pierce to John Thomson, July 20, 1861, Papers of Franklin Pierce.

192. *and his army's departure by eight days.:* BL, 1:175.

192. *to witness a Fourth of July procession.":* Poore, *Reminiscences,* 84.

192. *swelling his ranks by nine thousand soldiers.:* BL, 1:181–83.

192. *Some regiments were in plain clothes.:* BL, 1:167 Editorial note; BL, 1:176.

193. *seeking to turn the Confederate left flank.:* McPherson, *Battle Cry,* 340.

193. *"powder, smoke, and dust.":* BL, 1:235.

193. *features of the fight," according to one general.:* Ibid., 1:189.

193. *no matter when it may overtake me.":* Ibid., 1:238.
193. *began to walk, and finally to run away.:* Ibid., 1:191–92.
193. *at this juncture," she answered.:* Helm, Katherine. *Mary, Wife of Lincoln* (New York: Harper Brothers, 1918),179.
193. *taking notes, planning his next move.:* Nicolay and Hay, *History*, 4:355.
194. *to the health of Confederate generals.:* Chitwood, *Tyler*, 461.
194. *of the Confederate forces could be offered.":* Buchanan, *Works*, 11:213–14.
194. *with their business very badly.":* Correspondence to Millard Fillmore, July 23, 1861, Papers of Millard Fillmore.
194. *twenty-five officers and 362 enlisted, with 1,519 wounded.:* BL, 1:193 Editorial note.
194. *which before was but a political assertion.":* Ibid., 1:219.
194. *be invaded for eight more months.:* McPherson, *Battle Cry*, 347.
194. *placed their banners upon its public buildings.":* McCullough, Hugh. *Men and Measures of a Half Century* (New York: Charles Scribner's Sons, 1888), 161.
195. *to grant under any conceivable circumstances.":* Buchanan, *Works*, 11:216.
195. *patriotic volunteers who are already in the field.":* Ibid., 11:222–23.
195. *"'Old Buck' Sound at the Core!":* Hartford Daily Courant, October 8, 1861.
195. *I cannot but think you ought to have made it."* Buchanan, *Works*, 11:226.
195. *and to all others who have asked to be informed of them.":* Martin Van Buren to John Halberton, November 1861.
196. *find arms to put into their hands.":* CW, 5:20.
196. *recruits into a professional fighting force.:* McPherson, *Battle Cry*, 349.
196. *and placed in charge of the Army of the Potomac.:* McClellan, George, *McClellan's Own Story* (New York: Charles L. Webster and Company, 1887), 2–3.
196. *greatest results with the weakest instruments.":* Nevins, *Ordeal*, 5:272–73.

Chapter 23: To Lose Kentucky Is Nearly the Same as to Lose the Whole Game

198. *his order to conform to the Confiscation Act.:* CW, 4:506.
198. *and the job on our hands is too large for us.":* Lincoln to Orville Browning, September 22, 1861, CW, 4:532.
198. *Confederate coinage, weights, and measures.:* Journal of the Confederate Congress, 1:492.
198. *secretary of war and the commander of the navy.:* Chitwood, *Tyler*, 459.
198. *you are elected, sir! You are elected!":* Tyler, *Letters and Times*, 2:665.
199. *such names as James Buchanan and Frank Pierce?":* Springfield Weekly Republican, November 30, 1861.
199. *must respectfully advise against it.":* Millard Fillmore to James Sill, September 16, 1861, Papers of Millard Fillmore.
199. *neighbors will understand him better.":* CW, 4:505.
199. *and cherished purpose to visit the Great West.":* Wallner, *Pierce*, 2:340.
200. *likely to be forced to defend St. Louis.:* Nicolay Memorandum, October 2, 1861.
200. *are ready to meet them at any moment.":* Isaac Newton to Millard Fillmore, October 14, 1861, Papers of Millard Fillmore.

200. *cast a gloom over the people of this place.":* Isaac Newton to Millard Fillmore, October 23, 1861, Papers of Millard Fillmore.

200. *Union commanders, and he was not alone.:* Isaac Newton to Millard Fillmore, October 26, 1861, Papers of Millard Fillmore.

200. *failed, and that he ought to be removed.":* Nicolay to Lincoln, October 21, 1861.

200. *the men and artillery as his opponents.:* McPherson, *Battle Cry*, 365.

201. *soon be called upon to save my country?":* Nicolay and Hay, *History*, 4:445.

201. *or will not see the true state of affairs.":* McClellan to his wife, Whipple, *Story Life*, 440.

201. *more than a well meaning baboon" and an "idiot.":* Donald, *Lincoln*, 319.

201. *points of etiquette and personal dignity.":* Burlingame, *Inside Lincoln's White House*, November 13, 1861.

201. *hold McClellan's horse if he will only bring us success.":* Whipple, *Story Life*, 461.

201. *smaller vessels" across thirty-five hundred miles of coast.:* McPherson, *Battle Cry*, 369.

201. *Key West and Hampton Roads, the navy required another.:* Ibid., 369–70.

201. *Both forts surrendered four hours later.:* McPherson, *Battle Cry*, 371.

202. *wait patiently and anxiously for his first blow.":* Millard Fillmore to Isaac Newton, October 26, 1861, Papers of Millard Fillmore.

Chapter 24: Capture on the High Seas

203. *relations between England and your country.":* Buchanan, *Works*, 11:218–19.

204. *were about to intersect once again.:* Monaghan, Jay. *Diplomat in Carpet Slippers* (Indianapolis: Bobbs Merrill, 1945), 166.

204. *at Fort Warren, Massachusetts, with prisoners aboard.:* *Annals*, 794–800, eyewitness account of R. M. Hunter.

205. *aware of the potential unwanted consequences.:* Bates, David. *Lincoln and the Telegraph Office* (New York: The Century Company, 1907), 98–99.

205. *broadside from the English journals," he wrote.:* Buchanan, *Works*, 11:231–32.

205. *transport his troops or his despatches.":* Ibid., 11:234.

205. *apologize for the act as a violation of our doctrines.":* Nicolay and Hay, *History*, 5:26–27.

205. *in Britain as a consequence of the* Trent *affair.:* McPherson, *Battle Cry*, 390.

205. *Additional ships were sent to American waters.:* Nicolay and Hay, *History*, 5:27.

205. *would purposely insult the country.:* Ibid., 5:28.

206. *beyond question the master-mind of the cabinet.":* Whipple, *Story Life*, 431.

206. *would-be emissaries in solitary confinement.:* Bates, *Lincoln and the Telegraph Office*, 98.

207. *will then hold her responsible for the consequences.":* Millard Fillmore to Abraham Lincoln, December 16, 1861.

207. *to grant his nephew a commission in the army.:* CW, 5:33.

207. *close the embassy and withdraw from Washington.:* Donald, *Lincoln*, 323.

207. *chairman of the Senate Foreign Affairs Committee, was included.:* Nicolay and Hay, *History*, 5:35.

207. *dearest interest, probably the existence, of the nation.":* Beale, Howard. *The Diary of Edward Bates* (Washington, DC: Government Printing Office, 1933).

207. *and a pleasant dinner with his housekeeper.:* Buchanan, *Works*, 11:241–42.

207. *"we ought to have done it gracefully and without pettifogging."*: Ibid., 11:244, 246.
208. *the subject of the defense of our city and frontier."*: Millard Fillmore Papers, 2:398.
208. *and necessary to defend the city against attack.*: Ibid.

Chapter 25: The Bottom Is Out of the Tub

209. *Will try to hope for the best."*: Millard Fillmore to Dorothea Dix, January 23, 1862, Papers of Millard Fillmore..
209. *and on the Continent, that I fear for the blockade."*: Buchanan, *Works*, 11:248.
210. *withdraw his own letter, allowing Cameron to resign.*: Donald, *Lincoln*, 326,
210. *restore the Union which your heart can desire."*: Buchanan, *Works*, 11:256.
210. *to produce great and, we trust, happy results."*: *Buffalo Commercial Advertiser*, January 24, 1862, Papers of Millard Fillmore.
210. *but unquestioning obedience would satisfy."*: Nicolay and Hay, *History*, 5:140.
211. *who knew that they had less than a third of the Union's men).*: Nicolay and Hay, *History*, 5:152.
211. *"and will adjourn this council."*: Meigs, *Benten*, 292–93; Donald, *Lincoln*, 330.
211. *the keen intelligence of his questions."*: Nicolay and Hay, *History*, 5:156.
211. *mandated that this occur on or before February 22.*: CW, 5:115.
211. *and sent for the General to come to him."*: Burlingame, *Inside Lincoln's White House*, March 1862.
211. *reveal his plans to the administration.*: Nevins, *Ordeal*, 6:41.
212. *"I shall gladly yield my plan to yours."*: CW, 5:118–19.
212. *or accept his judgment. He chose the last.*: Nevins, *Ordeal*, 6:42.
212. *"I really believe she knows me," he delighted.*: Tyler, *Letters and Times*, 2:671.
213. *"Perhaps, it is best."*: Chitwood, *Tyler*, 465.
213. *were made to bury him next to James Monroe.*: *Richmond Examiner*, January 20, 1862.
213. *marched to the tune of "a solemn dirge."*: Tyler, *Letters and Times*, 2:682; Crapol, *Accidental President*, 268.
213. *a last glimpse of the departed statesman."*: *Richmond Examiner*, January 22, 1862.
213. *a ripple to the rushing current of events."*: *Albany Evening Journal*, January 22, 1862.
213. *which he devoted the last ill-spent hours of his life."*: *New York Herald*, January 22, 1862.
214. *through in this great struggle in our country."*: Isaac Newton to Millard Fillmore, February 9, 1862, Papers of Millard Fillmore.
214. *and the necessary accoutrements to accompany the same."*: Public announcement, February 10, 1862, Papers of Millard Fillmore.
214. *read the first president's famous Farewell Address.*: *Buffalo Morning Express*, February 19, 1862.
214. *on my part, will be faithful to you."*: *Annals*, 80.
214. *he is the target for fanatical malevolence."*: John Pendleton Kennedy to Millard Fillmore, March 5, 1862, Papers of Millard Fillmore.
214. *"the best man to lead our armies to victory."*: Fillmore to John Pendleton Kennedy, March 7, 1862, Papers of Millard Fillmore.
215. *well-fortified structure protected by fifteen thousand troops.*: BL, 1:406.

215. *answer for his actions in the previous administration.:* Ibid., 1:426.

215. *to move immediately upon your works.":* Nicolay and Hay, *History,* 5:199.

215. *come to blows in our discussions over Fort Sumter.":* Nicolay journal entry, February 17, 1862.

216. *when the heart hath bled."':* Franklin Pierce to Abraham Lincoln, March 4, 1862, Papers of Franklin Pierce.

Chapter 26: Greenbacks and Ironclads

217. *but such as I have give I thee."':* Hertz, *Lincoln Talks,* 224.

217. *making it a legal tender,"Buchanan wrote.:* Buchanan, *Works,* 11:233.

218. *'From which end would you pay, Chase?"':* Hertz, *Lincoln Talks,* 223.

218. *was an instrument of God to destroy slavery.:* Nicolay and Hay, *History,* 5:202.

218. *and with the best judgment I can bring to it.":* Lincoln to Bancroft, November 18, 1861; Nicolay and Hay, *History,* 5:203.

218. *$400 per slave, for a total of $719,200.:* Nicolay and Hay, *History,* 5:206.

218. *Delaware, Maryland, Kentucky, Missouri, and the District of Columbia.:* Ibid., 5:210.

218. *that he did not want to delay the message.:* Sumner, Charles. *Memoir and Letters* (Boston: Roberts Brothers, 1877), 4:64.

219. *institution in some satisfactory way,"Lincoln said.:* Nicolay and Hay, *History,* 5:216.

219. *the* Congress, *and run the* Minnesota *aground.":* Bates, *Telegraph,* 116.

219. *a drowned body floats up to the surface.":* Atlantic Monthly, June 2, 1862.

219. *force the government to give up the capital.:* This seemed to be the view in cabinet; Whipple, *Story Life,* 450.

219. *to read the danger and find the remedy.":* Bates, *Telegraph,* 116.

219. *McClellan sat silently.:* Nicolay and Hay, *History,* 5:226.

219. *it also had five times as many guns.:* Ibid., 5:228.

220. *shells bounced off the sides of each ship.:* Ibid., 5:228.

220. *nine barges, whose contents were saved.:* Ibid., 5:184.

220. *McClellan left nineteen thousand.:* Ibid., 5:186.

Chapter 27: Any Explanations Which You May Offer Would Be Acceptable

222. *pronounce your letter perfect," one friend replied.:* Wallner, *Pierce,* 2:344.

223. *as a simple act of justice been placed before me.":* Franklin Pierce to William Seward, January 7, 1862, Papers of Franklin Pierce.

223. *contemptible knavery of this political mountebank.":* Correspondence to Franklin Pierce, January 15, 1862, Papers of Franklin Pierce.

223. *suffer any breach of the Constitution to pass unnoticed.":* Correspondence from Franklin Pierce, January 16, 1862, Papers of Franklin Pierce.

223. *now felt it necessary to correct the record.:* Nichols, *Young Hickory,* 520.

223. *the entire correspondence to be published.:* Franklin Pierce to Milton Latham, March 24, 1862, Papers of Franklin Pierce.

224. *who authorized the publication of the letter.:* Franklin Pierce to Milton Latham, March 25, 1862, Papers of Franklin Pierce.
224. *"dignified and manly" response, and condemning the administration..:* For one example see A. O. Brewster to Franklin Pierce, April 4, 1862, Papers of Franklin Pierce.
224. *as he [Seward] winced under your hands.":* Belle Dunne to Franklin Pierce, April 4, 1862, Papers of Franklin Pierce.
224. *to an Ex-President of the United States.":* Pittsfield Sun, April 10, 1862.

Chapter 28: West and East

225. *welcome they would not receive from man..:* BL, 2:189.
226. *"would drink hot blood" before laying eyes on Richmond.:* Ibid., 2:189–91.
226. *preparing for an all-out assault.:* Nevins, Ordeal, 6:81.
226. *in the direction of Pittsburg Landing.:* Grant, Ulysses. *Personal Memoirs of U.S. Grant* Volumes I–II (New York: Charles L. Webster, 1885), 1:277.
226. *fell into their hands," Grant remembered.:* Ibid., 1:280.
226. *giving each side a small measure of protection.:* Ibid.
226. *"sometimes at several points at once.":* BL, 1:484.
226. *into their camp, every fifteen minutes until sunlight.:* Ibid., 1:485.
226. *torrential rain may have done anyway.:* Grant, Memoirs, 1:287.
226. *Grant returned outside to the rain.:* Ibid.
227. *without a foot touching the ground.":* BL, 1:479.
227. *dead was Lincoln's brother-in-law, Samuel Todd.:* Grant, Memoirs, 1:302.
227. *than he has for some time.":* Isaac Newton to Millard Fillmore, May 2, 1862, Papers of Millard Fillmore.
227. *But you must act," Lincoln concluded.:* CW, 5:184–85.
228. *and to do what he thought best.:* Bates, Telegraph, 103–4.
228. *the crucial port of New Orleans, fell to the Union navy.:* Nicolay and Hay, History, 5:255.
228. *subsequent Confederate attempt to retake Louisiana.:* Lincoln Log, August 20, 1862; Washington Star, August 20, 1862.
228. *battle against thirteen thousand Confederates.:* McPherson, Battle Cry, 427.
228. *protection of Julia Tyler and her children.:* Chitwood, Tyler, 466.
228. *and Presidents Jefferson, Monroe, and Tyler.:* BL, 2:199.
228. *to join McClellan before Richmond.:* McPherson, Battle Cry, 460.
228. *four desperate battles, and winning them all.":* BL, 2:297.
229. *Let me hear from you instantly.":* CW, 5:235–36.
229. *watching each other in front of Richmond.":* BL, 2:271.
229. *after General Johnston was wounded.:* Ibid., 2:272; History.com, www.history.com/this-day-in-history/jeb-stuart-rides-around-the-union-army.
229. *of the wounded" could be heard in the Union camp.:* BL, 2:331.
229. *contemplated no such thing.:* Ibid., 2:362.
229. *before relaying the message to Secretary of War Stanton.:* Bates, Telegraph, 109.
230. *in the advance, was masterly in retreat.":* BL, 2:395.
230. *as close to Richmond for three years.:* Whipple, Story Life, 462.

230. *when all is unraveled McClellan will be justified.*": Buchanan, *Works*, 11:273.

230. *or Congress or the country forsakes me.*": Lincoln to Seward, June 28, 1862, CW 5:292–93.

231. *and stick to your purpose.*": Lincoln to Campbell, June 28, 1862, CW, 5:288.

231. *a call for three hundred thousand volunteers.*: CW, 5:296–97.

Chapter 29: The Very Vortex of Hell

232. *studying carefully each sentence.*": Bates, *Telegraph*, 138–42.

232. *expect to see a large and interested audience.*": Undated article in the Papers of Millard Fillmore.

233. *the dead, reflects honor upon the living.*": Papers of Millard Fillmore, 69–84.

233. *than any other necessary result of war.*": Article from January 20, 1862, Papers of Millard Fillmore.

233. *our woe has proceeded from their foolishness.*": *Buffalo Commercial Advertiser*, January 13, 1862.

233. *plantation slaves of the south for regulated freedom.*": Editorial of *The World*, New York, February 1862, Papers of Millard Fillmore.

234. *Lincoln's project in the telegraph office.*: *Baltimore Sun*, July 14, 1862.

234. *to agree with Lincoln. Welles concurred.*: Welles, *Diary*, 1:70–71.

234. *this game leaving any available card unplayed.*": Lincoln to Reverdy Johnson, CW 5:342–43.

234. *of military news since his indisposition.*": *New York Daily Tribune*, July 29, 1862.

234. *utmost confidence in that of Mr. Lincoln.*": *Western Reserve Chronicle* (Warren, OH), July 30, 1862.

235. *to have been . . . 'there is but one Reliance.'*": *New York Daily Tribune*, July 29, 1862.

235. *Another Statesman has departed for the Silent land.*": *Albany Evening Journal*, July 24, 1862.

235. *fullness of years and with a fame undimmed.*": *Milwaukee Morning Sentinel*, July 26, 1862.

235. *and for peace and good will among his fellow citizens.*": CW, 5:340–41.

235. *with an eye on the election returns.*": Niven, *Romantic Age*, 612.

236. *and our sacred honor?*": *New York Tribune*, July, 29, 1862.

236. *the moment he heard I was engaged.*": BL, 2:456.

236. *to General John Tyler by General Winfield Scott.'*": *San Francisco Bulletin*, August 26, 1862.

237. *remained to attend Washington College).*: *New York Daily Tribune*, September 4, 1862; *Boston Semi-Weekly Courier*, September 11, 1862.

237. *she was easily able to sell upon her arrival.*: Jones, *Rebel War Clerk's Diary*, 2:9, Official Records of the Union and Confederate Navies in the war of Rebellion, series I, volume 9, 270.

237. *minor engagements with Lee's Army of Northern Virginia.*: BL, 2:462.

237. *none of the promised reinforcements would arrive.*: BL, 2:461.

237. *seemed to think him a little crazy," Hay recalled.*: Burlingame, *Inside Lincoln's White House*, September 1, 1862.

237. *will be able to hold his men.":* Ibid., September 5, 1862.

237. *straggled into Washington "in large numbers.":* Welles, *Diary,* September 1, 1862.

237. *this was the very vortex of Hell.":* Kennedy Francis. *The Civil War Battlefield Guide* (New York: Houghton Mifflin, 1998), 2448.

238. *"I hope I mistake them.":* Welles, *Diary,* September 7, 1862.

238. *their common fame and the welfare of the country.":* Undated entry, mid-September, Burlingame, *Inside Lincoln's Whitehouse,* 1862.

238. *Yet the contest proceeds.":* CW, 5:403–4.

Chapter 30: Destroy the Rebel Army, If Possible

239. *the Potomac singing, "Maryland, My Maryland.":* McPherson, *Battle Cry,* 535.

239. *the planned movement of his army.:* BL, 2:603.

240. *12,500 troops at Harper's Ferry.:* CWB, 2503.

240. *McClellan could bring seventy-five thousand to the fight.:* Ibid., 2573.

240. *like the unbroken roll of a thunder storm.":* BL, 2:682.

240. *the ground strewn with prostrate forms.":* Ibid., 2:684.

240. *the broad, green leaves were sprinkled and stained with blood.":* Ibid.

240. *died or were injured in the first four hours.:* CWB, 2587.

240. *bridge to the south, hitting Lee to the right.:* Ibid., 2596.

240. *carnage at Antietam would have to do.:* Randall, James. *Lincoln the President,* Volumes I–IV (Gloucester, MA: Peter Smith, 1965), 2:159.

241. *McClellan refused to give battle again.:* CWB, 2604.

241. *believed that Lee had 120,000 men.:* BL, 2:658.

241. *first day, two-thirds of Lee's entire force.:* Ibid., 2:685.

241. *Destroy the rebel army, if possible.":* Correspondence of September 20, 1862, between Lincoln and McClellan can be found in CW 5:426 and footnote.

241. *"Carry Me Back to Old Virginny" as they left.:* McPherson, *Battle Cry,* 545.

241. *Things would have to change a different way.:* Whipple, *Story Life,* 465–69.

242. *his cabinet laughed along, Stanton excepted.:* Donald, David Herbert, ed. *Inside Lincoln's Cabinet* (New York: Longmans, Green, 1954), September 22, 1862.

242. *"a little paper of much significance.":* Whipple, *Story Life,* 481–82.

242. *and I am going to fulfill that promise.":* Donald, September 22, 1862.

242. *read his proclamation to the cabinet.:* Welles, *Diary,* September 22, 1862.

242. *shall be then, thenceforward, and forever free.":* Whipple, *Story Life,* 482.

243. *novel sensation of appropriating that horrible name.":* Burlingame, *Inside Lincoln's White House,* , September 24, 1862.

243. *being within the entrenchments of Richmond.":* Lincoln to McClellan, October 13, 1862, CW, 5:461.

243. *done since the battle of Antietam that fatigue anything?":* Lincoln to McClellan, October 26, 1862, CW, 5:474

243. *"Twenty Years Ago…":* Lamon, *Lincoln,* 150.

Chapter 31: A Continuation of War by Other Means

245. *It never rains but it pours.":* Nicolay to Bates, October 16, 1862.

246. *administration's "criminal" acts against civil liberties.:* McCabe, James Dabney. *The Life and Public Services of Horatio Seymour* (New York: United States Publishing Company, 1868), 40.

246. *306,649, to 295,897 for the Republican.:* Ibid., 42.

246. *in the late election, was given for Governor Seymour.":* Charles Davies to Millard Fillmore, November 8, 1862, Papers of Millard Fillmore.

246. *and oppose all those who violate it.":* Millard Fillmore to Ephraim Hutchins, February 9, 1863.

246. *the US Senate from all three states in 1863.:* Heidler, David, and Jeanne Heidler. *Encyclopedia of the American Civil War: A Political, Social, and Military History* (New York: W.W. Norton, 2000), 640.

247. *with Burnside to assume his place.:* CWB, 3100.

247. *find some one whom I don't understand.":* BL, 3:70.

247. *from there to the capital of the Confederacy.:* CWB, 3105.

247. *the creative backlash of their holders.:* Salem Register, August 10, 1863.

247. *perfidious close of his inglorious public career.":* New York Tribune, September 12, 1862.

247. *wait for peace to publicly make his case.:* Buchanan, *Works*, 11:258–59.

248. *war in my time; and this they well knew.":* Ibid., 11:260–61.

248. *sustaining it one day after Scott requested it.:* Ibid., 11:279–93.

248. *dragged him deeper in the slough of shame.":* Reprinted in the *Richmond Examiner,* November 8, 1862.

248. *Is there no one to protect him against his own folly?":* *Albany Evening Journal,* November 26, 1862.

249. *nor would they ever be, receptive to his defenses.:* Buchanan, *Works*, 11:317.

Chapter 32: A Storm of Lead

250. *and "solid shot rained like hail.":* CWB, 3116; BL, 3:73.

250. *marched into Fredericksburg the next day.:* CWB, 3127.

250. *twenty days had been preparing their welcome.:* BL, 3:73.

250. *Jackson "grimly awaited the onslaught.":* Ibid., 3:76.

250. *Behind this wall Longstreet placed twenty-five hundred men.:* Ibid., 3:78.

251. *and heavily fortified position began.:* Ibid., 3:126.

251. *piled as high as three bodies deep in some places.:* Ibid., 3:80–82.

251. *dying of cold, freezing the bodies to the ground.:* Ibid., 3:101.

251. *southernmost instances in history of the northern lights.:* Donald Pfanz, "The Union Army Retreats," http://fredericksburg.com/CivilWar/Battle/0915CW.

251. *and back across the Rappahannock.:* BL, 3:82.

252. *"Where are my 15,000 sons—murdered at Fredericksburg?":* Whipple, *Story Life*, 494.

252. *suffers more than I do, I pity him!":* Ibid., 499.

Chapter 33: If My Name Ever Goes into History, It Will Be for This Act

253. *only junction connecting every part of the Confederacy.:* Grant, *Memoirs*, 1:351.

253. *"the nail head that holds the South's two halves together.":* National Park Service article on Vicksburg, www.nps.gov/vick/index.htm.

253. *but to go forward to a decisive victory.":* Grant, *Memoirs*, 1:370.

254. *he said, "That will do!":* Whipple, *Story Life*, 491.

254. *Of thee I sing!":* New York Times, January 9, 1863; Camp Diary of Thomas Wentworth, January 1, 1863.

255. *"My heart is sick of the contemplation.":* Franklin Pierce to Colonel George, January 2, 1863.

256. *and fast" against these and all unconstitutional measures.:* Franklin Pierce to Millard Fillmore, October 3, 1862. In the collection of the Albany Institute of History and Art, to whom I am indebted for their speedy production of a copy of this letter.

256. *carried through the midst of a civil war.":* Springfield Republican, September 24, 1862.

256. *have his damned black heart cut out.":* Lincoln Log, August 13, 1863; Lincoln to Holt, August 13, 1863, CW, 6:385.

256. *fight for the Union, Lincoln asked that he be restored.:* Lincoln to Hunter, April 30, 1863, CW 6:191–92.

257. *a war of invasion in the most efficient manner.":* Buchanan, *Works*, 11:331–32.

257. *sleepless vigilance, go forward, and give us victories.":* Lincoln to Hooker, January 26, 1863, CW 6:78–79.

257. *defense of the Union," praising his "esprit de corps.":* Correspondence of the Union Continentals to Millard Fillmore, December 6, 1862, Papers of Millard Fillmore.

257. *and I am not in the way of earning more.":* Millard Fillmore to E. D. Morgan, February 16, 1863.

258. *remainder of my days in peace up north.":* March 19, 1863, letter printed in the *Commercial Advertiser*.

258. *banks of the Mississippi would end the rebellion at once.":* Lincoln to Johnson, March 26, 1863, CW, 6:149–50.

258. *any military success to speak of before the election.":* Hartford Courant, January 31, 1863.

259. *by the administration in its prosecution of the war.":* New York Times, March 12, 1863.

Chapter 34: We Are Ruined

260. *on any Civil War battlefield, 130,000 to sixty thousand,:* CWB, 4169–75.

260. *believed his chances of ending the war were 90 percent.:* BL, 3:174–75.

260. *attacking Hooker's superior numbers.:* Ibid., 3:175.

260. *highest ground for miles at Zoan Church.:* Kennedy, *The Civil War Battlefield Guide*, digital edition, 4180.

261. *woods," a quarter of a mile in front of Union lines.:* BL, 3:179–80.

261. *fire sent them back into the woods.:* Ibid., 3:181.

261. *twice in his left arm and through his right hand.:* Ibid., 3:211.

261. *Jackson's attack, his last, had all but sealed its outcome.:* Ibid., 3:213.

261. *What will the people say?":* Hertz, *Lincoln Talks,* 209.
262. *Oh, what will the country say?":* Whipple, *Story Life,* 510.
262. *instructions urging Hooker to renew the fight again.:* Ibid., 512.
262. *have an opportunity to show his innocence.":* Millard Fillmore to Abraham Lincoln, May 16, 1863, Papers of Millard Fillmore.
262. *President Fillmore, who writes the within letter.":* CW, 6:222.
262. *with execution or exile as possible punishments.:* McPherson, *Battle Cry,* 596.
262. *to weaken the government's war effort.:* Donald, *Lincoln,* 420.
262. *the Rebels with whom he sympathizes.":* Welles, *Diary,* May 19, 1863.
263. *glad to correct, on reasonably satisfactory evidence.":* CW, 6:261.
263. *nominated Vallandigham for governor.:* Donald, *Lincoln,*421.

Chapter 35: The Brave Men, Living and Dead

264. *the accomplishment of this one object.":* Grant, *Memoirs,* 1:401.
264. *average of 180 miles to reunite at this place.:* Ibid., 1:446–47.
264. *including from his longtime friend and sponsor.:* Ibid., 1:452.
264. *Lincoln would stick by his general.:* Lamon, *Lincoln,* 185.
265. *his life was "tranquil and monotonous,":* Buchanan, *Works,* 11:333.
265. *"to the privations inseparable from old age.":* Ibid., 11:337.
265. *to be found from the War Department.:* Welles, *Diary,* June 15, 1863.
265. *her Uncle Edward's and not to come home.:* Buchanan, *Works,* 11:338.
265. *within eleven miles of us," Buchanan wrote in horror.:* Ibid., 11:338.
265. *though he was not sure for what.:* BL, 3:243.
266. *the extreme right was thirty miles away in Maryland.:* Nicolay and Hay, *History,* 7:234.
266. *The first reinforcements came around noon.:* BL, 3:284.
266. *final resting place of the town's founders.:* Ibid., 3:338.
266. *or they are going to whip me.":* Ibid., 3:339–40.
266. *Union lines by the light of a full moon.:* Ibid., 3:291.
267. *and the two forces met at the summit.:* Nicolay and Hay, *History,* 7:254.
267. *scattered "like a herd of wild cattle.":* BL, 3:315.
267. *curved south along Culp's Hill.:* Nicolay and Hay, *History,* 7:255; BL, 3:342.
267. *whom had to stand due to a lack of seats.:* BL, 3:313.
267. *if Lee did, he would defeat him.:* Ibid., 3:314.
268. *other than those indicated above.":* Grant, *Memoirs,* 1:465.
268. *next movement in the struggle for Gettysburg.:* Nicolay and Hay, *History,* 7:261.
268. *responded for the next hour.:* Ibid.
268. *"vomited their iron hail upon each other.":* BL, 3:327.
268. *who could make that attack successfully.":* Ibid., 3:342.
268. *"My heart was heavy when I left Pickett.":* Ibid., 3:343.
269. *"high water mark of the Confederacy" had receded.:* Kennedy, CWB, 4435.
269. *where tomorrow would bring a new battle or a retreat.:* Nicolay and Hay, *History,* 7:272.

Chapter 36: The Fourth of July

270. *had resorted to eating rats and tree bark.:* Grant, *Memoirs,* 1:472.

270. *fighting for the same cause,"* Grant noted.: Ibid., 1:477.

270. *promise not to take up arms against the Union.:* Ibid., 1:476.

270. *and 172 cannon were taken.:* Ibid., 1:479.

271. *celebrate the Fourth of July until after World War II.:* *Baltimore Sun* reprinted story from the *Dallas Morning News,* July 4, 1997; *Time,* July 9, 1945.

271. *Democratic Mass Convention which meets in this city [Concord] on July 4.":* *New York Herald,* July 3, 1863.

271. *and perhaps in all of New England.:* *Sun* (Baltimore, MD), July 7, 1863.

271. THE CONSTITUTION AS IT IS; THE UNION AS IT WAS.: *New Hampshire Patriot,* July 8, 1863.

272. *to the sacred shrines of the Holy Land.":* Miller, Marion Mills, ed. *Great Debate in American History* (New York: Current Literature Publishing Company, 1913), 325–26.

272. *5th New Hampshire regiment had been killed at Gettysburg.:* Nichols, 523.

272. *compared with such a copperhead as Franklin Pierce.":* *Hartford Courant,* July 9, 1863.

272. *occupied Concord, N.H., on the 4th of July.":* *Vermont Phoenix,* July 23, 1863.

273. *being reminded that it ever had such a president.":* *Boston Daily Advertiser,* July 7, 1863; *Constitution,* July 15, 1863.

273. *he concluded, "I will now take the music.":* Response to a serenade, July 7, 1863, CW, 6:319–20

273. *intercepting the retreating rebel army.:* Welles, *Diary,* July 7, 1863.

273. *Man-in-the-Moon as any part of Lee's Army.":* Lincoln to Lorenzo Thomas, July 8, 1863, CW 6:321–22.

274. *across the lawn to telegraph the news to General Meade.:* Welles, *Diary,* July 7, 1863.

274. *other late successes, have ended the war.":* Lincoln to Meade (unsigned and unsent), July 14, 1863, CW 6:327–28.

274. *The whole country is our soil.":* Burlingame, *Inside Linoln's White House,* July 14, 1863.

274. *without criticism for what was not done.":* Lincoln to Oliver Howard, 6:341.

274. *"from a soldier to a soldier's friend.":* *New York Herald,* July 27, 1863; Martin, David G., *The Vicksburg Campaign* (New York: Da Capo, 1990); *Sun,* July 28, 1863.

275. *myself in his opinions on the subject of southern rights.":* *Albany Journal,* August 21, 1863.

275. *was "a great ado," in the words of one newspaper.:* *Columbian Register,* September 26, 1863.

275. *than Franklin Pierce gives him in this letter.":* *New York Daily Tribune,* September 19, 1863.

275. *there "as in the days of my power.":* Buchanan, *Works,* 11:346.

275. *living in a separate confederacy from them.":* Ibid., 11:344; *Philadelphia Daily Age,* August 18, 1863.

276. *recruiting drive for black soldiers and regiments.:* Donald, *Lincoln,* 430–31.

276. *shall have the same pay as white soldiers.":* Whipple, *Story Life,* 514.

276. *against their prisoners should that not be the case.:* CW, 6:401–10.

276. *one hundred thousand blacks were serving the Union cause in uniform.:* Donald, *Lincoln,* 471.
277. *scenes through which we are now passing.":* Lincoln to Banks, August 5, 1863, CW, 6:364–65.

Chapter 37: A New Birth of Freedom

278. *aspired to the Presidency of the United States.":* Reprinted in the *Daily Evening Bulletin,* October 17, 1863.
279. *and I was going to his house.'":* Hertz, *Lincoln Talks,* 269.
279. *displaying "a good deal of emotion.":* Welles, *Diary,* October 14, 1863.
279. *and made to stand on a barrel for two hours.:* J. H. Moore to Millard Fillmore, October 23, 1863, Papers of Millard Fillmore.
279. *saying he was pledged to Lincoln.:* Burlingame, *Inside Lincoln's White House,* October 17, 1863.
279. *as the head of the Treasury Department.":* Ibid., October 18, 1863.
280. *can spare time for personal contention.":* Lincoln to Cutts, October 26, 1863, CW, 6:538.
280. *murderer in the very place where he would be assassinated.:* Burlingame, *Inside Lincoln's White House,* November 9, 1863.
280. *there won't be any fun till I get there.'":* Lamon, *Lincoln,* 133.
281. *and the people are disappointed.":* Ibid., 173.
281. *through crowded and cheering streets.":* Burlingame, *Inside Lincoln's White House,* November 19, 1863
281. *aims of the war from Union to Equality and Union.":* Donald, *Lincoln,* 465–66.

Chapter 38: Our Old Home

283. *customers were very much fans of Hawthorne.:* Boulard, *Expatriation,* 2380.
283. *cut out the dedication before reading.:* "Our Old Home," Introduction, Eldritch Press Edition, www.eldritchpress.org/nh/ooh.html#pref.
283. *graveside at the Old North Church in Concord.:* Nichols, *Young Hickory,* 524.
283. *hoping that he had made her happy.:* Wallner, *Pierce,* 2:355.
283. *Hawthorne's coat to shield him from the bitter cold.":* Ibid., 2:354.
284. *having resumed its former role in the Union.:* CW, 7:54–56.
284. *Tell him from me God Bless him.":* Burlingame, *Inside Linoln's White House,* December 9, 1863
284. *The crowd cheered in agreement.:* *Courant* (Boston, MA) February 17, 1863.
284. *formed to modernize the Army Medical Bureau.:* McPherson, *Battle Cry,* 323.
284. *voluntary association in the history of the United States.:* Ibid., 480.
284. *and the event netted an incredible $25,000.:* Rayback, *Fillmore,* 427.
285. *amongst the bitterest opponents of the war.":* *Buffalo Commercial Advertiser,* February 23, 1864.
285. *the favor of sympathy with rebellion and slavery.":* Correspondence to Millard Fillmore from Lewistown, March 5, 1864, Papers of Millard Fillmore.

286. *still more ghastly name of James Buchanan.": New York Daily Tribune*, March 1, 1864.
286. *however, carried, "to much laughter.": Farmer's Cabinet*, March 10, 1864.
286. *they were willing to return to the Union.:* Renda, Lex. *Running on the Record: Civil War Era Politics in New Hampshire* (Charlottesville: University of Virginia Press, 1997), 120.
286. *nominee for governor, was for "perpetual war.":* Ibid., 121.
286. *features with hypocritical smiles in New Hampshire.":* Ibid., 119.
287. *at Fredericksburg, and were now in Virginia.:* NPS Soldiers and Sailors Database, www.nps.gov/civilwar/search-regiments-detail.htm?regiment_id=UNH0013RI.
287. *country's cause on many a bloody field.": Farmer's Cabinet*, February 25, 1864.
287. *Democrats would send Pierce to the Senate.:* Renda, *Running*, 122.
287. *and "skedaddled" by train after voting.:* Wallner, *Pierce*, 2:356.
288. *New Hampshire Union ticket had prevailed by three thousand votes.:* Nicolay Memorandum, March 8, 1864.
288. *The spirit of liberty dwells among my people.":* Papers of Abraham Lincoln, March 9, 1864.
288. *worthy of a better fate.":* Buchanan, *Works*, 11:358.
288. *their bark is upon the breakers.": Hartford Courant*, March 12, 1864.
288. *"cast among the rubbish.": Daily Evening Bulletin*, May 11, 1864.
289. *generous, brave heart beat no more.":* Wallner, *Pierce*, 2:357.
289. *the final honor of bearing his friend to the grave.:* Nichols, *Young Hickory*, 525.

Chapter 39: Those Not Skinning Can Hold a Leg

290. *relations towards each other as . . . when the war began.":* Grant, *Memoirs*, 2:125.
290. *towards a common center.":* Grant to Sherman, April 4, 1864; Ibid., 2:130.
290. *provisioned by railroads in their interior lines.:* BL, 4:250.
291. *enjoying the blessings of peace.":* Millard Fillmore to Mary McClellan, March 24, 1864.
291. *say is, the fault is not with you.":* Lincoln to Grant, April 30, 1864, CW, 7:324–25 and footnote.
292. *just as well by advancing as standing still.:* Grant, *Memoirs*, 2:143.
292. *can hold a leg.":* Burlingame, *Inside Lincoln's White House*, 180.
292. *amassing north of the Rapidan.:* BL, 4:118.
292. *which reduced Lee's numerical disadvantage.:* Ibid., 4:154.
292. *the sound of the firing.":* Ibid., 4:122.
292. *died from fire alone.:* Ibid., 4:162.
292. *no man's land were burned or suffocated.:* Grant, *Memoirs*, 2:201.
292. *strewing the Wilderness with human wrecks.":* BL, 4:125.
292. *withdrew on the evening of May 6.:* Grant, *Memoirs*, 2:202.
292. *"Our cat has the longest tail.":* Burlingame, *Inside Lincoln's White House*, May 9, 1864.
293. *and perhaps to bring him out into the open.:* Grant, *Memoirs*, 2:211.
293. *"fight it out on this line if it takes all summer.":* Ibid., 2:226.
293. *forcing Lee into the defenses around Richmond.:* BL, 4:248–49.

293. *ambulances trapped by washed-out roads.:* Grant, *Memoirs*, 2:237.

293. *this is now the hope of our country.":* Whipple, *Story Life,* 574.

293. *were with him about four hundred men.":* Bates, *Telegraph,* 194–95.

293. *expertly, leaving nothing behind, delaying Sherman.:* BL, 4:252.

Chapter 40: Not Unworthy to Remain in My Present Position

294. *the temerity" to advance and fight Lee's forces again.:* BL, 4:230.

294. *which they clipped to their uniforms.:* McPherson, *Batlte Cry,* 735.

294–95. *period of time throughout the war.":* BL, 4:217.

295. *or wounded to seventeen hundred for the Confederates.:* Ibid., 4:249.

295. *are brought daily to Washington by hundreds.":* Welles, *Diary,* June 11, 1864.

295. *to compensate for the heavy loss we sustained.":* Grant, *Memoirs,* 2:276.

295. *from the south—Grant opted for the latter.:* Ibid., 2:278.

295. *thought, he rose and left the room.:* Bates, *Telegraph,* 268.

296. *give it legal form, and practical effect.":* Lincoln's reply to notifying committee, June 9, 1864, CW, 7:380–81.

296. *swap horses when crossing streams.":* Lincoln's reply to New York Union League, June 9, 1864, CW, 7:383–84.

296. *have not placed it beyond hope.":* Franklin Pierce correspondence, June 14, 1864.

297. *grant her the pass she had been seeking to return.:* *Philadelphia Inquirer,* August 19, 1864; *New York Daily Tribune,* August 18, 1864; *New York Herald,* August 18, 1864.

297. *and live to take his bride back to Buffalo.:* *Worcester Daily Spy,* January 15, 1903.

297. *Pontoon bridges were laid down.:* Grant, *Memoirs,* 2:292–93.

297. *since Grant set forth from Washington.:* McPherson, *Battle Cry,* 742.

297. *as he is of anything in the world.":* Burlingame, *Inside Lincoln's White House,* June 23, 1864.

297. *inspired confidence in the general and army.":* Welles, *Diary,* June 24, 1864.

297. *sooner he could have seized the capital.:* Grant, *Memoirs,* 2:306.

298. *"riddled to pieces with musketry.":* Burlingame, *Inside Lincoln's White House,* July 13, 1864.

298. *an expensive lesson for the Confederates.:* BL, 4:253.

298. *"because soldiers, like other mortals, must have food.":* Ibid., 4:254.

298. *of interest in Millard Fillmore and Franklin Pierce.:* One representative article can be found in the *Daily Constitutional Union DC,* August 3, 1864.

298. *"The Constitution as it is and the Union as it was.":* George Read Riddle to Millard Fillmore, July 2, 1864, Papers of Millard Fillmore.

298. *"beyond the Constitution . . . the sole object.":* Millard Fillmore to George Read Riddle, July 5, 1864, Papers of Millard Fillmore.

299. *insisted that the letter be kept private.:* Millard Fillmore to A. B. Norton, August 10, 1864, Papers of Millard Fillmore.

299. *and give peace to our bleeding country.":* Millard Fillmore to J. T. Stuart, August 10, 1864, Papers of Millard Fillmore.

299. *confess I am far from being prepared.":* Buchanan, *Works,* 11:370.

299. *and chew and choke as much as possible.*": Bates, *Telegraph*, 128.

299. re-*electing Mr. Lincoln 'unless something is done.'*": Nicolay to Bates, August 21, 1864.

299. *sign the back of a memorandum, sight unseen.*: Memorandum, August 23, 1864, CW, 7:514–15.

300. *too high a price at the expense of the Union.*": Buchanan, *Works*, 11:373.

300. *to preemptively surrender the war than to lose the race.*: Nicolay to Bates, August 28, 1864.

300. *"depends the salvation of our country."*: Millard Fillmore Papers, 2:433.

300. *make a first class Copperhead."*: *Albany Evening Journal*, October 5, 1864.

301. *among the rebels in justification of their course."*: *Albany Journal*, October 8, 1864; October 17, 1864.

301. *and bands of music in the north."*: Grant, *Memoirs*, 2:176.

301. *"The elections carried him off."*: Burlingame, *Inside Lincoln's White House*, October 12, 1864.

301. *for returning reason and patriotism?"*: Franklin Pierce to Millard Fillmore, November 2, 1864.

302. *"She is more anxious than I."*: Burlingame, *Inside Lincoln's White House*, November 8, 1864.

303. *before my own conscience."*: Ibid., November 11, 1864.

Chapter 41: The Last Full Measure

304. *and decisive utterances of the national will."*: Marquis de Chambrun, "Personal Recollections of Mr. Lincoln," *Scribner's*, January 1893.

304. *He ought to desire nothing more."*: Buchanan, *Works*, 11:377.

305. *greatness of the President, in this age of little men."*: Nicolay to Bates, December 4, 1864.

305. *He wrote a pass and handed it to me."*: Welles, *Diary*, December 24, 1864.

305. *your Christmas gift, the capture of Savannah."*: Lincoln to Sherman, December 26, 1864.

305. *fame than any single act of my life."*: BL, 4:257.

305. *slavery to the lame duck Congress that had rejected it.*: Lincoln's Fourth Annual Message, December 4, 1864.

306. *urged Congress to enact the mandate of the people.*: Donald, *Lincoln*, 553.

306. *lobbying members personally for passage.*: Ibid., 554.

306. *necessary for passage was limited to members present.*: Burlingame, Michael. *Abraham Lincoln: A Life* (Baltimore: Johns Hopkins University Press, 2008), unedited edition hosted online by Knox College, 3877.

306. *was perhaps the worst news possible.*: Ibid., 3881.

306. *commissioners in the city, or likely to be in it."*: CW, 8:248.

306. *pass that Lincoln issued the day before.*: Ibid.

306. *by the narrow margin of 118–59.*: Burlingame, *Life*, 3882.

306. *"loud and long applause" upon passage.*: Nicolay to Bates, February 4, 1865.

306. *his own great work, the Emancipation Proclamation."*: Arnold, *Life*, 1:366; Burlingame, *Life*, 3883.

306. *the national government which was irresistible.":* BL, 4:259

307. *and who was so reluctantly dragged into their support.":* Buchanan, *Works,* 11:380.

307. *through which men and horses plodded wearily.":* Poore, *Reminiscences,* 157.

307. *obscured by rain clouds, burst forth in splendor.":* Whipple, *Story Life,* 617.

307. *and with all nations.":* CW, 8:332–33.

307. *He "slept no more that night.":* Lamon, *Lincoln,* 116–17.

307. *streets of Richmond," wrote one Confederate captain.:* BL, 4:725.

308. *thereafter announced that evening services would be cancelled.:* St. Paul's Church, "Who We Are." www.stpauls-episcopal.org/index.php/who/history_architecture.

308. *would find Lee had escaped him.:* Grant, *Memoirs,* 2:424.

308. *and one foot out of bed for many weeks.":* BL, 4:708.

308. *he could force them to surrender before long.:* Grant, *Memoirs,* 2:454.

308. *the ghostly streets of Petersburg to his commander.:* Cooking, William. "Lincoln's Last Day," *Harper's Magazine,* Volume 115, 41–42.

308. *that you intended to do something like this.":* Grant, *Memoirs,* 2:459.

308. *had the honor to be the first to enter.:* NPS Soldiers and Sailors Database.

308. *have put out our hands and touched them.":* Crook, 520.

309. *when he is ready for whatever may come.":* Ibid., 521.

309. *and attempted to kiss his feet.:* Donald, *Lincoln,* 576.

309. *been deprived of it for so many years.":* Whipple, *Story Life,* 627.

309. *with a serious, dreamy expression.":* BL, 4:728.

309. *very success the end of a terrible responsibility.":* Chambrun, Marquis de. "Personal Recollections of Mr. Lincoln," January 1893, 28

310. *there in peace and tranquility.":* Ibid., 85.

310. *Appomattox Courthouse and accepted his surrender.:* Crook, 522.

310. *great purpose of his life had been achieved.":* Whipple, *Story Life,* 637.

311. *"more cheerful and happy than I had ever seen him.":* Whipple, *Story Life,* 639.

311. *day the war has come to a close.":* Lamon, *Lincoln,* 120.

311. *his law practice and time on the circuit.:* Whipple, *Story Life,* 643.

311. *"torchlight processions" and music.:* Chambrun, "Recollections," 37.

311. *though I would rather stay.":* Hollister, James. *The Life of Schuyler Colfax* (New York: Funk and Wagnalls, 1886), 253.

Epilogue: Do Not Despair of the Republic

312. *deepest regrets and sorrows with yours.:* Wallner, *Pierce,* 2:361.

312. *exhibition as the enquiry suggests.":* Nichols, *Young Hickory,* 526.

312. *responded with "three cheers" for Pierce.:* Wallner, *Pierce,* 2:361.

313. *atoned for remained between him and God.:* Boulard, *Expatriation,* 3376, 3386, 3408, 3431.

313. *where he was looking.:* New York Daily Tribune, April 19, 1865.

313. *and the Union has not been broken.":* Tyler, *Letters and Times,* 2:685.

313. *—for which I had toiled for years.":* Ibid., 2:686.

314. *heart," an impression that never changed.:* Buchanan, *Works,* 11:384–85.

314. *whom he had "known . . . for many years.":* Ibid., 11:382–83.

314. *rebellion," quipped the* Lowell Daily Citizen.: *Lowell Daily Citizen,* November 27, 1865.

314. *of the hero of the last sensational murder.":* Philadelphia Inquirer, July 15, 1865.

314–15. *Fillmore was simply out of town.:* Raybeck, *Fillmore,* 430.

315. *house your house during your time in the city.":* Millard Fillmore to Mary Lincoln, April 21, 1865, Papers of Millard Fillmore.

315. *and will not be able to travel for some weeks.":* Robert Lincoln to Millard Fillmore, April 25, 1865.

316. *succeed the storm if we do our own duty.":* Millard Fillmore Papers, 2:106–8.

316. *itself remains greater yet than they.":* Chambrun, "Recollections," 38.

BIBLIOGRAPHY

BOOKS

Annals of War by Leading Participants North and South (Philadelphia: Times Publishing Company, 1879).

Bancroft, George. *Martin Van Buren to the End of His Public Career* (New York: Harper and Brothers, 1889).

Basler, Roy, ed. *The Collected Works of Abraham Lincoln* (Springfield, IL: Abraham Lincoln Association, 1953). Referred to in notes as CW.

Bates, David. *Lincoln and the Telegraph Office* (New York: The Century Company, 1907).

Beale, Howard, ed. *The Diary of Edward Bates* (Washington, DC: Government Printing Office, 1933).

Benton, Thomas Hart. *Thirty Years' View*, Volumes I–III (New York: D. Appleton and Company, 1854).

Boulard, Gary. *The Expatriation of Franklin Pierce* (Bloomington, IN: iUniverse, 2006).

Bridgman, Edward Payson, and Parsons, Luke Fisher. *With John Brown in Kansas* (Madison, WI: J.N. Davidson, 1915).

Buchanan, James. *Mr. Buchanan's Administration on the Eve of the Rebellion* (New York: D. Appleton, 1866).

———. *The Works of James Buchanan*, Volumes I–XI (Philadelphia: J.B. Lippincott Company, 1911).

Burlingame, Michael. *Abraham Lincoln: A Life*, Volumes I–II (Baltimore: Johns Hopkins, 2008). References are to unedited manuscript hosted by Knox College online,

———, ed. *At Lincoln's Side: John Hay's Civil War Correspondence and Other Writings* (Carbondale: Southern Illinois University Press, 2006).

———. *Inside Lincoln's White House: The Complete Civil War Diary of John Hay* (Carbondale: Southern Illinois University Press, 2009).

———. *With Lincoln in the White House: Letters, Memoranda, and Other Writings of John G. Nicolay* (Carbondale: Southern Illinois University Press, 2000).

Chitwood, Oliver. *John Tyler: Champion of the Old South* (Newtown, CT: American Political Biography Press, 1990).

Cole, Donald. *Martin Van Buren and the American Political System* (Fort Washington, PA: Eastern National, 2004).

Crapol, Edward. *John Tyler, the Accidental President* (Chapel Hill: University of North Carolina Press, 2012).

Crawford, Samuel Wylie. *The Genesis of the Civil War: the Story of Sumter, 1860–1861* (New York: Charles L. Webster, 1887).

Curtis, George Ticknor. *Life of James Buchanan* (New York: Harper and Brothers, 1883).

DeRose, Chris. *Congressman Lincoln: The Making of America's Greatest President* (New York: Simon & Schuster/Threshold, 2013).

Donald, David Herbert, ed. *Inside Lincoln's Cabinet: The Civil War Diary of Salmon Chase* (New York: Longmans, Green and Company, 1954).

———. *Lincoln* (New York: Simon & Schuster, 1995).

Etcheson, Nicole. *Bleeding Kansas: Contested Liberty in the Civil War Era* (Lawrence: University Press of Kansas, 2004).

Grant, Ulysses. *Personal Memoirs of U.S. Grant,* Volumes I–II (New York: Charles L. Webster, 1885).

Guelzo, Allen. *Lincoln and Douglas: The Debates that Defined America* (New York: Simon & Schuster, 2008).

Helm, Katherine. *Mary, Wife of Lincoln* (New York: Harper Brothers, 1918).

Herndon, William, and Jesse Weik. *Herndon's Lincoln: The True Story of a Great Life* (New York: Da Capo, republished 2008).

Hertz, Emanuel. *Lincoln Talks: An Oral Biography* (New York: Viking Press, 1939).

Hollister, James. *The Life of Schuyler Colfax* (New York: Funk and Wagnalls, 1886).

Holt, Michael. *The Rise and Fall of the American Whig Party* (New York: Oxford University Press, 2003), 17280 (digital version).

Holzer, Harold. *Lincoln President-Elect* (New York: Simon & Schuster, 2009).

Howard, Robert Lorenzo. *American State Trials,* Volume IX (St. Louis: Thomas Law Book Company, 1919).

Johnson, Robert Underwood, ed. *Battles and Leaders of the Civil War,* Volumes I–IV (New York: The Century Company, 1887). Referred to in notes as BL.

Jones, J. B. *A Rebel War Clerk's Diary,* Volumes I–II (Philadelphia: J.B. Lippincott, 1866).

Julian, George. *The Life of Joshua R. Giddings* (Chicago: McClurg, 1892).

Kennedy, Francis. *The Civil War Battlefield Guide* (New York: Houghton Mifflin, 1998) Referred to in notes as CWB.

Lamon, Ward Hill. *Recollections of Abraham Lincoln 1847–1865* (Washington, DC: Published by his daughter, Dorothy Lamon Teillard).

Lawson, John David. *American State Trials,* Volume XIII (St. Louis: Thomas Law Book Company, 1921).

Mackay, Charles. *Through the Long Day* (London: W.H. Allen, 1887).

Martin, David G. *The Vicksburg Campaign* (New York: Da Capo, 1990).

McCabe, James Dabney. *The Life and Public Services of Horatio Seymour* (New York: United States Publishing Company, 1868).

McClellan, George. *McClellan's Own Story* (New York: Charles L. Webster and Company, 1887).

McCullough, Hugh. *Men and Measures of a Half Century* (New York: Charles Scribner's Sons, 1888).

McPherson, James. *Battle Cry of Freedom: The Civil War Era* (New York: Oxford, 1988).

Meacham, Jon. *American Lion: Andrew Jackson in the White House* (New York: Random House, 2008).

Meigs, Montgomery. *The Life of Thomas Hart Benton* (Philadelphia: J.B. Lippincott Company, 1904).

Merry, Robert. *A Nation of Vast Designs: James K. Polk, the Mexican War, and the Conquest of the American Continent* (New York: Simon & Schuster, 2009).

Miller, Marion Mills, ed. *Great Debates in American History* (New York: Current Literature Publishing Company, 1913).

Miner, Margaret, and Rawson, Hugh. *The Oxford Dictionary of American Quotations* (New York: Oxford University Press, 2006).

Monaghan, Jay. *Diplomat in Carpet Slippers* (Indianapolis: Bobbs Merrill, 1945).

Nevins, Allan. *Ordeal of the Union*, Volumes I–VIII (New York: Scribner's, 1947).

Nichols, Roy. *Franklin Pierce: Young Hickory of the Granite Hills* (Philadelphia: University of Pennsylvania Press, 1969).

Nicolay, John, and Hay, John. *Abraham Lincoln: A History*, Volumes I–X (New York: The Century Company, 1914).

Niven, John. *Martin Van Buren: The Romantic Age of American Politics* (Newtown, CT: American Political Biography Press, 2000).

Official Proceedings of the Democratic National Convention (Cincinnati: Enquirer Company Steam Printing Establishment, 1856).

Parton, James. *The Life of Andrew Jackson* (New York: Houghton, Mifflin, and Company, 1888).

Poore, Benjamin Perley. *Reminiscences of Sixty Years in the National Metropolis* (Philadelphia: Hubbard Brothers, 1886).

Potter, David. *The Impending Crisis: America Before the Civil War* (New York: Harper and Row, 1976).

Pryor, Sarah. *Reminiscences of Peace and War* (New York: Macmillan, 1905).

Quaife, Milton, ed. *The Diary of James K. Polk During His Presidency*, Volumes I–IV (Chicago: McClurg, 1910).

Randall, James. *Lincoln the President*, Volumes I–IV (Gloucester, MA: Peter Smith, 1965).

Rayback, Robert. *Millard Fillmore: Biography of a President* (Buffalo: Publications of the Buffalo Historical Society, 1959).

Remini, Robert. *Henry Clay, Statesman for the Union* (New York: W.W. Norton, 1991).

Renda, Lex. *Running on the Record: Civil War Era Politics in New Hampshire* (Charlottesville: University of Virginia Press, 1997).

Rhodes, John Ford. *History of the United States from the Compromise of 1850 to the Restoration of Home Rule at the South in 1877*, Volume III (New York: Macmillan, 1907).

Riddle, Albert Gallatin. *Recollections of War Times* (New York: Putnam's Sons, 1895).

Scarry, Robert. *Millard Fillmore* (Jefferson, NC: McFarland and Company, 2001).

Seale, William. *The President's House* (Washington, DC: White House Historical Association, 2008).

Severance, Frank, ed. *The Papers of Millard Fillmore*, Volumes I–II (Buffalo: Buffalo Historical Society, 1907).

Silbey, Joel. *Martin Van Buren and the Emergence of American Popular Politics* (Lanham, MD: Rowman and Littlefield, 2002).

Smith, Elbert. *The Presidencies of Zachary Taylor and Millard Fillmore* (Lawrence: University of Kansas Press, 1988).

Stoddard, William. *Inside the White House in War Times* (New York: Ogilve, 1895).

Sumner, Charles. *Memoir and Letters* (Boston: Roberts Brothers, 1877).

Taney, Roger. *The Merryman Habeas Corpus Case Baltimore: The United States Government a Military Despotism* (Jackson, MS: J.L. Power, 1861).

———. *The Proceedings in the Case of John Merryman* (Baltimore: Lucas Brothers, 1861).

Tyler, Lyon Gardiner, ed. *The Letters and Times of the Tylers,* Volumes I–III (Richmond: Whittet & Shepperson, 1884).

Van Buren, Martin. *The Autobiography of Martin Van Buren* (Washington, DC: Government Printing Office, 1920).

Wallace, William Warden. *The Pen and Pencil,* Volume I (Cincinnati: Publisher unknown).

Wallner, Peter. *Franklin Pierce,* Volumes I–II (Concord: Plaidswede Publishing, 2007).

Welles, Gideon. *Diary of Gideon Welles: Secretary of the Navy Under Lincoln and Johnson* (New York: Houghton, Mifflin, 1911).

Whipple, Wayne. *The Story Life of Lincoln* (Philadelphia: John C. Winston, 1908).

MANUSCRIPT COLLECTIONS

Papers of Millard Fillmore, Library of Congress, Washington, DC.

Papers of John J. Hardin, Chicago Historical Society, Chicago, IL.

Papers of Franklin Pierce, Library of Congress, Washington, DC.

Papers of Martin Van Buren, Library of Congress, Washington, DC.

ARTICLES

Chambrun, Marquis de. "Personal Recollections of Mr. Lincoln." *Scribner's,* January 1893.

Crook, William. "Lincoln's Last Day," *Harper's Magazine,* Column 115.

Gineapp, William. "Abraham Lincoln and the Border States." *Journal of the Abraham Lincoln Association,* Vol. 13, No. 1, 1992.

Hawthorne, Nathaniel. "Chiefly About War Matters." *Atlantic Monthly,* June 2, 1862.

Milton, George Fort. "Stephen A. Douglas' Efforts for Peace." *Journal of Southern History,* Vol. 1, No. 3 (August 1935), 269.

Nevins, Allan. "Stephen A. Douglas: His Weaknesses and His Greatness," *Journal of the Illinois State Historical Society,* Vol. 42, No. 4 (December 1949).

Omohundro Institute of Early American History and Culture. "Edmund Ruffin's Visit to Sherwood Forest." *William and Mary Quarterly,* Vol. 14, No. 3 (January 1906).

Pfanz, Donald. "The Union Army Retreats," http://fredericksburg.com/CivilWar/Battle/0915CW.

Somit, Albert. "Jackson as Administrator." *Public Administration Review,* Vol. 8, No. 3 (Summer 1948).

Digital

American Memory, Memory.loc.gov
American Presidency Project, www.presidency.ucsb.edu
Blackjack Battlefield, BlackJackBattlefield.org
Fredericksburg, Fredericksburg.com
Georgia Encyclopedia Online, www.georgiaencyclopedia.org
The History Channel, History.com
Kansas State Historical Society Online, kshs.org
The Lincoln Log, Lincolnlog.org
National Park Service, Nps.gov
St. Paul's Church, Richmond, VA, www.stpaulsepiscopal.org
Territorial Kansas Online, territorialkansasonline.org
United States House of Representatives, House.gov
United States Senate, Senate.gov
Virginia Secession Convention, University of Richmond, collections.richmond.edu/
secession

Newspapers

Albany Evening Journal, Albany, NY
Baltimore Sun, Baltimore, MD
Boston Courant, Boston, MA
Boston Courier, Boston, MA
Boston Semi-Weekly Courier, Boston, MA
Buffalo Commercial Advertiser, Buffalo, NY
Buffalo Morning Express, Buffalo, NY
Columbian Register, New Haven, CT
Congressional Globe, Washington, DC
The Constitution, Atlanta, GA
Daily Confederation, Montgomery, AL
Daily Constitutional Union, Washington, DC
Daily Evening Bulletin, San Francisco, CA
Daily Ohio Statesman, Columbus, OH
Daily Picayune, New Orleans, LA
Farmer's Cabinet
Fremont Journal, Fremont, OH
Glasgow Weekly Times, Glasgow, MO
Hartford Daily Courant, Hartford, CT
Liberator, Boston, MA
Litchfield Republican, Litchfield, CT
Lowell Daily Citizen, Lowell, MA
Milwaukee Morning Sentinel, Milwaukee, WI
National Intelligencer, Washington, DC
New Hampshire Patriot, Concord, NH

New York Daily Tribune, New York, NY
New York Herald, New York, NY
New York Times, New York, NY
New York Tribune, New York, NY
Philadelphia Daily Age, Philadelphia, PA
Philadelphia Inquirer, Philadelphia, PA
Richmond Dispatch, Richmond, VA
Richmond Examiner, Richmond, VA
Richmond Times, Richmond, VA
Richmond Whig, Richmond, VA
Salem Register, Salem, MA
San Francisco Bulletin, San Francisco, CA
Springfield Weekly Republican, Springfield, MA
St. Louis Missouri Republican, St. Louis, MO
Vermont Phoenix, Brattleboro, VT
Washington Star, Washington, DC
Western Reserve Chronicle, Warren, OH
Wisconsin Daily Patriot, Madison, WI
Worcester Daily Spy, Worcester, MA
The World, New York, NY

OFFICIAL PUBLICATIONS

The Journal of the Confederate Congress
The Journal of the United States House of Representatives
The Journal of the United States Senate
Report of the Committee on Reconstruction
Report of the Special Committee to Investigate the Troubles in Kansas ("Howard Report")

INDEX

About the Author

Chris DeRose is the author of the highly acclaimed *Congressman Lincoln: The Making of America's Greatest President* and *Founding Rivals: Madison vs. Monroe, the Bill of Rights, and the Election that Saved a Nation.* DeRose is an assistant professor of law at Arizona Summit Law School and political strategist who for the past seventeen years has served in nearly every capacity on campaigns up and down the ballot in five different states. He lives in Phoenix, Arizona.

Visit him at chrisderosebooks.com or @chrisderose on Twitter.